Emily Davies and the Mid-Victorian Women's Movement

Emily Davies and the Mid-Victorian Women's Movement

JOHN HENDRY

OXFORD
UNIVERSITY PRESS

Great Clarendon Street, Oxford, OX2 6DP,
United Kingdom

Oxford University Press is a department of the University of Oxford.
It furthers the University's objective of excellence in research, scholarship,
and education by publishing worldwide. Oxford is a registered trade mark of
Oxford University Press in the UK and in certain other countries

© John Hendry 2024

The moral rights of the author have been asserted

All rights reserved. No part of this publication may be reproduced, stored in
a retrieval system, or transmitted, in any form or by any means, without the
prior permission in writing of Oxford University Press, or as expressly permitted
by law, by licence or under terms agreed with the appropriate reprographics
rights organization. Enquiries concerning reproduction outside the scope of the
above should be sent to the Rights Department, Oxford University Press, at the
address above

You must not circulate this work in any other form
and you must impose this same condition on any acquirer

Published in the United States of America by Oxford University Press
198 Madison Avenue, New York, NY 10016, United States of America

British Library Cataloguing in Publication Data
Data available

Library of Congress Control Number: 2023951790

ISBN 978-0-19-891023-7

DOI: 10.1093/oso/9780198910237.001.0001

Printed and bound in the UK by
Clays Ltd, Elcograf S.p.A.

Links to third party websites are provided by Oxford in good faith and
for information only. Oxford disclaims any responsibility for the materials
contained in any third party website referenced in this work.

For Philomena, Sophie, Emma, and Florence

Preface

Emily Davies has long been recognized as a key figure in the emergence and early development of a women's 'movement' in mid-Victorian Britain. A central member of the Langham Place group, editor of both the *English Woman's Journal* and the *Victoria Magazine*, she directed the first campaign for female suffrage in 1866–7, was one of the first women elected to public office in 1870, campaigned successfully for the admission of girls to school-leaving examinations, played a significant part in the reform of girls' secondary school provision, and established Girton College, Britain's first university-level college for women. It has also long been recognized that in some respects Davies was an unusual kind of feminist activist—deeply conservative, both socially and politically, shying away from anything radical or unchristian, and from any talk of women's 'rights', and focusing much of her attention on educational opportunities rather than legal reforms. Perhaps for this reason, she has been relatively neglected in recent years. The standard biography is still that of Barbara Stephen, written nearly a hundred years ago, and few treatments go beyond what can be found there.

Davies was not only an important figure in the movement, however. In some respects she was a pivotal one. One striking, and under-examined, feature of the movement's history is its rapid transformation from what was essentially a Unitarian phenomenon in the 1850s into what quickly became a much more mainstream affair, cutting across religious divides but firmly implanted within the established church. Davies was not only a committed Church of England Christian, daughter and brother of distinguished clergymen. She was also closely connected through her brother to the broad church movement, which at just this time was coming to dominate liberal elite discourse, challenging the church's traditional interpretations of the position of women and opening it up to scientific, social and intellectual change. Her broad church connections facilitated her own work for women, and broad church support more generally acted to legitimize the aims of the women's movement within the educated, upper-middle-class establishment.

Davies was also at the heart of debates within the women's movement about strategy and tactics, and of an apparent fragmentation of the movement in the late 1860s and early 1870s, leaving it divided into three more or less separate arms, one focused on legal reforms, a second on the protection of vulnerable women, and the third on education. The division was not absolute. The legal campaigners wanted both to protect the vulnerable and to improve education; the

viii PREFACE

educational reformers wanted the franchise and property rights. But there seems to have been a marked split in terms of strategic priorities. There were different views, too, as to the purposes of improved education, which could be located either in the original Langham Place agenda of employment opportunities for single women; or in a liberal Millian context of the importance of letting women develop their potential to the maximum; or in the need to enhance and demonstrate women's rational capability and so their suitability for the franchise. As a member of the Langham Place group; philosophically a Millian but, at the same time, politically a Burkean conservative; and an early suffragist who then chose to devote herself to education, Davies sits as the very centre of these issues.

The question of strategy relates to another under-examined aspect of the women's movement, namely the resistance to it. Much has been written about Victorian values, but relatively little about how these were expressed, not so much in outright attacks upon the women's movement as in more moderate reasoned defences of the status quo. The key point about Davies here is that she largely shared the values of her opponents. She was, intellectually, a Millian, in that she believed that reason should take precedence over social conventions and that society should be ordered so as to give everyone the greatest possible opportunity of development, from which society as a whole would benefit. But she was also, politically, a Burkean, who believed that conventions were generally there for a reason, and should only be overturned gradually and cautiously, when the time was ripe.

In this book I have sought to explore these features of the women's movement through a focus on Emily Davies and her place in it, and two aspects of this approach perhaps require comment: what it includes, or the use of biography in history; and what it perforce excludes, in terms of spatial, temporal, and thematic limitations.

The relationship between history and biography has long been contentious. This is partly a question of style and norms. History tends towards the analytical, biography to the narrative. Historians tend to be relatively rigorous in their use of evidence, biographers to allow themselves much more freedom of interpretation, especially in exploring the motives and psychology of the subject. There are also differences of focus. Historians tend to focus on deep societal changes, often over long periods. Biographers attend to the accidental, the short term, the shifting surface of events. Biographers have also tended to focus overwhelmingly on the powerful and privileged, whose names are familiar and whose lives are well documented, shutting out from view the great mass of society. The aims and interests of the historian and biographer are often different and, from the historian's perspective, biography too often manifests as a literary genre that distorts our view of the past and has little to contribute to history proper.[1]

---

[1] For a substantial treatment of the historical relationship between history and biography see Barbara Caine, *Biography and History* (Palgrave Macmillan, 2010).

PREFACE ix

This is a valid concern, but it is one that relates to the conventional practices of biography rather than to a biographical focus in itself. People are part of history, and we have seen in the last few decades that biography can make a distinctive historical contribution, and not only in those areas—political or intellectual history, for example—in which individual achievement plays a prominent part. Kathryn Kiss Sklar showed half a century ago how biography can be used to explore the roles and relationships that shape a society,[2] and there is now a substantial body of work that uses biography to rescue the marginalized elements of society from neglect. Women's history has led the way in this respect, together with Black history, post-colonial history, and other specialisms. A biographical approach also allows us to explore the interplay between individuals and society and in doing so to counter the 'great man' tradition in other ways. It showcases the role of luck, serendipity, and chance encounters and helps us to understand the complex reasons why some projects flourish while others of apparently equal potency flounder.[3]

As historians we can rarely say with any confidence what drove people to act as they did. Motives, intentions, feelings, and reasons are often unclear to the person experiencing them, never mind to an external observer. But they are as much a part of history as the blind forces of economic change or class conflict. Indeed, they are precisely where those forces converge and are enacted.[4] Even if we cannot pinpoint an individual's thoughts, moreover, we can use the study of individuals to get some handle on the multiple ways in which people thought about things, in that social milieu and at that time: how they thought about moral duties, for example, and not just how intellectual authorities or popular authors told them to think about them.

While a focus on a particular individual can often give us useful historical insights into the wider world in which they lived, it also entails compromises. Having begun my career in the history of science in the 1980s, in the thick of debates around internal and external approaches, I have always taken the view that both are valuable, providing each recognizes the other. The world is complex; the accounts historians offer can only ever be partial, in both meanings of that word; and any one approach needs complementing by others. It is impossible to do everything at once, however. Biographical insight comes through detail, but that very detail, much of it providing context to the questions of interest rather than addressing those questions themselves, can easily distract from the wider historical focus. To keep the account offered here within bounds I have maintained a relatively narrow focus. I have focused, for example, on a very narrow

---

[2] Kathryn Kiss Sklar, *Catherine Beecher: A Study in American Domesticity* (Yale University Press, 1973).
[3] For a paradigm case see Janet Browne, *Charles Darwin: Voyaging* (Princeton University Press, 1995) and *Charles Darwin: The Power of Place* (Jonathan Cape, 2002).
[4] See Ludmilla Jordanova, *History in Practice*, 3rd ed. (Bloomsbury Academic, 2017).

time scale, essentially the period of stable and mainly Liberal rule from 1859 to 1874. These were both the formative years of the women's movement and the years of Davies's activism. It was also a very distinctive period, the features of which can easily get lost in the context of a historiography that tends to address much longer-term developments. I have also restricted myself to a narrow geographical scope, reflecting Davies's own experience and concerns. I have not attempted any international comparisons, though all the main actors would have been well informed of contemporary developments in America, France, and elsewhere.

I have also limited my treatment in two other respects, which require further comment. Focusing on the main actors and their immediate social and intellectual context, I have not gone in any depth into issues of either class (and the effects of industrialization, for example) or race. I take it for granted that the discursive categories associated with class, gender, race, and religion are deeply interwoven, in this time and place as in any other.[5] People routinely carried epithets associated with one area of discourse into others, speaking and thinking of race in gendered terms, for example, or class in racial terms, or gender in religious terms, and so on. This was a time, moreover, when each area was under active debate and each debate impinged on the others. This was most obviously and explicitly the case in the debates leading up to the 1867 Reform Act, covered in Chapter 9 and explored in detail by Catherine Hall, Keith McClelland, and Jane Rendall.[6] Here John Stuart Mill was at the head of campaigns to give the vote to working men, to give it to propertied women, and to defend the rights of Black Jamaicans against imperial oppression following the Morant Bay 'rebellion'. In the wake of the American Civil War, with the Indian Rebellion still in people's minds, with the government trying at the same time to respond to a Fenian rising against protestant British rule in Catholic Ireland, and with the unrest in Jamaica widely attributed to evangelical Baptist missionaries, the resulting public discourse was a veritable soup of class, gender, racial, and religious elements. At other moments in time and in other contexts, the blend of ingredients was less visible, but it was always there.

This interweaving of discursive categories, and interweaving of prejudices, is clearly relevant to the present study, but we need to be careful how we treat it. Catherine Hall's much more detailed work on the Baptist missionary communities of Birmingham and Jamaica suggests that even in a context where both the religious and gender dimensions are effectively fixed (the community held a rigidly conservative, biblically inspired view of the nature and role of women) and where people's views on race were explicit and well documented, those views were

---

[5] Joanna de Groot, '"Sex" and "race": the construction of language and image in the nineteenth century', in Susan Mendus and Jane Rendall, eds., *Sexuality and Subordination* (Routledge, 1989).

[6] Catherine Hall, Keith McClelland, and Jane Rendall, eds., *Defining the Victorian Nation: Class, Race, Gender and the British Reform Act of 1867* (Cambridge University Press, 2000).

immensely complex, variable, and conflicted. Together with Hall's earlier pioneering work on the emergence of separate spheres, it also suggests that, in those contexts at least, the transfer of epithets was overwhelmingly one way. It was class and race that were gendered, not the other way around.[7] Women, Black men, and indigent white men might all be described as inferior beings in much the same terms: as being innocent or childlike, for example, incapable of reason or of ruling themselves. In that sense the categories clearly intersected, and we need to be alert to the consequences. But it seems always to have been a case of Black men, for example, being ascribed qualities thought to be typical of women—of being thought effeminate—and never of middle-class women being ascribed qualities thought typical of Black people. This was partly just because women, being much more familiar, provided the base point for any comparison. But it was also the case that no English gentleman would ever describe an English woman as being like a Black person. Both might be deemed inferior in many respects, but English women were universally honoured and respected, for all their perceived weaknesses, in ways that Black people very rarely were.

One way in which racial distinctions impacted more directly on the issues addressed by the women's movement was through a characterization of English women in particular, and North European women more generally, as superior both to their South European and to their oriental counterparts. This was something that Frances Power Cobbe played on in her claim for the franchise,[8] but from a male perspective it was also a reason for denying women the franchise. English women were superior, on this view, not so much on account of any innate qualities but because of the superior governance of English gentlemen; and being better treated than women of other nations, they had less need of the freedoms claimed. The core racial distinction here was between men: between the English gentleman, on one hand, and the 'foreigner', typically of Latin, oriental, or Jewish appearance or heritage, who was apt to be considered suspect of almost any misdemeanour. The same distinction lay behind fantasy discourses of male over female domination, which often drew on racial tropes—the oriental harem, for example—that English gender relations did not allow.

Almost everybody in the women's movement was an active supporter of abolition, and a few linked this with female emancipation. A tradition culminating in Mill saw the liberation of women as a further stage in a long-term process of civilization that had already abolished enslavement.[9] The likelihood is that most nevertheless held the racial prejudices common to English middle-class society:

---

[7] Catherine Hall, *Civilising Subjects: Metropole and Colony in the English Imagination 1830–1867* (Polity, 2002); Leonora Davidoff and Catherine Hall, *Family Fortunes: Men and Women of the English Middle Class, 1780–1840*, 2nd ed. (Routledge, 2002).

[8] Frances Power Cobbe, 'Criminals, idiots and minors', *Fraser's Magazine*, 78 (December 1868), 777–94.

[9] Clare Midgley, 'Anti-slavery and the roots of imperial feminism', in Clare Midgley, ed., *Gender and Imperialism* (Manchester University Press, 1998), 161–79.

xii PREFACE

that they viewed the races as essentially, not just accidentally different, and that they viewed not only Black people but most non-Anglo-Saxons as in some sense markedly inferior. But we don't know. We simply have no record of any comments by Emily Davies on the subject, or of any comments, outside the abolitionist context, by her colleagues in the women's movement.

The situation in respect of class is more complicated. Helen Taylor and Mentia Taylor in London, and Elizabeth Wolstenholme and Lydia Becker in Manchester, were working in a context of long traditions of class agitation going back to the Chartist movement. In the politics of the day, moreover, working-class male suffrage was generally considered a far more salient issue than female suffrage. Perceptions of women and the social relations between women were highly class-based, and the whole system of education was built upon fine class distinctions. The world of the women's movement in this period, however, was a world of upper-middle-class women working entirely within the existing class structure and the prejudices and preconceptions that embodied. Where they were concerned for the working class, it was overwhelmingly in a traditional philanthropic mode. Whether campaigning for rights or opportunities, their focus was very much on their own class.

As noted above, the standard biography of Emily Davies is still that of Barbara Stephen, which was published in 1927 and suffers more than most from the prejudices of that age. Lady Stephen was for many years a governor of Girton College and her portrait was explicitly a portrait of Davies as she thought she would want to be remembered, with almost everything of a personal nature left out. It probably *is* how Davies would have wanted to be remembered, but it is frustrating for the historian, the more so since much of the material on which Stephen relied is no longer extant. Whether it was lost or destroyed is unknown, but the latter seems more likely, as anything left amongst Stephen's papers would almost certainly have found its way back to the college after her death. The missing items include a large volume of letters to regular correspondents, close friends, and colleagues, which may well have included much more personal content than Stephen cites, and one hundred pages of Davies's 'Family Chronicle', an account of her life and achievements prepared for her nephews and nieces. The missing pages cover her late teens and the entirety of her twenties, a formative period in anyone's life, and constitute the section of the memoir most likely to have included insights to her character, friendships, and formative influences.

The only modern biography, by Daphne Bennett, published in 1990, purports to give more insight into the person. Unfortunately, almost everything that Bennett adds to Stephen's account appears to the be the product of her vivid imagination. Whole sections on her life in Gateshead, her relationship with Henry Tomkinson (who helped in the foundation of Girton), and other matters are completely unreferenced, with the 'facts' cited having no basis that I can find in the archival record. An account of her relationship with George Eliot is not

PREFACE xiii

only largely made up but in key respects simply wrong. Here and elsewhere Bennett mistakes names and dates, presumably misreading her own notes, and mixing up notes made in the archives with notes of her own ideas.[10]

Meanwhile, a 1979 article by Andrew Rosen set Davies's involvement in the 1866-7 suffrage campaign in context, and in the wake of Bennett's biography Barbara Caine, in her 1992 book *Victorian Feminists*, drew attention to the fact that Davies was not just an organizer but an intellectual too. This was a significant contribution, but it also highlighted a significant omission. Like other historians of Victorian feminism, Caine naturally enough attributed the influence of John Stuart Mill, the great philosopher of the era, to his writing on women, and so saw no significant influence on Davies, or others. Together with Barbara Bodichon and the Garrett sisters, however, Davies was very strongly influenced, as I hope to show, by Mill, but by his philosophy and political economy much more than by his feminism.[11]

Many things have changed since these early accounts. First, we now have an excellent scholarly edition of Davies's letters from her campaigning years, 1861-75. Edited by Ann Murphy and Deirdre Raftery, this appeared only in 2004 and there have been few significant studies since, but it is both comprehensive and reliable. It includes only letters *from* Davies, not those *to* her, but it is an invaluable starting point.

Second, we now have modern well-referenced biographies of many of Davies's colleagues and contemporaries, including amongst others Barbara Bodichon, Elizabeth Garrett Anderson, Millicent Garrett Fawcett, Frances Power Cobbe, Elizabeth Wolstenholme, Josephine Butler, Lydia Becker, and Henry Sidgwick.[12]

Third, we have definitive scholarly accounts of some of the key institutions that form the backdrop to the Davies's work in the women's movement, including in particular Tod Jones on the broad church movement; Lawrence Goldman on the Social Science Association; Sheila Fletcher on the Endowed Schools Commission; Patricia Hollis on the school boards; and official histories of the universities of Cambridge and London.[13]

---

[10] I have not attempted to detail and rebut Bennett's errors: they are too many and the book is not worth it. Suffice to say that the book contains nothing new and is not to be relied upon. Though presented as a scholarly biography it is best read as historical fiction.

[11] Dependent on Bennett, Caine's account is also peppered with minor errors of fact, but these don't significantly affect her analysis.

[12] See Hirsch on Bodichon; Manton and Crawford on Garrett Anderson; David Rubinstein, *A Different World for Women: The Life of Millicent Garrett Fawcett* (Harvester, 1991), on Fawcett; Sally Mitchell on Cobbe; Maureen Wright, *Elizabeth Wolstenholme Elmy and the Victorian Feminist Movement: The Biography of an Insurgent Woman* (Manchester University Press, 2011); Jane Jordan on Butler; Joanna Williams on Becker; Bart Schulz on Sidgwick.

[13] Tod Jones, *The Broad Church: A Biography of a Movement* (Lexington Books, 2003); Lawrence Goldman, *Science, Reform and Politics in Victorian Britain: The Social Science Association, 1857-1886* (Cambridge University Press, 2002); Sheila Fletcher, *Feminists and Bureaucrats: A Study in the Development of Girls' Education in the Nineteenth Century* (Cambridge University Press, 1980); Patricia Hollis, *Ladies Elect: Women in English Local Government, 1865-1914* (Oxford University

xiv PREFACE

Fourth, there is a substantial literature on the women's movement generally, as well as its forebears and followers, and their social, political, and economic contexts. This literature will be referenced as appropriate in the footnotes and bibliography, but a few contributions are worth highlighting here as providing the essential context within which a study such as this sits, even when it's not referenced directly. These include Catherine Hall's seminal work on the ideology of separate spheres (with Leonora Davidoff) and the interplay of views on gender and race;[14] Martha Vicinus's works on female sexuality;[15] Judith Walkowitz on prostitution;[16] John Tosh and Ben Griffin on masculinity;[17] Margot Finn and Eugenio Biagini on the liberal politics of the period under study;[18] and the many penetrating studies of Jane Rendall.[19] Whatever aspect of the women's movement of the long 1860s I looked at for this book, I almost always found that Rendall had been there before me.

Fifth, interlocking with the literature on mid-Victorian culture and the women's movement, but somewhat separate (reflecting the history of education as a separate sub-discipline) is a substantial literature on girls' schooling, in which the works of Carol Dyhouse and Sara Delamont are particularly worth noting.[20]

Finally, the growth of online databases has made much accessible that wasn't before, both in terms of ephemeral publications and in terms of simple factual information.

Between them, these advances have made possible a much more reliable and more analytical treatment of Emily Davies and her work in the women's

---

Press, 1987); Peter Searby, *A History of the University of Cambridge*, vol. 3: *1750–1870* (Cambridge University Press, 1997), on Cambridge; Willson on the University of London.

[14] See especially Catherine Hall, 'Competing masculinities: Thomas Carlyle, John Stuart Mill and the case of Governor Eyre', in Catherine Hall, *White, Male and Middle Class: Explorations in Feminism and History* (Polity, 1992), 255–95, 'The nation within and without', in Hall, McClelland, and Rendall, eds., *Defining the Victorian Nation*, 179–233, *Civilising Subjects*; Davidoff and Hall, *Family Fortunes*.

[15] See especially Martha Vicinus, *Suffer and be Still: Women in the Victorian Age* (Indiana University Press, 1972); *Intimate Friends: Women who Loved Women, 1778–1928* (University of Chicago Press, 2004).

[16] Judith Walkovitz, *Prostitution and Victorian Society: Women, Class and the State* (Cambridge University Press, 1980).

[17] John Tosh, *A Man's Place: Masculinity and the Middle-Class Home in Victorian England* (Yale University Press, 1999); Ben Griffin, *The Politics of Gender in Victorian Britain: Masculinity, Political Culture and the Struggle for Women's Rights* (Cambridge University Press, 2012).

[18] Margot Finn, *After Chartism: Class and Nation in English Radical Politics, 1848–1874* (Cambridge University Press, 1993); Eugenio Biagini, *Liberty, Retrenchment and Reform: Popular Liberalism in the Age of Gladstone, 1860–1880* (Cambridge University Press, 2004).

[19] See especially Jane Rendall, 'The citizenship of women and the Reform Act of 1867', in Hall, McClelland, and Rendall, eds., *Defining the Victorian Nation*, 119–78, 'A moral engine? Feminism, liberalism and the English Woman's Journal', in Jane Rendall, ed., *Equal or Different: Women's Politics 1800–1914* (Blackwell, 1987), 112–40, 'Friendship and politics: Barbara Leigh Smith Bodichon (1827–91) and Bessie Rayner Parkes (1829–1925)', in Mendus and Rendall, eds., *Sexuality and Subordination*, 136–70.

[20] See especially Carol Dyhouse, *Girls Growing up in Late Victorian England* (Routledge & Kegan Paul, 1981); Sara Delamont and Lorna Duffin, eds., *The Nineteenth-Century Woman: Her Cultural and Physical World* (Routledge, 2014).

movement than has hitherto been available and one that will, I hope, shed new light on the evolution of that movement and its reception, in the context of the changing attitudes and institutions of the 'long' 1860s.

My main debt in writing this book has been to the many historians who have gone before me, including but by no means limited to the ones named above. I have not attempted to give an exhaustive bibliography of the area, but have listed there the works I have both read and drawn upon. History is both a cumulative and a collaborative venture, each writer bringing their own perspective, both building and reinterpreting what's gone before. I am also indebted, like most historians, to the archivists past and present who have created and curated the collections on which I've drawn, and to the institutions that have devoted scarce resources to housing, maintaining, and providing access to those collections. The Women's Library at the LSE, in particular, is an invaluable open resource. I am grateful to the Mistress and Fellows of Girton College for permission to quote from the Emily Davies material in the archive collection there, and to the archivist Hannah Westall both for her general help and for assisting with other permissions. I should like to thank the Hancox Archive for permission to quote from the letters of Barbara Bodichon and the copyright holders of letters from Joseph Parkes, Bessie Rayner Parkes, George Eliot, Elizabeth Garrett Anderson, and Henry Tomkinson for permission to quote from those letters, and to apologize for those copyright holders of other letters from the 1860s and 1870s I have been unable to trace.

I am also particularly grateful to the various colleagues, editors, and reviewers who have encouraged the venture and commented on different versions of the manuscript, including especially Tom, my editor at OUP, and my Girton colleagues Marilyn and Susan. A final acknowledgement is to the motivation provided by writers and activists still fighting misogyny and other forms of hatred today. A century and a half after the pioneering work described here it shouldn't still be necessary, but it is.

Contents

List of Abbreviations	xix
1. Introduction	1
2. Institutions of Engagement and Debate	22
3. The Rector's Daughter	41
4. Joining the Movement	61
5. A Woman Set Free	80
6. The Demise of Langham Place	94
7. From Educating Women to Examining Girls	108
8. The Education of Girls: 'Not a "Woman's Question"'	129
9. Votes for Women?	144
10. Towards the Higher Education of Women	163
11. Rival Projects	184
12. Girton and Newnham	202
13. Property, Prostitutes, and Public Service	221
14. 'A Good Age for Retiring into Private Life'	247
15. Conclusion	268
Select Bibliography	285
Index	295

List of Abbreviations

Databases, Archive Sources, Reference Works, Reports

AC — *Alumni Cantabrigienses: A Biographical List of All Known Students, Graduates and Holders of Office at the University of Cambridge, from the Earliest Times to 1900* (Cambridge University Press, 1922–54).

AO — *Alumni Oxonienses: The Members of the University of Oxford, 1715–1886* (Parker & Co, 1888–92).

BL — British Library archive collection.

CCEd — Clergy of the Church of England Database: theclergydatabase.org.uk.

DNB — *Dictionary of National Biography* (Smith, Elder & Co., 1885–1900 plus later supplements).

FC — Emily Davies, 'Family Chronicle', Girton GCPP Davies 1.

Girton — Girton College Cambridge archive collection.

LMA — London Metropolitan Archives.

LSE — London School of Economics archive collection.

ODNB — Oxford Dictionary of National Biography online: oxforddnb.com.

SIC Report — *Report of the Schools Inquiry Commission (Taunton Report)* (HMSO, 1868).

Journals

EWJ — *English Woman's Journal.*

TNAPSS — *Transactions of the National Association for the Promotion of Social Science.*

Biographies, Memoirs, etc. (Full References in Bibliography)

Amberley Papers — Bertrand Russell and Patricia Russell, eds., *The Amberley Papers.*

Clough — Blanche Athena Clough, *A Memoir of Anne Jemima Clough.*

Crawford — Elizabeth Crawford, *Enterprising Women.*

EDCL — Ann Murphy and Deirdre Raftery, eds., *Emily Davies Collected Letters.*

Fawcett — Millicent Garrett Fawcett, *What I Remember.*

Haight — Gordon W. Haight, *The George Eliot Letters.*

Hirsch — Pam Hirsch, *Barbara Leigh Smith Bodichon.*

Jordan — Jane Jordan, *Josephine Butler.*

Kamm — Josephine Kamm, *How Different From Us.*

Lowndes — Emma Lowndes, *Turning Victorian Ladies into Women.*

Manton — Jo Manton, *Elizabeth Garrett Anderson.*

Mitchell — Sally Mitchell, *Frances Power Cobbe.*

Richardson — Anna Richardson et al., *Memoir of Anna Deborah Richardson.*

Pyle — Andrew Pyle, *The Subjection of Women.*

xx   LIST OF ABBREVIATIONS

Sidgwick	Arthur Sidgwick and Eleanor Sidgwick, *Henry Sidgwick*.
Stephen	Barbara Stephen, *Emily Davies*.
Stuart	James Stuart, *Reminiscences*.
Thoughts	Emily Davies, *Thoughts on Some Questions Relating to Women, 1860–1908* (Bowes and Bowes, 1910).
Williams	Joanna Williams, *The Great Miss Lydia Becker*.
Willson	F. M. G. Willson, *The University of London*.

Correspondent names

AC	Anne Clough
AP	Adelaide Procter
AR	Anna Richardson
BB	Barbara Bodichon
BLS	Barbara Leigh Smith
BRP	Bessie Rayner Parkes
CB	Charlotte Burbury
CG	Charles Gray
CM	Charlotte Manning
EB	Eliza Bostock
EC	Ebenezer Charles
ECC	Edwin Clark
ED	Emily Davies
EG	Elizabeth Garrett
EGA	Elizabeth Garrett Anderson
EM	Edmund Morgan
EP	Edward Plumptre
ERG	Emilia Russell Gurney
ES	Emily Shirreff
EW	Elizabeth Wolstenholme
FB	Frances Buss
FM	Fanny Metcalfe
FPC	Frances Power Cobbe
FWHM	Frederick Myers
GL	George Liveing
HA	Henry Alford
HM	Henry Manning
HR	Henry Roby
HRT	Henry Tomkinson
HS	Henry Sidgwick
HT	Helen Taylor
JB	James Bryce
JD	John Davies
JG	John Griffiths
JH	James Heywood
JLD	John Llewelyn Davies

JP	Joseph Parkes
JS	John Seeley
JSA	James Skelton Anderson
JSM	John Stuart Mill
KA	Kate Amberley
MA	Matthew Arnold
MB	Marian Bradley
MD	Mary Davies
MF	Millicent Fawcett
ML	Marian Lewes (George Eliot)
MT	Clementia (Mentia) Taylor
PT	Paul Tidman
RHH	Richard Holt Hutton
RP	Robert Potts
TDA	Thomas Dyke Acland
TM	Thomas Markby
WD	William Davies
WS	William Shaen

1

Introduction

When a new women's movement began to emerge in the late 1850s, Emily Davies knew nothing about it. She may well not even have thought of any such thing. A spinster in her late twenties, the only surviving daughter of an evangelical rector in the industrial north-east of England, she lived at home with her parents and occupied herself with home and parish duties. Socially and politically conservative and utterly conventional in her habits and beliefs, she was the most unlikely of rebels. Yet in the space of just over fifteen years she would do as much as anyone of her generation to free women from the bonds that society imposed on them. It was through her campaigns of the 1860s that schoolgirls were first allowed to take public examinations, their teachers mobilized, and the way opened for the massive expansion and improvement of secondary girls' education that followed. It was also mainly through her efforts that women were first allowed to take university degrees, and in Girton College in Cambridge she created Britain's first university-level college for women. Along the way she directed the first major campaign for votes for women and was one of the first women elected to public office, as a member of the London School Board.

This book is partly the story of a remarkable woman. Quiet and conventional she may have been, but Emily Davies was, as we shall see, fiercely determined, and utterly ruthless when it came to getting her way. She was also formidably intelligent, with a very clear view both of what she wanted to achieve and of what it might be possible to achieve. It is also a story, as many are, of chance and serendipity. It was only due to a very particular set of circumstances and events that she first became aware of the women's movement, then became involved in it, and then was able to take the leading role she did.

Much more significantly, it is also a story of major social and intellectual changes that impacted not only on the possibilities of reforms but also on the possibilities with respect to how and by whom those reforms might be proposed and debated. Focusing on the long-term history of feminism and the relatively stable attitudes to gender roles across much of the nineteenth century, some historians have seen the development of the women's movement from the mid-1850s through to the early 1870s as no more than incremental change, the key turning point coming later, with the campaign against the treatment of prostitutes through the 1870s and beyond.[1] It was in the

---

[1] See for example Barbara Caine, *English Feminism, 1780–1980* (Oxford University Press, 1997), 90–1.

Emily Davies and the Mid-Victorian Women's Movement. John Hendry, Oxford University Press. © John Hendry 2024.
DOI: 10.1093/oso/9780198910237.003.0001

2 DAVIES AND THE MID-VICTORIAN WOMEN'S MOVEMENT

1850s and 1860s, however, that the institutional structures developed that made this campaign possible, and it was through the discourses enabled by those structures that the different aims and objectives of the movement were delineated.

Two developments at the beginning of the period were critical. One was the creation of the National Association for the Promotion of Social Science, generally known as the Social Science Association (SSA), which gave women for the first time a public *voice*. They had long been able to publish books and articles, but this was the first public forum in which they could present their ideas, in person, for debate. Some people found it shocking; some found it ridiculous. The *Saturday Review* found it both and laid in year after year to the pointlessness and impropriety of the 'Universal Palaver Association'.[2] But the women were heard, and as often as not they were given a fair hearing.

The other development, harder to pin down but every bit as important, was the growing influence within elite discourse of the broad church movement within the Church of England. The broad churchmen were always a small minority within the church, and when they gained high office it was typically as cathedral deans rather than bishops, responsible for the fabric rather than for the clergy. But even within the church they were influential way beyond their numbers and in the pages of the more intellectual monthly magazines, quarterly reviews, and other vehicles of elite debate they were, from the late 1850 through the 1860s and into the 1870s—the precise period of Davies's activism—the dominant voice of the established church. And in contrast with the conservatism of the mass of the clergy—but in tune with many of the educated laity—their voice was consistently liberal and progressive. They were not only open as to biblical interpretation and religious doctrine but also welcoming of scientific, technological, and social change, including changes to the education, status, and roles of women.

This had implications both generally, for the women's movement as a whole, and more specifically, for Davies's part in it. Generally, it opened up the women's movement, which until the mid-1850s had been almost entirely the province of Unitarians and Quakers, to members of the established church. The SSA also contributed to this, by creating public networks to supplement and supplant the existing private ones. But the broad church intellectuals, through their public support, made women's causes and the women's movement respectable for the first time from an establishment Church of England perspective. More specifically, they provided a network of support for Davies and her colleagues. Her brother, Llewelyn, was both a close associate of F. D. Maurice (who though not counting himself a member of the broad church was generally seen as one of its leaders) and a prominent advocate of liberal broad church causes. Davies herself

---

[2] *Saturday Review*, 13 (14 June 1862), 668.

was more conservative, more orthodox, but many of her friends and supporters were either Mauricians or broad church intellectuals.

In this chapter I shall set the scene for what follows with a short introduction to the society in which Emily Davies and her colleagues in the women's movement lived and worked, focusing in particular on the laws and social conventions relating to women. In the next chapter I shall look at the history of the women's movement in the years before Davies encountered it and at the institutions that were to sustain it during her period of activism. I shall then take up the story of Emily Davies's early life and her induction into the women's movement.

Emily Davies lived into her nineties. She played an active role in Girton College for half a century and was quietly active in the women's suffrage movement of the late nineteenth and early twentieth century. Her signal achievements, however, fell within a relatively short period, from the late 1850s to the mid-1870s—what I shall call for convenience the long 1860s. In political terms, this was a period of Liberal dominance and relative stability. It opened with Palmerston's second administration of 1859–65, the first that could properly be termed 'Liberal' rather than 'Whig', and closed with Gladstone's first, modernizing administration of 1868–74. The years 1866–8 saw a brief return to minority Conservative government, under Derby and Disraeli, but even this was a forward-looking, indeed reforming government, marked more by compromise than by conflict.

Across the period the political mood in general was increasingly forward- rather than backward-looking, and increasingly focused on domestic affairs rather than the foreign entanglement that had characterized the 1850s. It was the period in which the age of Palmerston, Russell, and Derby, all members of the old aristocracy and all born in the eighteenth century, gave way to that of Disraeli and Gladstone, and in which political leadership shifted decisively from the House of Lords to the House of Commons. The Palmerston administration was transitional in this respect, with the prime minister focused, as he always had been, on foreign affairs and prone, as he always had been, to sabre rattling, while Gladstone as chancellor of the exchequer acted as a budget-minded restraining force. When Derby became prime minister for the third time in 1866, however, it was Disraeli, leading the House of Commons, who was effectively in charge.

Tied in with the domestic focus, the period was also one in which Britain was at peace, albeit perhaps in the early years as much by luck as by judgement. Mainland Europe was far from peaceful. France, Austria, and Prussia were repeatedly at loggerheads, initially in the context of Italian unification and independence (in the wars of 1859 and 1866) and subsequently on their own account (in the Franco-Prussian War of 1870). The French emperor, Napoleon III, was both belligerent and unpredictable, and though France had been an ally in the Crimean War of 1853–6, she was widely seen in the early 1860s as a threat. But the experience of the 1850s had been salutary. The Indian Rebellion of 1857–8 had been effectively if brutally suppressed, and skirmishes against Persia and

China had caused relatively little trouble, but the Crimean War had been hugely embarrassing. Britain had ended up on the winning side, but only thanks to her French allies, whose professionalism had put to shame the ramshackle shape of the British military. Quite apart from incompetent leadership and tactical and strategic misjudgements, including most famously the confusions that resulted in the calamitous 'Charge of the Light Brigade', the British troops were hopelessly under-supplied and under-fed, and totally unequipped for the Crimean winter. Arrangements for the evacuation and treatment of the wounded and diseased were equally ill thought out and under-supplied, with doctors, nurses, medicines, field hospitals, and troop ships all hopelessly inadequate. Florence Nightingale had become a national heroine and made noble efforts to improve the sanitary conditions, but to very little effect.[3] In response, Palmerston spent heavily on modernizing and enlarging the British armed forces, but resisted any further engagement.[4]

In America, meanwhile, the secession of southern states in early 1861 was followed by four years of civil war, and a succession of diplomatic incidents threatened to draw Britain in. But opinion was sharply divided. Government sympathies, and aristocratic sympathies more generally, were with the South, and had Britain been pulled in it would most likely have been on that side.[5] But popular opinion was strongly with the North, and in particular against the institution of slavery, and while reinforcements were sent out to Canada, Britain maintained its neutrality.

Britain was at peace internationally, and it was relatively at peace at home. England was still, in Disraeli's famous phrase, 'two nations', rich and poor, powerful and powerless.[6] It was a country of sharp class distinctions and huge inequalities of wealth and power. The condition of the Manchester working classes chronicled by Friedrich Engels in the 1840s and fictionalized for the British public in Elizabeth Gaskell's *North and South* had improved but not greatly.[7] The London poor, chronicled by Henry Mayhew in 1849, were still desperately poor.[8] But the strikes and violence of the Chartist uprisings of that period had long since subsided. The interests of the working classes were represented in Parliament by the Radicals, and while not much was done to substantially advance those

---

[3] Trevor Royle, *Crimea: The Great Crimean War 1854–1856* (Little, Brown, 1999); Orlando Figes, *Crimea: The Last Crusade* (Allen Lane, 2010).

[4] For a general treatment, see K. Theodore Hoppen, *The Mid-Victorian Generation, 1846–1886* (Oxford University Press, 1998), chapter 7.

[5] Don Doyle, *The Cause of All Nations: An International History of the American Civil War* (Basic Books, 2015).

[6] Benjamin Disraeli, *Sybil, or The Two Nations* (Henry Colburn, 1845).

[7] Elizabeth Gaskell, *North and South* (Chapman & Hall, 1855); Frederick Engels, *The Condition of the Working Class in England* (London, 1892).

[8] Reprinted as Henry Mayhew, *London Labour and the London Poor* (George Woodfall & Son, 1851).

INTRODUCTION 5

interests, enough was done to show some progress and keep the peace. Both middle-class perceptions of the working classes and working-class perceptions of the democratic process were significantly more favourable than they had been in earlier decades.[9]

One marked characteristic of this period was a strong interest, especially amongst the middle classes, in improvement. This impacted on the poor through philanthropic activities, which in the 1860s far outweighed the support provided by the state, as well as through improving legislation, such as the 1870 Elementary Education Act (see Chapter 13). It was manifest in the huge success of self-help manuals, such as Samuel Smiles's *Self-Help* (first edition 1859), Mrs Beeton's *Book of Household Management* (1861), and many more, and in a strong public interest in science and technology.

Popular science writing had been a staple of the reading public since the 1830s. At that time it had been closely associated with radical politics and the diffusion of useful knowledge to the working classes. As class conflict had subsided, however, it had become a middle-class interest. By the time of the Great Exhibition of the Works of All Nations in Hyde Park in 1851, which Davies may well have visited with her parents as a young women, science was seen as the handmaiden of empire, and as part of a stable, hierarchically structured order, but also increasingly as the foundation for liberal visions of progress.[10] The University of Cambridge had introduced a Natural Sciences Tripos in 1849 and while take-up had been slow, by the 1860s it was beginning to gather pace. Darwin's *Origin of Species*, published in 1859, may have upset some churchmen, most notably Samuel Wilberforce, Bishop of Oxford, but the public interest was in its standing as science, and within a very few years it was widely accepted. The women of the 1860s may not have been able to attend university, but they could attend public lecture series by leading scientists such as Thomas Huxley or John Tyndall. The literary periodicals reviewed scientific as well as literary works and specialist journals provided professional scientific updates for the general reader.[11] And across society was an evident pride in the progress in technology and public works.

The railways, great symbol of the Victorian age, were already well established but were still expanding rapidly, with increasing speeds and frequencies, and changing people's lives. Journeys that had taken several days by coach could now

[9] Eugenio Biagini, *Liberty, Retrenchment and Reform: Popular Liberalism in the Age of Gladstone, 1860–1880* (Cambridge University Press, 2004).

[10] James Secord, *Visions of Science: Books and Readers at the Dawn of the Victorian Age* (Oxford University Press, 2014). The Davies family passed through London en route to and from the continent at the time of the exhibition, and Emily's father had a strong amateur interest in science, so a visit seems likely.

[11] The most successful of these, *Nature*, commenced publication in 1869. See A. J. Meadows, *Science and Controversy: A Biography of Sir Norman Lockyer, Founder Editor of Nature*, 2nd edn (Macmillan, 2008); Janet Browne, *Charles Darwin: The Power of Place* (Jonathan Cape, 2002).

be accomplished in hours. London could be reached from Exeter in just four hours, from Edinburgh in ten and a half hours, and from much of England in a day trip. The London newspapers could be delivered across the country on the same day, and post overnight on the mail trains (which also carried passengers). In London itself, construction of the underground railway began in 1860, and by 1868 Emily Davies could take underground trains from Gloucester Road to St John's Wood, changing at Baker Street, a journey she found 'very convenient'.[12]

Over the same period, in response to the 'great stink' of 1858, when the banks of the Thames piled high with sewage, the Thames embankment and pumped London sewage system were constructed. With the increasing separation of drinking water and effluent, hygiene improved dramatically. These technological changes had yet to impact significantly on the poor. It was the middle and upper classes, and to a large extent only the upper and upper middle classes, that reaped the benefit. But this was the world in which the women's movement operated. The activities and concerns of women activists ran across the social spectrum, from the educational and employment opportunities for middle-class women to the rights of working-class wives and the protection of child prostitutes. But the debates and campaigns took place, and the battles were fought, in the much more rarefied world of the upper and middle classes, and more specifically still in that of the educated upper middle classes.

This was, in essence, the world of Anthony Trollope, as portrayed in his contemporary novels: the last five Barchester chronicles (1858–67), the six Palliser novels (1864–76), *The Way We Live Now* (1873), and three dealing explicitly with the position of women: *The Belton Estate* (1865), *He Knew He Was Right* (1868–9), and *The Vicar of Bullhampton* (1870). All were set or published in the period and all focused on the class of which he was himself a member.[13] It was a world in which the boys went to private schools—the so-called public schools—or if resources were scarce to endowed grammar schools. From there they went on to Oxford and Cambridge universities, or University College London for dissenters, or else into the law or the armed forces. They ended up typically in the professions: in the church, law, medicine, or the army and navy; or else as writers, artists, or scientists. Their fathers might also have been professionals, or landed gentry, or successful bankers or businessmen, and some inherited large estates or continued in business, but all laid claim to the status of gentlemen. To rank as a gentleman one needed to be reasonably well off, or the son of well-off parents, and reasonably well educated, but more important than these was a certain moral code. A gentleman knew how to dress and present himself, and how to behave,

---

[12] ED to CB, 17 November 1868, *EDCL*, 294.

[13] Trollope is particularly valuable as a social commentator because while he had (and repeatedly stated) his own strong views he was the most sympathetic of satirists. He consistently chronicled both the social conventions of society and their limitations; how people were expected to behave and how real people often failed, for good reasons as well as bad, to live up to those expectations.

not only with his peers but also with regard to his servants or workers. He was courteous to women, generally trustworthy, and with a visible sense of public responsibility. He kept abreast of public affairs, and concerned himself with the issues of the day.[14]

The girls of this class were not so well educated, at least in a narrowly academic sense. They were typically taught no Greek, Latin, or theology, no science, and little mathematics. And what they were taught they were generally taught rather poorly. They were not expected to show any interest in politics and were more likely to read the latest novels than the high-minded quarterly reviews. But by the time they grew up they were often highly literate, with some French and even Italian, and a reasonable if sanitized cultural and historical awareness. They may not have read the classics, but they would probably have read bowdlerized digests. The writers of more serious fiction could include quite sophisticated cultural references as well as passages in French, untranslated, quite confident that their mainly female readers would be able to cope. And as their menfolk were gentlemen, the women of this class were unmistakably ladies.

Emily Davies's friend Anna Richardson drew a nice distinction between the lower, upper and upper middle, and middle classes as between women who had never had stays, those who knew how to use them but when not to and, in between, that 'vast incomprehensible steel-encased middle class'.[15] Another familiar characterization of a lady was a woman who dressed for dinner. But this was a world in which the status of women was derived from that of their menfolk. In a formal sense, a 'lady' was such either on account of her husband, as the wife of a lord or baronet, or on account of her father, as the daughter of an earl. And in general parlance a lady was the female appendage to a gentleman: the wife or daughter of a gentleman, or a woman whose presentation and behaviour conformed to what society expected of a gentleman's wife.

While the women's movement looked for its audience towards this educated upper middle class, its immediate battleground was an even narrower segment of society, made up of academics, writers, artists, intellectuals, journalists and politicians: the intelligentsia of the day. And here the rules were more fluid. As with any intelligentsia this segment of society encompassed a wide range of opinion, from the reactionary to the radical, but in general terms it was socially more liberal than the class to which it belonged. Of the great luminaries of the period, John Stuart Mill, Charles Dickens, Wilkie Collins, and George Eliot all lived or had lived with partners to whom they were not married, while John Ruskin and (reportedly) Thomas Carlyle married women with whom they did not partner. The first leader of the new women's movement, Barbara Bodichon,

---

[14] See for example Shirley Robin Letwin, The Gentleman in Trollope: Individuality and Moral Conduct (Palgrave Macmillan, 1982).

[15] AR to ED, 1 March 1868, Richardson, 222.

8 DAVIES AND THE MID-VICTORIAN WOMEN'S MOVEMENT

was illegitimate, and quite a few of her colleagues were known by their friends (and suspected by their enemies) to be homosexual, as were numerous Cambridge and Oxford academics.[16] Bodichon and her friends shocked their more straight-laced peers by dressing, for comfort rather than fashion, in ways that were considered distinctly unladylike. And while nobody accused the men of not being gentlemen, the women were more vulnerable. Eliot was spurned by 'respectable' society. Bodichon and her sisters were spurned by her family (including her cousin Florence Nightingale) until marriage brought a degree of respectability. (Barbara's husband, being French, was not automatically accorded gentleman status, but he was a qualified doctor, which helped; one of her sisters married a general.) An intellectual woman was always at risk of being thought a 'strong' woman, and a strong woman, with a mind and opinions of her own, was always at risk of not being thought a lady. If she openly questioned accepted notions as to the position of women in society, that could only make matters worse.

The position of women in English society at the beginning of our period, in the late 1850s, was determined both by law and by established social norms, and to understand the challenges faced by the women's movement of the long 1860s it is necessary to understand the effects of each and how they interacted.

In purely legal terms, women suffered under two main sets of disabilities. In the first place, the principle of coverture meant that when a woman married, her property, her earnings, if any, and the income from any property she might have inherited all became the property of her husband. More fundamentally, so did she. To quote from Blackstone's *Commentaries on the Laws of England*:

> By marriage, the husband and wife are one person in law: that is, the very being or legal existence of the woman is suspended during the marriage, or at least is incorporated and consolidated into that of the husband: under whose wing, protection, and cover, she performs every thing.[17]

A married woman could not enter into contracts on her own right, nor could any agreement between husband and wife (since they were legally the same person) be enforced. Some critics compared her state to that of enslavement, which was inaccurate: she retained her humanity and was no mere chattel. But in the sense in which a man's body was considered to be his own property, she was the property of her husband, bound not only to obey him in all things but also to suffer

---

[16] For the men see, for example, Bart Schultz, *Henry Sidgwick: Eye of the Universe* (Cambridge University Press, 2004); Phyllis Grosskurth, *John Addington Symonds: A Biography* (Longmans, 1964). For the women, see below.

[17] William Blackstone, *Commentaries on the Laws of England* (1765), 430.

whatever violence or other kind of cruelty he chose to inflict on her, within rather broad limits.[18]

For the rich, some of the legal provisions on property could be mitigated through the use of trust funds, but even here the trustee of a wife's property was almost always a male relative and very often her husband. And for the great majority of women there was no such escape. A typical middle-class woman, on marrying, lost all control over her property. If a working-class woman married a man who turned out to be idle or a drunkard, her wages had by law to be given over to him. A single woman could own property, but where was she to get it from? Middle-class women were not expected to work—or rather they were expected not to work—and remained as they had been as minors, dependent on their parents, or failing that on other males in the family. If all that failed, and they were reduced to working as governesses, they were paid a pittance and could not hope to save anything. Nor could single working-class women.

Provisions for divorce also distinguished sharply between the sexes. A woman could be divorced for adultery, and the corespondent sued by the husband for infringing his property rights. (A father could similarly sue his daughter's seducer for depriving him of her services.) A man could be divorced only if he were both adulterous and guilty of substantial cruelty or desertion. When a couple separated, it was the man who was automatically granted legal custody of children, even if he was at fault. They were *his* children, not hers: indeed, one of the justifications for treating adultery by the wife as infinitely worse than adultery by the husband was that it threatened to usurp, through a son who was not his own, the husband's property. Similarly in the case of the nomination of guardians in case of the parents' death, it was the father, not the mother, whose wishes prevailed in law.

The second set of disabilities was political. A woman could not legally vote for or sit in Parliament or hold any public office. Women could vote in parish vestries, which were considered non-political, and after the passing of the Municipal Corporations (Elections) Act in 1869 this right was extended to municipal elections, but even here it was soon ruled, after some confusion, that that applied to single or widowed women only.[19] Politics and the public sphere were by law an entirely masculine domain, in which women had no place. Even amongst men, the franchise was severely restricted. The Reform Act of 1832 had increased its scope, partly through a restructuring of constituencies and partly through a broadening of property qualifications, but that had only increased the electorate to around 650,000, out of a total population of about 12 million: about one in seven adult males. Politics was, in effect, the preserve not merely of men but of middle- and upper-class men. But as Frances Power Cobbe put it in an article

---

[18] Mary Poovey, 'Covered but not bound: Caroline Norton and the 1857 Matrimonial Causes Act', *Feminist Studies*, 14 (1988), 467–85.
[19] See Chapter 13 below.

written in 1868, anybody could vote who met the property qualifications—providing that they were not idiots, criminals, minors, or women.[20]

Alongside and underpinning the laws relating to women was a set of widely shared assumptions and social conventions. There were assumptions, first, as to male and female nature. Men were supposed to be naturally active, women passive; men strong, mentally as well as physically, women weak and fragile; men rational and in command of their thoughts, women intuitive, emotional, and easily led. Both men and women were assumed to be heterosexual, but while men were recognized to be sexually charged, women—if properly brought up—were not. Those exposed to the crammed sleeping accommodation of slum living, or to mixed-sex factory working, might have their sexuality unnaturally aroused, but the idea that a lady might experience the sort of sexual urges that a gentleman knew only too well was unthinkable. If middle-class women experienced sexual attraction at all it was, by conventional agreement, only very mildly and only in response to a loving husband and their natural maternal instinct. People knew, in private, that these assumptions were all idealizations, that there were many exceptions to the rules, but in public and political discourse they went largely unchallenged. Even if they were challenged, they could be readily justified in historical or biological terms or, to put it another way, on the authority of male historians and scientists.[21]

The core assumption underlying the law on women was that of male authority and willing female compliance. This both supported and was supported by assumptions as to male and female nature, but its main ground was in the biblical teaching of St Paul: 'wives obey your husbands'.[22] A key point here was the willingness of women to comply. That they should comply, that they had a duty to comply, was taken almost as self-evident. But it was also essential to the maintenance of the social fabric and the ideology underlying it that women should desire to be what men desired them to be, that wives should want to sacrifice themselves in the interests of their husbands, to adapt to their needs, to yield when they disagreed.[23]

Complementing this assumption of the virtuous, willingly dutiful wife was that of the virtuous, willingly dutiful husband. The duties were different, but in a society in which moral virtue was held high it was assumed that a husband's legal control over his wife carried with it a duty of care, and that charged with the protection of his wife a husband would do everything he could, willingly, to protect

---

[20] Frances Power Cobbe, 'Criminals, idiots and minors', *Fraser's Magazine*, 78 (December 1868), 777–94.

[21] Jeffrey Weeks, *Sex, Politics and Society: The Regulation of Sexuality since 1800*, 3rd ed. (Pearson, 2012); Michael Mason, *The Making of Victorian Sexual Attitudes* (Oxford University Press, 1994).

[22] Ephesians 5:22–4; Colossians 3:18, 1 Corinthians 11:3, 1 Timothy 2:12.

[23] Mary Poovey, *Uneven Developments: The Ideological Work of Gender in Mid-Victorian England* (Chicago University Press, 1988).

INTRODUCTION   11

her—as indeed would a father protect and care for his daughter.[24] That the rougher elements of the working classes might fail here was acknowledged as a problem to be addressed, and even amongst the better off there might be isolated exceptions, as there were in all things. But it was assumed as a general rule that no respectable husband, and no trustee of a woman's estate, would abuse the position the law gave him.

Beyond the law and its interpretation, these assumptions had various consequences. One was a moral, and especially a sexual double standard that demonized the fallen woman while exempting men from serious blame.[25] It was not that the moral standards applied to men were in principle any looser. A single gentleman was expected to conserve his semen for marriage and work off his energy in sport and exercise. But male authorities, having mainly failed to live up to this ideal themselves, condoned lapses in others. For a woman to lapse was, however, unforgivable. Along with this went a code of conduct by which middle-class young women, at least, were protected. They may have enjoyed more freedom than their continental counterparts, but they could not meet with men alone, cousins excepted (as Trollope put it, 'there is certainly a great relief in cousinhood'), or attend social functions unchaperoned.[26] The protection was not perfect, however, and it created its own problems: how to commit or respond to a proposal of marriage when one had spent little or no time alone with the prospective spouse. So the rules might be broken with good intent, and then heaven help the woman of any class who allowed herself to be seduced, especially if it led to a pregnancy outside of marriage. For a woman of the respectable middle or skilled working classes, a single transgression, even if there were no physical consequences, would if discovered seal her fate for life. Amongst the labouring classes of the countryside, customs might be less harsh. It was commonplace for sex to follow a declaration of betrothal and only be followed later by marriage, and if the man reneged a child might be taken in by the family and pity shown. But even that rested, in effect, on an acknowledged and approved betrothal to a respectable man. And in all cases it was the woman who suffered, the man who escaped.

[24] Gertrude Himmelfarb, 'The Victorian trinity: religion, science, morality', in *Marriage and Morals among the Victorians: And Other Essays* (I. B. Tauris, 1989), 50–75; *The De-Moralization of Society* (Institute of Economic Affairs, 1995). Himmelfarb is rarely cited nowadays, partly because of her right-wing politics and extreme moral conservatism. She was no friend of feminism, but she did understand very well the forces within Victorian society that resisted and opposed it.

[25] Keith Thomas, 'The double standard', *Journal of the History of Ideas*, 20 (1959), 195–216; Weeks, *Sex, Politics and Society*.

[26] Anthony Trollope, *The Vicar of Bullhampton* (Bradbury and Evans, 1870). This was one reason why marriages between cousins were so common. For others see Simon Goldhill, *A Very Queer Family Indeed: Sex, Religion, and the Bensons in Victorian Britain* (University of Chicago Press, 2016); Adam Kuper, *Incest and Influence: The Private Life of Bourgeois England* (Harvard University Press, 2009). For detailed analysis of the often conflicting evidence on these issues see Mason, *The Making of Victorian Sexual Attitudes*.

Particularly condemned, of course, were those women driven to prostitution to survive. That men visited prostitutes was considered unfortunate. But with the average age of marriage for a man around twenty-nine in mid-century, it was also thought (by men!) to be understandable, and from a health perspective greatly preferable to masturbation. Men were born with their sexuality and it had to be satisfied. The women who satisfied it, however, and those suspected of satisfying it, were condemned out of hand. They had to live not only with the fear of violence and sexually transmitted disease, but in utter opprobrium as well.

More generally, the double standard was not restricted to sex. Both men and women were held to high moral standards, but the standards were set by men. Men decided what was and was not 'manly'. They also decided what was and was not 'womanly', and this imposed particular notions of femininity. Men should be morally virtuous, but women should be paragons of virtue. Men should go out into the world and make a place for themselves; women should know their place. Men should make decisions, women follow them, and so on.

One expression of these differences was through an ideology of what historians have termed separate spheres. Originating in the evangelical revival of the late eighteenth century, this characterized emerging provincial middle-class society in terms of two spheres. One was the sphere of work and politics, a sphere in which men had necessarily to act but one that was fraught with temptation and vice. The other was the private sphere of domestic life, in which women could maintain their moral purity and provide a refuge for their husbands in which true religion could flourish and they could find protection from the dangers outside.[27] Marriage, it should be noted, was assumed.[28]

In the historiography of the women's movement, this concept of separate spheres has played a prominent role. Identified by Leonore Davidoff and Catherine Hall with processes of class formation under the early nineteenth-century growth of capitalism, it has been employed variously as a stifling constraint on women's freedom, a source of feminist solidarity, or the primary ground for men refusing women the vote. It is now recognized that it was in general none of these things, though it might well have been in particular cases.[29] As Jane Rendall has observed, the public–private dichotomy conflates multiple distinctions, with

[27] See especially Catherine Hall, 'The early formation of Victorian domestic ideology', in Sandra Burman, ed., *Fit Work for Women* (Croom Helm, 1979), 15–32; Leonora Davidoff and Catherine Hall, *Family Fortunes: Men and Women of the English Middle Class, 1780–1840*, 2nd ed. (Routledge, 2002); Martha Vicinus, ed., *Suffer and be Still: Women in the Victorian Age* (Indiana University Press, 1972); Sara Delamont and Lorna Duffin, eds., *The Nineteenth-Century Woman: Her Cultural and Physical World* (Routledge, 2014).

[28] Children born out of marriage accounted for just 5–6 per cent of the total. See Peter Lazlett, *The World We Have Lost*, 2nd ed. (Methuen, 1971).

[29] Davidoff and Hall, *Family Fortunes*, and for extensions and critiques see Caine, *English Feminism*; Amanda Vickery, 'Golden age to separate spheres? A review of the categories and chronology of English women's history', *The Historical Journal*, 36 (1993), 383–414; Ben Griffin, *The Politics of Gender in Victorian Britain: Masculinity, Political Culture and the Struggle for Women's Rights* (Cambridge

the 'public' realm including and often dominated by very private business interests, while the private domestic realm spilled over into all sorts of public community engagement.[30] The basic argument, that industrialization intensified the
sexual division of labour, stands, however, and for all its analytical flaws the concept of separate spheres, crudely understood (and understood, in particular, as
suited men), clearly underpinned what had by the 1850s become a dominant
ideology of middle-class culture. It is reflected both in the volume of advice
books, addressed to both men and women, through which it was propounded
and in the voluminous anecdotal evidence of diaries, letters, and novels.

Unless possessed of a large private income (in which case he was expected not
to sully himself with paid employment), a man was expected to earn enough to
keep himself and his dependents in comfortable circumstances, providing not
only for his wife and pre-adult children but also for any adult unmarried daughters and even, where necessary, sisters and nieces. A woman was expected not to
work, and above all not to go out (and so be seen) to work for money. With a few
exceptions that was seen as unwomanly and, perhaps more important, as embarrassing to their menfolk. Households were structured around the needs of the
working man, even if, perforce, his wife also worked. Children were inducted to
the ideology from the cradle, receiving different educations and occupying different roles in the home. Sisters deferred to and served their brothers, and in poorer
homes they helped with the housework while their brothers idled or played. In
wealthier homes, the brothers studied and went out in the world while the sisters
'visited' with their mothers or (they could not go out unchaperoned) sat at home
with their 'work' (embroidery).[31]

Even as commonly understood, the ideology was a caricature, as is apparent
from the novels and satirical writing of the period. Not all women were minister-
ing angels, though they might casually be referred to as such. Nor did all men
wish them to be so. Human nature was as various in its details in this time and
place as in any other. A strict separation of spheres might be compromised, as
friends and partners recognized each other as people with thoughts and abilities
that were not just determined by their genders. And in one very important
respect, the very term 'separation of spheres' is misleading. Women might be
barred from the public sphere, but men were far from barred from the domestic
sphere. On the contrary, that is precisely where they ruled, where they expected
to be obeyed.[32] While the notion of separate spheres may have limited value as an

---

University Press, 2012), chapter 2; Joyce Thomas, 'Women and capitalism: oppression or emancipation? A review article', *Comparative Studies in Society and History*, 30 (1988), 534–49.

[30] Jane Rendall, 'Women and the public sphere', *Gender and History*, 11 (1991), 475–88.

[31] Carol Dyhouse, *Girls Growing up in Late Victorian England* (Routledge & Kegan Paul, 1981),
chapter 1.

[32] Poovey, *Uneven Developments*; John Tosh, *A Man's Place: Masculinity and the Middle-Class
Home in Victorian England* (Yale University Press, 1999); Griffin, *The Politics of Gender*.

14   DAVIES AND THE MID-VICTORIAN WOMEN'S MOVEMENT

explanatory concept, it remains useful as a descriptive generality, but only with this last qualification.

One respect in which the spheres of men and women were quite sharply defined was that of intimate friendship. In a culture in which intimate relationships between unmarried men and women were regarded as inherently dangerous, people's needs for intimacy were met predominantly through relationships with their own sex, and it was perfectly normal for these to be both highly emotional and more physical than we might now imagine. Men would no longer kiss each other in public as they might have a half century earlier: that was now thought effeminate. But they would still walk arm in arm. Women would kiss on the lips and cuddle, there was nothing unusual in them both living and sleeping together, and this held no necessary implications for their sexuality.

In the case of men, there was a widespread fear of what we would now term homosexuality. It was well known (amongst men—women were supposed to be ignorant of such things) that the friendships of teenage schoolboys sometimes took on a sexual charge, but that was just a phase of growing up, and so much safer than if they had become intimate with girls. It was known, too, that homosexual activities were rife in the armed forces (guardsmen were famous for it), and that the care of masters for their pupils sometimes became sexually charged, which was considered much more serious. It was an accusation of this kind that lost Charles Vaughan, a close acquaintance of Emily Davies's brother, his headship of Harrow and preferment in the church. But there was nothing amiss in young men going on holidays or reading trips together and displaying their affections very openly. The conventional assumption was that such relationships remained asexual and in the upper middle class within which Davies moved, for the most part they probably did. The homosexual was not yet a recognized identity, men were expected to live out heterosexual roles, whatever might be their feelings, and the combined forces of powerful social convention and intense guilt were severely constraining. Some of the homosexual men we know of in this class, mainly academics, no doubt engaged in homosexual activities, either with their peers or through readily available casual encounters with working-class youths. They seem, however, to have pined much more than they performed.[33]

When it came to women, sexual purity was assumed. When women not only entered into 'marriages' but also dressed up in male clothes and flaunted their affections, their Bohemian friends knew perfectly well what was going on and

---

[33] The law also played its part. In the period with which we are concerned here, however, the principal crime with which they might have been charged was that of buggery. It was only with the Labouchère Amendment of 1885 that the specific crime of gross indecency between men was introduced. There is an enormous and contentious literature on male homosexuality in Victorian England, but for a balanced overview see Weeks, *Sex, Politics and Society*, chapter 6. For academics and intellectuals in the 1860s and 1870s see, for example, Schultz, *Henry Sidgwick*; Grosskurth, *John Addington Symonds*; Goldhill, *A Very Queer Family*.

others had a good guess. But polite society viewed them as 'strong women', their behaviour signalling a rejection of men—which was disgraceful in itself—rather than anything more sinister. And if female couples did not display themselves in this way, no one questioned their behaviour. Kissing and cuddling were fine, sex was unthinkable, but because sex was unthinkable the fluid boundary between one and the other—and it must, in the nature of humans, have been very fluid—was also unthinkable. Looking back from later centuries, by when lesbian sex had become thinkable, observers have tended to draw sharp distinctions between the sexual and merely affectionate, and quite often to assume the former.[34] But we need to remember that in a world in which physically intimacy between the sexes was condemned, women had good reason to be physically afraid of male sexuality, and that what looks like an attraction to other women may often have started out (and may or may not have continued) as a rejection of men. We would also do well to take note of Virginia Woolf's warning: 'Where people mistake, as I think, is in perpetually narrowing and naming these immensely composite and wide flung passions—driving stakes through them, herding them between screens.... What is the line between friendship and inversion?'[35] Answer: very permeable. Some of the intimate friendships between women would have been highly sexual, some not at all, some chaste but erotically charged, some just occasionally crossing the line, and some completely muddled. In many cases we just cannot know which.

Another way in which the concept of separate spheres provides a useful insight is in respect of attitudes to work. There was a broad consensus across the upper middle class that men were born to work and to govern in a public sphere, women to be wives and mothers in a domestic sphere. In class terms this was blinkered. Working-class women had to work when they could, to make ends meet, and seem to have done so to a much greater extent than elite opinion recognized.[36] In the lower middle classes, too, while the husband might be the proprietor of a shop, farm, or small business, he would often be reliant on the work of his womenfolk. Within the upper middle classes, however, there was a strong prejudice against women working, unless they had to from absolute necessity.

---

[34] Martha Vicinus, *Intimate Friends: Women Who Loved Women, 1778-1928* (University of Chicago Press, 2004); and see also her *Independent Women* and 'Lesbian perversity and Victorian marriage: the 1864 Codrington divorce trial', *Journal of British Studies*, 36 (1997), 70–98. But while doing much to uncover the homosexuality within Victorian female relationships, Vicinus also seems at times to read too much into the evidence. For a broader coverage of intimate female relationships see Lilian Faderman, *Surpassing the Love of Men: Romantic Friendship and Love between Women from the Renaissance to the Present* (Women's Press, 1985); Sharon Marcus, *Between Women: Friendship, Desire and Marriage in Victorian England* (Princeton University Press, 2007).

[35] Virginia Woolf to Ethel Smyth, 15 August 1930, in Nigel Nicholson and Joanne Trautmann, *The Letters of Virginia Woolf*, Vol. 4 (Harcourt, Brace and Jovanovich, 1978), 200, quoted in Vicinus, *Intimate Friends*, 136.

[36] This became apparent following analysis of the 1851 census: see John Duguid Milne, *The Industrial and Social Position of Women* (Chapman & Hall, 1857; reprinted by Forgotten Press, 2018).

There was something of a prejudice, indeed, against gentlemen working unless they had to, and for their female appendages—their wives and daughters—to do so was unthinkable. A key marker of manhood was being able to maintain one's family, and there was also, perhaps, a fear that the vice associated with female employment in the working classes might somehow taint middle-class women workers.[37]

There was a prejudice, too, against girls getting the kind of education that might enable them or dispose them to work or enter the public sphere. If asked why, people would respond either that that was not what God intended, or that it would do them harm. They were not physiologically cut out for it. Too much brain work would make them ill. It would injure their femininity, and so damage their ability to be good wives and mothers. The general assumption was that a girl's education should be designed, first, to prepare her for motherhood and a domestic role; and second, to attract and then please, but never to challenge, a husband. Domestic skills, musical and artistic accomplishments, a broad spattering of knowledge were all important. The ability to think logically and form her own judgements were thought on the one hand to be beyond her and on the other to risk discord.

This prejudice reigned across the middle class and was strongly reinforced at local level by the Church of England clergy, who took primary responsibility for the education of boys but none at all for that of girls. Only in Unitarian and Quaker circles, where the privileges of rational dissent were extended to all, was it thought appropriate to educate girls along similar lines to boys. There was one notable exception, Queen's College in London, where girls were taught to more or less secondary level by professors from King's College. But that had been set up originally for a very specific purpose, the education of governesses for the upper and upper middle classes. And such governesses were a very special case: middle-class women, typically, with no other means of support: Wilkie Collins's Norah Vanstone in *No Name* (1861) or a latter-day Jane Eyre, women who had to work but according to the values of elite society should not have had to.[38]

Beyond school, the universities were completely closed to women by their statutes, and so, without exception, were the professions. A women could not qualify

---

[37] Weeks, *Sex, Politics and Society*; Tosh, *A Man's Place*. For the notion that the ideals of femininity followed from those of masculine gentility see Maria Grey, 'Idols of society', *Fraser's Magazine*, n.s. 9 (1874), 377–88.

[38] The creation of Queen's College was followed by that of Bedford College, but in providing a secular secondary education for girls, Bedford was rooted in a strong tradition of Unitarian schooling. What was novel about Queen's was that it was a Church of England foundation. The term 'governess' covered a wide range: those working for the upper classes (for whom Queen's was intended) would often be reasonably well educated, by the standards of women's education at the time; those working in middle-class homes might have very little education themselves. See Christina de Bellaigue, 'The development of teaching as a profession for women before 1870', *The Historical Journal*, 44 (2001), 963–88.

as a doctor or a lawyer. Like the universities these were male preserves and unsurprisingly men wished to keep them as such. Quite apart from the bar on upper-middle-class female labour, it was assumed that women would have neither the brain power nor the worldly experience that would be needed, and, moreover, that they *should* not have these. If the core university curriculum of Greek, theology, and mathematics was not fit for women, the hostile adversarial nature of the English legal system, the unspeakable details of case law, and the anatomy and physiology of the human body were certainly not.

The women's movement of the 1860s had its origins in developments of the mid- to late 1850s and in particular in an attempt to change the law on married women's property, and the responses to that provide a good illustration of how the laws and social conventions pertaining to women interacted.

Back in the 1830s, Caroline Norton had left her husband, who sued her successfully for her earnings, which were legally his, and then abducted their children, also legally his. He also claimed that she had had an affair with the then prime minister, Lord Melbourne, and sued him for damages to his property, i.e. his wife. In this he was unsuccessful, but it gave the case notoriety and in its wake Parliament passed the Custody of Infants Act, which introduced some modest changes: legally separated mothers, if they had the financial resources, could apply to court for custody of their children up to the age of seven, and for limited access thereafter.[39]

After this the issue of married women's property rights faded from view, but it came to prominence again in the 1850s.[40] A commission set up to review the law on divorce reported in 1853, following which Parliament began to debate the possibility of moving divorce proceedings from the ecclesiastical courts (for legal separations) and Parliament itself (an absolute divorce, allowing remarriage, required an act of Parliament) to a new civil divorce court. That year J. J. S. Wharton published a solid legal tome, *An Exposition of the Laws Relating to the Women of England, Showing their Rights, Remedies, and Responsibilities in Every Position in Life*, and in 1854 Caroline Norton published a new pamphlet reviewing her case.[41]

Noting that nobody other than a lawyer was going to read Wharton, Barbara Leigh Smith, a young woman well connected in Unitarian intellectual circles, with feminist leanings and anxious to do something useful with her life, and especially to dispel the ignorance she saw around her, decided that what was needed to overcome ignorance in this case was an accessible digest. So she wrote one. *A Brief*

---

[39] Poovey, 'Covered but not bound'.

[40] Lee Holcombe, *Wives and Property: Reform of the Married Women's Property Laws in Nineteenth Century England* (University of Toronto Press, 1983); Mary Shanley, *Feminism, Marriage and the Law in Victorian England, 1850–1895* (I. B. Tauris, 1989).

[41] Caroline Norton, *English Laws for Women in the Nineteenth Century* (privately printed, 1854).

Summary in Plain Language, of the Most Important Laws Concerning Women was published (anonymously) as a substantial pamphlet in 1854, by John Chapman.

Chapman was the owner and editor of the influential radical quarterly the *Westminster Review*. He was also a friend, neighbour, would-be lover (a renowned philanderer, he tried to persuade Barbara that sex would be good for her health), would-be debtor (he was nearly bankrupt and had already borrowed from her relations), and keen to promote Leigh Smith's work.[42] In preparing it, she had also consulted Matthew Davenport Hill, a close friend of her father's and father of a friend, who was a key figure in the Law Amendment Society (LAS). Chaired by Lord Brougham, friend and associate of Barbara's father and grandfather, this was an organization that had taken on itself the task of expertly reviewing proposals put before Parliament and, where appropriate, making proposals of its own.

Through Hill and the Liberal MP Richard Monckton Milnes, the book was brought to the attention of a committee of the LAS. Encouraged by their support, and by the reviews of her pamphlet, and drawing on her wide Unitarian network, Leigh Smith then began collecting evidence from women who had suffered under the law. With the help of Tottie Fox, daughter of the famous Unitarian minister William Johnson Fox, she also circulated a petition calling for reform. In the early months of 1856 the petition attracted 26,000 signatures, and in October that year it was put before Parliament by Lord Brougham and Sir Erskine Perry.[43] Perry, in the House of Commons, and Brougham, in the Lords, subsequently introduced a bill to change the law so as to give married women rights over their own property and earnings and the income from their inherited real estate. Meanwhile, debate over the proposed divorce bill also continued to rage, with strong church opposition to the secularization of proceedings, seen both as a challenge to church authority and as an attack on the sacrament of marriage, as the proposed new civil divorce would allow remarriage as if the divorce were absolute.[44]

The divorce bill was eventually passed, as the Matrimonial Causes Act of 1857, but divorce remained a rare and expensive remedy, carrying a strong social stigma, and the asymmetry between husband and wife remained effectively unchanged. A man could divorce his wife on the grounds of adultery, but a woman had to prove excessive cruelty or desertion. In response to the property

---

[42] He made his own contribution through an essay review in which he pointed out that English law still lagged behind ancient Rome: 'The position of women in barbarism and among the ancients', *Westminster Review*, 64 (October 1855), 378–436. For his relationship with Leigh Smith see Pam Hirsch, *Barbara Leigh Smith Bodichon, 1827–1891: Feminist, Artist and Rebel* (Chatto & Windus, 1998), 105 ff.

[43] Petitions to Parliament were commonplace, with many arriving every day. In 1856 some seventy petitions were received with respect to women's property rights and what marks out Bodichon's is the number of signatures.

[44] *Quarterly Review*, 102 (October 1857), 251–88. Ostensibly a review of recent literature but in fact a commentary on the current bill, this was probably written by Samuel Wilberforce, Bishop of Oxford, who also opposed the bill in the House of Lords. Wilberforce argued that marriage should be sacrosanct and adultery a criminal offence.

INTRODUCTION   19

rights debate, a clause was included to give women who had been granted a legal separation on the grounds of desertion by their husbands ownership of their own property. But with this concession made, parliamentary support for any more substantial reforms to the law on women's property dropped away.

In response to the proposals under debate, the recently founded *Saturday Review*, which was quickly becoming required reading for the educated middle and upper classes, set out its stall against what it called a 'feminine insurrection' and 'petticoat rebellion', lambasted the LAS and asserted that the 'rights of women' risked taking up so much time and attention as to be an impediment to progress in general.[45] The *Saturday Review*'s positioning can be hard to read. It was certainly socially conservative, and throughout the 1850s and 1860s it was to be consistently scathing of any attempt to advance women's causes, but it always had a satirical edge and was not beyond mocking its own readers, many of whom were women. A much more considered and more moderate conservative response came from Margaret Oliphant, writing (anonymously) in *Blackwood's Magazine*.

Oliphant pursued four main themes, all characteristic of mainstream middle-class opinion of the period. The first was that men and women were different— and yet not so different as to justify a 'women's movement'. On one hand, they were 'primarily human creatures, answering to the unity of an indivisible race'. There was no ground for any special pleading by or about women, no ground for exempting them from the established social mores. But on the other hand, that unity was expressed through the union of sexes and roles, not through any kind of equality: 'God has ordained visibly, by all the arrangements of nature and of providence, one sphere and one kind of work for a man and another for a woman. He has given them different constitutions, different organisations, a perfectly distinct and unmistakable identity.'[46] An identity, she suggested, that women campaigners refused to recognize.

The second theme was that the lot of women was really not so bad. Civilization was no harder on women than on men; indeed, it was probably kinder. Needlewomen were no worse off than clerks. Old maids at least had their respect. Feminine education could be criticized, but it didn't seem to unfit young women for what they had to do. Of course there were exceptional cases, in which some woman did suffer injustice, but for one thing they were exceptional cases, and no principle should be built on such; and for another, there were cases in which men suffered injustice too.

The third theme was that there was no conspiracy by men to keep women down, keep them out of work, deprive them of what was rightfully theirs, or anything of that sort. If the law of property seemed to favour men over women, it was

---

[45] 'Law for ladies', *Saturday Review*, 2 (24 May 1856), 77–8; and see also 'Woman's rights', ibid., 87.
[46] Margaret Oliphant, 'The condition of women', *Blackwood's Magazine*, 83 (February 1858), 139–54: 145; 'The laws concerning women', ibid., 79 (April 1856), 379–87.

not through any intent or bias. The law was there to provide a secure and stable basis for the social world, in which marriage was the core institution. Given the nature of the marriage sacrament, the law could only recognize one person. One or other party to the marriage had to be given priority, and it just made practical sense for all sorts of reasons for that to be the man.

The fourth theme, and the one that most deeply reflected the attitudes of the period, was that it was not anyway the law that mattered, but morality. There were inevitably cases in which, thanks to the law, a few women suffered injustice, but in the vast majority of real-life marriages the law was an irrelevance. True marriage was based on a union of souls, on genuine sharing and reciprocal moral duty, and such things were beyond the reach of the law. If a marriage broke down and custody of the children was disputed, that was already a tragedy for all concerned—father, mother, and children—that could only be properly addressed by decent people acting decently. All that the law could do was provide an artificial solution, in cases 'horrible and extreme'. More generally, while laws and conventions were necessary for the stability of the social order, they were inevitably artificial and so relatively unimportant. The wrongs suffered by women were due to men behaving badly, and bad behaviour could not be legislated against.

One further point is worth raising in this context. In the course of her argument, Oliphant made very brief reference to the rather different marriage laws pertaining in France. Leigh Smith in her pamphlet had noted, again very briefly, that it was possible in France for a woman to marry, if she chose, without losing control over her property. Oliphant's response was that this seemed 'the most miserable and revolting of bargains', a hundred times more humiliating than the sacrifice made under English law. What she could also have responded was that, as anyone who read George Sand would know, while women in theory had significantly greater legal rights and freedoms in France, in practice they were on the whole much worse treated there. But respectable English ladies didn't read George Sand. Indeed, they didn't read French novels at all. Over the period covered by this book the intellectual elite, both women activists and their opponents, were well aware of developments in France and America, in both of which women had greater rights than in Britain. But they were also well aware that the mere word 'rights', especially in those contexts, conjured up thoughts of revolution, and that public opinion was firmly of the view that Britain was a much more civilized country than either France or America, that its men were more respectful and its women happier and better provided for. Any talk of legal rights would be met on the one hand with a riposte as to the awfulness of strong-minded American women, and on the other with an insistence that legal rights were not the issue. What mattered in Britain were moral duties, not rights.

One consequence of this was that while female activism in this period was far from being confined to Britain, and while events in America, in particular, occasionally impinged, the story of Emily Davies and the women's movement of the long 1860s is very much a British, indeed an English, story. To a large extent, it's even narrower than that, a story focused on London and Cambridge, with occasional references to Manchester and Oxford. The women's movement as a whole was much broader than that. By the later 1860s it was being led as much from Manchester as from London, arguably more so, and there were activist groups around the country. Where the main focus was educational, these were often set up or encouraged by Davies herself, but it was quite rare for the influence to go the other way round. Reading Davies's letters and reminiscences, it seems clear that her interest in the women's movement was overwhelmingly in her own contribution to it. In an historical account, that needs to be balanced against broader perspectives, but in a biographical account (and a book like this is inevitably both) it cannot but be reflected.

2

Institutions of Engagement and Debate

The political discourse of women's rights can be traced back at least to Mary Wollstonecraft and her *Vindication of the Rights of Women* in the 1790s, and there are continuing echoes of Wollstonecraft in the early nineteenth-century novels of Jane Austen and beyond. Wollstonecraft's claims were quickly overshadowed, however, by her husband William Godwin's candid *Memoir of the Author of A Vindication of the Rights of Women*, written after her death: before they married she had given birth to an illegitimate daughter to an American adventurer, Gilbert Imlay, and this put her beyond the pale for any respectable woman reader.[1]

A generation later, the question of female suffrage had arisen in the context of debate over the Reform Act of 1832 and had cropped up again throughout the 1830s and 1840s in the context of the Chartist movement, of the model communities proposed by the utopian socialist Robert Owen, and of the progressive politics of the Unitarian minister William Johnson Fox and his followers. A number of women—Anne Knight, Marion Reid, Margaret Mylne, Catherine Barmby—wrote in this period in support of votes for women, either as only just in itself or as opening the way to the removal of wider disabilities. A little later still, female suffrage was also the subject of an 1851 article by Harriet Taylor Mill in the *Westminster Review*.[2]

None of this made any significant impact in political terms,[3] but by the early 1850s the idea that women and, in consequence, society as a whole were held back by a patriarchal system of law and custom was commonplace in radical and Unitarian intellectual circles. There was also, within these circles, a close-knit

---

[1] Mary Wollstonecraft, *A Vindication of the Rights of Women with Strictures on Political and Moral Subjects* (Joseph Johnson, 1792); William Godwin, *Memoir of the Author of A Vindication of the Rights of Women* (Joseph Johnson, 1798); Anne K. Mellor, 'Mary Wollstonecraft's *A Vindication of the Rights of Woman*', in Claudia L. Johnson, ed., *The Cambridge Companion to Mary Wollstonecraft* (Cambridge University Press, 2002), 141–59.

[2] [Margaret Mylne], 'Woman, and her social position', *Westminster Review*, 35 (1841), 34–52; Mrs Hugo Reid, *A Plea for Women: Being a Vindication of the Importance and Extent of her Natural Sphere of Action* (William Tait, 1843); [Harriet Taylor Mill], 'Enfranchisement of women', *Westminster Review*, 55 (July 1851), 289–311. See Kathryn Gleadle, *The Early Feminists: Radical Unitarians and the Emergence of the Women's Rights Movement 1831–1851* (Macmillan, 1995) and 'British women and radical politics in the late nonconformist enlightenment, c.1770–1830', in Amanda Vickery, ed., *Women, Privilege and Power: British Politics, 1750 to the Present* (Stanford University Press, 2001), 123–51; Jutta Schwarzkopf, *Women in the Chartist Movement* (Macmillan, 1991); Gail Malmgreen, 'Anne Knight and the radical subculture', *Quaker History*, 71 (1982), 100–13.

[3] See Ruth Watts, *Gender, Power and the Unitarians in England, 1760–1860* (Longman, 1998), 205 ff.

Emily Davies and the Mid-Victorian Women's Movement. John Hendry, Oxford University Press. © John Hendry 2024.
DOI: 10.1093/oso/9780198910237.003.0002

familial network of intellectual Unitarian and Quaker women committed both to improving the lot of women and to contributing as women to the common good.

To the extent that we can talk of an English or British women's movement before the late 1850s, it is with reference to this network, but while sympathetic to the rights and freedoms of women, its main concern was with the abolition of slavery. Elizabeth Jesser Reid, Julia Smith, Jane Smeal Wigham, Harriet Martineau, Charlotte Manning, Marion Reid, Anne Knight, Elizabeth Pease Nichol, Mary Carpenter, Clementia Taylor, Priscilla Bright Mclaren, Anna and Elizabeth Blackwell, Eliza Bostock, Mary Estlin, and Eliza Wigham were all prominent abolitionists. Some of them also engaged in other causes. Elizabeth Jesser Reid, with help from Eliza Bostock and money from Lady Byron, founded Bedford College, which provided young women from (mainly) Unitarian families with a secondary-level education. Mary Carpenter founded a ragged school and reformatories. Harriet Martineau, a prolific author, wrote on a range of social as well as historical and philosophical topics. But these were not politically motivated, and to the extent that these women were part of any movement it was the abolitionist movement. With the exception of Martineau, Elizabeth Jesser Reid, and a few others, moreover, they operated firmly within the established gender roles. The women organized support and raised funds for the male activists and cast themselves in caring maternal roles in respect of the enslaved, especially the women and girls. Light-skinned girls of mixed race sold as concubines were a particular concern. They did, however, establish a precedent for the formation of women's societies and associations, mainly at the local level.[4]

In the American context, the women's movement of the second half of the nineteenth century emerged directly from this abolitionist engagement, the question being whether it was proper for women to engage publicly in politics. In Britain prior to the late 1850s, the answer was a clear 'no'. They might engage in fundraising and support roles, but it would be unthinkable for them to speak in public meetings. America was less hidebound. In the Northern states, at least, women generally received a broader education and were allowed greater social freedom. They could be more visible publicly and more vocal privately. Political participation was still thought to be unfeminine and unseemly, but in the context of the anti-slavery movement of the 1830s that view was already being challenged. In some states women were excluded, but in others they were attending meetings, and they were taking part.

In 1840 the British and Foreign Anti-Slavery Society held a World Anti-Slavery Convention in London. American delegates were invited, but women were

---

[4] Clare Midgley, *Women against Slavery: The British Campaigns, 1780–1870* (Routledge, 1992); Gleadle, *The Early Feminists*; Ruth Watts, 'Rational religion and feminism: the challenge of Unitarianism in the nineteenth century', in Sue Morgan, ed., *Women, Religion and Feminism in Britain, 1750–1900* (Palgrave Macmillan, 2002), 32–52.

explicitly excluded. Some turned up anyway, as delegates or as individuals, but while they were allowed to watch from a gallery they were not allowed to sit in the main hall or to participate in the proceedings.[5] Out of this rejection grew an American movement for women's rights, focused on a series of women's rights conventions, the first in Seneca Falls and Rochester, New York State, in 1848, with the first National Woman's Rights Convention following in Worcester, Massachusetts, in 1850. On the agenda was the full panoply of female equality, in property rights and marriage, education and employment, and the franchise.

In England, the 1850 convention provided the hook for Harriet Taylor Mill's article in the *Westminster*, but no parallel women's movement emerged. As noted in the last chapter, the language of rights, so natural in the American context, played badly in Britain, a country ruled by duties, and in which rights were still strongly associated with revolution. There was a general suspicion of American mores, and the mere phrase 'American woman' was enough to drive the press into a frenzy. The women's movement of the early1850s remained essentially what it had been a decade earlier: a loose network of intellectual and reform-minded friends, mostly Unitarian with some Quakers and the occasional atheist, trying to improve the world with their writing and projects, but with little or no political impact.

The people who did more than anyone to change this and pave the way for the politically engaged women's movement that was to follow were two close friends, Barbara Leigh Smith and Bessie Parkes—and especially Leigh Smith.[6] The Smiths were a prominent Unitarian family who had grown rich through trade and commerce. Barbara's paternal grandfather, William Smith, had managed to lose much of the fortune he inherited but had made his mark as a Radical MP and leading abolitionist, closely associated with the Clapham Sect. Her father, Ben, who restored the family business, was also an MP, whose particular passions were for Owenite socialism and working-class education.

They were an irregular family. Ben Smith never married Barbara's mother, Anne Longden, but after an attempt to set up an Owenite community in America he established her and their five children as the 'Leigh Smith' family back in England. Anne died when Barbara, the eldest child, was just seven, and the mother role was filled by two of Barbara's aunts, one of whom, Julia Smith, was an active member of the women's abolitionist movement. All five children, girls as well as boys, received an excellent if unstructured education through a combination of Unitarian schools and private tutors, and on reaching the age of

---

[5] For details see Catherine Hall, *Civilising Subjects: Metropole and Colony in the English Imagination 1830–1867* (Polity, 2002), 330.

[6] For what follows see Pam Hirsch, *Barbara Leigh Smith Bodichon, 1827–1891: Feminist, Artist and Rebel* (Chatto & Windus, 1998), and Jane Rendall, 'Friendship and politics: Barbara Leigh Smith Bodichon (1827–91) and Bessie Rayner Parkes (1829–1925)', in Susan Mendus and Jane Rendall, eds., *Sexuality and Subordination* (Routledge, 1989), 136–70.

twenty-one each received a portfolio of investments, sufficient to make them independent. Barbara also received the title deeds to an infant school that had been set up by her father.

The context of this was an Infant School Society that had been set up thirty years earlier by Henry Brougham, later Lord Brougham, and others. Ben Smith had been introduced to Brougham by his father. Following a visit to Robert Owen's school for mill workers in New Lanark, he had persuaded the society to open a school in Westminster and had persuaded Robert Buchanan, the teacher from the New Lanark school, to teach there. When the eccentricities of the teacher, a mystical Swedenborgian, had proved too much for the society, Ben had taken over the school himself.

Buchanan had become a friend of the family and was a formative influence on Barbara. By the time she inherited the school, however, he had long since left the country and the school was no longer a source of innovation. She consequently immersed herself in the various innovative educational ventures of the time— William Ellis's Birkbeck schools, Bertha Ronge's kindergartens, Caroline Hill's Pestalozzian school, the schools run by Mary Merryweather for the Unitarian Courtauld family, and a variety of ragged and reformatory schools—and opened a new school herself close to her family's London house in Marylebone, where she was then living.

Meanwhile, in her late teens, Barbara had become close friends with two girls whose own Unitarian families had, like hers, taken properties in Hastings on the south coast. One was Anna Mary Howitt, whose parents were prolific and successful writers. The Howitts had travelled widely and Anna Mary had little formal education but an excellent grounding in languages and the arts, and was set on a career as an artist. The other was Bessie Parkes, whose father, Joseph Parkes, was a parliamentary solicitor and journalist, a political Radical and close associate of Brougham. A maternal great grandfather was Joseph Priestley, whose *Institutes of Natural and Revealed Religion* was one of the core texts of Unitarian theology. Bessie had been, if anything, even better educated than Barbara and had ambitions to be a writer. Barbara, whose energy and enthusiasm were extraordinary, pursued both writing and art. By 1850 she had exhibited at the Royal Academy and was in due course to become one of England's most successful female artists—unlike Anna Mary Howitt, who retreated from public view after one of her paintings was cruelly condemned by Ruskin. Meanwhile she started writing, contributing with Bessie to two local papers, one in Hastings and one in Birmingham, of which Joseph Parkes had once been proprietor. Bessie wrote mainly poetry. Barbara wrote on public health, the education of women, the subjection of women, and the folly of fashion.

In the late 1840s and through most of the 1850s Barbara and Bessie were intimate friends. Their circumstances were different. Bessie Parkes was an only daughter, living with and dependent on quite conventional and aging parents.

Barbara Leigh Smith had the use of her father's London house, but she also built a country cottage of her own and was in every respect independent. Much of the time they were in London together, or travelling in Europe together (unchaperoned!), and when they weren't together they wrote to each other at length. Barbara painted, Bessie wrote poetry, but they also talked and wrote endlessly about the things that concerned them: politics, law, education, the state of women, and what, as single women, to do with their lives. And when Barbara wrote her pamphlet on the laws concerning women, Bessie wrote one on the education of girls.

Remarks on the Education of Girls, which was also published anonymously by Chapman, did not have the immediate impact of the *Brief Summary*, but it set out an agenda for the future.[7] The main thrust was in favour of a full and broad education for girls, such as she had received herself but much more so, with plenty of physical exercise (a particular concern of Barbara's) and unfettered reading. Along the way, however, Bessie touched on the social restrictions under which women lived, and stirred the prejudices of those who supported them. Her physical ideal was not just a physically healthy girl but a strong and muscular woman. She not only argued for unfettered reading, with nothing hidden or forbidden, but positively recommended the sexually explicit classics of past ages as an education in the relationships between the sexes. And she condemned the social ban on young men and women spending time alone together. She proposed social and political science as the most appropriate subject for girls to study, and suggested that even more important than this study was engagement in the world—the public sphere of employment and responsibility.

Barbara Leigh Smith and Bessie Rayner Parkes slotted naturally into the existing Unitarian network of women. They were also widely connected beyond it, through their own parents and the Howitts, to literary and artistic circles and, most significantly, to the world of radical and progressive politics. And with their publications of 1854 they began the progress of mobilizing those networks. Their relationship was always lopsided. Leigh Smith, with her friends as with her siblings, was always the leader: charismatic, adventurous, practical, an organizer. She was much the more politically engaged of the two, but also more measured in her writing and public pronouncements. Parkes was much more emotional, in both her friendships and her writing. Adoring and deeply in awe of her friend, she always tended to follow her lead, and as a women's movement developed in the second half of the 1850s and early 1860s she would be the faithful lieutenant. She would also be, more often than not, the one in the firing line.[8]

---

[7] Bessie Rayner Parkes, *Remarks on the Education of Girls* (John Chapman, 1854). A later edition bore the author's name and a longer and more provocative title: *Remarks on the Education of Girls, with Reference to the Social, Legal, and Industrial Position of Women in the Present Day,* 3rd ed. (John Chapman, 1956).

[8] For an exploration of the relationship between the two women see Rendall, 'Friendship and politics'.

By the time the petition on married women's property was presented to Parliament in October 1856, Chapman had put out new editions of both the 1854 pamphlets, now with their authors' names. In Leigh Smith's case this brought recognition and respect. Amongst those who had met to organize the petition, she was already seen as the leader, but she was now known to a wider audience for a work which, when originally published, had been widely praised. In Parkes's case it brought recognition and opprobrium. The *Saturday Review* took aim at the 'species of vermin', the 'strong-minded women', in the mould of the heroines of Aristophanes, that the proposed education would be likely to produce.[9] This prompted another damning notice in the (normally moderate) *National Review*, in the wake of which Parkes's father castigated her, not for the last time, for writing about things she could as yet know nothing about, and publishing something without letting him vet it first: for unmarried women to read such things was, he said, outrageous.[10] Parkes, it should be noted, was now twenty-seven.

Whatever the responses elicited, both women were now well known, and known to be on a mission. The question was how to pursue it. It happened that that October Parkes was visiting Edinburgh, where she ran into another aspiring young woman writer, Isa Craig, who drew her attention to a local fortnightly paper that had been set up the previous year. The *Waverley Journal*, though owned by a man, was edited by women and published 'for the cultivation of the memorable, the progressive and the beautiful'. She began submitting articles and when, that same winter, she joined the Leigh Smith family on a long holiday in Algiers, the two friends hatched up a plan. Parkes would apply for the position of editor, which she must have known was vacant. They would then move the offices to London and establish the *Waverley* as a national journal for working and would-be working women, with a particular focus on the education and training of middle-class women and the opportunities for their employment. Using Leigh Smith's financial resources, they would also seek to buy out the owners.

In the end it made more sense to set up a new journal of their own than to buy out the *Waverley* and in February 1858 the *English Woman's Journal* was set up as a joint stock company, with offices and a small reading room in Princes Street, near Oxford Circus, Parkes as editor and the funding provided mainly by Leigh Smith.[11] In December 1859, the *Journal* moved to much larger premises round the corner from Princes Street at 19 Langham Place, which also housed a reading room, luncheon room, and the offices of a new venture, the Society for Promoting the Employment of Women (SPEW), as well as residential accommodation.

---

[9] 'Bloomeriana', *Saturday Review*, 4 (19 September 1857), 238–9.

[10] [Willam Caldwell Roscoe], 'Woman', *National Review*, 7 (1858), 333–61, especially 353–4; JP to BRP, 6 October 1858, GBR/0271/GCPP Parkes 2/64.

[11] The title may have come from George Holyoake, the Owenite and secularist whom Parkes consulted at this time: Laura Schwarz, *Infidel Feminism: Secularism, Religion and Women's Emancipation in England, 1830–1914* (Manchester University Press, 2013), 157.

The Langham Place building provided a physical meeting point for the new movement and acted as the nerve centre for a range of activities, including two women-run businesses, a copying agency, and a printer and publisher, the Victoria Press.

Several features of these developments are particularly worth noting. First and most obviously, this was the first time there had been such a women's organization in Britain, with a physical headquarters, a journal and publisher through which to advance its cause, and a mailing list of subscribers—about a thousand by 1860.

A second point to be noted is Leigh Smith's role. She was still the leader and chief funder, either herself or through her contacts, and an article she wrote for the *Waverley* on 'Women and work', reissued shortly afterwards as a short book, was to be a seminal work.[12] But besides all her other commitments she had married, in spring 1857, a French doctor she met in Algiers, had spent the following year travelling in America, and from 1859 would be in England only for the summers. She was now Madame Bodichon, her majority stake in the *English Woman's Journal* had to be placed in her sister, Nannie's name, and both her married state and her residence inevitably set her somewhat apart.

A third point is the particular focus on women and work, and in particular on work opportunities for middle-class women. This had long been a concern of both Leigh Smith and Parkes, both of whom wished to earn their own living. In the literary and artistic world in which they grew up, women sometimes did earn their living: as writers like Harriet Martineau or Elizabeth Gaskell, both from Unitarian families, or their friend Marian Evans (i.e. George Eliot), whom they had met through John Chapman; or as artists, sculptors, or actors, such as the friends they had made when travelling in Rome and Florence. But even here there were restrictions. A woman could respectably sell her paintings, but she could not take life drawing classes or be a member of the Royal Academy. An artist's model, such as Bodichon's friend Lizzie Siddall (also an artist in her own right), was definitely not considered respectable, and nor was an actress, though the very people who disapproved might flock to see her. They were also friends with the Blackwell sisters, relatives of the Parkes family, who had qualified and practised as doctors in America, but could not have done so in England. Even if it had been possible, these were, however, elite roles. For the ordinary middle-class woman, the only jobs open were as a teacher or governess, both insecure and very poorly paid. The plight of such women was widely recognized and had been vividly described in Charlotte Brontë's novels, *Jane Eyre* and *Villette*, attention to which had been newly drawn by Elizabeth Gaskell's biography.[13] Their Unitarian circle also included women who worked hard without pay: the reformatory pioneer Mary

---

[12] Barbara Leigh Smith, *Women and Work* (Bosworth and Harrison, 1857).
[13] Elizabeth Gaskell, *The Life of Charlotte Brontë* (Smith Elder, 1857).

Carpenter, Parkes's teacher Lucy Field, and the teacher and social worker Mary Merryweather, with the latter two of whom Bessie Parkes had very close, emotional relationships.

Three contemporary publications also acted as immediate inspiration. One was Elizabeth Barrett Browning's 1856 *Aurora Leigh*, an epic poem or novel in verse centred on the frustrated creativity of a woman writer and noting the ways in which established ideas of women's work serve to force them into uselessness.[14] A quotation from the poem headed both *Women and Work* and the editorial pages of the *Waverley*: 'The honest, earnest man must stand and work; / The Woman also, otherwise she drops / At once below the dignity of man, / Accepting serfdom.' The others were two short books by Anna Jameson: *Sisters of Charity* and *The Communion of Labour*.[15] Jameson was a writer and art critic who had cast herself as a 'motherly friend' to the young Barbara and Bessie and helped mobilize support for the campaign on married women's property.[16] Her own emphasis was on voluntary work. She wrote partly in the context of the recent work in Crimea by Barbara's cousin Florence Nightingale and shared Nightingale's view— and the more general presumption—that middle-class women would always be the *unpaid* supervisors of working-class nurses. Barbara criticized her roundly for this, but she also had a great respect for her as someone who had always earnt her own living, first as a teacher and governess and then, during and after her failed marriage, as a writer. And she warmly endorsed her underlying message:[17]

> We require in our country the recognition,—the public recognition,—by law as well as by opinion, of the woman's privilege to share in the communion of labour at her free choice, and the foundation of institutions which shall train her to do her work well.

Jameson's books attracted the attention of others, too, including a long and sympathetic article in the *North British Review* in February 1857,[18] and a few months later a Scottish lawyer, John Duguid Milne, brought out a work on which he'd apparently been working for some time, *The Industrial and Social Position of*

---

[14] See Gillian Beer, *George Eliot and the Woman Question* (Edward Everett Root, 2018), 158.

[15] Anna Jameson, *The Communion of Labour: A Second Lecture on the Social Employments of Women* (Longman, 1856); *Sisters of Charity, Catholic and Protestant, Abroad and at Home* (Longman, 1855). Abridged versions had earlier been given as lectures to friends.

[16] Lowndes, 41; Lawrence Goldman, *Science, Reform and Politics in Victorian Britain: The Social Science Association, 1857–1886* (Cambridge University Press, 2002), 49.

[17] Jameson, *Sisters of Charity*, 32. For nursing, class, and paid employment see Gillian Sutherland, *In Search of the New Woman: Middle-Class Women and Work in Britain, 1870–1914* (Cambridge University Press, 2015), 48.

[18] 'The employment of women', *North British Review*, 26 (February 1857), 291–338. Though nominally reviewing, as was the norm, a range of books, including a second edition of Bessie Parkes's *Remarks of the Education of Girls*, the focus was very much on Jameson's *Communion of Labour*.

Women.[19] A comprehensive survey of women's lives in relation to their social context and employment, this was notable for several features. It gave, for the first time, a statistical summary of women's employment based on the 1851 census, which demonstrated that far more working-class women, several million in all, were employed than was generally assumed by middle-class commentators. It argued the case for the employment of middle-class women in their late teens and early twenties as being strongly beneficial to their health, development, and well-being in all sorts of respects, irrespective of whether they continued in employment. It cast these young middle-class women as disadvantaged, compared not only with the upper classes but also with the better-off working classes, through their lack of training and employment and, generally, of useful things to do. And it very carefully made the case for the equality of capabilities of men and women, once their different social contexts and constraints were allowed for. Along the way it questioned the legal disabilities under which women suffered, in respect of property rights and the lack of the vote, and quietly demolished the grounds for their defence. It was an impressive work, and if written by a woman would probably have been mocked and condemned out of hand. Written by a man it was largely ignored, but it provided an invaluable resource on which others would draw.

A fourth point of note concerns the networks that were connected and mobilized by the *English Woman's Journal*, which went well beyond the dissenting and radical communities of Barbara and Bessie's parents' generation. These still played an important part. Samuel Courtauld, Peter Taylor, and Elizabeth Reid all became shareholders in the *Journal*. But most of the financial support came from independently wealthy women outside that circle. Helena, Comtesse de Noilles, of the Baring and Bingham families, who had supported the Blackwell sisters in America, was the second largest shareholder. Theodosia Blacker, the Dowager Lady Monson, an artist and regular amongst the circle of British artists in Rome and a friend of Anna Jameson and Mary Howitt, not only lent the Langham Place house, apparently for free, but fitted out and furnished the offices and club rooms herself, as well as buying shares in the *Journal*.

The campaign on married women's property rights had also brought in various young women from outside dissenting circles, who would play key roles in Langham Place. Maria Rye, who acted as secretary to the campaign committee, came from a background in Church of England parochial work. Adelaide Proctor, reputedly Queen Victoria's favourite poet and a regular contributor to Dickens's *Household Words*, who had got to know Barbara and Bessie through the Howitts, was a Roman Catholic. At Princes Street and Langham Place, Isa Craig was an Anglican. Jessie Boucherett, the main force behind SPEW, was from the landed

---

[19] John Duguid Milne, *The Industrial and Social Position of Women* (Chapman & Hall, 1857; reprinted by Forgotten Press, 2018). A revised edition with updated statistics was published in 1870 as *Industrial Employment of Women in the Middle and Lower Ranks.*

country gentry. Emily Faithfull, who ran the Victoria Press, was like Emily Davies the daughter of a Church of England rector. SPEW would have the evangelical Earl of Shaftesbury as its president, and the chancellor of the exchequer and high churchman William Gladstone, head of the Court of Chancery Sir William Page Wood, and two bishops (Wilberforce of Oxford, high church, and Tait of London, liberal) amongst its vice presidents. A movement created and led by dissenting Unitarians was quickly finding both support and patronage from within the established church.

The broad and distinguished representation on SPEW was linked to its being taken up by the National Association for the Promotion of Social Science, more commonly known as the Social Science Association (SSA), which provided the second important institutional foundation for the new women's movement.

This new organization, an outgrowth of the Law Amendment Society, would have come about independently of the married women's property campaign but was deeply affected by it. The LAS had been founded in 1844, with Lord Brougham as its president and leader and George Hastings, a liberal lawyer, as its secretary. Amongst the founders was Matthew Davenport Hill, a Unitarian barrister, sometime Liberal MP and Recorder of Birmingham. Hill was both a long-term associate of Brougham and a long-term supporter of women's rights. By the mid-1850s the LAS had about three hundred members, nearly half of whom were lawyers and around a fifth of whom were MPs or peers, most of them Liberals or moderate Tories. Its declared purpose was to remedy the defects of legislation both by reviewing government proposals and by preparing the ground for private members' bills. It concerned itself, amongst other things, with court procedure, the reform of commercial law, and clarification and consolidation of the law generally.[20]

A particular interest of Hill's was the reform of penal policy, away from punishment and towards reform, and while there was strong resistance to such a move in the case of adult criminals, thought to be hardened and irrecoverable, there was more support in the case of juveniles.[21] In the early 1850s a network of reformatory schools grew up, funded by wealthy philanthropists. Conferences were organized to promote the movement, the LAS gave its support, and in 1854 the Youthful Offenders Act recognized the endeavour, giving judges and magistrates power to send offenders to the reformatories and providing for certification and inspection. To coordinate the movement and defend it to a still sceptical public (an 1853 act had introduced a system of probationary release for criminals, which was causing a law and order panic), a National Reformatory Union was

---

[20] Goldman, *Science, Reform and Politics*, chapter 1.
[21] For the classic treatment see Martin Wiener, *Reconstructing the Criminal: Culture, Law and Policy in England 1830–1914* (Cambridge University Press, 1990).

32 DAVIES AND THE MID-VICTORIAN WOMEN'S MOVEMENT

created in 1856, with Brougham as president, Hastings as secretary, and Hill as the driving force.[22]

Meanwhile, as governments stumbled through the mid-1850s, the influence of the LAS, which relied on stable government, waned. The experience of the married women's property campaign also showed up its limitations. It was all very well generating legislative proposals, but if Parliament just ignored them, nothing was achieved. Both in respect of the LAS and in respect of the reformatory movement, Brougham and Hastings saw the need for a forum in which discussion could be taken into the public realm and looked to a new organization for this purpose. A promising model was the British Association for the Advancement of Science (BAAS), which had long established itself as the dominant institution for intellectual debate in the country, but restricted itself to the natural and mathematical sciences, refusing to accept contributions on the social, political, and moral sciences. Taking this as a model Hastings proposed a new association, initially focused on legal and criminal reform but soon recognizable as what was to become the SSA. In July 1857 the new organization was founded at a meeting held at Brougham's London house, and in recognition of their contribution to both the reformatory movement and the LAS's recent campaign, women were invited. Fifteen women attended, out of a total attendance of forty-three.

The meeting was held at short notice and there was a slightly random quality to the list of names, as some women clearly came as representatives of others, or on some similar pretext. By far the largest group, however, came from Hill's connections amongst the established Unitarian women's network, including Barbara Leigh Smith and Bessie Parkes but mainly members of the older generation. Indeed, of the twelve who are identifiable, ten were Unitarians, one Jewish, and the other a Quaker. Of the twenty-seven men present, in contrast, between twenty and twenty-five were members of the established Church of England.[23]

This inclusion of women was revolutionary. From the beginning they would be accepted as full members of the SSA (which they could not be of the BAAS) and would be invited to give papers to the annual congresses and so admitted, on almost equal terms, to a public forum for debate. Deeply entrenched conventions ensured that the terms were not quite equal. At the very first congress, Mary Carpenter not only gave a paper but read it herself, to an overflowing room. A vote of thanks, however, was acknowledged by her brother, as for a woman to acknowledge applause would have been thought immodest. Many women, especially in the early years, would have their papers read for them by men, and few would dare to speak from the floor. The very idea of women contributing to a

---

[22] This was a non-sectarian body: Hill, Mary Carpenter and others involved were Unitarians; the pioneer whose model was being followed, Auguste Demetz, was a French Catholic; while others were members of the Church of England. Church of England clergy who could not tolerate this formed a rival Reformatory and Refuge Union.

[23] Goldman, *Science, Reform and Politics*, appendix 1: 378–81.

INSTITUTIONS OF ENGAGEMENT AND DEBATE 33

debate was enough to bring out the chauvinist satire. Referring to the association a few years after its founding as the Universal Palaver Association, the *Saturday Review* suggested that it was 'to Lord Brougham's credit that he is the first person who has dealt upon this plan with the problem of female loquacity.... It is a great idea to tire out the hitherto unflagging vigour of their tongues by encouraging a taste for stump-oratory among them...We heartily wish the strong-minded ladies happiness and success in their new alliance; and do not doubt that they will remember and practice the precept of one of their debaters "not to mind being thought unladylike". It is always better not to mind that which is inevitable.'[24] When the meeting was held in Edinburgh, the *Edinburgh Evening Courant* mocked the 'stale virgins of mature years and ferocious aspect who expound violent views of "women's rights" '.[25] But an important barrier had been crossed.

While Langham Place would provide a meeting point for the women of the new movement and the SSA would provide a largely sympathetic audience for their papers, the debates they wished to influence took place largely in the print media. And while the *Saturday Review* would remain unremittingly hostile,[26] this too was becoming more sympathetic to their views. Middle- and upper-class Victorian Britain was a print culture in which the contents of newspapers, periodicals, and books were widely shared and provided the basis for discussion and debate. By the late 1850s the lowering and abolition of taxes such as paper duty, stamp duty, and advertisement duty had led to a profusion of daily and weekly newspapers and weekly, monthly, and quarterly reviews with growing circulations, carrying various combinations of news, opinion, reviews, features, poetry, short stories, and serialized novels.[27]

For the upper and upper middle classes, the *Times* newspaper was required reading: the accepted paper of record, it was also the only one carrying serious editorial weight and tended, like most of its readers, to be socially conservative and religiously orthodox. But as a daily it was inevitably ephemeral, focused more on the short than the longer term, and for more considered comment and debate people looked to the weekly and fortnightly reviews, the monthly magazines, and the quarterly reviews.

Amongst the up-market weeklies, that with the highest circulation, the *Athenaeum*, was devoted mainly to science and literature with little political content. The *Saturday Review*, by far the best-selling literary and political review, was like the *Times* socially and religiously conservative and, as already noted,

[24] *Saturday Review*, 13 (14 June 1862), 668.
[25] *Edinburgh Evening Courant* (9 October 1863), 2.
[26] For attacks on both women and the SSA see *Saturday Review*, 4 (1857), 343; 6 (1858), 375; 10 (1860), 386–7; 13 (1862), 680–1; 16 (1863), 479; 18 (1864), 406–7; 20 (1865), 450–1.
[27] For analysis see Alvar Ellegård, 'The readership of the periodical press in mid-Victorian Britain, II: directory', *Victorian Periodicals Newsletter*, 13 (September 1971), 3–22.

consistently hostile to women's causes and to the SSA. But the *Examiner*, the *Economist*, and the *Spectator* were all politically liberal in their tendencies.

The monthly magazines were mainly literary, with substantial space devoted to poetry, serialized novels, travel writing, and history, but most also included political articles. The leaders in this respect in the 1850s, catering in measured, thoughtful tones to the intellectual elite, were *Blackwood's Magazine*, politically conservative, and *Fraser's Magazine*, politically liberal. They were joined in 1859–60, however, and rapidly outsold, by two more liberal publications. The *Cornhill* was overwhelmingly literary but *Macmillan's Magazine* was from the outset a major political journal. Launched later in the 1860s, the *St Paul's Magazine* also took a socially liberal line.

The prestigious quarterlies were in theory devoted to book reviews, but these often acted as hooks for long articles on contemporary politics, in which the books supposedly under review might be barely mentioned. Of these the *Quarterly Review* was high church Tory, but the *Edinburgh Review* and *North British Review* were both liberally inclined, in both politics and religion, while the *Westminster Review* was radical and rationalist. These would be joined, moreover, in 1865, by the *Contemporary Review*, again liberal.

Throughout the period under discussion, there was a discernible shift in balance across these periodicals, not only from Tory to Liberal but from socially conservative to socially liberal. There was also a shift in religious balance, from traditional high church or evangelical standpoints to a predominance of broad church perspectives.

Alongside the institutional bases of Langham Place and the SSA, this rise of broad church influence on elite debate was to be a third important feature of the institutional context of the women's movement. The term 'broad church', coined by Arthur Stanley in 1850,[28] is descriptive of an attitude rather than a party. Not all who were given the label agreed with it, their opinions differed widely, and their main concern with the church as it stood was precisely that it was divided into parties, working against rather than with each other and losing touch with the educated laity in the process. Their initial inspiration came from Samuel Taylor Coleridge, the poet and religious writer, and Thomas Arnold, the famous headmaster of Rugby, and they shared, more or less, a number of characteristics.[29]

---

[28] [Arthur P. Stanley], 'The Gotham controversy', *Edinburgh Review*, 92 (July 1850), 138–53: 140; see also William John Conybeare, 'Church parties', *Edinburgh Review*, 98 (October 1853), 273–342; Edward Plumptre, 'Church parties, past, present and future', *Contemporary Review*, 7 (1868), 321–46. For a lighter contemporary account, see Anthony Trollope, *Clergymen of the Church of England* (Chapman and Hall, 1866). This was condemned as 'ignorant' in the *Contemporary Review* but captured well the realities of the clergy on the ground, as opposed to the more intellectual leadership: 'Mr Anthony Trollope and the English clergy', *Contemporary Review*, 2 (1866), 240–62.

[29] For a detailed exploration of some of the key figures and their interactions see Tod Jones, *The Broad Church: A Biography of a Movement* (Lexington Books, 2003).

First, they were intellectuals, familiar with current biblical scholarship and of the view that any interpretation of the scriptures must take account of history as well as textual criticism. Arnold had argued that God's commandments were adapted to circumstances, and that while they might be applied to different circumstances by analogy they couldn't simply be taken literally and without question, as the evangelical wing of the church was inclined to do.

Second, on the other hand, they were conscious of the limitations of human reason and sceptical of theologians' attempts to impose specific interpretations of doctrine, such as some in the high church sought to do. They valued theology, and some were prominent theologians, but they resisted any claim to theological certainty. A common distinction was between religious truth and theological opinion. Religious truth was a matter of fact, and could be accessed only through faith: a combination of will, trust, and moral conscience. Theological argument could explore that truth, but could never determine it. This stance led to repeated arguments over subscription to the Church's 39 Articles, the point at issue being what specific commitments subscription entailed, and a rather porous dividing line between broad church clergy and some sceptical agnostics, who differed mainly in respect of whether or not they felt able in conscience to subscribe.

Third, they believed that Christianity embraced the whole of humanity: that Christ, as revelation of God's love, was present in all, and that the forgiveness of sin was a fait accompli: it had only to be recognized. This was often associated with a belief in a National Church, embracing all who could call themselves Christians, including dissenters. Key figures such as Coleridge and F. D. Maurice had come to the church from Unitarian backgrounds and the broad church approach was often in sympathy with leading Unitarians such as James Martineau. This led to sometimes to accusations of heresy and more often to accusations that they put the state above the church, but from a religious perspective they argued that the state was the church and vice versa: in practice, both should work together. There was some uncertainty as to Roman Catholics, who recognized a higher authority than the Crown, but the broad church approach in general was to welcome them with love and let that love do its work.

Fourth, and most significant in our context, in line with their recognition that circumstances changed through history, they were welcoming of scientific, technological, and social change, arguing that it could pose no threat to true religion. On the contrary, new circumstances offered new opportunities for religious enlightenment.

In composition, the broad church comprised two roughly delineated and overlapping groups, one rooted in Oxford and the other in Cambridge. Key Oxford figures, all associated in some way with Arnold, included Arthur Stanley, Regius Professor of Ecclesiastical History from 1856 and Dean of Westminster from 1863; Benjamin Jowett, Regius Professor of Greek from 1855 and, after years of opposition, Master of Balliol College from 1870; Mark Pattison, Rector of Lincoln

College from 1861; Frederick Temple, appointed Bishop of Exeter in 1869; and Benjamin Brodie, Professor of Chemistry from 1865. Archibald Tait, who became Bishop of London in 1856 and Archbishop of Canterbury in 1868, was more a conciliator than a broad churchman and more orthodox on theological matters, but he too was committed to a broad church. All were socially as well as religiously liberal.

The dominant influence in Cambridge was F. D. Maurice, whose main influences in turn were Julius Hare, a disciple of Coleridge, and Thomas Erskine, a Scottish lay theologian.[30] Maurice was a controversial figure, who had founded the Christian Socialist movement in the late 1840s with John Ludlow and the novelist Charles Kingsley. The label is misleading. While champions of the working classes and of cooperative over competitive business models, Maurice and Kingsley in particular were Tory traditionalists, believing in fellowship between the classes rather than any break-up of the class system. An all-embracing broad church was, for them, the solution to class unrest, and indeed to the pressures of a changing society more generally.[31]

A professor at London's King's College, Maurice had also been the key figure in the establishment of Queen's College, had established programmes of lectures for working men, and, after being sacked from King's in 1853 for denying the possibility of eternal damnation (only God was eternal, and God was love), had founded the Working Men's College.[32] In theological terms, he was actually fairly orthodox, but he believed in a church that was not merely broad but universal and he had a devoted group of followers and disciples, both clerical and, especially, lay, including Queen Victoria. Kingsley, who was his most popular advocate, was appointed to a royal chaplaincy in 1859 and to the Regius Chair of Modern History at Cambridge the following year. Maurice followed him as Professor of Moral Philosophy in 1866.

The direct involvement of broad church members in support of the women's movement will become apparent in the chapters that follow. Meanwhile its growing influence more generally can be seen through the periodicals discussed above. In the 1850s and early 1860s, both the *Quarterly Review* and *Blackwood's Magazine* were reliably hostile to anything that smelt of the broad church, but by the mid-1860s their attacks had completely ceased. And elsewhere there was general support.

Richard Hutton, editor of the *Spectator* from 1861, was a broad church adherent and popularizer of Maurice, who had switched from Unitarianism to the

---

[30] For Maurice see especially Jeremy Morris, *F. D. Maurice and the Crisis of Christian Authority* (Oxford, 2005), and Frank McClain, *Maurice, Man and Moralist* (SPCK, 1972).

[31] For the Christian Socialist movement see especially Edward Norman, *The Victorian Christian Socialists* (Cambridge University Press, 1987). For Kingsley see Frances Kingsley, ed., *Charles Kingsley. His Letters and Memories of his Life* (Kegan Paul, 1878); Brenda Colloms, *Charles Kingsley: The Lion of Eversley* (Constable, 1975).

[32] Frederick Denison Maurice, *Theological Essays* (Macmillan, 1853).

INSTITUTIONS OF ENGAGEMENT AND DEBATE   37

Church of England under his influence. He turned the paper into a leading organ for serious debate, broadly liberal in both politics and theology but always sympathetic to contrasting views, providing they were reasonably and fairly expressed. Two committed disciples of Maurice were the Macmillan brothers, booksellers and publishers in Cambridge, and *Macmillan's Magazine*, launched in 1859, was very much an outlet for liberal, broad church views. The first editor, David Masson, was broad church and Maurice, Stanley, Kingsley, and Ludlow were all regular contributors. Other contributors, all broad church adherents, included Tom Hughes (Christian Socialist, pupil of Arnold, author of *Tom Brown's Schooldays*), Llewelyn Davies (also a Christian Socialist and brother of Emily), and Henry Hart Milman (Dean of St Paul's). The *Reader*, a short-lived magazine edited by Ludlow, and the *Contemporary Review*, edited initially by Henry Alford, Dean of Canterbury, both began as broad church mouthpieces. The *Contemporary* was published by Alexander Strahan, whose first London venture had been the monthly *Good Words*, a popular and religious weekly/monthly, suitable for family reading on Sundays. Both publications featured a roster of broad church writers, and the *Contemporary* was difficult to distinguish, either politically or religiously, from *Macmillan's*. *Fraser's Magazine*, the *Edinburgh Review*, and *North British Review*, moderate in their politics, were also all solidly broad church in their sympathies, finding there a sound combination of spirituality and reasoned good sense.[33]

On the political left, the *Westminster Review* tended to the view that broad church thinking did not go far enough in countering religious dogma, that its leaders should probably leave the church altogether. But that came across more as a criticism of the body of the church than of the broad church itself.[34] The *Fortnightly Review*, edited initially by George Lewes and then by John Morley, set out explicitly to act as a non-partisan sounding board, welcoming a wide range of ideas and discussion and debate on questions of reform. In practice, it had like the *Westminster* a radical, atheist bent, but that did not stop it from publishing work by the likes of Ludlow, Hughes, Hutton, and Llewelyn Davies alongside atheists and agnostics like Amberley, Mill, Crompton, Beesly, and Huxley.

A good indication of the influence of broad church attitudes can be seen in the response to two revolutionary books published at the beginning of our period: Darwin's *Origin of Species* in 1859 and the compilation of theological writings, *Essays and Reviews*, in 1860.[35]

---

[33] See, for example, *Fraser's Magazine*, 56 (1857), 657–72; 60 (1859), 563–78; 62 (1860), 228–42; 66 (1862), 695–709; 67 (1863), 549–62; 68 (1863), 277–91; 74 (1866), 277–96. *Edinburgh Review*, 113 (1861), 461–500; 128 (1868), 128–46; 137 (1873), 100–15. *North British Review*, 28 (1857), 123–39; 50 (1868), 99–122.

[34] See, for example, 'Jowett and the broad church', *Westminster Review*, n.s. 16 (1859), 41–67; 'Battles in the church', ibid., n.s. 39 (1871), 353–83.

[35] Charles Darwin, *On the Origin of Species by Means of Natural Selection* (John Murray, 1859); *Essays and Reviews* (John W. Parker, 1860).

38   DAVIES AND THE MID-VICTORIAN WOMEN'S MOVEMENT

Darwin's theory was met by robust reviews by Thomas Huxley in the *Westminster Review* (strongly pro) and by Richard Owen in the *Edinburgh Review* (strongly anti).[36] The main focus of the reviews was scientific rather than religious, but the religious dimension was clearly implicit and it broke out forcefully in a spat between Huxley and Samuel Wilberforce, Bishop of Oxford, at the British Association for the Advancement of Science meeting at Oxford in 1860. A subsequent article by Wilberforce raised the stakes,[37] and two much more accessible books, Charles Lyell's *Geological Evidences of the Antiquity of Man* and Thomas Huxley's *Man's Place in Nature*, both published in 1863, prompted further discussion and debate.[38]

This was not the first time that more literal readings of the Bible had been challenged by science, and for broad church Christians, Darwin's theory was no threat. The Christian Socialist Charles Kingsley, who was a keen amateur scientist, was one of Darwin's first supporters, and one of F. D. Maurice's disciples (and Darwin's niece), Julia Wedgwood, set out to write a book showing how evolution and Christianity could be reconciled. Darwin's own Christianity was considered suspect, however; the idea that humans had evolved from lower animals was emotionally troubling to many; and for dogmatic churchmen already reeling from the impact of German biblical criticism and of the schisms within the Anglican church the new development was deeply unsettling. But remarkably, within a few years the panic had completely subsided. By 1870, Darwin had been awarded an honorary doctorate at the predominantly orthodox Oxford and was recognized even by his religious opponents as an eminent scientist whose work had to be taken seriously.[39]

Essays and Reviews was the brainchild of Benjamin Jowett and Frederick Temple, who decided it was time that issues in biblical scholarship were discussed openly in the Church of England. Seven essays were collected, and while the views expressed were largely unexceptional they were not entirely so. There was the suggestion, for example, that the Bible could be 'true' without being historically accurate, that while it was the word of God, not every word had to be the word of God. There was a critical treatment of miracles. And there was a repeat of Maurice's claim that a loving God was incompatible with the doctrine of eternal punishment.

Within private discussion, the points made might not have caused much concern, and the intellectual press was broadly sympathetic. *Fraser's Magazine* noted

---

[36] *Westminster Review*, n.s. 17 (April 1860), 541–70; *Edinburgh Review*, 111 (April 1860), 487–532; see also *North British Review*, 32 (May 1860), 455–86. All these reviews were anonymous, but the authorship of the first two was unmistakable.

[37] *Quarterly Review*, 108 (July 1860), 225–64.

[38] Charles Lyell, *Geological Evidences of the Antiquity of Man* (John Murray, 1863); Thomas Huxley, *Evidences as to Man's Place in Nature* (Williams and Norgate, 1863).

[39] Janet Browne, *Charles Darwin: The Power of Place* (Jonathan Cape, 2002).

that there was nothing in the book that would startle the educated laity and expressed the hope that it might bridge a growing gap between clergy and laity. The *Edinburgh Review* thought the volume a tactical mistake, but again found nothing new, and nothing that was not perfectly acceptable to the most eminent theologians of deep and sincere faith. The radical *Westminster Review*, however, was in a sense too effusive in its praise. These were the leading minds within the church, the younger members of which had thoroughly welcomed the volume. But it didn't follow through on its own arguments, the thrust of which was to totally undermine official dogma.[40] Probably prompted by this suggestion, Wilberforce (again) went on the attack with a series of condemnatory articles in the *Quarterly Review*, bringing the volume to wide attention, prompting ortho-dox responses and pushing the church hierarchy to react.[41]

The twenty-five bishops, high church and evangelical, issued a unanimous dec-laration questioning how the authors could hold their views and at the same time subscribe to the 39 Articles of the Church. 10,906 clergymen, drawn from both Tractarian and evangelical wings, signed a further declaration upholding the divine authority of the Bible without reservation and the doctrine of everlasting punishment. There was pressure for prosecution, and pressure on those authors whose contributions were inoffensive, most notably Temple, to dissociate them-selves from the work. Prosecutions did in fact proceed against two of the authors, and though they were ultimately cleared by a court with a lay majority, the convo-cations of Canterbury and York both issued condemnations of the book. And Temple did eventually commit, reluctantly, to withdrawing his contribution from any future editions.[42] Meanwhile, the temperature was kept high by a parallel case involving a book by John William Colenso, Bishop of Natal, which again ques-tioned the inspiration of parts of the Bible and again argued against eternal dam-nation. Colenso was deposed by his metropolitan bishop, a high church Tory, appealed successfully to the Privy Council, was then excommunicated and replaced, but remained, leaving the South African church in schism.[43]

For Maurice and his associates, especially, this was all quite alarming. Maurice found both *Essays and Reviews* and Colenso's work disappointing, both as lacking in rigour and as raising unnecessary discord, but he was dismayed by the strength of the reaction. There was a fear that the whole thing could divide the church

---

[40] *Fraser's Magazine*, 62 (August 1860), 228–42; *Edinburgh Review*, 113 (April 1861), 461–500; *Westminster Review*, n.s. 18 (October 1860), 293–332.

[41] *Quarterly Review*, 109 (January 1861), 248–305; 112 (October 1862), 445–99; 115 (April 1864), 529–80.

[42] For a full account see J. L. Altholz, *Anatomy of a Controversy: The Debate over Essays and Reviews, 1860–1864* (Scolar Press, 1994).

[43] John Colenso, *The Pentateuch and Book of Joshua Critically Examined* (Longman et al., 1862); this was dutifully condemned in the *Quarterly Review*, 113 (April 1863), 422–47.

even more than the Tractarians had a generation earlier.[44] In the event, however, the opposite was the case. Although the South African situation was not resolved until Colenso's death, hostilities in England soon abated, and after nearly a decade of argument the end result would be a clear victory for openness. The one bishop to have defended *Essays and Reviews*, Tait of London, ended the decade as Archbishop of Canterbury. Soon after, Temple was appointed to a bishopric and many years later he too would be Archbishop of Canterbury. Meanwhile, in the same year as the volume was published, few people objected to Maurice's appointment as Rector of St Peter Vere Street. And when, six years later, he was appointed to a Cambridge professorship, nobody criticized his orthodoxy. At the end of the decade, in 1869 a new discussion group would be formed, called the Metaphysical Society, with a membership that included many of the leading minds of the age, intellectuals of every religious persuasion and none. Admittedly there were no women, religion still being considered beyond their remit, but there were Anglicans high, low, and broad; Roman Catholics; Unitarians; deists, agnostics, and outright atheists; all happy to discuss their differences, calmly and courteously, in a spirit of genuine enquiry and a genuine effort to understand one another's positions.

What arguably held such a group together was something by no means new in Victorian society: a common sense of morality and moral duty that overrode religious differences. For some this was rooted in God, for others in mankind, but for all it was peremptory, not accidental. In the spats over the *Origin of Species* and *Essays and Reviews* this was lost sight of, but as tempers cooled, and under the powerful moderating influence of the broad church, people became aware of it as never before. By the end of the 1860s, the scientific and religious elites had by and large come to recognize that they were not at war, either with each other or amongst themselves, but engaged in different ways in an honest search for truth.[45]

---

[44] Altholz, *Anatomy of a Controversy*, 73. The Mauritians (Maurice himself, Ludlow, Hughes, Llewelyn Davies) responded with a series of *Tracts for Priests and People*, presenting a liberal but moderate perspective.

[45] See Gertrude Himmelfarb, 'The Victorian trinity: religion, science, morality', in *Marriage and Morals among the Victorians: And Other Essays* (I. B. Tauris, 1989), 50–75.

3

The Rector's Daughter

Sarah Emily Davies was born in Southampton on 22 April 1830, the fourth of five children of John Davies, a Welsh evangelical clergyman, and his wife Mary, née Hopkinson.[1] For the first ten years of her life the family lived mainly in or around Chichester, with spells in Brighton, the Isle of Wight, and Avranches in northern France. In 1840 the Revd Davies was appointed rector of Gateshead, in England's industrial north-east, and for the next twenty years, throughout her teens and twenties, Emily lived with her parents in the Gateshead rectory.

Our knowledge of the family in this period is scrappy. In later life Emily Davies put together a 'Family Chronicle' compiled partly from memory but largely from papers kept by her mother and herself, but this contains precious little personal information, and the volume covering the later 1840s and the 1850s was either lost or destroyed by her first biographer. As far as we can tell, however, her upbringing was in many respects fairly typical of that of an upper-middle-class girl of the period, in a devoutly evangelical family.

Her world was certainly one of separate spheres. While her brothers were educated at public school and at Cambridge University, she received very little formal education, and none at all in classics, mathematics, or science. While they travelled abroad and left home to make their way in the world, she was stuck at home into her late twenties, her only foreign excursion being a single trip with her parents to Geneva, visiting Swiss pastors. As a rector's daughter, and a passionately evangelical rector's daughter at that, she was more than usually subject to the constraints imposed on young women to 'protect' them from temptation, and in her case these were amplified by circumstance. She had cousins, but she seems to have met only one of them, an older niece of her mother's, and to have had no close contact with her. Her father's evangelicalism was not popular in Gateshead and Newcastle society, and she seems to have made no close friends as a teenager. Even through her twenties we know of no male friends or acquaintances at all, romantic or otherwise. She read avidly, but even that must have been circumscribed: one would not expect to find novels in an evangelical rectory.

None of this was unusual for her time, class, and gender, though it was, perhaps, towards the closeted end of the spectrum. What were unusual, and were to

---

[1] FC, 13, 28.

Emily Davies and the Mid-Victorian Women's Movement. John Hendry, Oxford University Press. © John Hendry 2024.
DOI: 10.1093/oso/9780198910237.003.0003

42 DAVIES AND THE MID-VICTORIAN WOMEN'S MOVEMENT

influence her life strongly in different ways, were her father—who was very unusual—and her older brother.

John Davies was born in 1895 in Llandewi-brefi, in mid-Wales, the eldest child of a gentleman farmer. At some point in his early teens his mother died and his father remarried and emigrated to America, leaving John in the care of his mother's family. He had at least five siblings, but whether they too stayed in Wales or moved with their father to America is unknown. At any rate they were not close. From her later recollections it seems that Emily had no contact whatsoever with anyone on her father's side of the family.[2]

At fourteen, Davies was sent to a grammar school established by the Revd Eliezer Williams in Lampeter with the aim of preparing pupils for ordination. A bright pupil, he almost certainly stayed on as a student teacher, teaching the younger children, but the first formal record we have is of him matriculating aged twenty-two at St Edmund Hall, Oxford, a unique evangelical stronghold in a pre-dominantly high church university, in December 1817.[3]

What was behind this rather late university entry we don't know. It may just be that funds became available that hadn't been before, but Davies was to spend the next quarter century hopelessly torn between scholarship and the ministry, and struggling to combine the two. For whatever reason, Oxford didn't work for him, and he never completed his degree. In June 1819 he was ordained deacon and six months later priest. The following year he entered Queens' College Cambridge as a 'ten year man': a curious arrangement that allowed men over twenty-four to register for a Bachelor of Divinity degree, which they could take ten years later without taking the BA, with minimal residence and without any examinations.[4] Matriculating in 1830, he would receive his BD in 1831, but already in the late 1820s he would describe himself as 'of Queens' College Cambridge'.[5] There were two ways of looking at this route to a Cambridge degree. Davies himself seems to have viewed it as a mark of distinction, and a stepping stone to the higher degree of Doctor of Divinity, which was indeed conferred on him in 1844. In other people's eyes, however, it did not count as a 'proper' degree at all: he never studied for a tripos and was never an MA of the university.

Davies's clerical career reads like something out of Trollope's Barchester Chronicles. His first appointment, in 1820, was as stipendiary curate at St Peter the Great and Sub-Deanery, Chichester, where Bartholomew Middleton was sub-dean and perpetual vicar, released from his pastoral duties but retaining an

---

[2] FC, 1–5; Cardigan Baptisms; AC, Pt. 2, Vol. 2, 241.

[3] AO, Vol. 1, 348; see also George Armstrong Williams, *The English Works of the Late Revd Eliezer Williams with a Memoir of his Life* (Cradock & Co, 1840): subscription list.

[4] The BD was normally awarded only after graduation. Davies's route made use of a loophole originally intended for monks and friars: Peter Searby, *A History of the University of Cambridge*, Vol. 3: *1750–1870* (Cambridge University Press, 1997), 263.

[5] AC, Pt. 2, Vol. 2, 241. He appeared as such on the title page of his 1828 book, *An Estimate of the Human Mind* (John Hatchers & Son, 1828; Forgotten Books, 2018).

THE RECTOR'S DAUGHTER   43

'excellent residence' as well as the income from two other livings in the area.[6] We know nothing about why or how Davies came to be appointed to the curacy—it must have been through some personal connection—but it was no sinecure. The original parish of Chichester, the parish of St Peter the Great predated the arrival of the cathedral and its satellite churches and covered the old Roman town and much of the surrounding area, with around four thousand inhabitants.[7]

Amongst Davies's parishioners were a retired businessman from Derby, John Hopkinson, his wife Sarah and his daughter Mary, a devout young woman, active in the Bible Society. Mary Hopkinson and John Davies will have met as a matter of course and in 1823 they married. They moved into a house in Tower Street, close to the cathedral, and Davies set up a school and took boarders, either on his own account or as a house master for the Prebendal Free School, where he had taught before his marriage and where the master, George Bliss, was a fellow evangelical and part of the same social and familial circle as Mary's parents: a network of intermarrying evangelical, Quaker, and Quaker-turned evangelical families, most prominent of whom were the Bartons and Hacks.[8]

This network provided the social and religious context for Emily Davies's first decade. At this time, before Newman and the Tractarians, before the rise of the broad church, there were roughly speaking two parties in the Church of England, corresponding to two responses to the tensions in a church that proclaimed itself both catholic, maintaining the apostolic succession, and protestant, rejecting both the pope's authority and significant parts of Roman doctrine. The liturgy and the Book of Common Prayer steered a careful path between these two poles, but much was open to interpretation and individual clergy naturally leaned one way or the other. Most, described as 'high' or 'orthodox', preferred not to lean too much, at least in public. For them the church was less a vocation, more an occupation or career, one of few considered suitable for a gentleman. These were university-educated gentlemen, who mostly performed their duties conscientiously but didn't trouble their parishioners with doctrinal issues or over-long sermons. Some sought promotion and preferment up the career hierarchy, others were content to be country parsons, devoting themselves to their small communities, to family life, to natural history, to antiquarianism, or whatever their particular bent happened to be. Almost to a man they were Tories in politics, and the novels of Anthony Trollope and George Eliot are full of them.

There were also clergymen, however, who took religion much more seriously, and while some of these might be described as the energetic orthodox or high church, the most prominent in this period described themselves as evangelicals. Evangelicals came in many varieties, but all stressed the severity of the Last

---

[6] CCEd; Richard Dally, *The Chichester Guide* (P. Binstead, 1831).
[7] www.chichestercathedral.org.uk/heritage/history-cathedral; *Clerical Guide* (1929).
[8] FC, 12–13. For Bliss, a heavily committed teacher, see Funtington Archive: https://sites.google.com/site/funtingtonarchive/general-history/george-bliss; *Chichester Directory* (1809); CCEd.

Judgement and the need for constant vigilance in this world to evade the temptations of the devil, ensure salvation in the next, and avoid the torments of everlasting hellfire. Redemption could come only through, first, conversion to faith in Jesus Christ, and then an ongoing and active fight to stop backsliding. Whereas Anglican orthodoxy emphasized the redemptive power of the sacraments, beginning with infant baptism, so that salvation was in a sense done for you, evangelicals emphasized the active faith of the individual and the need for spiritual conversion. Evangelicals were active proselytizers, promoting missions and distributing bibles and cheap religious tracts. They stressed the need for discipline, self-control, and self-denial, whether in people's own lives, in the upbringing of children, or in the examples set by the rich to the poor. In all this they had much in common with some of the dissenting protestant churches: the Presbyterians, Congregationalists, Quakers, and various branches of Methodism.

A common caricature of the evangelical minister at this time was of an uneducated zealot, but the leaders of the movement were educated gentlemen. Most notable in the early nineteenth century were those known later as the Clapham Sect, which brought together evangelical clergymen and politicians and led the movement for the abolition of slavery as well as promoting such organizations as the Church Missionary Society and the British and Foreign Bible Society.

The Chichester group would have identified with this heritage. They were intellectuals as well as evangelicals, and Bliss's mother-in-law, Maria Barton Hack, a well-known writer of educational books for children, was the daughter of John Barton, a famous Quaker abolitionist. Their politics were broadly liberal, but their private lives would have been marked by evangelical religious fervour and strict moral vigilance, combined with Quaker humility and simplicity.

The first two Davies children, Jane and Llewelyn, were born in Chichester, but in late 1827 John Davies resigned his curacy and moved thirty miles down the coast, taking a rather fine villa in Carlton Crescent, Southampton, a fashionable area of a growing and fashionable resort. We don't know what prompted this. Emily speculated much later that he may have fallen out with George Bliss, but this seems unlikely: they remained close associates. He may have fallen out with others in the cathedral hierarchy, or hoped for preferment from Charles Sumner, the young evangelical Bishop of Winchester. He most likely just wanted, and somehow had the funds available, to free himself from parish duties and focus on his writing. He had already published a number of pamphlets and had been working on a large book, *An Estimate of the Human Mind*, a talk based on which was delivered in November 1828 at the inaugural meeting of a new Southampton Literary and Philosophical Institution.[9]

---

[9] Davies, *An Estimate of the Human Mind*; see also *The Cultivation of the Mind: An Object of Prime Importance. Introductory Lecture at Southampton Literary and Philosophical Institution 12th December 1828* (Baker & Son, 1828). Earlier works included *An Inquiry into the Just Limits of Reason in the Investigation of Divine Truth* (Seeley & Son, 1823); *Christian Preaching; as Exemplified in the Conduct of St Paul: A Sermon* (Seeley & Son, 1827).

THE RECTOR'S DAUGHTER   45

This book was evidently an attempt to establish a reputation as a man of both intellectual breadth, up to date with all the latest scientific and philosophical learning, and strong Christian convictions. It might be summed up as 'philosophy as handmaid to religion'. God gave us minds. It is our duty to cultivate them, through philosophy—a term which in this period covered the sciences, or natural philosophy, as well as ethics, politics, and psychology. And when we do so, when we study in particular the achievements of contemporary science, we find the gospel message reinforced.

Davies circulated the book widely, and in 1829 he applied on the strength of it for a chair in moral and political philosophy at the new 'London University', forerunner of University College London, set up to provide a non-sectarian alternative to the existing Church of England universities. A largely self-educated man, ordained in the established church, yet with no degree to his name and a book that was neither original nor authoritative, his chances of success must always have been negligible. Zachary Macaulay, father of the historian, an ardent evangelical who had been a prominent member of the Clapham Sect earlier in the century, was a member of the college's council and keen to have an evangelical in the post, and he sponsored the application. But after a few months of inaction, he wrote to Davies to the effect that a mooted stipend was not in fact guaranteed, and Davies withdrew his application. The college having been set up on the Scottish model, whereby professors were not paid but charged for their lectures, there probably never was a chance of a stipend, but the story allowed Davies to withdraw without sacrificing his self-esteem.[10]

However unrealistic the application, it was clearly a source of pride (if pride can be allowed to an evangelical) that it was supported, however blandly and politely, by some of the distinguished men to whom Davies had written: Thomas Chalmers, leader of the evangelical wing of the Church of Scotland and Professor of Theology at the University of Edinburgh; and Michael Maurice, a prominent Unitarian (and father of Frederick), then living in Southampton. Seventy-five years later Emily Davies would transcribe some of the correspondence into her Family Chronicle—the only correspondence of her father's, apart from a few family letters, to have survived.[11] Having failed in his objective, however, Davies turned to more purely church matters, publishing in 1830 what would be his bestselling work, *Splendid Sins*, a passionate evangelical attack on the violation of the Sabbath by the upper classes, worthy of Trollope's Revd Slope.[12]

At just thirty-two pages, *Splendid Sins*, which was published under the nom de plume of Latimer Redivivus, was more a substantial pamphlet than a book and took up what was then a hot topic. Like many evangelicals, Davies was a strict Sabbatarian, and was horrified by the way in which members of the upper classes

---

[10] FC, 14 ff.   [11] FC, 20–38.
[12] John Davies, *The Elements of Greek Versification* (Simpkin, 1829). Latimer Redivivus, *Splendid Sins: A Letter Addressed to his Grace the Duke of Wellington* (Hatchard, 1830).

not only treated Sunday as a day of ostentatious enjoyment and entertainment, rather than rest and prayer, thus setting a bad example for everyone else, but in so doing required the working classes who served their needs to work on Sundays, when they too should have been at rest and prayer.

This was followed in 1832 by Davies's most substantial purely religious work, *The Ordinances of Religion Practically Illustrated and Applied*.[13] The general theme here was that while in the past people had observed the forms of Christian worship and neglected the substance or meaning, the danger now was of people neglecting the forms. Whereas Christianity had long been in danger of being reduced to mere show, as people went automatically and unthinkingly through the motions of observance, it was now in danger of being reduced to mere sentiment. Davies doesn't name his targets here, but while the crime of unthinking observance would have been readily associated with the orthodox high church, the evangelicals' established bêtes noires, the perceived purveyors of mere sentiment, can only have been the likes of Samuel Taylor Coleridge and Thomas Arnold, progenitors of what was to be the broad church movement. Coleridge's main religious works had been published within the last few years, and were becoming increasingly influential, and while Arnold's first volume of sermons would not appear until the following year, his reputation was already growing.

Meanwhile, in 1829–30, Davies completed the residence requirements for his Cambridge BD and in 1830 the family, augmented by William, aged two, and Emily, newborn, moved back to Chichester, to a house in North Street, which once again became also a school house, and the following year John Davies was installed as rector of Chichester St Pancras.[14] This was a small parish outside the Roman walls, of which George Bliss had recently become patron.[15] Before Davies's arrival there was no rector but a stipendiary curate, and when Emily was christened in September it was at St Peter the Less, the parish church for the house in North Street.[16] It seems as though the St Pancras curate had been found another position, however, as he vacated the parish that October and soon after that Davies was installed as rector.[17]

By 1831, then, the Davieses were back in Chichester amongst friends. John Davies had a living. He had his degree. By October of that year he also had a new and sympathetic bishop, Edward Maltby, appointed with almost unseemly haste by the new prime minister, Earl Grey, to provide an additional Whig vote in the

---

[13] John Davies, *The Ordinances of Religion Practically Illustrated and Applied* (J. Hatchard & Son, 1832).

[14] FC, 13; CCEd; *Clerical Guide* (1836).

[15] The previous patron had fled the country after accumulating enormous debts and Bliss presumably acquired the patronage as part of the winding up of his assets. See James Dalloway, *A History of the Western Division of the County of Sussex*, Vol. 1 (1815); H. J. Green, 'The Westgate Brewery', at westgate.org.uk/2016/03/10/the-westgate-brewery-1/.

[16] FC, 14; *Clerical Guide* (1829); CCEd.   [17] *Clerical Guide* (1836).

THE RECTOR'S DAUGHTER   47

House of Lords in support of his Reform Bill. That failed. Maltby joined the octogenarian Bishop Bathurst of Norwich in voting for the bill but twenty-one bishops voted against, enough to defeat the measure, briefly bring down the government, and postpone suffrage reform for nearly a year. But Davies could not have asked for a more congenial bishop.

Maltby was most famous for his wealth, a plurality of church positions bringing him, at the height of his career, an income in excess of £20,000. Even if much of this was spent on church and charity, it made him very rich. But he was liberal in his politics (a close associate of Brougham), an able scholar, and with evangelical sympathies. He evidently became good friends with Davies, who should now have been well settled, but was actually deeply unsettled.

Emily recalled that her father's writing, on top of school and parish work, made him ill; but when he sought to recover it was once again the school and parish work he gave up. A sojourn in Brighton failed to restore him and in April 1833, and evidently with Maltby's agreement, he recruited a newly ordained curate, Thomas Speck, and effectively handed over the parish to his care. The whole thing was done at a speed that made Maltby's own elevation look pedestrian, but it must have been well prepared. Speck was appointed curate the day after he was ordained deacon, and the Davies family left the country three days after that. Only eight months later was Speck ordained priest.[18]

The family, augmented by a fifth child, Henry, moved to Avranches, a small town at the foot of the Cherbourg peninsular with a resident Anglican clergyman and an established English community, amongst whom were close friends of the Davieses, Dr William Vassall, a physician, and his wife Anne, Emily's godmother.[19] Emily recalled much later that they lived there for about a year, in order that her father, who was ill from overwork, could rest and recuperate, and illness was certainly the excuse given for deserting his parish. He wrote and published a letter to his parishioners, apologizing for his enforced absence and ordering them to be diligent while he was away.[20] It seems to have been an unusual form of rest, however, for as far as we can tell the restless reverend parked the family and set off on his travels. A letter from a seven-year-old Llewelyn to his father the end of 1833, reporting on his progress at a local school and on the Christmas season, makes it clear that John Davies spent the season elsewhere,[21] and his recuperation seems to have consisted primarily in the writing of yet another, substantial book, *First Impressions: A Series of Letters from France, Switzerland and Savoy*.[22] As one reviewer commented, this was much better than the typical clergyman's travel

---

[18] FC, 39; CCEd.   [19] FC, 40; Lowndes, 90.

[20] John Davies, *A Brief Address to the Inhabitants of the Parish of St. Pancras, Chichester, in the Prospect of a Temporary Absence* (1833).

[21] JLD to John Davies, 31 December 1838, in FC, 40–1.

[22] John Davies, *First Impressions: A Series of Letters from France, Switzerland and Savoy, Written in 1833–4* (Seeley & Co, 1835).

48 DAVIES AND THE MID-VICTORIAN WOMEN'S MOVEMENT

writings.[23] But it was very much the writing of an evangelical clergyman. The main thrust was that the morals of a people could be determined by the degree to which they observed the Sabbath.

After a year in Avranches the family appear to have returned to Chichester, but two years later Davies again claimed ill health and they removed to a cottage in Shide, on the Isle of Wight. December 1836 found Davies writing to his parishioners again, regretting that he had been separated from them for so long, and offering them the benefit of his earnest reflections.[24] By the spring of 1838 they had moved again, to Ashling, a village outside Chichester, the idea presumably being to be close to friends and family—George Bliss was nearby and Mary Davies's parents were still living in Westgate—but not too close to John Davies's parish. While he didn't resume parish duties, however, he did engage in church controversy. Amongst the documents copied in Emily's Family Chronicle is a fiercely anti-papist letter to *The Record*, an evangelical magazine, published that June, and marked 'JLL D'.[25] Llewelyn was precociously intelligent but still only twelve and we must at least suspect his father's influence, and shortly afterwards Davies senior entered a public dispute, lashing out in a printed sermon against the 'papist dogmas' of the Tractarians, and in particular of Henry Manning.

Manning had moved into the area a few years earlier, becoming rector of Woolavington and Graffham, about 12 miles outside Chichester, and marrying the daughter of the previous, strongly evangelical, incumbent. He and Davies became friends. After his wife died in 1837, however, he shifted his ground quickly towards the high church doctrines of Henry Newman, the Oxford Movement, and the Tractarians (so named after a series of *Tracts for the Times*, promoting an extreme catholic version of Anglicanism), and when he published a sermon on the subject Davies responded in print, with no holds barred.[26]

Meanwhile at home, in Ashling from 1838 and wherever they were based before that, the boys were taught by their father and the girls by their mother. In 1839, Emily went very briefly to a local girls' day school, presumably for reasons other than educational. She also picked up what she could from her brothers' books and lessons, including a little Latin. John Davies also read aloud to the family in the evenings, Emily recalling later that the only book she remembered with certainty was Charles Rollin's *Ancient History*—already a hundred years old,

---

[23] *The Monthly Review*, 4th series, 3 (1835), 406–18.

[24] John Davies, *A Pastoral Letter Addressed to the Parishioners of St. Pancras, Chichester, at the Close of the Year* (1836).

[25] FC, 51–2.

[26] Henry Manning, *The Rule of Faith: A Sermon Preached in the Cathedral Church, Chichester, June 13, 1838* (reprinted by BibioLife, 2010). For the friendship see FC, 41–2, and for Manning's friendly but hurt response, HM to JD, 1 October 1838, in FC, 53–7. Two of Manning's sisters-in-law were also married to evangelical clergy, Samuel and Henry Wilberforce, sons of the famous abolitionist; they too turned to the Tractarians, Samuel becoming the high church Bishop of Oxford and Henry converting, like Manning, to Rome.

THE RECTOR'S DAUGHTER   49

but a popular and relatively accessible work. There were visits to family friends, in particular the Hacks, and a letter from Rhoda Hack gives us our first glimpse of the young Emily. It was August 1837 and Jane, then thirteen, and Emily, seven, had been staying at the Hacks' farm together. Rhoda reported to their mother that she thought Jane much improved in respect of her order and neatness, and that there was 'no fear of her not being quite respectable in that department of female excellence'. But 'She is never likely to have <u>my sweet</u> Emily's precision.'[27] Cleanliness and precision, in manner and appearance, were classic Quaker virtues, but one can't help feeling somewhat for Jane, not quite living up to the standards set by a sister only half her age!

It's not hard to see why Emily's mother should have kept this particular letter, nor why Emily should have included it in her Family Chronicle. Apart from the warm praise, the word 'precision' is perfect. If you had to describe the adult Emily in a single word, 'precise' would probably be it. She was precise in her appearance and manners, precise in her writing, and precise in her thinking, and it was a quality she evidently valued. She dressed, spoke, argued, wrote, behaved with enormous care that things should be just right. She had no truck with woolliness in speech or writing, and she always preferred facts, about which one could be precise, to feelings. And what was true of the adult was evidently true of the child.

Meanwhile, in February 1836, the Bishop of Durham, William Van Mildert, had died, and the following month Edward Maltby had been translated to the see in his place. His departure must have been a loss for John Davies, whose peculiar position must surely have been helped enormously by his bishop's support. But they kept in touch, and in the autumn of 1839 Maltby invited Davies to be rector of Gateshead.[28]

As with the appointment to St Pancras, this must all have been worked out in advance. When Maltby had arrived in Durham, the rector of Gateshead had been John Collinson, an orthodox churchman, father of fifteen but now approaching retirement, living in an enormous but decrepit old rectory at the centre of the old town. Reorganizing the diocese to his own satisfaction, Maltby had commissioned a new Gateshead rectory in Bensham, then a semi-rural area of mills and quarries about a mile to the west of Gateshead town centre. He then moved Collinson to the nearby village of Boldon and in November 1839 offered the Gateshead living to Davies. At the end of January the family travelled north, four days by a mixture of coach and rail, and moved straight into the new house. On 8 February, Davies was inducted.[29] Having spent the first ten years of her life in the rural south of England, Emily was to spend the next twenty in the industrial north.

In many respects this was an extraordinary move: from a country parish of a thousand souls in the shadow of an old cathedral to a parish of around fifteen

[27] Rhoda Hack to MD, 23 August 1837, in FC, 47–51: 48–9.
[28] FC, 60.   [29] *Clergy List* (1841); FC, 60–1.

thousand in a rapidly expanding industrial conurbation, 350 miles from friends and family. At the north end of the parish were the industrial banks of the River Tyne, with its shipyards, collieries, and chemical, engineering, and manufacturing works. Away from the river was a sprawling network of quarries and collieries.[30] The benefits, apart from a sympathetic bishop, were financial. It was a generous living—at least ten times the income of St Pancras—and came with a large new rectory: eight bedrooms, four reception rooms, servants' accommodation, garden, shrubbery, and meadow. The family employed a cook (their maid-of-all-work from Chichester), housemaid, and a gardener-cum-coachman-cum-handyman, George Lister, and while two indoor servants would have been hard put to keep up a house of that size—Emily recalled later that 'we were not much waited upon & did a good deal for ourselves'—they would have been pretty comfortable.[31]

As far as Davies's workload was concerned, only a very small minority of the population would have been Church of England, the great majority being Methodists of one kind or another. He had the luxury of a pony and trap, with driver, to take him round the parish, took with him his dependable curate, Thomas Speck, from Chichester and kept on another, William Bennett. There was a small school, the Anchorage, above the vestry of the big old church of St Mary's, of which Bennett was already master, and a hospital or almshouse with a dozen beadsmen attached to another of the churches, St Edmund's Chapel, of which Davies was master but Speck took charge. Speck also took a number of pupils, including for a time the Davies boys. Freed from teaching himself and with the curates able to undertake much of the parish work, Davies had time for both writing and projects. As the town expanded in the direction of his rectory he would oversee the building of a new church, St Cuthbert's, and a new school associated with it, as well as supervising the establishment of state-aided national schools for the poor across the town.[32]

What the family lacked—and what the teenage Emily lacked—was anything like the kind of friendship network they had been lucky to find in Chichester. Gateshead was an overwhelmingly working-class town, with a just a few big houses for the factory and shipyard owners, and they made no close friends. Newcastle had a much larger middle-class population and Emily recalled that they became intimate with a banker and his family, but the children were older and it is striking that this was recalled as if unusual.[33] Maltby will have been able to provide introductions to the gentry and nobility of the area, but they are unlikely to have warmed to an evangelical pastor with a chip on his shoulder.

---

[30] FC, 63; *Clerical Guide* (1836); www.genuki.org.uk/big/eng/DUR/GatesheadHistory/Ch6. In Davies's twenty years as rector, Gateshead would double in population: *Bradshaw's Descriptive Railway Handbook* (1863).

[31] FC, 62.

[32] FC, 64; inscription on monument to John Davies at St Cuthbert's Church, Bentham.

[33] FC, 65.

THE RECTOR'S DAUGHTER   51

And the Newcastle clergy, who would have been the natural entry point to Newcastle society, certainly didn't warm to him.

In 1842 Edward Pusey, one of the leaders of the Tractarians, published a long letter—in effect a substantial book—addressed to the then archbishop of Canterbury complaining that certain evangelical bishops had been using intemperate language to condemn the *Tracts for the Times* as enticing people to convert to Rome, and doing so, moreover, for political rather than truly religious reasons.[34] (Some of the leading Tractarians, including Newman, Henry Manning, and Henry Wilberforce, would in fact later convert.) Davies had taken up the evangelical case in the form of a published letter to Maltby, one of the bishops accused,[35] and the Tory high church faction of the region had responded with a pamphlet by one 'P.N.': *Remarks on the Letter Lately Written by Rev. John Davies, (Ten-Year-Man) B.D., Rector of Gateshead, to the Bishop of Durham, in Reply to Dr Pusey's to the Archbishop of Canterbury: With a Few, Previously, on the Rector and His Lordship Themselves.*[36] The meat was in the 'few, previously, on the rector'.

P.N. began by mocking the 'snobbish trisyllable' ten-year-man Davies, who had made the curious decision to describe himself thus on his title page, and continued:

> The "first impressions" this odd Bachelor or Divinity made upon his parishioners, when he arrived, were anything but favourable; as they could not imagine what could have induced the Bishop of Durham to send them such an undignified, unclerical, ungentlemanly-looking man.

This first gibe may not have been personal. Davies, presumably, would have worn the short tails, white shirt front, and high collar of an evangelical pastor and not the frock coat and cassock waistcoat of the orthodox or high church gentlemen clergy. What followed was very personal, however. Having criticized Maltby for landing on such a large parish a man in such bad health, the writer went on to attack Davies for insisting on bringing in his own curate, a 'not sick-visiting, but sickly-looking man', and making him a full-time schoolmaster, 'in order that he might get his own children instructed at a low rate, or, for ought I know, gratuitously'.

'The next piece of economy', he continued, 'that struck the scheming Rector, was to discontinue the Afternoon Service in the Mother Church.' Why, he

---

[34] E. B. Pusey, *A Letter to His Grace the Archbishop of Canterbury on Some Circumstances Connected with the Present Crisis in the English Church* (J. H. Parker, 1842).

[35] Edward Maltby, 'Salutary cautions against the errors contained in the Oxford tracts', *Newcastle Courant*, 13 August 1841 (reprinted by J. Blackwell, 1841).

[36] *Remarks on the Letter Lately Written by Rev. John Davies, (Ten-Year-Man) B.D., Rector of Gateshead, to the Bishop of Durham, in Reply to Dr Pusey's to the Archbishop of Canterbury: With a Few, Previously, on the Rector and His Lordship Themselves* (Currie & Garthwaite, 1842). I have been unable to establish who P.N. was.

speculated. To save the cost of a curate? Or was he too heavy after his dinner to go through the duty without too much yawning? Not the latter, because he was 'a most miserable, poor, tame, preacher', who could never liven up a congregation anyway. Perhaps he did it to encourage the dissenters (who tended to meet on a Sunday afternoon), and so please his bishop, who supports dissenters simply because they are Whigs, and he is a Whig?

The living was worth over £1,000 p.a., P.N. asserted, yet one curate was tied up teaching the rector's children, another properly engaged in the Anchorage school, and a third had been summarily dismissed when he got sick. So who did the parish work? 'As to the Rector himself, he has ever been, and still is, I believe, incapable of much visiting, owing partly to his mania for making books, but principally, I rather think, to ill health'—which didn't however prevent him from working hard in the '*Bensham Book-Manufactory*'. This was an allusion, presumably to the pamphlet, but also perhaps to Davies's past history and with the strong suggestion that he was neglectful of his parish duties.

The first few years in Gateshead must have been very difficult for Mary Davies. Her father had died just before the move, leaving her mother a widow in Chichester. She had five children at home with no friends or family to help out, and her husband was making enemies rather than friends. They seem to have kept in close touch with Chichester friends and family, however, at least for the first couple of years, while Mary's mother and brother were still alive. (They died in October 1842 and May 1843, respectively.) Early in 1842, John Davies took Jane down for a long stay with the Hacks, then wintering in Torquay, he going on to Chichester, and in May Jane joined her mother for an extended tour of friends and family in the south. They also had friends to stay. Still, Mary must have felt cut off.[37]

For the younger children, in contrast, it must all have been quite fun. They had plenty of space, indoors and out, and in effect a second family in the Listers. George Lister was, on Emily's recollection, 'a very clever and cultivated Scotchman'.[38] He lived with his wife in a cottage just outside the rectory gates and they presumably acted as housekeepers when Mary was away. 'During all the early years at Gateshead,' recalled Emily, 'Lister & his wife…were our constant companions.'

John Davies did not believe in schooling for girls. Indeed, Emily claimed later that the Anchorage school originally had girls as well as boys, but that her father got rid of them as lowering its status.[39] She later summarized the education of her sisters and herself in terms recalled from an account by the Oxford liberal Mark Pattison:

---

[37] FC, 69–84; Chichester death records.   [38] FC, 62.   [39] FC, 64.

THE RECTOR'S DAUGHTER   53

> Our education answered to the description of that of clergymen's daughters generally…Do they go to school? No. Do they have governesses at home? No. They have lessons & get on as they can….I learnt a little Latin for my own pleasure, simply because the boys were doing it, but I think this had ceased before we reached Gateshead [i.e. by the time she was ten]. William and I used to do what we called Themes. i.e. bits of English composition, once a week, looked over by my father, & the practice was no doubt very useful.[40]

The 'lessons' included French and Italian, as well as the obligatory music, and the 'Themes' probably took her at least as far as and probably beyond what she would have learnt at a typical girls' school. Moreover, she evidently picked up a lot from William's education. Her oldest brother, Llewelyn, was four years older than she was and intellectually outstanding. He would have been well ahead of her in his studies and growing through adolescence might well have had little time for his little sister. William, however, was just two years older, and while academically capable was not exceptional as Llewelyn was, and as Emily certainly would have been if given the chance. Formidably intelligent herself, she would probably have been well able to keep up with his studies, and they were evidently close. She lacked the formal education she would have got as a boy, especially in mathematics, classics, and theology. Her learning was untutored, and it may not have been encouraged. But she will certainly have learnt.

In October 1841, as the arguments around the Tractarians exploded, and when they were eleven and thirteen, respectively, Emily and William started to compose weekly newspapers, closely modelled on those read in the house (hers was *The Herald*), complete with news, reviews, correspondence, and advertisements. Copies of these appear not to have survived, but Barbara Stephen in her biography quotes excerpts, which are instructive.[41] There were denunciations of popery and high church excesses, no doubt reflecting the rector's comments, and a favourable review of one of his sermons, presumably linked to his published letter to Maltby, in which he laid into the Tractarians. There were advertisements for curates, required to be sound evangelicals. There was also a lot of political content, in the form of 'Parliamentary Intelligence', which revealed the eleven-year-old Emily, unlike her father (but like Lister, with whom she evidently shared her thoughts), to be a Conservative, albeit of a liberal or Peelite mould.[42] This would have been in the last months of Melbourne's Whig administration in late 1841 or early 1842. Melbourne finally agreed to a general election following

---

[40] FC, 65.
[41] In the Family Chronicle, Emily reports having three surviving issues of the *Herald*, and quotes an advertisement from one of them. These must still have been extant when Barbara Stephen prepared her account, but like much of what she used no longer are.
[42] Stephen, 23–4.

54 DAVIES AND THE MID-VICTORIAN WOMEN'S MOVEMENT

successive defeats in May 1842 and in the election that took place in July the Conservatives, led by Robert Peel, came home with a strong majority.

Perhaps most revealing, the children's papers included an advertisement for a governess for Emily herself:

> Wanted, a Governess in a gentleman's family. The lady who is to fill this situation must be a person of great firmness and determination, as the young lady who is to be the object of her care is rather inclined to be self-willed. Phrenologically speaking she has the organ of self-esteem rather largely developed and it will require the utmost care on the part of her governess to prevent this organ from being unduly developed. The lady who is to fill this situation must be a person well skilled in the languages and sciences, as Miss D. is ambitious to excel all her contemporaries in these departments of knowledge.[43]

A letter to Emily from her mother from around the same period, written when her mother and Jane were staying with friends on the south coast, suggests that the portrayal in the advertisement, though it may have been partially self-mocking, was also quite accurate:

> I am delighted to receive your letters....I am glad to hear you intend to be such a proficient in the various branches of education by the time I return. I shall hope to find you grown in everything good. Above all my own dear Emily remember that 'one thing is needful.' Be watchful over yourself & pray to be enabled to overcome your most besetting sins. Then you will indeed grow in that which is the most important of all things.[44]

The slight note of reproof here is characteristic of an evangelical parent, but also a warning against the pride and self-esteem Emily herself notes in the advertisement. This is clearly a very precocious eleven-year-old, highly intelligent and hungry for learning, and there are strong shades here of her father. But it is also a highly self-aware eleven-year-old. We must always remember that Emily kept only a minute fraction of the documents that might shed light on her childhood, choosing those she kept with care. But we still get the sense that she knew herself well: knew what she was capable of, and what, in educational terms, she was missing. There is no evidence yet of any resentment that she is not getting the same education as her brothers, but she is certainly aware of a lack. The letter also tells us that while her mother and Jane were away she was entrusted to some extent with the housekeeping: there are instructions as to payments that might be made

---

[43] Stephen, 24.   [44] MD to ED, early 1842, in FC, 69–74: 71.

THE RECTOR'S DAUGHTER   55

and work to be commenced. All practical matters were normally handled by her mother.

In the autumn of 1842, Llewelyn Davies went off to boarding school at Repton, where a Durham clergyman, Thomas Peile, had recently been appointed master. Two years later, Llewelyn went on to Trinity College, Cambridge, and William went to Repton.[45] They presumably returned home during the vacations, but with William's departure Emily was left educationally to her own devices. Neither Jane nor Henry seems to have been academically inclined. That she had continued to progress meanwhile is indicated by another mock newspaper, the 'North of England Record', composed in 1844 and notable not so much for its strong evangelical views (reflecting those of the real *Record*, one of the main evangelical publications, as well as of her father, who contributed to that) as for articles in French, German, Italian, and Latin.[46]

By this time, aged fourteen, Emily must have been teaching at Sunday school, and was no doubt engaged in 'work' for charity: sewing, netting, or knitting items to be sold amongst the middle-class congregation to raise money for charitable causes. There must also have been visits to and from her parents' friends, though they are not recorded. But term times especially must have dragged. The strict evangelical household would have held no novels to pass the time, and as far as we know she had no close friends. She would have had the newspapers, and perhaps some periodicals, and given what we know of John Davies's intellectual interests, there must have been a substantial and wide-ranging library, but we have no idea of what access she had to it. Many clergymen would have kept their libraries locked with daughters in the house.

In the summer of 1846, Anne Gravely, one of Rhoda Hack's nieces, got married. Emily was invited down to Torquay, where the Hacks now lived permanently, to act as a bridesmaid, and she stayed on afterwards for about six months, her brother William, by then in his first year at Gonville and Caius College, Cambridge, joining them for Christmas. Whether this was for a change of scene or to help out, we don't know, but it must at least have been a change, and with Henry starting school that year, at Rugby, the rectory would have been a dull place.[47] Then, for the next thirteen years, from the age of seventeen to thirty—when we would most like to know what was happening to her—we know only what the little Stephen chose to note, all records having been lost or destroyed.

In some respects there is enough to draw a picture. As Emily grew older she must have become more engaged in parish life. She recalled meeting through parish work a schoolmistress, Isabella Fedden, who introduced her to other teachers and schools and became a friend. She even did a little teaching herself.

---

[45] FC, 82; F. C. Hipkins, ed., *The Repton School Register, 1620–1894* (Bemrose & Sons, 1895). G. S. Messiter, ed., *Records and Reminiscence of Repton* (Repton, 1907).
[46] FC, 84.   [47] FC, 85.

'I remember making some attempts at getting to know lower middle-class people,' she recalled, 'and as one means of doing so I got leave to teach something, I think Arithmetic, in a small private girl's school.'[48] Isabella Fedden seems to have moved to Gateshead from Houghton-le-Spring sometime in the 1850s, and lived with her mother and brother very close to the rectory and just round the corner from the Lady Vernon school with which John Davies had been involved, so it is likely that she taught there.[49] The teaching seems to have made little impression on Emily, however, and her recollection tells us more about her class consciousness than anything.

The visits to and from Torquay and the south coast must have continued, as both the Hacks and the Bartons remained close friends of the family. There were also other visitors. Two visitors of Emily's own generation, Hannah and Annabella Monck-Mason, friends of a Newcastle surgeon's widow, are mentioned partly because of their ancestry—part of the local aristocracy, their grandfather was a brother of the Whig prime minister, Earl Grey—and partly because they left behind a sketch of Emily. Drawn by Annabella, this is the only likeness we have of her as a young woman. It shows a serious and rather sad-looking person, lost in thought.

There was also, in 1851, an extended trip to Geneva, as the Davies parents took Jane and Emily on what was probably intended as a kind of 'finishing', though Jane was already past her mid-twenties. It was certainly a change from Gateshead and Emily recalled it later as a 'stimulating time': 'besides taking lessons in languages, we saw much of the leading Swiss pastors and their friends and families....From Geneva we ascended Mont Salève, and also made an expedition to Chamonix...We returned by the Rhine, reaching home on August 5th.'[50] Relative to home life it must indeed have been stimulating, but more so, I suspect, for John Davies, meeting up with protestant pastors who had maybe read his books and with whom he had no doubt corresponded, than for his daughters. Given the timing of the trip, the family may well have taken in the Great Exhibition, then in London's Hyde Park and showcasing all the latest technologies of the time, but either Emily didn't think that worth recalling or Stephen didn't think her recollection worth committing to print.

The most important development in Emily's life around this time was the arrival in Gateshead of the Crow family. Francis Crow and his family moved to Gateshead in 1848 from Haughton-le-Skerne, near Darlington, about 30 miles away. Crow's father had been a wealthy businessman, and after he died Crow used his inheritance to go into partnership with a local shipbuilder, George Gray, and buy the Friars Goose chemical works on the south shore of the Tyne.[51] This was a large establishment boasting the highest chimney in England, employing about

---

[48] Stephen, 30.   [49] 1851 census; 1861 census.   [50] Stephen, 26–7.
[51] www.gracesguide.co.uk/Friars_Goose_Chemical_Works; www.tynebuiltships.co.uk.

THE RECTOR'S DAUGHTER   57

five hundred men and sitting on land leased from the almshouse of which John Davies was technically master. The Crows were a large family, including four daughters from Francis's first marriage, the eldest, Elizabeth, being a year older than Emily and the youngest, Annie, five years younger. Their mother having died young, he had remarried and by 1851 there were another six children, with a seventh on the way. They lived in considerable style in Park House, an eighteenth-century mansion set in extensive parkland, with about ten servants. At some point the Davies and Crow families inevitably met and Emily became close friends with the older Crow girls.[52]

In the early 1850s, the Crow family fell apart. Two of the older girls seem to have died and the business failed. In late 1853, the family moved out of Park House and into the more modest Usworth Hall, about 4 miles out of Gateshead, presumably for financial reasons.[53] A few months later, Francis Crow died of a heart attack and within another four years George Gray had been declared bankrupt and the business sold off at auction to the Jarrow Chemical Works.[54] What was a tragic time for the family, however, might well have helped to bond the friendship between Emily and the surviving older sisters, Jane and Annie, who would be her intimate friends, and faithful supporters in her various projects, for the rest of their lives. Through the Crows, she also met Elizabeth Garrett (Lizzie to friends and family, later Elizabeth Garrett Anderson), who had been a pupil at the same girls' boarding school as they had and a contemporary of Annie's.[55]

Lizzie Garrett grew up in Aldeburgh on the Suffolk coast, where her father, Newson, was a dynamic and extremely successful entrepreneur. Setting out more or less from scratch, he had become a prominent maltster (he built the Snape maltings, now home to the Aldeburgh Festival concert hall), shipowner (owner or part-owner of twelve of the twenty-four ships operating out of Aldeburgh on the London–Newcastle run), builder, developer, and Lloyds agent. The second child of another large family, Lizzie was fiercely intelligent, outgoing, capable, and mature beyond her years. Her mother was evangelical, but her father had little time for religion and encouraged adventure; she seems to have had a very free and easy upbringing. She evidently thought her schooling a waste, but she made friends there and made use, like Emily, of a brother's tutor to supply some of what

---

[52] FC, 94; 1841 census; 1851 census; Teesside Archives, U/HD/53.

[53] William Whellan & Co, *History, Topography and Directory of Northumberland* (Whittaker & Co, 1855).

[54] John Sykes and T. Fordyce, *Local records : or, Historical Register of Remarkable Events, which have Occurred in Northumberland and Durham, Newcastle-upon-Tyne, and Berwick-upon-Tweed from the Earliest Period of Authentic Record to the Present Time; with Biographical Notices of Deceased Persons of Talent, Eccentricity, and Longevity* (Privately printed, 1867), 340; Crawford, 32–3. The Great Fire of October 1854 destroyed much of Gateshead's riverside industry, and may well have contributed to the firm's woes, but Crow had died a few months earlier.

[55] This was a renowned girls' boarding school in Dartmouth Row, Blackheath, run by Louisa Browning and her sister Sarah and taking about thirty to forty girls at a time, mainly aged between ten and fifteen.

was missing. She also read voraciously, in poetry, history, and novels, as well as in papers and periodicals, and regaled her family with what she learnt.[56] Her baby sister Millie (later Millicent Fawcett) recalled that she would gather her younger siblings together on Sunday evenings for 'Talks on things in general', covering everything from her historical readings to current proceedings in Parliament and the fight for Italian unification.[57]

In October 1856, Annie Crow married an architect, Thomas Austin, son of the family's former curate at Haughton-le-Skerne. Jane, Emily, and Lizzie were bridesmaids, and all spent several weeks together at Usworth Hall, after which Emily and Lizzie also became intimate and lifelong friends. Had they been contemporaries, Emily might well have run scared of the outgoing Lizzie, but the age gap allowed her to see her as a brilliant younger sister and to see herself as her leader or guide, even when Lizzie was in fact doing the leading. They became and remained fast friends, personally sympathetic and intellectually well-matched, but it was a friendship that always had a touch of the tutor/tutee or sensible older/ precocious younger sister about it.

Elizabeth Garrett and the Crow sisters must have brought a whole new dimension to Emily's life. They were from industrial, not clerical backgrounds, much more worldly and much less constrained by convention. They would have gone to parties and dances, and read whatever they wanted. In one way they were stuck in the same state as Emily was: grown-up but unmarried sisters, living at home; but with crowds of younger siblings they would have had much more to occupy them. The Crows' home would have been stocked with novels, not sermons, and it was almost certainly there that Emily began to read them—and enjoy them—herself. Once her reading broadened out, moreover, nothing could really stop her. She was a grown woman, and if she wanted to bring home a novel she could hardly be forbidden. And at least when at home she would have had both space and time to read.

Meanwhile, Emily must also have been acutely conscious of her older brothers, making their way in the world outside. Llewelyn had always been her father's pride and joy, and didn't disappoint. At Trinity College he found himself in a stellar set that included his close friend David Vaughan, Brooke Foss Westcott (later Regius Professor of Divinity and Bishop of Durham), Fenton Hort (Hulsean and then Lady Margaret's Professor of Divinity), Joseph Lightfooot (also Hulsean and then Lady Margaret's Professor of Divinity, and also Bishop of Durham), and Edward Benson (Archbishop of Canterbury). Davies and Vaughan shared the 1845 Bell's scholarship, were placed equal fifth in classics in 1848, and were elected together to Trinity fellowships in 1850, Llewelyn serving twice meanwhile

---

[56] Manton, 17–39; Crawford, 13–42.   [57] Fawcett, 41–2; Manton, 36–8.

as president of the Cambridge University Union.[58] In 1852 they published a new translation of Plato's *Republic*, which didn't quite attain the fame of Jowett's Oxford rival, but was still in print ninety years later.[59]

This was the kind of academic success of which his father would have dreamt, and he followed it up, as his father would certainly have wished, by entering on a pastoral career. Ordained deacon in December 1851 and priest a year later (both by Maltby in Durham), he moved to London, first taking an unpaid curacy in Limehouse and in 1853 being appointed perpetual curate of St Mark's in neighbouring Whitechapel, a poor and densely populated parish with a large population and a high proportion of immigrants.[60] In 1856 he was instituted as rector of Christ Church, Marylebone, an even larger parish than Whitechapel (population in 1865: 30,000). Geographically, much of this parish comprised recently built upper-middle-class squares and villas stretching up from the New Road, now Marylebone Road, to St John's Wood, but the vast majority of its population was crowded into a small area between Edgware Road and Lisson Grove, where five families crowded into each narrow terraced house.[61]

The one respect in which his father might not have been quite so proud of his son's achievements was in the direction of his religious conviction. For at Cambridge Llewelyn, together with most of his set, had come under the influence of the broad church. His was not quite the religion of pure sentiment that John Davies had condemned in his earlier publication, for the guiding authority in Cambridge was F. D. Maurice, who was more orthodox in doctrine than his Oxford peers. And some aspects of the broad church would have appealed to father as well as to son: the liberal politics and the close bond between church and state, for example, both of which had formed part of his allegiance to Maltby. Llewelyn was not, at any rate, a high churchman. But he was socially as well as politically liberal, and under Maurice's influence he became one of the most active of the Christian Socialists, working by choice amongst the working classes, a supporter of the co-operative movement, and a teacher in the Working Men's College.

---

[58] A. F. Hort, 'Davies, (John) Llewelyn', ODNB/32739; *Times*, 19 May 1916. W. G. D. Fletcher, 'Vaughan, David James', ODNB/33332; Graham A. Patrick, 'Westcott, Brooke Foss', ODNB/6839; Arthur Westcott, *Life and Letters of Brooke Foss Westcott* (Macmillan, 1903). C. K. Barrett, 'Lightfoot, Joseph Barber', ODNB/16650; Graham Patrick, 'Hort, Fenton John Anthony', ODNB/13824; Graham Patrick, *F. J. A. Hort: Eminent Victorian* (Bloomsbury Academic, 2015). For Benson see ODNB 2139; Simon Goldhill, *A Very Queer Family Indeed: Sex, Religion, and the Bensons in Victorian Britain* (University of Chicago Press, 2016); Geoffrey Palmer and Noel Lloyd, *Father of the Bensons: The Life of Edward White Benson* (Virgin Books, 1998).

[59] Plato had been largely ignored by Oxford and Cambridge teaching in the first half of the century, at least partly because of worries that his writing would inspire 'Greek love', i.e. homosexuality. By the 1850s, however, new translations were beginning to appear and the choice of the *Republic* reflects Davies's and Vaughan's political as well as religious interests.

[60] For the parish and Davies's time there see www.stgitehistory.org.uk/stmarkwhitechapel.html.

[61] *Crockford's Clerical Directory*, 1865.

60 DAVIES AND THE MID-VICTORIAN WOMEN'S MOVEMENT

Emily's favourite brother, William, fared less well. He failed to qualify for the Bell prize, which required a long explanation to his father,[62] indulged in gambling at cards, ran up bills with the local tradesmen, was conned by a loan shark, and had to borrow £15 from the Macmillan brothers—part of the same broad church network as Llewelyn—to pay off debts.[63] This episode remained for Emily, even late in life, a source of great sorrow. She was acutely sensitive both to moral lapses and to questions of reputation.[64] By the standards of undergraduate life of the time, however, William's sins seem modest, and he went on to graduate, work off his debts, and be ordained. In February 1855, whether out of patriotism, a sense of adventure, or to escape his father's disapproval, he enlisted as a navy chaplain and embarked for the war in Crimea.[65] Thus began a period which must, for Emily, have been dominated by concern for her siblings.

[62] WD to JD, 20 March 1847, in FC, 88–9.
[63] WD to JD, 28 July 1849, 4 August 1849, in FC, 95–100.   [64] FC, 95.
[65] He was appointed on 22 February 1855: *The Navy List, Corrected to the 20th June, 1856* (John Murray, 1856).

4

Joining the Movement

William Davis was not long in Crimea. Falling sick, he was invalided home, and by the time the war ended, in February 1856, he was chaplain to *HMS Invincible*, a training ship in Devonport.[1] By this time, however, both Jane and Henry were showing symptoms of tuberculosis.[2]

In the nineteenth century, tuberculosis, commonly called consumption, was a killer disease with no known cure, and the most common cause of death in adults. So prevalent was it that few families escaped it completely, and many lost more than one member, typically in their twenties or thirties. It was almost certainly what caused the deaths of two of the Crow sisters and the Davies family, like everyone else, would have been acutely aware of its dangers. It was generally attributed to a combination of inborn weakness and bad air, and the most common treatment for those who could afford it was to move somewhere with 'good air'.

It was generally agreed that the best air was to be found in North Africa, in Algiers, and in 1856 that is where Henry went. The railways had made it relatively accessible, with good services from London to Dover, Calais to Paris, and Paris to Marseille, and it had become a popular destination for Englishmen in bad health, trying to get away from the dampness and humidity of their home country, as well as for tourists seeking a taste of the exotic. It was where the Leigh Smith family would go for a mix of painting, rest, and recuperation later that same year.

Jane Davies, being a woman, hadn't that option. It would have been unthinkable for her parents to send her off to somewhere so foreign. A recognized English alternative was Torquay, with its sea breezes and mild winters, where their friend Rhoda Hack had moved for her own health. Rhoda had since died, but her sister and sister-in-law now lived in the house and took Jane into their care. Emily went with her to provide help and companionship and William, stationed just a few hours ride away, must have visited regularly.

How Emily occupied herself during this time we don't know. She will have kept Jane company. She will, presumably, have walked out. She will have done her knitting or needlework, keeping company with her hostesses and making and receiving whatever visits were common to their circle. Her mother must surely have visited from time to time. She will certainly have read, and probably subscribed to

---

[1] *The Navy Lists, Corrected to the 20th June, 1856* (John Murray, 1856).   [2] Stephen, 28.

Emily Davies and the Mid-Victorian Women's Movement. John Hendry, Oxford University Press. © John Hendry 2024.
DOI: 10.1093/oso/9780198910237.003.0004

Mudie's Library for that purpose, but she is unlikely to have had the private space and time to herself that she had at home. Nursing someone through consumption, when there were always faint hopes of recovery but also the near certainty that it would prove fatal, must also have been enervating, and might well have precluded all but light reading. We can be confident, anyway, that she wouldn't have read, wouldn't even have noticed, the works then issuing forth from Ann Jameson, Barbara Leigh Smith, and Bessie Parkes.

This period of suspended animation came abruptly to an end at the beginning of 1858. In December 1857, William Davies was appointed chaplain of *HMS Cambrian*, a thirty-six-gun frigate assigned to the East India and China Station, which left home soon afterwards to join the British fleet in China. Then in January Jane died.[3] Soon after, word reached home that Henry's health had taken a turn for the worse, and it was decided that Emily and Llewelyn should go out to see him and, if appropriate, bring him home. Emily's close friend, Jane Crow, also joined the party, providing support and companionship to Emily and reassurance to her parents. Two young women were always considered safer abroad than one.

In the event, Llewelyn returned on his own. He will have needed to get back to his parish duties and may well have taken the opportunity to detour via Switzerland in preparation for a visit later in the year, when he would make the first recorded ascent of the Dom, Switzerland's second-highest mountain.[4] It was left to Emily and Jane to accompany Henry home, he acting presumably as both invalid and chaperone. He would die in Gateshead the following summer. Meanwhile on the Canton River, William Davies also sickened, presumably from some kind of fever, and on 5 August he too died, the news reaching Gateshead in October.[5] In less than two years, Dr and Mrs Davies had lost three of their five adult children, and Emily had lost three of her four siblings. Meanwhile, however, by pure chance, she also found her future.

One of the many fascinations of foreign travel in these times was that it brought you into contact with people from your own country, whom you wouldn't otherwise meet. Henry Davies, in Algiers, must inevitably have run into the Leigh Smith family. They had returned to England in the spring of 1857 and when Emily Davies arrived, Barbara, now Barbara Bodichon, was still on her extended honeymoon in America. But her sister Nannie was staying in the Bodichon house and the women met. Emily's recollection was as follows:

> On my return to Gateshead I went back to parish work, but tried to combine it with some effort in another direction. After making acquaintance at Algiers with Annie Leigh Smith (Madame Bodichon's sister)—the first person I had ever

---

[3] Stephen, 28.
[4] Stephen, 28; *Times*, 19 May 1916. A keen climber, he was a founder member of the Alpine Club.
[5] *AC*, Pt. 2, Vol. 2, 246; Stephen, 28.

met who sympathised with my feeling of resentment at the subjection of women—I corresponded with her and she introduced me to others of the same circle and kept me up to what was going on. In 1858 the first organised movement on behalf of women was set on foot.[6]

Nannie Leigh Smith was an artist, from an illegitimate family and unfettered by the social conventions of 'respectable' English society: unchaperoned in a foreign country, mixing freely with whom she chose, dressing for practicality and comfort, ankles on show. Described by a friend a couple of years later as 'utterly untutored', she was prone 'to scream at the sun or leap about at the sight of the clouds'. 'She prefers climbing gates to opening them, & when 2 yards off there is a bridge, will coolly pull off her stockings & wade through a river in preference.'[7] She was not the kind of person Davies would ever have come across as a rector's daughter in Gateshead. She was, however, a well brought up young woman from the upper middle class, well educated, intelligent, warm, sociable, and affectionate, and Davies evidently took to her.

Nannie Leigh Smith was almost certainly *not* the first person Emily had met who sympathized with her views on the subjection of women. If she had formed such views she would certainly have shared them with Jane Crow and Elizabeth Garrett. The likelihood is, however, that while she might well have felt a sense of dissatisfaction, perhaps even harboured a grudge in respect of her own lack of education and opportunity compared with her brothers, she had never articulated that dissatisfaction in the way in which Nannie, full of enthusiasm for her sister's projects, would have. What Davies certainly will have found in Nannie was someone who would have expressed, and in considerable detail, feelings with which she could strongly sympathize—or with which, at least, she would very soon come to strongly sympathize. At some point, whether in Algiers, on the journey home with Jane Crow, or after reaching home, meeting up with Elizabeth Garrett, and embarking on some of the reading Nannie must surely have suggested, she was attracted to the cause.

Although we cannot know exactly what passed between the two, Garrett's role in this may well have been critical. She recalled herself in this period as being

full of...the discontent which goes with unemployed activities. 'The obscure trouble of a baffled instinct' as Coleridge finely calls it....Everything seemed wrong to me.[8]

---

[6] Stephen, 29.   [7] AP to Bella Leigh Smith, 6 August 1859, Girton GCPP Bodichon 4/5.
[8] EGA, notes for a speech *c*.1888, LMA H72/EGA/01/003, quoted in Manton, 44. The quotation is from *The Friend*, 3rd ed. (1837), second section, essay eleven.

She was twenty-two. Her elder sister, Louie, had married and moved to London, leaving her as the eldest at-home daughter, in effect second mother to her younger siblings. She was under no external pressure, but with her restless energy the role of an at-home daughter was never going to be enough, and the prospect of marriage may not have been much more appealing. Though more at ease socially than Davies she was apparently reserved, fiercely independent, and apt to be short. Much like Davies, she must have been something of a frightening prospect for the men of her acquaintance, most of whom were perforce less bright and less able than she was, and brought up to expect dutiful acquiescence from a wife.

The conclusion Garrett reached was that she had to find some occupation. As she put it in a letter to her Aunt Elizabeth in 1860,

> During the last two or three years, I have felt an increasing longing for some definite occupation, which should also bring me, in time, a position and a moderate income. I think you will not be surprised that I should feel this longing for it is indeed far more wonderful that a healthy woman should spend a long life in comparative idleness than that she should wish for some suitable work, upon which she could spend the energy that now only causes painful restlessness and weariness.[9]

At what point Garrett read Barbara Leigh Smith's *Women and Work* we don't know—almost certainly not until after Davies returned from Algiers—but it must have made an impression. While it addressed such issues as the 'surplus women' problem (an excess of 500,000 women over men in the 1851 census) and the problem of women married to men unable to support their families, the central theme was that women benefitted from seriously working at something just as much as men, and suffered just as much from idleness, which in the case of middle-class women was pretty well enforced and thoroughly debilitating. In the eyes of her peers, Elizabeth Garrett didn't need an income. The Garretts were wealthy and she would have been well provided for, even if unmarried. But she desperately wanted the freedom to work, to be active, to do things. As she recalled in later life, 'I was a young woman living at home with nothing to do in what authors call "comfortable circumstances". But I was wicked enough not to be comfortable.'[10]

In January 1859, the papers reported on a forthcoming lecture series by Dr Elizabeth Blackwell, Barbara Bodichon's friend and Bessie Parkes's cousin. A remarkable and determined woman, Blackwell had qualified as a doctor at a minor American medical college and founded an infirmary for women and

---

[9] EG to Elizabeth Garrett, 13 June 1860, quoted in Anderson, 57. There are strong shades here of Charlotte Brontë's Caroline Helstone.
[10] Manton, 44.

JOINING THE MOVEMENT 65

children, staffed only by women. She had been the subject of one of the cases studies Bodichon had used in *Women and Work* to illustrate the possibilities that might be opened up: this was a profession, Bodichon suggested, that was particularly appropriate for intelligent, middle-class women, and particularly needed by women patients. She was also the subject of an extended profile in the second number of the *English Woman's Journal*, published in April 1858,[11] and medicine was one of the professions considered in a subsequent article on professions for women.[12]

Meeting up with Blackwell in America, Bodichon had persuaded her to visit England in an attempt to open up the medical profession there to women. Towards the end of 1858, she travelled to Europe for the winter to spend time with family, friends, and supporters, and while in London she agreed to give a series of lectures on the theme of 'Medicine as a profession for ladies', the first to be held on 2 March at the Marylebone Literary and Scientific Institute.

To the English establishment, the idea of a woman doctor was seen not merely as an invasion of male territory but as inherently preposterous. How could a mere woman possibly acquire the necessary medical knowledge and experience? And even if she could, how could she do that, let alone practise, and still retain her feminine qualities? Strange things sometimes happened in America, but they couldn't be allowed to happen in England. (Indeed, the criteria for entry to the new Medical Register were changed to exclude holders of foreign degrees, specifically so as to rule out Dr Blackwell.) Bodichon's cousin, Florence Nightingale, would have liked Blackwell to take charge of a training programme for nurses, but women doctors, never. The papers published mocking reports of the 'Doctrix' and the story goes that when her father repeated one of these Elizabeth Garrett charged him with judging someone he knew nothing about and challenged him to write to his business partner, Valentine Smith, who was Bodichon's first cousin and might well know Elizabeth Blackwell personally. He did so, and Valentine Smith came back with a letter of introduction, either to Elizabeth Blackwell herself or, more plausibly, to Barbara Bodichon.[13]

Meanwhile, returning from Algiers to Gateshead, Emily Davies's overriding priorities will have been to support her parents, nurse her brother, and help out in the parish. Her father, never in good health, was into his sixties, and both parents must have been devastated by their losses. She must have subscribed to the *English Woman's Journal*, however, and educated herself in the emerging women's movement and its background, and she had a standing invitation to call on Barbara

[11] 'Dr Elizabeth Blackwell', *EWJ*, 1 (April 1858), 80–100.
[12] 'On the adoption of professional life by women', *EWJ*, 2 (September 1858), 1–10. This article also noted the particular problem of the middle-class woman, made famous in the twentieth century by Virginia Woolf, in not having a room of her own. The working classes had work; the upper classes had space in which to build their own lives; the middle classes had neither.
[13] Manton, 42; Stephen, 55.

Bodichon, back in London after her honeymoon. In February 1859 she and Garrett visited London together, partly to visit their respective siblings, Llewelyn and Louie, but primarily to go to tea with Bodichon, where they were also introduced to Bessie Parkes and Adelaide Procter, and to visit the offices of the *English Woman's Journal*.

A few weeks later they returned, Garrett with an eye on a possible career and Davies out of general interest and in support of her younger friend, and took their places in the front row for Dr Blackwell's first lecture. They then went back to Bodichon's house in Blandford Square for a reception and Garrett was introduced to Elizabeth Blackwell, who assumed that she was already set on a medical career. In fact her mind was far from made up. She wanted to do something, but it was chance circumstances that had led her to the lecture, not any particular interest in medicine. She did, however, stay on in London for the remaining two lectures of the series before returning home to think about her future. Davies also stayed on for the remaining lectures before returning to Gateshead and the care of her brother, and she too began pondering Garrett's future. For the moment, nothing much seems to have happened, but Davies and Garrett may well have visited each other and Davies will certainly have discussed matters with Jane Crow. It also seems likely, from the confused accounts we have, that at some point Garrett stayed with the Crows, still at Usworth Hall, enabling the three women to plot together.

By late summer 1859, Emily Davies's brother Henry had died, but she had gained a sister. That September Llewelyn Davies resigned his fellowship at Trinity and married Mary Crompton, eldest daughter of a rich and renowned judge, Sir Charles Crompton. They probably met through Mary's brother, Charles, who was himself a fellow of Trinity at the time and would go on to become a QC, marry one of Elizabeth Gaskell's daughters, and serve briefly as a Liberal MP. A sister, Caroline, would marry the Scottish philosopher George Croom Robertson, a disciple of John Stuart Mill who would become actively involved in the campaign for women's suffrage. Two brothers, Henry, who married the daughter of Sir John Romilly, Master of the Rolls, and Albert, became ardent positivists, followers of the French philosopher Auguste Comte. Positivism as then practised combined scientific rationalism with political socialism in a kind of atheist equivalent to Llewelyn Davies's Christian Socialism, though with a peculiarly anti-feminist slant. Women were idolized but to be confined entirely to domestic duties and on no account educated, let alone allowed to work.[14] Henry also became a prominent advocate of the trades union movement and the reform of labour laws,

---

[14] For a stinging critique see Frances Power Cobbe, 'The final cause of woman', in Josephine Butler, ed., *Woman's Work and Woman's Culture: A Series of Essays* (Macmillan, 1869), 1–26. Josephine Butler had recently been the subject of a vicious positivist attack for her unwomanly views and behaviour and may well have encouraged Cobbe to include her critique in this, the first essay in her collection. See Mitchell, 92–3.

working closely in this with Edward Beesly, Professor of History at University College, and Professor of Latin at Bedford College for Ladies, who married the youngest of Mary's sisters, became a friend of Karl Marx, and was instrumental in the setting up of the First International.

It was an interesting set of in-laws. It also provided Emily Davies with a London base. Her brother's Christ Church living was worth £550 a year, but there was no residence attached and with a large population of 30,000 that also had to support at least two curates.[15] As a single man, Llewelyn Davies was not rich, and presumably lodged in suitable bachelor accommodation. Mary must have come with a considerable settlement, and his married home, at 18 Blandford Square, just across the corner from Barbara Bodichon, was a sizeable, recently constructed town house, with room for a growing family and their visitors and servants. The sisters-in-law seem to have got on very well, and Emily was no doubt made very welcome.

Her first extended visit came some time during the winter following the marriage, when she spent her time 'at Langham Place, helping in work either for the *Englishwoman's Journal* or the Employment of Women Society, and in helping E. Garrett in the first steps of her enterprise'.[16] She paid further visits to London in June and July, the following winter, and again the following summer, staying either with Llewelyn in Blandford Square or with Garrett's sister, Louie, initially in Bayswater and later in Manchester Square, Marylebone. These visits seem to have been combined with visits to family friends, in Chichester and elsewhere, and also served to increase her London acquaintance. In the summer of 1861 she socialized with Barbara Bodichon and her friends, met John Chapman, the publisher, and went with Llewelyn and Mary Davies to a party at Charlotte Manning's.[17] James Manning, known as a Sergeant Manning, was a radical lawyer who had been involved with the promotion of the bill on married women's property; Adelaide, his daughter, would become a close friend and associate alongside her stepmother Charlotte, who came from a Unitarian family with strong abolitionist associations.

Davies also went, probably for the first time, to the theatre, and clearly enjoyed the social life London offered, so different from that at home. Her main focus, however, was now very firmly on joining the women's movement. She was not working alone. Elizabeth Garrett, Jane Crow, and her sister Annie Austin were all becoming engaged too, in different ways, and Garrett and Crow on a much more full-time basis than Davies, but it's hard not to see Davies as director of operations of this little group of friends.

---

[15] *Crockford's Clerical Directory* (1865).
[16] Stephen, 55, presumably taken from the missing section of the Family Chronicle.
[17] FC, 214 ff.

Jane Crow was a free agent. Her stepmother had moved out of Gateshead with her own children and she had no home of her own, but she had been well provided for by her grandfather, with an independent income. She probably went down to London with Davies in January–February 1860 and must have got involved with her in the work of Langham Place, as within a few months she had taken over as secretary of SPEW and was soon living in the Langham Place flat with Emily Faithfull and Max Hays.[18]

Garrett, meanwhile, was still uncertain what she wanted to do. Egged on by Davies, she was taking preparatory steps to the training that would be needed to becoming a doctor: getting coaching in Latin and Greek from the local schoolmaster and using Davies to critique her English composition. But she hadn't yet raised the question with her father, and for all her energy and determination she seems to have found the prospect rather daunting. A short article by Elizabeth Blackwell in the January number of the *English Woman's Journal*, 'A Letter to Young Ladies Desirous of Studying Medicine', laid out what would be involved, and made it clear how big the challenge would be.[19] Davies, however, who had no thought of undertaking such a challenge herself, was not at all daunted. She thought Garrett admirably suited to the task and set about helping her.

Her first step, after consulting her brother, was to speak to Emilia Russell Gurney, an acquaintance of Barbara Bodichon who had become one of Elizabeth Blackwell's group of supporters. Emilia's brother-in-law was rector of St Mary, Marylebone, the adjacent parish to Llewelyn's, and she herself was a devotee of F. D. Maurice, whom she had come to know through shared pilgrimages to the Scottish home of the theologian Thomas Erskine. Llewelyn Davies was able to provide an introduction. Emily called, made her acquaintance, and laid the ground for a further visit with Garrett.[20]

Emilia Gurney was never at the forefront of the women's movement, but she was often in the background and she and her husband were to be important allies in Davies's projects, and even more so in Garrett's.[21] In her late thirties, the daughter of an assistant master at Harrow and the granddaughter on her mother's side of John Venn, rector of Clapham and leader of the Clapham Sect, she was the wife of Russell Gurney, a distinguished lawyer and Recorder of London. They lived in Kensington Palace Gardens, had no children, and were extremely well off, but their personal style was modest.[22] While Russell presided over the London courts, Emilia devoted herself to religion, to caring for friends and relatives, and very quietly to philanthropy, using her money, connections, and personal charm

---

[18] Girton GCIP SPTW 2/1/1: 1 and 2; FC, 214 ff.

[19] *EWJ*, 4 (January 1860), 329–33.   [20] Stephen, 56.

[21] Elizabeth J. Morse 'Gurney [née Batten], Emilia Russell', ODNB/56343; Ellen Mary Gurney, ed., *Letters of Emilia Russell Gurney* (James Nisbet, 1902).

[22] EG to ED, 17 May 1861, FC, 215–16: 216.

to support causes ranging from female artists to Elizabeth Blackwell and the Ladies Sanitary Association, which lobbied for public health improvements.

By midsummer, Garrett had raised the prospect of attempting to qualify as a doctor with her father.[23] Predictably, her father was horrified. He found the very thought disgusting. Equally predictably, when he raised the matter himself with some visiting cousins and they objected on principle to women doctors, he launched into his daughter's defence, and father and daughter were soon in London together, seeking the help and advice of leading consultants. They found no help, and only unwelcome advice, some of it barely civil, but to the combative Newson the challenge was irresistible. From that point on he was on Elizabeth's side, supporting her financially and in any way he could.

In early July, Garrett and Davies met with Emilia Russell Gurney. Davies returned home soon afterwards, but Garrett had several more meetings with Mrs Gurney, with whom she formed a close bond, based partly on religion. Elizabeth Garrett had been brought up by an evangelical mother, but had never warmed to that stern creed.[24] What had attracted her was the broad church approach of Thomas Arnold as portrayed in Arthur Stanley's *Life*, a book she had read and reread over six months.[25] The message she took from it was that one could be 'at once as liberal and as Christian as Arnold was', that religion need not be bound by dogma and could be combined with action, innovation, and social responsibility. In London, both she and her sister Louie became followers of Maurice, joining Emilia Gurney in attending his services. Elizabeth Garrett took notes, which she wrote up as essays for Davies to copy-edit.[26] The idea was apparently that Davies's critiques would improve her writing skills, as part of her general education, but she was also anxious to share the insights she received with her close friend. In February 1861, she went to a party at Llewelyn Davies's home, where Maurice and Emilia Gurney were both present, and reported enthusiastically back to Emily:[27]

> I enjoyed Mrs. Davies's party very much, seeing Mr Maurice in some kind of private life was very pleasant. He & Mrs. Gurney talked together for some time & I stood as near as I could & took in the sights & sounds to my heart's content. There was nothing particularly interesting talked about I think, the party was too large for that, but perhaps it is the sociable, less earnest side one chiefly wishes to see after being familiar with the other in books & sermons.

She was also very tempted to go with Emilia Gurney to Maurice's bible classes, though in the end her own medical studies proved too demanding.

---

[23] This section is based on Stephen and Manton.
[24] EG to ED, 30 November 1861, Anderson Family Papers, quoted in Crawford, 25.
[25] EG to ED, 12 September 1865, LSE 9/10/055, and see Manton, 42.
[26] Fawcett, 43–4; Manton, 97.
[27] EG to ED, 14 February 1861, LSE 10/9/024; FC, 202–3; and Anderson, 75.

70 DAVIES AND THE MID-VICTORIAN WOMEN'S MOVEMENT

Armed with an introduction from Mrs Gurney, Garrett next saw William Hawes, a governor of the Middlesex Hospital (and also, as it happened, a former business acquaintance of her father's). At the beginning of August she moved in with her sister Louie and began work at the Middlesex as an honorary surgical nurse. She had no intention of nursing, but this would be both a valuable learning experience and a chance to make sure that she would be able to cope with the horrors, dirt, and smells of contemporary surgery. It also provided introductions to potential teachers, and after three months nursing she turned her attention to study, spending half a day in the hospital dispensary and having a physician come to Louie's home to tutor her in anatomy and physiology.

Davies, meanwhile, received long and frequent reports of Garrett's progress and involved herself with the people and projects of Langham Place, visiting as much as she could and keeping in close touch with developments through Jane Crow.[28]

The recognized leader of the Langham Place enterprise was Barbara Bodichon, but she now spent the winters in Algiers and the summers mainly in Sussex and was only occasionally in her London house. The leader on the ground, editor of the *English Woman's Journal* and general mother hen, responsible in her own eyes for the group of women most closely involved, was Bessie Parkes. Those for whom she felt most responsible were Matilda (Max) Hays and Adelaide Procter. Hays was a writer and translator of George Sand who had been part of the bohemian artistic community in Rome and had had notorious affairs with both the sculptor Hatty Hosman and the actress Charlotte Cushman. (Elizabeth Barrett Browning described Hays and Cushman as making 'vows of celibacy and of eternal attachment to each other—they live together, dress alike...it is a female marriage'.)[29] Hays was emotionally demanding and unstable, but she was also kind and loving and when her affair with Cushman had come to a violent end Parkes had taken her under her wing, recruited her to the journal and given her a home and a salary, in the hope that she might in due course become editor.

Adelaide Procter, a poet protegée of both Dickens and Thackeray, friends of her father, had also been brought into the project by Bessie. Her main concern was with the evils of poverty and homelessness, and impressed by the charitable work of the Sisters of Mercy she had converted in the early 1850s to Roman Catholicism. By 1860 she must already have been suffering the effects of consumption, but she threw herself into the work of both SPEW and the Victoria Press.

---

[28] The only letters to have survived from this time are from Garrett to Davies, but there must have been an extensive correspondence between all three friends. Each would have known about everything the others were doing.

[29] Edward C. McAleer, ed., *Dearest Isa: Robert Browning's Letters to Isabella Blagden* (University of Texas, 1951), 27; Lisa Merrill, 'Hays, Matilda', ODNB/57829.

JOINING THE MOVEMENT 71

The driving force behind SPEW was Jessie Boucherett. Slightly older than the others, Jessie was the daughter of a Lincolnshire country squire, owner of the Ayscoghe estate. Her father had died and her brother inherited the estate, but she seems to have been left with money of her own, and would take various ventures into her own hands and her own pocket, beginning with a programme of classes to prepare women for the examinations in book-keeping offered by the Society of Arts, so that they might become cashiers and clerks.[30]

Under the auspices of SPEW, but funded by Bodichon, Maria Rye ran a legal copying office. A solicitor's daughter and strong evangelical, Rye had somehow got involved in the movement right at the beginning, helping with the married women's property petitions, but she was a strange fit, being opposed to women having the vote, getting involved in politics, or becoming doctors. Overwhelmed by the number of women seeking jobs in the copying office, she soon turned her attention to the possibility of addressing the surplus women problem through emigration, setting up in 1861 a Female Middle Class Emigration Society. She would eventually turn her attention, with Lord Shaftesbury's support, to the care of pauper children, setting up homes in which destitute girls could be trained and educated for domestic work and placing them with middle-class families in the colonies.[31]

The other business set up specifically to employ women was the Victoria Press, which printed both the *English Woman's Journal* and the SSA's *Transactions*. In the autumn of 1859, Bessie Parkes had visited a printing press, observed the work being done, and come to the view that printing was an area well suited to women, as compositors as well as designers and editors.[32] George Hastings had prepared a plan for setting up a business and they had agreed with Bodichon that Emily Faithfull had the skills to run it. Investors were found, a house was taken in Great Coram Street in Bloomsbury, a printing press acquired, and a few skilled compositors found who could teach others.[33] SPEW then provided funding for apprenticeships. The business was named the Victoria Press in honour of the Queen, who sent an approving letter, and Emily Faithfull was subsequently rewarded with a royal warrant, as Printer and Publisher in Ordinary to the Queen.

Emily Faithfull, 'Fido' to her friends, was the daughter of Ferdinand Faithfull, rector of Headley in Surrey (her grandfather, two uncles, and brother were also clergymen), but she somehow escaped the normal lot of a clergyman's daughter.

---

[30] This began as a SPEW project but was continued by Boucherett as the Commercial School for Girls. Bessie Rayner Parkes, 'A year's experience in women's work', *EWJ*, 6 (October 1860), 112–21; *Englishwoman's Review*, 33 (15 May 1876), 224–5.

[31] Hirsch, 195; SPEW minutes, Girton GCIP SPTW 2/1. Lowndes states that Maria Rye's emigration work was supported financially by Lady Byron, but Lady Byron was dead, so this seems unlikely.

[32] 'Letters on the employment of women', *EWJ*, 4 (December 1859), 270–82.

[33] Emily Faithfull, 'The Victoria Press', *TNAPSS*, 4 (1860), 819–22, reprinted in *EWJ*, 6 (October 1860), 121–6. James Stone, *Emily Faithfull: Victorian Champion of Women's Rights* (P. D. Meany, 1994); SPEW minutes, 6 March 1860, Girton GCIP SPTW 2/1.

72 DAVIES AND THE MID-VICTORIAN WOMEN'S MOVEMENT

Her immediate family seem to have been comfortably off but no more, but her uncle, Francis Faithfull, had gone from Oxford to Hatfield House as tutor to Viscount Cranborne, only son of the Marquess of Salisbury, after which he became rector of Hatfield, and her cousins moved in very high circles.[34] The baby of the family, Emily went at age eighteen in 1853 to stay in the London home of the well-known novelist and society figure Sydney Owenson, Lady Morgan, whose provocative historical study, *Women and her Master*, would soon be published in a new edition.[35] Here she will have met Lady Morgan's close friend and companion, the Irish writer Geraldine Jewsbury: the cross-dressing, probably bisexual lover—platonic or otherwise—of Jane Carlyle and Charlotte Cushman amongst others, and an entrée to literary London.

The following year, while staying with relations, she met and became close friends with Helen Codrington, the young and vivacious wife of Commodore Henry Codrington, and in 1854 she moved in with Helen and her two baby daughters, Henry being posted overseas. She stayed there for about three years, enjoying the parties and balls of society life and being presented at Court (admitted to the Queen's Drawing Room) in 1856. In 1858, following Codrington's appointment as Admiral Superintendent of the Malta Dockyard, his family moved to Malta and soon after Faithfull landed at Langham Place, eager to work. 'Emily Faithfull', reported Parkes to Bodichon, 'is the nearest approach to my idea of a canvasser I have yet got hold of. A clergyman's daughter, aged 23, & rather strong-minded; carried her own huge carpet bag, etc.'[36] Over the next few years, while running the Victoria Press, Faithfull seems to have moved between her parents' home and the Langham Place flat, subsequently renting properties in Bloomsbury and Victoria, where she could entertain her many friends and acquaintances.

Two other central figures amongst the Langham Place group were Sarah Lewin, who was a niece of Harriet Grote and admirer of the secularist reformer George Holyoake and kept the books for both the *Journal* and SPEW;[37] and Isa Craig, whose main job was with the SSA but who also directed a SPEW programme training women to act as telegraph operators.

Visiting Langham Place, Davies found, as did all visitors, immense energy, enthusiasm, and excitement. She also found people she could get on with, reporting in particular how much she liked Adelaide Procter and Emily

---

[34] See LSE 7EFA, *passim*, for correspondence of her cousin, also Emily, who became close friends with the Cecils (Marquesses of Salisbury) and Balfours, and with whom she is occasionally confused.

[35] Lady Morgan, *Woman and Her Master*, 2nd ed. (David Bryce, 1855).

[36] BRP to BB, 30 January 1859, Girton GCPP Parkes 5/88. For Emily Faithfull see Stone, *Emily Faithfull*; Eric Ratcliffe, *The Caxton of Her Age: The Career and Family Background of Emily Faithfull (1835–95)* (Images, 1993).

[37] For the Holyoake connection see Laura Schwarz, *Infidel Feminism; Secularism, Religion and Women's Emancipation in England, 1830–1914* (Manchester University Press, 2013), 157.

Faithfull.[38] And she found work she could get involved with. The *English Woman's Journal* was already struggling and would have benefitted both from her discipline and from her copy-editing. SPEW, on the other hand, offered an object lesson in how to go about setting up a campaigning institution, an activity in which Davies found herself quite at home. Her time in London, however, was necessarily limited. Her parents will have wanted her at home, and she was soon asking herself what she might do in Gateshead and Newcastle to join in the work going on at Langham Place.

The obvious way forward was through some extension of SPEW, for three reasons. First, with Crow as secretary, she had an inside track. Second, with the involvement of senior church figures as vice-presidents it could be presented as an extension of parish work. Third, with the evangelical Shaftesbury as president she could hope for the support of both her father and the then Bishop of Durham, Henry Montagu Villiers, another evangelical. Coincidentally, events on the Davies's doorstep may have made Emily's father and his colleagues particularly sympathetic to an initiative focused on the women of the district, and must also have impacted on Emily's thoughts about what women might do.

In Gateshead at this time, the most populous churches were the dissenting Methodists: the Primitive Methodists and the New Connexion Methodists. Most populous of all was the Bethesda New Connexion Methodist Chapel, where the minister from 1858 to 1861 was the charismatic revivalist preacher William Booth, subsequently founder of the Salvation Army. This chapel, in the centre of Gateshead and on a direct route from the Davies rectory to the main St Mary's church, seated 1,300. The congregation before Booth's arrival had been around a hundred, but by 1859 he was attracting up to two thousand, three times a week.

This simply cannot have escaped Emily Davies's attention, or her father's, and it cannot have escaped their attention either that Booth's wife, Catherine, was no mere helpmeet. Inspired by the example of an American Wesleyan revivalist, Phoebe Palmer, she determined that she too would preach. In 1859 she wrote and had published a pamphlet, *Female Teaching*, and she followed this with a defence of Palmer, *Female Ministry: Woman's Right to Preach the Gospel*.[39] A month after this came out, in January 1860, she addressed the full congregation herself for the first time, and soon became an even more popular preacher than her husband.[40] To polite society this would have been an egregious crossing of the spheres. The daily practice of religion was generally assigned to the domestic sphere, to the angels of the house, but religious authority and the privilege of preaching in public was clearly assigned to the public or masculine sphere. (Female Quaker

---

[38] EG to ED, 15 June 1860, LSE 9/10/02. It is not clear how long she spent in London, as she also went down to stay with family friends in Chichester.

[39] At http://purl.dlib.indiana.edu/iudl/vwwp/VAB7105.

[40] The Booths left Gateshead in 1861.

74 DAVIES AND THE MID-VICTORIAN WOMEN'S MOVEMENT

ministers might be an exception, working with female congregations.) A woman preaching to a mixed audience would probably have horrified Emily Davies as much as it would have her father, but an activity that took members of the established church out into the female community might well have seemed timely.

By October 1860, Villiers had agreed to act as president of a Durham 'branch' of SPEW, also known as the Newcastle Society for the Employment of Women. A committee of eight men and eight women had been formed, including John Davies and two other clergymen, with a small management committee of women only and with Emily Davies as secretary.[41]

Various initiatives were undertaken. One was a book-keeping class, which opened the following March and was intended like its London equivalent to prepare girls for the examinations of the Society of Arts, which would qualify them for employment. A reading and discussion class aimed at raising the educational levels of domestic servants was started at Annie Austin's house. Davies herself conducted some research into the employment conditions of women in local factories, which demonstrated how much they suffered from a lack of any education: 'It is indeed no wonder that people who have not learned to do anything cannot find anything to do.'[42] As part of this research, Davies also discovered that the problem of 'surplus women' was not a problem in Newcastle and Gateshead, where numbers overall were roughly equal. The main issue in respect of women's employment was the lack of education and training—an issue that applied even in domestic service, where the opportunities for learning, in a large house with a large staff, were quite inadequate to meet the middle-class demand for well-trained girls.[43]

Davies later summed up the achievements of the Newcastle Society in dismissive terms: 'I do not think any work was done.'[44] And probably nothing of substance was achieved. But she herself was not only doing something, at last, but had found her metier. As Elizabeth Garrett wrote in response to a report of developments: 'I am glad...that you are fairly started now as a recognised worker for the cause. Miss Smith [i.e. Nannie] and I agreed the other day that it was just the work for your special powers.'[45] She also began at this time her own career as a writer, preparing a series of articles for one of the local papers, arguing the case for women working and calling for their education and training to this end.[46]

---

[41] FC, 210–11. Annie Austin's husband was treasurer. SPEW authorized the society to describe itself as operating 'in connection with' SPEW itself. It was more cautious about other proposed 'branches'. See SPEW minutes, Girton GCIP SPTW 2/1. Branches were also established in Edinburgh, in the wake of the 1860 SSA congress in Glasgow, and in Dublin in the wake of the 1861 congress there. See *EWJ*, 12 (February 1864), 427.

[42] Stephen, 53. Emily Davies, 'Northumberland and Durham branch of the Society for Promoting the Employment of Women, 1861', in *Thoughts*, 28–33: 32.

[43] Davies, ibid.   [44] FC, 210.

[45] EG to ED *circa* October–November 1860, quoted in Stephen, 53, presumably from the missing section of the Family Chronicle. It does not seem to be amongst the run of letters from this period held in the LSE archive.

[46] Emily Davies, 'Letters to a daily paper', in *Thoughts*, 1–18.

It is not clear whether these were actually published as newspaper articles, and even if they were their impact would have been minimal, but they were issued a little later in a pamphlet published by the Victoria Press, and they are the first evidence we have of Davies's distinctive voice on women's education and employment.

The most striking thing about these articles, reading them today, is how extraordinarily well written they are. There is nothing particularly original in the content, but of all the pieces written on the subject at this time, by women or men, for or against, they are the most lucid, the most clearly expressed, the most rationally coherent. The writing is simple but elegant. The argument is clear and well structured, one point following another through straightforward common sense. The examples are brief and to the point, doing exactly what is needed without going off on a tangent. The arguments against her view are fairly demolished, but calmly, reasonably, and with respect and restraint. We can see immediately why Garrett and others would send her their compositions for critique, and how Davies would prove invaluable on the *English Woman's Journal*.

The other things we learn from these articles are how the different arguments on women's education and employment fitted together in Davies's mind, and what kind of strategy she thought appropriate for advancing them. The most obvious feature of the strategy is the avoidance of anything that might set the interests of women against those of men. She was clearly mindful of the *Saturday Review* attacks, and wrote explicitly against women banding together as being not only implausible, given the force of convention, but positively undesirable. Her appeal was to the fathers of daughters, and her arguments were to the effect that the education and employment of young women would be to the common benefit, and in particular that it would make them better wives and mothers. In educating their daughters and directing them towards an occupation, indeed, parents should look for precisely those occupations that would *both* provide a living if needed *and* be useful in married life. Idleness and frivolity benefitted no one: neither the person concerned (whether man or woman), nor their future spouse and children. Even on the theme of governesses, her emphasis was not on their own plight—enough had been said about that—but on the plight of children placed under the care of women with neither the liking, nor the aptitude, nor the training to teach.

In listing—as had her predecessors—those occupations she thought suitable for women, Davies's emphasis was on those for which women had a proven capability and where the skills once acquired could be put to wider use, and here, unsurprisingly, she made a particular case for medicine. Women, she suggested, had a natural predilection to act as physicians and prescribe for their friends and neighbours: would it not be in everybody's interests if at least some of them were scientifically educated so as to do so competently?[47]

---

[47] Ibid., 10.

I believe that in imparting to a young woman a sound scientific medical education we should be bestowing a gift which would be of infinite value, whatever might be her lot in life. If she should marry, such a knowledge of medicine would enable her to prescribe wisely for her children and servants; if she should remain single, she would be free to exercise her talent for the benefit of women and children in general.

One of the side effects of all this activity was to broaden Davies's social sphere. She became friendly with the wife of one of the clergymen involved, Mrs Lintott, who had worked as a teacher under Frances Buss at the North London Collegiate School for Ladies, and it was probably through her introduction that she would later meet Miss Buss. Another new acquaintance became both a close friend and a kind of tutor, both broadening and deepening her own education. Anna Richardson came, on her father's side, from a prosperous Newcastle family of Quakers, and on her mother's side from another prominent Quaker family, the Wighams of Edinburgh.[48] She had grown up in a large house on the outskirts of Newcastle, but after the failure of a Newcastle bank in which her father was heavily invested the house had to be sold. Anna accompanied her brother to Edinburgh, where he was studying at the university, but returned briefly to Newcastle in 1860. Her name and address appeared on the list of subscribers to the *English Woman's Journal*, which would have been Davies's first resource in finding women for her SPEW committee, and she was recruited to it.[49]

Anna Richardson was two years younger than Emily Davies. She was a deeply emotional, deeply caring young woman who invested heavily in all her friendships, and was very deeply religious. She had fallen in love at seventeen and become engaged, but the engagement had been broken off abruptly and rather than risk earthly love again she had turned to Jesus Christ, and in particular to the Tractarian teachings of Keble and Pusey. An intellectual from an intellectual family, she read omnivorously and found connections everywhere, managing to combine her high church readings of scripture, which would later lead her into the Church of England, with a continuing loyalty to her Quaker roots. She took Davies to lectures, taught her some Greek, and encouraged her reading.

Davies was a willing learner. 'Though I did not care for the subject', she recalled of a lecture course for ladies in physiology, arranged by Anna's cousin Mrs Sturge, 'I very much enjoyed being associated with others in learning *anything*.'[50] And writing to Richardson she noted: 'My mind wants looking after dreadfully and I consider you responsible for it.'[51]

---

[48] Both extended families had strong abolitionist connections, but I can find no record of Anna's immediate family being involved. Her brother, John Wigham Richardson, became a prominent shipbuilder.
[49] Stephen, 53–4. See also Richardson.   [50] Stephen, 54.   [51] Stephen, 54.

Reading what remains of their correspondence, with each other and with others, it can be hard to put these two friends together. Richardson's letters are all full of spiritual reflections, of praise for others and deep concern for the wellbeing of friends and family; of Jesus Christ; and of the poetry of landscape. Davies's are all practical, matter of fact, to the point. There is a strong selection bias, but even if we make full allowance for context and circumstance the difference is marked.[52] Much of Davies's childhood and youth, however, had been spent amongst families that, even if they had joined the established church, retained many of their Quaker ways. She was comfortable in that context.

For Elizabeth Garrett in London, meanwhile, things went very well for a while. With the support of the dean of the Middlesex Hospital she was soon attending lectures there and working in the dissecting room, and in a letter she wrote to the *English Woman's Journal* in the spring of 1861, encouraging others to join her, she reported uniformly positive experiences of both the work and the support she was receiving.[53] She did very well, too, when exams came round. But in doing well in class she showed up the men, and this was too much for some of them. In June, over forty students submitted a memorial to the hospital. (A 'memorial' in this context was a letter signed by a number of people calling for a particular action—Davies was to prepare many of them in the years ahead.) They complained that Garrett's presence in the operating theatre was an outrage, that lecturers had to censor their lectures because of a lady present, and that her presence exposed the medical school to public ridicule.

This was hard. She could charm her teachers—indeed, she discussed with both Davies and Emilia Gurney the use of 'all kinds of little feminine dodges'. Emilia thought that the 'feminine arts' were very useful and had no compunction in using them herself.[54] But students were another matter. The authorities gave in. Garrett was allowed to finish that term, but not to return after the summer break. An editorial in the medical newspaper, *The Lancet*, mocked her ambitions and endorsed the students' position.[55] One of her teachers came (anonymously) to her defence, but this only stimulated another attack. What was the point in letting women study medicine, when no degree-awarding body would admit them to a medical degree? As various medical schools replied, in response to her request to attend lectures, since women couldn't qualify, admitting them to lectures would be tantamount to encouraging illegal practice. And indeed, when she wrote round the universities all refused to examine her.[56]

---

[52] Anna Richardson's letters were collected in a memoir put together for friends and family after her early death, aged forty, in 1873. Emily Davies and/or her first biographer kept only what contributed to the story of her campaigns and destroyed anything more personal.

[53] *EWJ*, 7 (June 1861), 282–3. The letter was signed 'AMS', i.e. A Medical Student.

[54] EG to ED, May 1861, FC, 205–6: 206.   [55] *The Lancet*, 6 July 1861.

[56] Manton, 115.

78   DAVIES AND THE MID-VICTORIAN WOMEN'S MOVEMENT

In fact, while this was a period in which medicine was fast professionalizing, most practising physicians were neither university men nor graduates of the Royal Colleges, but licentiates of the Society of Apothecaries. To become licensed you had to be nominally apprenticed for five years, take certain lecture courses (unexamined), and attend for six months at a hospital or dispensary.[57] It was not what Garrett had envisaged but it was something, and the society's legal advice when she enquired was that they could not refuse her. Their charter referred only to 'persons', and since it was drawn up to regulate the dispensing of drugs (which was indeed how most physicians traditionally earned their money) rather than the practice of medicine itself, the lawyer consulted could find no grounds for refusing to admit women. Garrett became formally the apprentice of one of the physicians she had met at the Middlesex, and had two lecture courses under her belt already. Returning to London after spending August and September at home, she signed up for three more: in botany at the Chelsea Physic garden, natural philosophy (i.e. physics) at the Royal Institution, and natural history and physiology at the South Kensington Museum. She combined this with private study of a more general kind, preparing herself to matriculate at a university should that ever become possible.

It was not clear at first that the South Kensington lectures would be open to women, but the lecturer was Thomas Huxley, Darwin's champion and a regular contributor to the *Westminster Review*. John Chapman provided an introduction and while Huxley, who would in due course become a notable advocate for the education of women,[58] seems to have been uncertain, he was probably glad of the fees and concurred.[59] And it turned out that Garrett was not the only woman attending. She was joined by Sophia Jex-Blake, who would be another medical pioneer, and two sisters of Octavia Hill, a friend of Barbara Bodichon's who had taught in her infant school. Sophia, who had been in a passionate affair with Octavia, was aggressive and outspoken, shocking the Hill sisters, but Garrett was glad to have someone to talk to who shared her commitments, both to medicine and, as it happened, to F. D. Maurice.[60]

For the most part Emily Davies followed all this from afar, but she got a blow-by-blow account in letters from Garrett, one every few days as she raised her plans with her parents and got her father on side, and during Garrett's early weeks at the Middlesex.[61] And she was in London when the students launched their memorial. Indeed, she seems to have taken this worse than Garrett did, and when the latter changed course and went for the apothecary route she appears to have seen this as

[57] The battle between scientifically trained and licentiate dispensing doctors is a common theme in the literature of this period, and is one of the main themes of George Eliot's *Middlemarch*.

[58] Thomas Huxley, 'Emancipation: black and white', *The Reader*, 5 (20 May 1865), 561–2, and in *Lay Sermons, Addresses and Reviews* (Macmillan, 1870), 23–30.

[59] FC, 236; Manton, 121–2. Sophia and Octavia had been involved in a passionate relationship for about a year, which was ended by Octavia's mother around this time.

[60] FC, 236–7. Octavia Hill was also a fan of F. D. Maurice.

[61] We only have one half of the correspondence, from Garrett to Davies: see LSE 9/10/001–042, and FC, 201–41 *passim*. Neither set is complete. Stephen, 57, notes that Davies's letters were destroyed, presumably by Emily herself.

JOINING THE MOVEMENT 79

tantamount to accepting defeat.[62] Her mood was not improved by a sense that her efforts back home were also not getting anywhere. She wrote to Anna Richardson in April, à propos of the lessons towards the Society of Arts examinations, 'it is questionable whether our Committee would even approve of it. I don't think they half believe in their own work.'[63] It also appears from this letter that she was struggling with what to do generally with her local SPEW branch, and in particular how to maintain control of it in the face of pressures from the church members of her committee, who had their own ideas about what was appropriate.

Trying to advance the women's movement in Gateshead and Newcastle was clearly deeply frustrating. Aside from Annie Austin, she had no real support and, we must suspect, a declining appetite for a thankless task. The action was in London, and so were her two closest friends, Elizabeth Garrett and Jane Crow.

Once again, however, tragedy brought opportunities. Emily's father, who had turned sixty-five in December, was feeling unwell. He had often felt unwell, of course, particularly when stressed, and he may well have been stressed now. The extraordinary success of the Bethesda Chapel must have been extremely trying, and he was at an age when his bishop might well have been encouraging him to vacate the living (and comfortable home) in favour of a younger man. Emily, at any rate, doesn't yet appear to have taken the illness seriously. At the time of her letter to Anna Richardson, her parents were in London to consult doctors, but while her father was gloom and doom her sister-in-law, with whom they were staying, could see nothing wrong with him:[64]

> It is difficult to make out how my father really is, the accounts are so contradictory. He writes of himself in the gloomiest tone, while on the other hand, Mary says they could not see anything the matter, & gives reports of what he was able to do &c., which certainly did not look like extreme illness. He has been to two doctors in London, who concur in saying there is nothing serious in the complaint & in recommending good food, & wine &c.... I have great hopes that the warm weather, which we may now look forward to, will soon set him to rights.

Unfortunately, the illness this time was serious. In September Emily's parents went for a holiday in Harrogate, in an effort to recover John's health. He got worse rather than better, however. They moved to a hydrotherapy establishment in Ilkley, where he went down with bronchitis.[65] On 20 October, Emily and Llewelyn were summoned, but by the time they arrived the next day he had died.[66] Emily and her mother now had to set up a new home, and where else to do it but London, near Llewelyn and his growing family.

---

[62] FC, 214 ff.   [63] ED to AR, 30 Apr 1861, *EDCL*, 1.   [64] Ibid.
[65] This may well have been the same cold-water cure establishment attended by Charles Darwin two years earlier. For an unwell man of Davies's age a cold-water treatment in Yorkshire in October sounds pretty awful and may well have been fatal.
[66] FC, 241–2.

5

A Woman Set Free

In January 1862, Mary and Emily Davies moved with a maid and their long-serving cook into 17 Cunningham Place, Maida Hill. Part of a small 1830s development that included a chapel of ease serving the northern end of Llewelyn Davies's parish, this small terraced town house would have been both affordable and respectable. About fifteen minutes' walk from Blandford Square, it was close enough for Mary to see her grandchildren regularly without being on top of them. Another fifteen minutes' walk in the same direction will have taken Emily to Louie Smith's home in Manchester Square and a further ten minutes beyond that to Langham Place. For the next few years this diagonal strip of London, from the north-west to the south-east of Marylebone, would be the heart of Emily Davies's London.

It took a couple of months to settle in, but sometime around April 1862 Emily could write to Barbara Bodichon in Algiers that 'we are quite settled now, & I hope soon to get into some work'.[1] Mary Davies had spent most of her life in support of her husband, running the household and engaging in parish work, and she continued with parish work in London. Emily had 'home claims' to attend to, which presumably included some companionship for her widowed mother and perhaps, now, the running of their household. She may also have felt a duty to help out her brother and sister-in-law in some way, and to contribute in a small way, at least, to the parish. At some point she ran a knitting circle. But she also wanted to do something herself. She doesn't seem to have been sure, at first, what this might be. She had contemplated following Elizabeth Garrett into medicine, but didn't feel cut out for it, though she did try to advance her general education, beginning lessons in Greek and Latin with Ellen Drewery, one of the Langham Place group, with a view to perhaps sitting the examinations of the Society of Arts.[2] In her letter to Bodichon she suggested modestly that the home claims and a 'want of nervous strength' would restrict her to an insignificant part in the fight for opportunities for women, but she also wrote that she 'would like to do something great'.

In the event, she threw herself into advancing Garrett's cause, and in particular into campaigning to get women admitted to the degrees of London University. She threw herself too into the work at Langham Place, and in particular into helping edit the *English Woman's Journal*. She got herself involved in the

---

[1] ED to BB, April 1862, *EDCL*, 3.   [2] FC, 244–5.

Emily Davies and the Mid-Victorian Women's Movement. John Hendry, Oxford University Press. © John Hendry 2024.
DOI: 10.1093/oso/9780198910237.003.0005

administration of committees of the Social Science Association's annual meeting, which that year was held in London. She was a founder member of Mentia Taylor's all-women Pen & Pencil Society. And she found herself on several committees, including those of SPEW; the Ladies' London Emancipation Society, an anti-slavery group set up by Charlotte Manning, Mentia Taylor, and others in support of the Unionist cause in the American Civil War;[3] and the Working Men's Club and Institute Union, founded by Charlotte Manning's brother, Henry Solly.

By July, Davies could report to her Newcastle friend Anna Richardson that she was now 'fairly embarked upon the work', of which she identified two aspects.[4] The first was routine administration and committee work, which played (as Garrett had earlier suggested) to her strengths: 'The amount of mechanical labour I see before me is stupendous, but I enjoy that kind of work.' The second was 'agitating' for change, which she described as 'hateful work' and 'horribly disagreeable', but a necessary part of 'fighting for people who cannot fight for themselves'. As things turned out, she seems to have quite quickly got over her hatred of agitating, but only if it was done in her own way, with courteous persistence and polite respect for her opponents, rather than through demands and accusations.

I shall look at Davies's various campaigns, and at how her approach to them played out, in the following chapters. First, though, it would be helpful to get some idea of the woman, now in her early thirties, her beliefs, attitudes, and ideals. The sources are limited, as little of her more personal correspondence survives, but we do have some correspondence from this period with two of her close friends, Anna Richardson and Jane Crow, the latter written while Crow was travelling. There are also personal snippets in her more businesslike correspondence with Barbara Bodichon and others, and combining all these with her published writings we can form some sort of a picture.

In physical appearance, Emily Davies was small, neat, feminine, perhaps a little plump, 'a dainty little figure and smiling face'. The few pictures we have give little away. She was apparently described by Bodichon at one point, in a context now unknown, as being 'ungracious as a sick porpoise crossed in love',[5] and there is something porpoise-like about her appearance. One of her early college students described her character as 'very indefinable.... I think she has very quick perceptions joined with good sense and sympathy underneath, very largely developed, yet seldom brought to the surface.'[6]

Compared with many of her colleagues in the women's movement she was socially very conservative. She thought that women should be modest, decorous,

---

[3] ED to AR, 19 April 1864, ED to BB, 14 November 1865, *EDCL*, 112, 161.
[4] ED to AR, 12 July 1862, *EDCL*, 4.
[5] Quoted in Margaret Crompton, 'Prelude to Arcadia', unpublished typescript biography of Bessie Parkes Belloc, Girton GCPP Parkes 15/70, pp. 175–6. This is quoted as from a letter from Bessie Parkes to Barbara Bodichon, but I cannot find it in the extant correspondence.
[6] Edith Lloyd, *Anna Lloyd* (Layton Press, 1928), 64.

and ladylike, as indeed she was herself (modest to a fault, according to Anna Richardson);[7] that they should always treat men with the greatest respect; and that they should not put themselves forward: indeed should not seek to advance themselves at all, but rather to help others. She didn't like self-seeking people, at least in part because it wasn't womanly.[8] Giving papers to the annual congresses of the Social Science Association, she preferred to have hers, and those of her friends, read for them by men. When Garrett proposed to read her own, she felt the need to explain in detail to Davies why that was a good idea, but still declared herself subject to her friend's veto.[9] When a few years later Garrett responded positively, if humorously, to the suggestion that she take the chair of the London School Board (having received the highest number of votes of those elected), Davies rebuked her strongly. It would be 'incongruous even to the point of absurdity'. It was primarily Garrett's youth and inexperience relative to the male board members that made it unseemly to preside over them, she suggested, but gender played its part too. To even think of it was 'indecorous'.[10]

Davies believed that women of her class should dress and behave in a feminine, ladylike, but modest and unassuming fashion. She expressed unease at any association with 'strong-minded women',[11] though in matters of appearance she must have made some allowances for friends such as Nannie Leigh Smith (artistic, casual) and Emily Faithfull (androgynous, tomboy). She would have wholeheartedly agreed with a male critic of the time that women should behave with 'prudence and decorum', and should never forget 'the amenities of [their] sex'.[12]

She certainly behaved with decorum herself, and always treated men with respect. She was not the sort of woman either to shrink away from them, as Bessie Parkes tended to, or to frighten them or put their backs up, preferring to look and behave as they would expect her to look and behave. She liked both male and female company and clearly loved London and (with qualifications) its social life. She enjoyed going to concerts, dinners, and parties, and moved within several social circles. Her connections with the women's movement opened up two overlapping female circles, one centred on Langham Place, the other on the long-established Unitarian network, including Charlotte Manning and Mentia Taylor. Emily Faithfull had a circle of society friends into which Davies was welcomed. And she also moved within her brother, Llewelyn's circles, which included his Christian Socialist friends like Tom Hughes, whose family were close to Llewelyn's; followers of F. D. Maurice, like Emilia Gurney; and friends of Llewelyn's wife, Mary, and the Crompton family.

---

[7] AR to Thomas Hodgkin, 24 October 1865, in Richardson, 200.
[8] ED to AR, 25 October 1865, *EDCL*, 158.   [9] EG to ED, 21 September 1866, FC, 495–8.
[10] ED to EG, 7 December 1870, *EDCL*, 539–40, and see FC, 426, 432–6.
[11] ED to HRT, 9 May 1864, *EDCL*, 118.
[12] George Whyte-Melville, 'Strong-minded women', *Fraser's Magazine*, 68 (November 1863), 667–78: 677.

The qualification with respect to parties was that she couldn't abide what she called 'chaff': light banter, or self-opinionated chatter with no underlying substance, a 'dreary subterfuge vainly used to hide the dullness of vacant minds'.[13] It was not the lightness she objected to—she would happily join in light-hearted gossip—but the vacant minds, to which 'The small things come uppermost, & I feel constantly as if I ought to be showing sympathy about things which are not of the slightest consequences, or they will call me severe or *exalté*.' This last was à propos of a family whose party she had been to with Emily Faithfull, one of whose daughters had to give up a course at Bedford College because there wasn't a footman to spare to accompany her. 'Their code of morals is...the most immoral I have ever come in contact with. It is very sad. Conventual stiffness, & carelessness, to say the very least, as to refinement in conversation. There could scarcely be a worse combination.'[14]

What Davies enjoyed most at parties were meeting the people whose books and articles she admired, and getting into serious discussion, whether about politics, literature, religion, or morals. Prominent amongst the former were Matthew Arnold, critic and poet, son of the headmaster, and especially Richard Hutton, editor of the *Spectator*, both of whom were broad church sympathizers and part of her brother's circle. What she enjoyed most about London was being in the mix of that kind of serious debate. Even if she wasn't meeting people, she was reading the elite periodicals as they came out. 'How London spoils one!', she wrote to Jane Crow. 'I feel quite injured now if I don't see everything that's going, the moment it comes out.' And again, 'I don't know how I should live without weekly & monthly stimulants. They do me a world of good.'[15]

Her approach to novels was similar. She loved a good story, providing it was intelligent and well-written, and read Trollope's in instalments as they came out. But it was the analysis that really interested her, not the description, which she tended to skip. Two examples make the point. In 1861, while still in Gateshead, she was reading George Eliot's *Silas Marner* and sharing thoughts with Anna Richardson:[16]

> In all that Mrs. Lewes writes, she shows the same marvellous power of dividing asunder, to the joints & marrow. I am afraid you will not understand this. I don't know how to express the merciless, yet merciful, way in which she cuts thro' plausible self-delusions. It *reminds* me of Thackeray, but he only exposes superficial meannesses, while she cuts deep down, & more than any writer I know, makes one thoroughly ashamed of oneself.

---

[13] ED to JC, 2 January 1864, *EDCL*, 84.   [14] ED to JC, 12 January 1864, *EDCL*, 90–3: 92.
[15] ED to JC, 2 January 1864, *EDCL*, 83.
[16] ED to AR, 30 April 1861, *EDCL*, 1. 'Mrs Lewes' was Marian Evans/George Eliot's preferred mode of address, as Davies will have known from Barbara Bodichon.

84 DAVIES AND THE MID-VICTORIAN WOMEN'S MOVEMENT

Three years later she was reading Charles Reade's *Hard Cash*. This is notable for a positive reference to the campaign for women doctors ('take me to a doctress next time', pleads the patient, exhausted by the doctors' analyses of her ailment, which the one sensible and empirically minded doctor in the story recognizes as just being in love). But Davies was also struck by one of the lead characters, 'a very beautiful & clever girl...such as a common man could not have imagined. Her characteristic is transparency, & it strikes me as singularly beautiful. It would be more so still, if she was the highest type of woman, but such as she is, the mere idea of perfect transparency is I think very beautiful & original.'[17] The character is in fact a fairly conventional Victorian heroine, and at the mercy of events around her rather than taking an active part, but she is open, honest, herself, with none of 'the opaqueness of the people one meets in society'.

On one hand openness, honesty with oneself as well as others and a lack of self-deluded pomposity; on the other hand, the ability to cut with precision to the marrow. These were some of the qualities Emily Davies looked for, whether in people, in novels, or in intellectual debate. She didn't always find them, of course. As we shall see, she was sometimes attracted to people who turned out to fall short, and shied away from people who had them in much greater measure than she realized. But Elizabeth Garrett had them, so did her brother Llewelyn, and so, in large measure, did she herself.

Morality was evidently important to Emily Davies. In common with society in general, she framed it in terms of moral virtues and their associated duties, and steered away from any talk of rights. Apart from the revolutionary associations of rights talk, it was just not, to her or most of her contemporaries, anything to do with morals, which were about how one should behave, not how one should be treated.

The big moral question of the day, at the most general level, revolved around a tension between a strict conventional moral code, on one hand, and a morality of sympathy and compassion on the other. This reflected the current tension within the church between a dogmatic Christianity and one based on God's love, but at a more practical level, and it ran through the novels of the period. Trollope in his novels of the 1860s, for example, routinely set conventional proscriptions against human charity and compassion and came out strongly and consistently in favour of the latter, with the important reservation that while compassion should qualify convention it should not condemn it. In the context of a novel his (mainly female) readers would have been with him. In practice, though, few would have stood out against convention quite as much as some of his heroines did, and he acknowledged this. The boundary between convention and compassion was hard to negotiate, and both sides mattered: to follow convention too strictly, lacking

---

[17] ED to JC, 2 January 1864, *EDCL*, 83–6: 86.

compassion, was a natural human weakness and as such forgivable. The same charity that should be extended to those condemned as immoral by society should also be extended to the condemners.[18]

This tension was one that Emily Davies would have to navigate, and one of the things that marks her out from some others in the women's movement is that she clearly recognized as much. Her own sympathies, however, were undoubtedly with the heroines. She was no sentimentalist. She believed in a rational, principled morality, consistently followed. But she objected strongly to a strict conventional morality that saw certain behaviours as automatically right or wrong, regardless of the circumstances, for no other reason than that convention so determined.

For Davies, again as for most of her contemporaries, morality was rooted in the Bible. This was so even for the atheist George Eliot, or for the self-proclaimed agnostic (seen by many as an atheist) Thomas Huxley. Huxley indeed made a point of insisting that moral education in schools should be based on the Bible, even though he was not himself a believer.[19] The question was what one took from the Bible: specific injunctions, as interpreted by orthodox clergy, or the teaching of Jesus, more broadly understood. For Emily Davies, as for the broad church generally, it was clearly the latter, albeit as a basis on which to build her own rational argument.

When it came to religion, Davies identified strongly as a Church of England Christian. She wrote to Barbara Bodichon, explaining of a letter filled with scriptural references that it was Sunday; that churches and prayers and sermons were among her sources of 'sweet waters'; and that while a younger generation might end up looking to science rather than religion, religion would see her out.[20] Her seminal writing, *The Higher Education of Women*, would be set explicitly in a Christian context, and her strong Church of England allegiance would, throughout her life, be an irritation to some of her colleagues in the women's movement.

As to what kind of Christian Emily Davies was, the answer can only be her own kind. She mixed easily with, and drew on the support of, the many Mauricians in her circle, and she clearly admired Maurice's spirituality, but he was not the guide for her that he was for many of her friends. There was a portrait of Maurice in Llewelyn's Blandford Square house and she quipped that her nephews and nieces were 'taught to adore the image of the Prophet before they can speak'.[21] But she was not one to follow prophets herself. As with most things she thought about,

---

[18] See, for example, *The Vicar of Bullhampton* (Bradbury, Evans, 1870), which treats of the 'fallen woman'; *The Belton Estate* (Chapman and Hall, 1865), about female subservience and a mistreated wife; *He Knew He Was Right* (Strahan, 1869), about unreasonable husbandly demands. On women's issue see also his lecture 'On the higher education of women', in *Four Lectures* (Constable, 1868).

[19] His wife was, however. She was a member of Llewelyn Davies's congregation, and when Huxley died, Davies conducted the funeral service.

[20] ED to BB, March 1868, *EDCL*, 267–8.   [21] ED to AR, 4 February 1868, *EDCL*, 260.

she tended to approach her religion intellectually rather than emotionally, and to make up her own mind. Anna Richardson wrote of her to a mutual acquaintance that 'I thoroughly believe she has the right feeling at the bottom; but…the teaching of her father's school, in which everything is blindly taken for granted, and all kinds of doubt alike looked upon as sin, has driven her to sympathy with the intellectual side of every religious question.'[22] Davies was inclined to question, and to work out everything for herself, whereas in Richardson's view it was much better just to be guided by the love of God and the wisdom of the Bible, interpreted according to one's own changing state of development, without trying to fix it in general principles.

Richardson by this time knew Davies well, and her analysis is persuasive. Davies did tend to approach things intellectually, analysing them for herself,[23] and it would be surprising if she didn't take the same approach to religion. She had certainly rebelled against the strict evangelicalism of her father, who had used his own intellect to defend his beliefs rather than to explore them, and when a new curate of her brother's preached what she saw as nonsense she had no qualms about saying so.[24]

Was she, then, broad church? That was certainly how she came across. Her prospectus for what would become Girton College described it explicitly as being established 'on Broad Church principles',[25] and looking at her family and male social circle most people would simply have assumed that she was herself broad church (the men in her life were, so she must be!). And in one sense, she was very much so—more, indeed, than she probably realized. One significant piece of broad church writing in this period was Llewelyn Davies's commentary on St Paul's letters to the Ephesians and Colossians, which included the injunctions habitually used to justify the subservience of wives to husbands.[26] Llewelyn rejected this interpretation, substituting one of equal and mutual duties, and when Emily came to argue the case for women's education, she would in effect take that for granted. Our duties, she argued, are primarily those of children of God, and in that men and women are equal. In her account this was straightforward, in much the same way that the morality applied by and to his heroines by Trollope was straightforward. And within the broad church context to which she was accustomed, it was straightforward. Outside that context, however, it went strongly against people's conventional habits and assumptions.

[22] AR to Thomas Hodgkin, 24 October 1865, in Richardson, 200.

[23] Bessie Parkes also described Emily's approach as 'intellectual' in the context of the *Journal*: ED to BB, 26 February 1863, *EDCL*, 40–1: 40.

[24] ED to JC, 27 January 1864, *EDCL*, 99–101. The curate had been recommended by Arthur Stanley, Dean of Westminster, but, as Emily Davies commented, he must have been taken in too.

[25] FC, 501.

[26] J. Llewelyn Davies, *The Epistles of St Paul to the Ephesians, the Colossians, and Philemon* (Macmillan, 1866), 58, 72–3.

While Emily Davies thought and wrote within a context of broad church assumptions, however, she would probably not have described herself as broad church.[27] She was interested in theological matters and well able to discuss them. Like many of her peers she will have followed the debates around *Essays and Reviews* and the writings of Colenso (the latter, indeed, were the context for the letter from Anna Richardson),[28] and she certainly sympathized with the broad church view of such matters. But in the context of broad church family and friends, where no one was going to dictate to her exactly what she should believe, she was more interested in what Christianity was to her than in what it should be to others, and in this she was perhaps more influenced by the Quaker elements of her upbringing—the very elements that Anna Richardson was moving away from. The Church of England was her church, certainly, and its breadth and openness were important to her, but the reason they were important was because of the freedom they allowed to form her own, personal beliefs.

One way of characterizing Emily Davies's religion would be to say that while her beliefs were idiosyncratic, the product of her own rationalization, her practices were entirely orthodox. To all appearances she was the model of a Christian lady. Something very similar can be said of her politics, which have puzzled both colleagues and commentators. She described herself as Liberal Conservative, a term that carries several connotations. Historically, it referred to the Peelite free traders, and that was probably where she started out, but by the 1860s they were mainly Liberals, whereas she remained a Conservative. A more contemporary association might be with Lord Stanley, son of the Earl of Derby (and later succeeding to the title), who served dutifully in his father's Conservative administrations in the 1850s and later under Disraeli, but whom everyone recognized to be a covert Liberal, who would have served under Palmerston had his father let him. Stanley would be one of the supporters of the admission of women to London University, and in that context Davies referred him as 'like me, a conservative, that is, a Liberal all the way round'.[29]

The description also brings to mind Trollope's 'Conservative Liberalism', which he characterized as aiming at Liberal ends but in a gradual conservative fashion, a kind of Burkean liberalism. In 1867 the idea was mooted of two companion volumes of essays on questions relating to women, one to be edited by Emily Davies and the other by Josephine Butler. This was at a time when they were engaged on separate—in Davies's mind rival—educational projects, and after meeting up they decided to go their separate ways with this project too. In summarizing their different approaches in a letter to Anna Richardson, Emily quoted the quintessential conservative philosopher Edmund Burke: 'Her contributors will be lively young

---

[27] ED to BB, 14 January 1863, *EDCL*, 29–33: 30.
[28] See, for example, ED to BB, 14 January 1863, *EDCL*, 29–33; ED to AR, 5 July 1865, *EDCL* 156–7.
[29] ED to AR, 27 March 1868, *EDCL*, 270–2: 271.

88 DAVIES AND THE MID-VICTORIAN WOMEN'S MOVEMENT

Radicals, mine, grave ancient women and men. Do you remember Burke's sentiments? "A disposition to preserve & an ability to improve." That is what my vol. is to show."[30]

As all these associations reflect in one way or another, Emily Davies's policies were broadly Liberal, but her politics were distinctly Conservative. Key changes should be achieved quickly, but as far as possible through traditional structures and institutions, through a rational reassessment of conservative arguments.

The 'rational' part of this was critical. Rationalism in politics in this period was associated with the Radicals, with the *Westminster Review*, and especially with John Stuart Mill. Emily Davies was not a Radical. In arguing for rights and seeking rapid and disruptive change, the Radicals went completely contrary to her own political instincts. In the debate over female suffrage and the 1867 Reform Act she would do everything she could to steer clear of Mill and the other radical causes he championed. But she nevertheless admired him enormously, both philosophically and, despite his atheism, spiritually. While she might have differed on specifics, the broad aims underpinning his political writings were her broad aims, and the structure of argument he built on them would be hers too. She was a Conservative, but she was a Millian (and in that sense a radical) rationalist Conservative.[31]

Whatever people may have thought of his politics, Mill was widely regarded by the early 1860s as Britain's premier philosopher of the age, his reputation built on two major works: *A System of Logic* (1843) and *Principles of Political Economy* (1848), both by then in their fifth editions. *A System of Logic* was in effect a thorough (1200-page) introduction to the philosophy of science, covering the rules and procedures of reasoning and the problems attendant on them, from logic itself through the natural sciences to psychology and the social sciences. The *Principles of Political Economy* was both the most authoritative economics text of the period (a status it would retain for many decades) and a defining work in political liberalism. The end point of economic policy for Mill was not merely wealth maximization but the creation of equality of opportunity and the social, educational, and other conditions necessary for the development of individual character.

Following his wife Harriet's death in 1858, Mill had also set himself to completing and publishing the works on which they had been engaged together over the

---

[30] ED to AR, 1 August 1867, 13 December 1867, *EDCL*, 244, 253, quotation on p. 253. Butler's volume came out in 1869 as *Women's Work and Women's Culture*. Davies's never happened.

[31] Barbara Caine, who made studies of both Mill's influence on Victorian feminism and Davies's particular approach to feminism, appears to have seen no connection, but that is perhaps due to her focus on *The Subjection of Women* rather than on Mill's earlier political and philosophical writings, which were those formative for Davies's approach. See Barbara Caine, 'John Stuart Mill and the English women's movement', *Historical Studies*, 18 (1978), 52–67; and her *Victorian Feminists* (Oxford University Press, 1992). For an astute treatment of Mill, feminism, and responses to them see Gertrude Himmelfarb, *The De-Moralization of Society* (Institute of Economic Affairs, 1995).

past few years, and in 1861 he published two new books: *On Liberty* and *Considerations on Representative Government*.

On Liberty addresses the relationship between the individual and the state and is one of the classics of political philosophy, as relevant now as it was 150 years ago.[32] The central theme is that the only ground on which society can justifiably constrain the actions or thoughts of an individual, whether by legislation or by social opprobrium, is to prevent harm to others. It is always legitimate to argue rationally for or against any position, whether it be a behavioural norm or an intellectual theory. It is never legitimate to impose such a position on others, whether as law, morality, or dogma, if their behaviour otherwise would not harm other people. The application of this principle depends critically on the notion of 'harm'. Many people would assert, over the coming years, that giving women property rights, or the vote, or a higher education would be harmful not only to those concerned (who would suffer from a loss of femininity) but to men generally and indeed to society at large. But that was at least something that could be challenged by evidence and argument, whereas simply asserting that those things were wrong could not. At a time when reasoned argument was making significant inroads into inherited dogma, most obviously in religion, but also in economics and the social sciences, Mill provided a basis on which to carry that into politics and the law. *On Liberty* was, in effect, the theoretical counterpart to, and philosophical justification of, the practical activities of the Social Science Association.

Considerations on Representative Government is concerned not so much with the principles of government as with the practicalities: what particular reforms would work best in practice, in 1860s Britain, given the realities of human nature. The underlying principles, as in Mill's other work, were the free development of the individual and the benefit to society as a whole, and these translated practically into forms of government that would maximize the scope for individual development and make best use of people's abilities for the common good. In the British context, he argued, this led to a form of representative government, but one that protected against the rule of the majority over the minority, and against the rule of the ignorant over the informed. On this basis he proposed several reforms, including the introduction of a system of proportional representation, as recently advocated by Thomas Hare and Henry Fawcett; and the extension of the suffrage to the working classes, but with an educational qualification replacing the current property qualification, and plural votes for the most educated. He also made it absolutely clear that in determining who should be granted the vote the sex of the person was completely irrelevant, and he referred repeatedly to the advantages of giving women the vote. The core argument here was that of *On Liberty*. It was not for society (in practice, men) to decide what women were or

---

[32] See, for example, Anthony Kwame Appiah, *The Ethics of Identity* (Princeton University Press, 2005).

90 DAVIES AND THE MID-VICTORIAN WOMEN'S MOVEMENT

were not good for, what they could or could not do. But even if it were right that women should be in subjection to men, they would for that very reason need to vote to protect themselves from abuse.

This picked up on, and brought back to attention, Harriet Taylor Mill's 1851 article,[33] the central argument of which was that the division of society into two castes, one ruling over the other, was harmful both to the development of the individual and to the wellbeing of society. The only arguments for it were custom, which for Mill was no argument, and the fact that men liked it that way. No part of society had the right to decide for another what was their proper sphere, and what they could or couldn't do.

Emily Davies didn't meet Mill until the mid-60s, but in the summer of 1861 she and Elizabeth Garrett (together, no doubt, with most of the Langham Place set) read his newly published *Considerations on Representative Government*, and they followed this up with his *Logic*. Davies seems to have been first into *Representative Government*, reporting in August that Mill was, as Garrett responded, 'so decided on our side'.[34] Having read the book herself, Garrett reported in early October that it 'is most delightful. It makes me full of joy and hope to know that perhaps most of the best young minds are now studying Mill & looking at him as a worthy teacher'.[35] Making an abstract of the book, she asked Davies to look over it and criticize.[36] (The reference to Mill being 'on our side' strongly suggests, incidentally, that both Davies and Garrett were already of the view that women should have the vote, something for which we have no other direct evidence.)

More significantly, perhaps, for Davies, was Mill's overall line of argument, which was to be fundamental to her own advocacy. Where others sought to create opportunities for women as women, with needs distinct from those of men, Davies, like Mill, insisted on the principle that no distinction should be made between men and women, unless a reasoned case could be made for it. Like Mill, too, she insisted that women should be given a good education, voting rights, and the freedom to choose their own paths, not in their own interests but for the benefit of society as a whole. Mill also meant something more to her. At some point, after rereading *On Liberty*, she wrote to her friend Anna Richardson of her deep debt to his writing:[37]

I met yesterday again in Mill a passage which made a great impression on me some years ago. 'Human beings owe to each other help to distinguish the better from the worse and encouragement to choose the former and avoid the latter.

[33] [Harriet Taylor Mill], 'Enfranchisement of women', *Westminster Review*, 55 (July 1851), 289–311.
[34] EG to ED, 21 August 1861, in FC, 227–9: 229; LSE 9/10/39.
[35] EG to ED, 3 October 1861, in FC, 232–4: 233.
[36] EG to ED, 8 October 1861, in FC, 234–6: 236; LSE 9/10/41.
[37] Stephen, 114. The letter is undated and, like many used by Stephen, no longer extant.

They should be for ever stimulating each other to increased exercise of their higher faculties, and increased direction of their feelings and aims towards wise instead of foolish, elevating instead of degrading, objects and contemplations.' That principle is at the bottom of everything I do (that is not bad) and perhaps accounts for what looks to you like love of power....I think there must be great fire in his writings tho' the form is so restrained, or they would not be so kind-ling. I feel glowing with hope and courage after reading Mill, tho' it would be hard to find a passage in which the enthusiasm is more than latent.

Engaging with the women's movements, these various attitudes, beliefs, and approaches all came to bear. The work was not, as some claimed, about rights. Late in 1865 she wrote to Henry Tomkinson that 'as to [women] "asserting their rights successfully and irresistibly," the idea is, if I may say so, rather revolting to my mind. It goes against me to think of it.'[38] Nor was it about equality. Men and women were roughly equal in numbers, and this was an issue, for example, in respect of school endowments, many of which had been created for 'children' but were almost exclusively being applied to benefit boys not girls. But Davies was perfectly happy to accept that men and women were generally different, and even that women were generally, in many respects, inferior.[39] But only generally. Women were individuals. They were interested in all sorts of things and possessed all sorts of abilities, both actual and potential, and she objected to men deciding, without any supporting evidence, what they weren't interested in, or what they were or weren't able to do. The only way to determine these things was to test them empirically. And she could see no grounds for depriving women of the free-dom to think for themselves, and make their own life choices.[40] 'Let the whole field of reality be laid open to woman as well as to man,' had pleaded George Eliot in conclusion to an 1854 article on 'Woman in France,'[41] and Davies would have concurred. When she launched the *Victoria Magazine* with Emily Faithfull in 1863, their chosen motto was 'Let every woman do that which is right in her own eyes.'[42]

Part of Davies's thinking was that women knew more about their values and desires than the men who claimed to choose for them—and even men tended to accept that women were *morally* superior. Her dominant theme, however, was a thoroughly Millian one. Giving women opportunities to learn, think for them-selves, make their own choices, work, and participate in the political process would benefit society as whole. The campaign for suffrage, for example, was not

---

[38] ED to HRT, 14 November 1865, *EDCL*, 161–2: 162.
[39] ED to HRT, 14 November 1865, *EDCL*, 161–2; ED to RHH, spring 1866, *EDCL*, 171–3.
[40] Ibid.
[41] 'Woman in France: Madame de Sablé,' *Westminster Review*, 62 (October 1854), 448–73, quoted in Gillian Beer, *George Eliot and the Woman Question* (Edward Everett Root, 2018), 11.
[42] ED to AR, 10 April 1863, *EDCL*, 45–6: 46.

92 DAVIES AND THE MID-VICTORIAN WOMEN'S MOVEMENT

in her view about rights or privileges, but about getting the best possible government, by drawing on whatever capabilities women might possess.[43] And telling women what they couldn't do could only ever be counter-productive: '[C]ontinually telling people that they cannot do things is apt to make them incapable, & in the interest of the human race it is not desirable for women to believe e.g. that they cannot be reasonable.'[44] The debt to Mill is confused here by Mill's own tendency, when discussing female suffrage, to insist on rights. As critics pointed out, however, following the publication of his *Subjection of Women*, this tendency, which they attributed to the excessive (to their minds) influence of his wife, was sharply at odds with the logic of his other writings. Emily Davies, in this respect, was a far more rigorous Millian than Mill.

It is notable that Davies's declarations of principle come from correspondence with men rather than women, and it might be that she was adapting her arguments to some degree to a male audience. But the views expressed are entirely consistent with her actions, and seem to be unfeigned. They are also consistent with her thoughts on how best to go about the work, found mainly in letters to Barbara Bodichon. The challenge, as she saw it, was to gain men's respect, so that women were *invited* to participate in public life, but to do so as women. To Anna Richardson she wrote that while agitating for change was disagreeable, part of her objective was about 'preserving women from becoming masculine, in a bad sense'.[45] Rather than trying to barge in where they were not wanted, which would just make things worse, they should aim to persuade men that providing women with a good education, allowing them to work and go to university, giving them control over their own property, and admitting them to at least some of those all-male institutions in which power resided—government and the professions in particular—was what they, the men, also wanted.

To this end it was important that women should take up those opportunities that *were* open to them (like voting for poor law guardians); work *with* men wherever possible, rather than with women against them, so as to earn their respect and get them used to the idea of women taking part in public affairs; and take them at their word, when they claimed to have women's interests at heart. They often didn't, of course, and it was natural to feel indignant, but one thing men could not, in her experience, stand was indignation. Much better to suppress it and try and persuade them that their views, while well-intended, were mistaken, than to charge them with intentional unfairness or abuse of power.[46]

It would be valuable, both in the context of the women's movement and in that of Victorian feminist studies more generally, to know something about Emily

---

[43] ED to HRT, 14 November 1865, *EDCL*, 161–2.
[44] ED to RHH, spring 1866, *EDCL*, 171–3: 172–3.   [45] ED to AR, 12 July 1862, *EDCL*, 3–4: 4.
[46] ED to BB, 14 January 1863, 14 November 1865, *EDCL*, 29–33, 160–1; ED to HRT, 14 November 1865, *EDCL*, 161–2.

Davies's sexuality. As noted in the introduction, the prevailing conventions make it very hard to tell whether or to what extent the many intimate homosocial friendships between women such as those in the women's movement were also homoerotic or homosexual. Sexual preference was not generally a marker of identity; emotional bonding and close physical contact were both commonplace; and distinctions we make now are not necessarily distinctions that would have been made by the parties concerned. There does seem to have been a strong homosexual or at least homoerotic thread running through parts of the movement. Max Hays and Emily Faithfull, while the latter would throughout her life preach family values, were almost certainly involved in relationships that were homosexual as well as homosocial, and proactively so, and the atmosphere at Langham Place must always have been erotically charged. What defines them, however, and the same can be said of Frances Power Cobbe, is not their sexuality so much as their determination to fill what society saw as a masculine role. They had no interest in men, either as sexual or as domestic partners, but wished to be free to live their lives and earn their living in the ways that men did.

Other women, including Bessie Parkes, appear to have been heterosexual but frightened by male sexuality—not surprising given the way it was sometimes characterized—and attracted by female sisterhood. Parkes did eventually marry and have children—the writer Hilaire Belloc was her son—but she spent many years engaged to someone with whom she had little physical contact and then married an invalid, for whom she could care.

Others again seem to have followed conventional heterosexual norms, fallen in love, and had apparently very happy marriages: Elizabeth Garrett and her sisters Louie and Millie, for example, or Josephine Butler. Emily Davies, however, is one of a group of spinsters (Anne Clough, Jessie Boucherett, Lydia Becker, and Helen Taylor were others) in respect of whom we have no idea whether they were so by choice or necessity, whether they were heterosexual, homosexual, bisexual, or asexual. In Davies's case, I think that she would have liked to be able to carry the authority, as the world saw it, of a 'Mrs' rather than a 'Miss'—and, indeed the authority of a mother. But that was not how things worked out. And if asked why, her instinctive response (though she would have put it far more politely) would have been: none of your business.

6

The Demise of Langham Place

Emily Davies's first priority, when she got to work in London, was to support Elizabeth Garrett in her efforts to advance in the medical profession, then focused on trying to gain admission to London University. Meanwhile, however, she also wanted to get involved in the women's movement more generally. Not knowing quite what she wanted to achieve, she threw herself into everything, but what evidently excited her most about her new environment was the intellectual milieu of the elite magazines and reviews. She wanted to be a part of it, and given that she had considerable editing skills, as well as organizational and administrative skills, she was drawn in particular to the *English Woman's Journal*.

The *EWJ* was struggling—or rather Bessie Parkes, as its editor and general standard bearer for the Langham Place group, was struggling, and increasingly stressed and unwell. There were three main sources of stress, each of which fed on the others. One was the interpersonal dynamic of the group. Another was external criticism of the group and its activities, which she took personally to heart. The third was disagreement amongst the group as to the aims and priorities of the journal.

Barbara Bodichon, effectively the proprietor of the journal, saw it as a political force, campaigning across the board for women's interests: on work, on education, on property, on divorce, and so on: a continuation and expansion of what she and Bessie Parkes had already begun. Max Hays, always intemperate, saw it more aggressively as a vehicle through which to attack male privilege. Bessie Parkes, while consistently defending Hays from attacks made on her, saw it quite differently: as an experiment in women working together and a showpiece for what they could do.

Against Bodichon's charge that the *Journal* was too timid, Parkes responded that 'you are not judging fairly of the success of my work in the Journal'. The 'Woman Cause', she wrote 'will probably never take in England the form of an abstract adhesion to justice & equality between men & women, because such a form is wholly opposed to the very genius of our national intellect.'[1] England was not France or America, in other words, and talk of women's rights, which she detested, would not get anywhere.[2] But this was secondary. The journal was written for working women by working women. It was about the ideal of a female

---

[1] BRP to BB, 5 January 1859, Girton GCPP Parkes 5/87.
[2] BRP to BB, 6 December 1857, Girton GCPP Parkes 5/86.

Emily Davies and the Mid-Victorian Women's Movement. John Hendry, Oxford University Press. © John Hendry 2024.
DOI: 10.1093/oso/9780198910237.003.0006

THE DEMISE OF LANGHAM PLACE   95

community, not unlike that portrayed (and satirized) in Tennyson's *Princess*, a working community based on love, not just mutual self-interest. It was, as Adelaide Procter put it, a 'moral engine'.[3]

From Bodichon's perspective, this was all very well, but not quite what was needed. The result was a journal that was timid, poorly edited—some of the articles contained factual errors—and in places just not good enough. Marian Evans (aka George Eliot), a sympathetic friend and supporter, complained that the writing was in general 'just middling', and that Hays in particular was hopeless: 'feminine rant of the worst kind'[4] or 'the application of feminine incapacity to Literature'.[5] 'I wish', she wrote to Bodichon, 'Bessie felt more keenly about the immorality of such slack writing as is sometimes admitted into [the review] department of the Journal.'[6]

These criticisms must have irritated, but far worse from Parkes's point of view were hostile criticisms from outside. In 1860 the *Saturday Review* had picked up on an advertisement of the reading room and dining facilities of Langham Place by mocking the idea of a 'ladies' club', and proceeding to warn men as to what might come of this kind of thing. 'We should not like to refer the committee-women of the ladies reading-room to the study of *Ecclesiazusae* and the *Lysistrata*, for it is very naughty reading, though it does describe what came of the ladies imitating a masculine institution, and combining against the other sex.'[7] In both plays, neither of them deemed suitable reading for women (and hence good reasons why women should not study the classics), the women triumph over the men by withholding their sexual favours. The unstated but clear reference is to the kind of women conceived as associating with such an institution—strong-minded, maybe lesbian, certainly far too sexually knowing, and quite certainly not respectable ladies. As Parkes noted, the suggestion was 'dirty and indecent to a horrible degree', the more so as it referenced, none too subtly, the earlier attack from the same source on her own book, and the reading it had recommended.[8]

The situation wasn't improved by her health—she was still recovering from a bad case of diphtheria—or by the fact that she was still living at home, with elderly parents and a cantankerous father who disapproved of anything that might be thought improper. Whenever she was attacked in public her father weighed in on the side of the attackers. He had strongly objected to an article in the very first number on the plight of former prostitutes, and objected too to an article by Hays in praise of George Sand, not because it was badly written (which was Marian Evans's complaint) but because Sand had in his view been a disreputable woman. To make matters worse, he had been neglecting his business interests and

---

[3] AP to BRP, 4 July 1862, Girton GCPP Parkes 8/24.   [4] Hirsch, 188.
[5] GE to Sarah Hennell, 2 March 1858, Haight, Vol. 2, 438–9.
[6] GE to BB, 5 December 1859, Haight, Vol. 3, 225–8: 226.
[7] 'The Ladies' Club', *Saturday Review*, 10 (7 January 1860), 12–13: 13.
[8] BRP to BB, 8 January 1860, Girton GCPP Parkes 5/96.

96 DAVIES AND THE MID-VICTORIAN WOMEN'S MOVEMENT

spending well beyond his means. The money was running out fast, and his temper was not improving as a result.[9]

A particularly stressful aspect of the criticisms that came Parkes's way was that they so often focused on Max Hays, whom she had made a point of befriending and supporting in her editorial role. And as Emily Davies got involved with the *Journal* in the summer of 1862 it was Hays again whose writing provoked. Lord Sydney Godolphin Osborne, or 'S.G.O.', brother-in-law to Charles Kingsley and James Anthony Froude, and a regular *Times* correspondent, had written plainly and positively about women's causes, about the work of Maria Rye and Emily Faithfull, and in support of a much better education for women. This should have been good news but, instead of welcoming it, Hays responded be letting fly at all *other* men. In England, she asserted, women were bought and sold as slaves, or sold themselves into a marriage that was no more than legalized prostitution. As Richard Hutton noted pointedly in the *Spectator*, if proof were wanted of the need for a better education for women, Hays's letter to the *Times* provided it, and it was fortunate that she didn't represent her colleagues.[10] But to many less informed people she *did* represent her colleagues. Parkes responded by setting out her own moderate position:

> To women of the educated classes I would give the freest opportunities to devote themselves to works of mercy, to literature, and to such professional pursuits as their own good sense and that of the public may end in allotting to them. But such women, even among the educated classes, will always be a minority, though an eminently useful and honourable minority. For the bulk of our female population, rich and poor, I entertain no other wish than that they may be happy in their homes.

The damage, however, had been done.

Unfortunately for Parkes's stress levels, Hays was not only a public nuisance but a private one too, as her strong and shifting passions made for a disrupting influence. What exactly happened is unclear, but it seems that soon after joining the *Journal* she made a play for Adelaide Procter, who then fell head over heels in love with her. She dedicated her first volume of poetry to her, and a love poem speaks of their blissful relationship. This may or may not have been sexual. It appears from her poetry that Procter had a morbid dread of male sexuality, and she had

---

[9] Jane Rendall, 'A moral engine? Feminism, liberalism and the English Woman's Journal', in Jane Rendall, ed., *Equal or Different: Women's Politics 1800–1914* (Blackwell, 1987), 127; JP to BRP, 15 October 1858, Girton GCPP Parkes 2/66; Lowndes, 32, 166.

[10] 'Women's platforms', *Spectator*, 35 (3 May 1862), 489–90. Hays's letter was in the *Times* on 29 April 1862. See also Osborne's letters on 3 April 1862 and 28 May 1862 and one by Isa Craig, 1 May 1862, explicitly disowning Max's views. Osborne, Kingsley, and Froude had all married daughters of Pascoe and Charlotte Grenfell.

THE DEMISE OF LANGHAM PLACE 97

had other close female relationships, including with Nannie Leigh Smith, but she comes across as a sexual innocent.[11] It was clearly turbulent, however, and disruptive. Later on Parkes would admit that Hays had a 'selfish unstable nature',[12] but at this time she was defensive:[13]

[Max] supplies all my deficiencies as if she had been created for the purpose. Every soul who works with her learns to love and respect her; to be patient with her faults & to acknowledge her virtues. It has been a long, & at first it was a very hard struggle to reorganise a life so shattered by her own & other's violence; & I must expect relapses from such a temperament so long as she is this side of the grave—But she is saved; and one must know my dear child to know the full meaning of that word.

Elsewhere she writes:[14]

It is very hard for women in England just now; men fail them & there is a terrible tacit division between the sexes. It is no wonder that the warm tender feelings cling too much to each other in default of natural ties...

Hays is recovering from a damaged past and her possessiveness and, perhaps, her homosexuality are understandable in the circumstances. All will be alright in the end.

It was not. By early 1861, when Parkes was visiting Bodichon in Algiers and Hays was in charge of the *Journal*, she seems to have shifted her attentions to Lady Monson, owner of the Langham Place house and an old friend, with whom she would go on to have an enduring relationship. Adelaide Procter was increasingly ill from tuberculosis, the symptoms of which had come on strongly after Hays split with her ('never question to yourself & others the effect of that friendship. It lies in the past inscrutable',[15] Parkes wrote later to Bodichon) and something evidently flared up. Writing on the way home, on a leisurely journey through France with some of Bodichon's paintings for a London exhibition, Parkes insisted to Bodichon that 'with all our faults & quarrels there is a real spirit of love at bottom, which is just what the outsiders cannot see'.[16] Writing again once back home she insisted that the office was flourishing, though Procter was still unwell.[17]

[11] Gill Gregory, *The Life and Work of Adelaide Procter* (Ashgate, 1998), 24–5 and chapter 1 *passim*.
[12] BRP to BB, 17 January 1864, Girton GCPP Parkes 5/126.
[13] BRP to BB, 8 January 1860, Girton GCPP Parkes 5/96.
[14] BRP to BLS/BB, 21 August ?, Girton GCPP Parkes 5/51a. The Girton archives have dated this around 1850, but Hirsch treats it as being contemporary with the travails of Langham Place, which strikes me as far more plausible.
[15] BRP to BB, 13 February 1864, Girton GCPP Parkes 5/127.
[16] BRP to BB, 19 April 1861, Girton GCPP Parkes 5/105.
[17] BRP to BB, 2 May 1861, Girton GCPP Parkes 5/106.

At some point, whether then or later, tensions were further raised as Emily Faithfull sought to take Hays's place in Procter's affections. She didn't succeed. Procter, whose health was continuing to deteriorate, was still in love with Hays, who now became her protector, professing friendship and affection. But it was another source of quarrels and left Parkes distraught. If it ever became known that the work of Langham Place was suffering because of quarrels amongst the women, the press would have a field day.

By the beginning of 1862, the emotional temperature had dropped, but not much. Barbara Bodichon had decided that, for the sake of the journal, Max Hays had to go, and her contract had been terminated at the end of the year.[18] She had moved in with Lady Monson, who had formally taken possession of the Langham Place flat. They don't appear to have been using it, but Emily Faithfull and Jane Crow had moved out to a house rented by Faithfull in Bloomsbury.[19] Adelaide Procter, still in love, was angry at the way Hays had been treated, and Bessie Parkes was exhausted. She was now sole editor of the *Journal*. She felt guilty about Hays. And she was deeply concerned about Procter, who even as her health was declining had been throwing herself into various projects: work with SPEW; a lavish presentation volume to showcase the skills of the Victoria Press; and a refuge for homeless women and children set up by her confessor, Father Daniel Gilbert.[20] Parkes was also increasingly concerned at this time about the behaviour of Emily Faithfull, writing to Bodichon, apparently in response to comments from Procter, that 'Emily, who is a splendid worker, full of energy & ability, is even more unsettled morally than Max.'[21] The precise reference is unclear, but after working closely with Faithfull at the press, Procter had broken off their friendship altogether—her mother told Robert Browning, a close friend of the family, that Faithfull had invented a lie to interest her daughter, 'about as pretty a specimen as I ever heard.'[22]

In March and April, Bessie Parkes took a long break, visiting her friend Mary Merryweather, engaged in social work in Liverpool, and Adelaide Procter's sister, who had become a nun, in Dublin, and apparently leaving Adelaide and Max (temporarily re-engaged) to hold the fort in Langham Place.[23] By the time she

---

[18] BRP to BB, 8 December 1861, 12 January 1862, Girton GCPP Parkes 5/108, 112.

[19] They stayed at the house, in Taviton Street, for about two years, Faithfull holding numerous parties and entertaining much of literary London: FC, 262; ED to BB, 28 December 1862, 3 January 1863, *EDCL*, 11–18, 23–7.

[20] BRP to BB, 8 December 1861, 12 January 1862, Girton GCPP Parkes 5/108, 112. *EWJ*, 13 (March 1864), 17–21. Gregory, *Adelaide Procter*, 12; AD to BRP, 1861 *passim*, Girton GCPP Parkes 8/11–29. The volume, *The Victoria Regia*, was dedicated to the Queen and included contributions from many well-known authors including Trollope, Thackeray, Arnold, and Maurice.

[21] BRP to BB, 8 December 1861, Girton GCPP Parkes 5/108.

[22] AP to BRP, 7 August 1862, Girton GCPP Parkes 8/26; Robert Browning to Isabella Blagden, 19 January 1865, in Edward C. McAleer, ed., *Dearest Isa: Robert Browning's Letters to Isabella Blagden* (University of Texas, 1951), 204; and see BRP to BB, 1 April 1862, Girton GCPP Parkes 5/114.

[23] BRP to BB, 1 April 1862, Girton GCPP Parkes 5/109, 114; and see ED to BB, 3 December 1862, *EDCL*, 7–10.

THE DEMISE OF LANGHAM PLACE   99

returned she had decided that she needed to step away for a while from the *Journal* and concentrate on her poetry, and on these other interests.[24] The question then arose as to who was to take over as editor. Procter wanted Hays to return, but Bodichon would not have it.[25] An obvious choice was Isa Craig, who had been in at the very beginning, but here Procter was strongly opposed. Whilst making it quite clear that personally she could see no reason why Hays should have had to leave, she objected in the strongest terms that 'anything which throws the EWJ into E. Faithfull's power, which giving it to Isa Craig does, is a positively wrong and wicked thing'. Indeed, the fact of Emily Faithfull being the ultimate destination of the journal turned all objections to Hays into 'smoke, not to say humbug'.[26] Parkes, while she loved Isa Craig dearly herself, backed Procter up. Asked by Bodichon for the relevant 'facts', she admitted that her opinion was based on many small things rather than clear facts, but it was nevertheless strong. Although Faithfull was 'not half so mad or tiresome' as Hays, and although she was 'very clever and very kind in many ways…she has that peculiar screw loose which might might [sic] in my opinion some day bring her to Millbank [Penitentiary]. This opinion has slowly formed itself in my mind during the last year and half, owing to numerous occurrences, great and small…'.[27]

While this debate was going on, Emily Davies was getting more and more involved in Langham Place, and no doubt demonstrating both her editing and her organizational skills. She offered her services, and at some point it was agreed that she should edit the September and October issues, albeit informally, unpaid and under Parkes's continuing oversight.[28] She continued on this basis to the following spring.

It didn't go well. On the positive side, Davies was able to take a disinterested view of the journal's reputation and viability, something that Parkes never had. It quickly became clear, however, that there were irreconcilable differences between them, both in respect of the journal content and positioning and in respect of the people involved.

With respect to content and positioning, Davies agreed with Bodichon that the *Journal* had been far too timid. At the beginning of her editorial stint, in September, she visited Bodichon in Sussex and she kept in very close touch thereafter, always representing herself as putting into practice Bodichon's policies.[29] But she felt constrained by Parkes's anxiety to avoid anything remotely controversial, or anything that Parkes or her friends didn't agree with. She had offers of all sorts of interesting articles, she claimed, that she didn't feel able to publish.[30]

---

[24] Bessie Rayner Parkes, *Ballads and Songs* (Bell & Daldy, 1863).
[25] BRP to BB, September 1862, AP to BRP, 4 July 1862, Girton GCPP Parkes 5/115, 8/24.
[26] AP to BRP, 4 July 1862, Girton GCPP Parkes 8/24; AP to BRP, 7 August 1862, Girton GCPP Parkes 8/26.
[27] BRP to BB, September 1862, Girton GCPP Parkes 5/115.   [28] FC, 263a.   [29] FC, 269.
[30] ED to BB, 3 December 1862, 3 January 1863, *EDCL*, 7–11, 23–6.

The *Journal*, she felt, was in a double bind. Thanks to the combination of Parkes's caution and Hays's intemperance, 'the EWJ has <u>two</u> bad characters, one for license,…the other for dullness'.[31] 'It is very unfortunate that in spite of Bessie's extreme care to avoid everything startling in the <u>matter</u> of the Journal, by which it was made less interesting & genuinely respectable than it might have been, it has got the credit of Bloomerism &c. <u>for nothing</u>, so to speak.'[32]

It didn't help matters that relations between Parkes and Faithfull were continuing to deteriorate, and that as they did so Davies increasingly took Faithfull's side. Parkes, spurred on perhaps by Procter, wanted to take the printing of the journal away from the Victoria Press. Faithfull responded by suggesting that if that happened she would publish a new magazine herself, implicitly in competition. Davies insisted both that the Victoria Press was printing it on the cheap and it would be financially crazy to move and, that if they did move, they could hardly fault Faithfull for her response. Indeed, she thought a new magazine would be rather a good idea and she might edit it herself.[33]

Davies insisted that despite their differences she and Parkes remained personally on the best of terms. 'You must not think we are not on perfectly good terms,' she wrote to Bodichon, after a long account of Parkes's ignorance and delusions. 'We get on extremely well together.'[34] 'We are the best friends in the world,' she wrote again, after reporting further irreconcilable differences.[35] This was ingenuous. Neither would dream of criticizing the other to their face, and no doubt all on the surface was sweetness and light. But it's clear that Parkes was criticizing not only Faithfull but also Jane Crow (who had gained a reputation for being nice but not very efficient) and Isa Craig (who was tied up with other projects and a close family bereavement) and that Davies felt a need to defend them. A visit by Frances Power Cobbe didn't help. A strong feminist herself and fast establishing herself as a prolific author and journalist, publishing frequently in elite monthlies, Cobbe would have been a valuable contributor and had ideas about the future of the *Journal* that Davies thought sensible. But she was forthright in her views, apt to stir controversy, and a critic of Roman Catholic sisterhoods. Parkes disagreed profoundly with her views and thought her 'dangerous'.[36]

For Davies, these were matters to be treated rationally. What were the objectives of the women's movement, how could the journal best serve those, and what did financial and business considerations suggest? For Parkes, it was always

---

[31] ED to BB, 3 January 1863, *EDCL*, 23–6: 24; ED to Nannie Leigh Smith, 2 January 1863, *EDCL*, 20–2.

[32] ED to BB, 3 December 1862, *EDCL*, 7–11: 8.

[33] ED to BB, 3 December 1862, 3 January 1863, *EDCL*, 7–10, 23–6.

[34] ED to BB, 14 January 1863, *EDCL*, 29–33: 31.

[35] ED to BB, 26 February 1863, *EDCL*, 40–1: 40.

[36] ED to BB, 14 January 1863, *EDCL*, 29–33: 30; and see BRP to BB, 1866, Girton GCPP Parkes 5/133.

more about community and personal relationships. At one point, she put it in religious terms.[37]

> I am induced by all I see more and more to believe that cohesion in work is next to impossible unless there be the inward binding of a common religious principle.
>
> I can work with Unitarians, because tho' I am not dogmatically a <u>Unitarian</u> I have been trained in & still retain in a great measure their view of life & its duties. And I could work with Catholics because of my intellectual sympathy with their doctrines, and the definiteness of their plans. [Bessie was by now in effect a practising Catholic herself, and would be baptized by Father Gilbert in 1864.] But I confess that when I get hold of minds which have been trained (or not trained) in the Church of England, I don't know how to deal with them— Emily Davies, Jane Crowe, EF, and to a certain extent my own little Isa, seem to me to have no floors to their interior domains!

Parkes and Procter were Catholic converts. Jessie Boucherett, with whom everyone seems to have remained on good terms, appears to have been brought up in the Church of England, and like Emily Davies had found the women's movement almost by accident, but she had been educated at a Unitarian school (run by the Miss Byerleys, where Elizabeth Gaskell had earlier been a pupil). Frances Power Cobbe had become a Unitarian, but of the Transcendentalist school of Emerson, Thoreau, and Theodore Parker, whose works she had edited—a form of deism that was quite alien to the Christian Unitarianism of Parkes's upbringing—and like Davies, Crow, Faithfull, and Craig had been brought up in the Church of England.[38]

What it came down to was that the whole venture, for Parkes, had always been idealized as a kind of sisterhood, something run by women for women, and almost an end in itself, the loss of which would be a disaster. For Davies, however, the *Journal* was no use if it was not read, and if it did not impact on the views of men, who had the power to change things, as well as women. Women working together was nothing new—it happened all over the place, most obviously in the schools and charitable ventures of the Church of England. 'The new & difficult thing is', she insisted, 'for men & women to work together on equal terms', and the *Journal* did nothing to advance that. Because it was seen as primarily a women's journal, it could just be dismissed by men as not worth listening to, and was. The name itself was a liability. The way forward was to assume that men and women were interested in the same things; to focus on the grievances of women as addressing practices that were injurious to society generally (Mill's argument,

---

[37] BRP to BB, 1863, Girton GCPP Parkes 5/121.   [38] Mitchell, chapter 6.

though she did not say so); and to have a publication that represented the viewpoints of good men as well as good women.[39] Or else to publish in the existing magazines, which were read in large numbers by both men and women and which were opening up to contributions on women's issues.

More prosaically, the *Journal* was just not viable. It wasn't paying an editor, it wasn't paying contributors—and was not, in consequence, getting quality contributions—yet it was still turning a loss. Davies's view, and the view of people she (very selectively) consulted, was that it had to be either put on a proper business foundation, with money spent on advertising, an editorial salary, and contributions, including a serialized story to draw in readers, or given up altogether. And while, she insisted, no one really wanted to see it go, spending a lot of money to make it better would probably still not make it viable.

By January 1863, Davies had concluded that the *Journal* should be wound up. Parkes, not surprisingly, was 'quite aghast at the idea, & is evidently in a state of delusion about it altogether',[40] and a decision was delayed until Bodichon was back in the country. In mid-March, however, Davies announced that she would edit the April edition of the *Journal* but then leave to become editor of a new magazine to be published by Faithfull. The *Victoria Magazine* would be managed jointly by men and women and would be a mainstream magazine along the lines of *Fraser's*, *Macmillan's*, and *Blackwood's*, seeking to publish the work of noted established authors on literature, science, art, theology, and politics. Pursuing Davies's Millian line, it would focus on 'those questions, which while more directly bearing on the condition of women, are in their wider aspects, of the highest importance to society generally'.[41] She hoped Bodichon would approve.

Meanwhile, Parkes was to edit the May issue of the *Journal*, and talks were under way to bring in the printing firm, Jarrold, as a new shareholder and a woman by the name of Ellen Barlee as editor. Davies had dearly hoped, she wrote to Bodichon, to continue helping with the work, but there was no way she could work with the likes of Ellen Barlee, who was energetic and pushy, qualities that were much needed, but irredeemably vulgar.[42] Not ladylike, in other words. In the event, nothing came of these talks, but the printing of the journal was moved from the Victoria Press to Jarrold in September.[43] Parkes meanwhile resumed the editorship and used a recent inheritance to invest heavily in the *Journal*, becoming the controlling shareholder.

For Davies, the *Victoria Magazine* looked like a much more promising venture than the *English Woman's Journal*. She got on well with and agreed on most things

---

[39] ED to BB, 14 January 1863, *EDCL*, 29–33: 30–1.

[40] ED to BB, 3 January 1863 and postscript of 8 January 1863, *EDCL*, 26.

[41] ED to BB, 12 March 1863, *EDCL*, 42–5: 43.   [42] ED to BB, 12 March 1863, *EDCL*, 42–5.

[43] Lowndes, 132, links this to the Codrington divorce case, but the change happened much earlier than that and had much more to do with the setting up of the *Victoria Magazine*.

with Faithfull,[44] and she had drawn up a formal agreement giving her both a salary and editorial control. 'I have no notion of friendly vagueness in matters of business,' she wrote to Bodichon, '& I believe a great deal of the trouble at L. P. has been caused by the want of distinct, definite arrangements. You may be as friendly as you like, *after* you have got your business-like basis, but let that be well defined, first.'[45] Positioned as a liberally inclined general interest magazine with occasional articles drawing attention to women's causes and a 'social science' section reporting on current affairs with a slant towards women's issues, the new venture attracted a much better quality of writing. Early contributors included Richard Hutton, F. D. Maurice, Nassau Senior, Edward Dicey, Christina Rosetti, Tom Taylor, Thomas Hood, Frances Cobbe, and Mrs Oliphant, all well-established writers. Davies herself contributed two articles, one on university degrees for women, the other on 'Needleworkers v. society', which argued that if needleworkers were to get a living wage, they must be able to strike, or else find sufficient employment elsewhere to improve their bargaining powers.[46] This rather strange piece was an exercise in economic reasoning that Elizabeth Garrett, for one, found distinctly unconvincing, and it was a theme to which Davies never returned.[47]

Unfortunately, though a much more professional product, the *Victoria* was, from a business perspective, far too ambitious, even foolhardy. It was a crowded market. Besides established competitors like *Blackwood's* and *Fraser's*, a whole host of monthlies had been set up in the last few years, including Thackeray's *Cornhill Magazine*, the *St James's Magazine*, *Temple Bar*, and *Macmillan's*. *Macmillan's Magazine*, moreover, was not only well-funded and with an exceptionally strong stable of writers; they were the very writers, broad church intellectuals and other forward thinkers, that Davies would have wanted to attract. There was also another new venture, *The Reader*, a weekly offshoot of *Macmillan's* edited by the Christian Socialists Tom Hughes and John Ludlow, which again fished from exactly the same pool of contributors, and to which Davies herself contributed book reviews—and which proved very quickly to be financially non-viable.

As if the environment were not challenging enough, Davies also fell foul of her attempt to source a good serialized novel, critical for a magazine of this kind. The best writers were all committed elsewhere and she resorted to commissioning a work from Thomas Adolphus Trollope, brother of Anthony, a prolific writer but not in the same league. This was unfortunately a disaster. Indeed, Richard Hutton

---

[44] ED to BB, 3 January 63, *EDCL*, 23–7: 24.
[45] ED to BB, 12 March 1863, *EDCL*, 42–5: 44. Their signed business agreement is preserved at FC, 288a.
[46] 'Needleworkers v. society', *Victoria Magazine*, 1 (August 1863), 348–60, copy at Girton GCPP Davies 11/20.
[47] EG to ED, 3 August 1863, in FC, 311–13.

told her emphatically that, in his opinion, ' "Thomas Adolphus" had murdered us, & that it was a great pity'.[48] Hutton suggested that they should cut their losses, pay off Trollope, get a first-rate story, and plug on, but it was not as easy as that. First-rate stories were snapped up well in advance and with the magazine by then clearly losing money they cost far more than Faithfull could afford.

It soon became apparent that the *Victoria* was no more viable, financially, than the *Journal*. Davies gave notice in the autumn that she would quit as editor at the end of January, and Faithfull began negotiations with the publishers Ward & Lock to sell the magazine.[49] Nothing came of the sale, however, and with Faithfull effectively absent Davies decided to continue for another few months. She had, she told Bodichon, nothing more useful to do.[50] Then, when Faithfull decided to try and make the magazine pay by cutting expenses and making it lighter, she pulled out: 'I could not edit a light Magazine, nor can I edit one at all, unless I may go to the best writers & pay them properly. So there was no alternative but to give up. I am sorry, but I have been so thoroughly inured to what you call the "discipline of disappointments" that nothing of that sort takes much hold of me.'[51]

Exacerbating their financial problems, both Bessie Parkes and Emily Faithfull were, by early 1864, struggling emotionally, for different but closely related reasons. Adelaide Procter's health had continued to deteriorate, and by the late summer of 1863 it was clear that she had not long to live.[52] For the next few months Parkes spent as much time as she could at her bedside. The journal was inevitably neglected, though Max Hays, who wrote daily to Procter but was prevented by the family from visiting, may well have helped out. When Procter died on 2 February, it left Parkes distraught. Writing to Mary Merryweather, she described the death as breaking her life into two halves and as setting the seal on her spiritual development over the last few years. Visiting Merryweather soon after, she went down with a bad bout of scarlet fever, from which it took her two months to recover. She then holidayed in France and was formally baptized a Roman Catholic when she returned in July. Meanwhile, she confessed to Bodichon how wonderful it was to be free of all her Langham Place women: Miss Lewin torturing her with hugs and finances, Emily Davies writing her letters about 'those awful University Examinations, which I certainly couldn't pass', and others pestering her about every cause under the sun.[53] By August, she had effectively resigned from the women's movement. The *Journal* was folded into another publication, the *Alexandra Magazine*, but even that only lasted a year.[54]

[48] ED to JC 2 January 1864, *EDCL*, 83–6: 83.
[49] ED to JC, 12 January 1864, 23 January 1864, *EDCL*, 90–3, 96–8.
[50] ED to JC, 12 January 1864, *EDCL*, 90–3: 91.
[51] ED to AR, 15 March 1864, *EDCL*, 106–7: 107.
[52] Lowndes, 133; AP to BRP, 23 August 1863, Girton GCPP Parkes 8/40. The doctor was probably Campbell de Morgan of the Middlesex Hospital, brother of the eminent logician Augustus de Morgan and uncle of the potter and tile designer.
[53] BRP to BB, 16 March 1864, GCPP Parkes 5/129.   [54] Lowndes, 132, 136.

THE DEMISE OF LANGHAM PLACE   105

Meanwhile, Emily Faithfull had her own troubles to content with. She too was hit by Procter's final illness and death, especially as she was not allowed to visit or even write, but she also found herself embroiled in a divorce case. The Codrington divorce case has been described in detail elsewhere,[55] but the bare bones are as follows. Commodore Codrington, son of an admiral, had married Helen Webb Smith while stationed in Lugano in 1848–9. She was an attractive and flirtatious woman twenty years his junior, whose father, a renowned ornithological artist, had moved to Florence after retiring from the East India Company. The marriage was not a success and in November 1863, Codrington, now a vice-admiral, sued for divorce on the grounds of adultery with two officers, both in Malta, where they had been stationed, and in London on their return. On a previous posting, to the Mediterranean and Crimea, when Helen had stayed at home with her small children, Faithfull had moved in as a friend and companion. They had remained close friends and Codrington's lawyers had gathered evidence to suggest that Faithfull had been instrumental in facilitating Helen's assignations.

Helen countered her husband's charges by charging him with cruelty and neglect, but also by claiming that one night in October 1856 he had entered her bedroom, where she was sleeping with Emily Faithfull, and 'got into the bed in which [she] and the said Miss Faithfull were then sleeping and then attempted to have connexion with the said Miss Faithfull while asleep.'[56] When the case came to court in July 1864, Faithfull, who had signed an affidavit in support of Helen's claims, went missing, almost certainly abroad. Other evidence was also wanting, the case was adjourned, and on its resumption in November, Faithfull withdrew her affidavit, claiming that she had signed it without reading it, on her friend's assurance.

At the beginning of the year, all that can have been known was that Faithfull was to be cited in a divorce case, but that was troubling enough, and it seems that the case, combined with Adelaide Procter's dying, distracted her completely from her work. Then, bit by bit, more details came out, and at some point they reached Bessie Parkes:[57]

---

[55] Martha Vicinus, *Intimate Friends: Women Who Loved Women, 1778-1928* (University of Chicago Press, 2004), 70–98; Martha Vicinus, 'Lesbian perversity and Victorian marriage: the 1864 Codrington divorce trial', *Journal of British Studies*, 36 (1997), 70–98; James Stone, *Emily Faithfull: Victorian Champion of Women's Rights* (P. D. Meany, 1994), 18–22. Vicinus gives a thorough account which she uses to explore contemporary attitudes to lesbianism but relies heavily for interpretation on parallels with a novel written by Emily Faithfull a few years later, *Change upon Change* (1868), which I find distinctly unconvincing. We know of the divorce case primarily through press reports: *Times*, 30 July 1864, 1 August 1864, 18 November 1864, 21 November 1864; *Daily Telegraph*, 24 November 1864; *Lloyds Weekly Newspaper*, 20 November 1864; *Law Journal Reports*, 34 (1864-5), 62; *Reynold's Newspaper*, 27 November 1864.

[56] Stone, *Emily Faithfull*, 18–19.

[57] BRP to BB, undated fragment, Girton GCPP Parkes 5/88a. 'She' is not named, and the letter is catalogued as from around 1859, but it seems almost certain that the reference is to Emily Faithfull, and that the letter dates from 1863–4, in which case the 'other two' are most likely to be Jane Crow and Emily Davies. 'Folie lucide' refers to the presence of strong and inexplicable emotional affect but with no delusion. The English term is 'moral insanity', but Parkes likely had in mind Ulysse Trélat, *La Folie Lucide, étudiée et considérée au point de vue de la famille et de la société* (Adrien Delahaye, 1861).

106 DAVIES AND THE MID-VICTORIAN WOMEN'S MOVEMENT

Isa burst out one day by accident with part of it to my astonished ears! and little by little the other two let out what they knew!

Sometimes I think she is mad; a mere case of "Folie Lucide"; but whether she is mad or bad, & whether what she says is true or false is more than I can tell.

Now this is all I can or dare tell you; and more perhaps than I ought to say. I do not think you will do harm by visiting her; but I am publicly involved; & must keep clear of the blow-up which I think must by all the laws of chances, come some day.

As Max, who is the most incurious and scandalous of talkers knows <u>the whole</u>, it is not in nature to suppose it will never come out.

Then, when the case came to court in July, tongues really started to wag, with attention shifting from the claims of adultery, in which Faithfull was implicated but secondary, to the claim of assault. Codrington claimed he had entered the bedroom to check on the fire, and this led, inevitably, to much talk of him 'poking the fire', but what really interested people was that Helen and Emily had not only slept together while the admiral was away (seen as quite normal) but had insisted on doing so after he returned (not at all normal). The rumour around the law courts, as Parkes's ever censorious father told her rather pointedly, was that Faithfull had not gone abroad at all but was 'still in London in Male attire'.[58]

When the case resumed in November, Faithfull was portrayed as an innocent young woman, misled by the wicked Helen Codrington. (Though the evidence was rather shaky, the admiral got his divorce, not perhaps surprisingly since divorce cases had, since the 1857 Act, been assigned to the Admiralty Court). Her reputation was not seriously affected, she got her act together with the business, and both the press and the magazine survived. Her friendships did not, however. For Emily Davies, in particular, but also for Barbara Bodichon and others, the association had become just too risky.[59] Good friends though they had been, Davies cut her off completely.

By the end of 1864, the Langham Place group was no more. Adelaide Procter was dead and Bessie Parkes had quit. Isa Craig and Jane Crow were still around, but both would now act primarily as Davies's lieutenants. Emily Faithfull continued to print and publish feminist writings, and to use the *Victoria Magazine* to give detailed reports of meetings, organizations, and campaigns, but she did not get directly involved with any of these. Jessie Boucherett continued her work with

---

[58] JP to BRP, 2 August 1864 and see also 4 August 1864, 11 August 1864, 19 November 1864, Girton GCPP Parkes 2/80, 81–3.

[59] FC, 337–8. In 1872, Faithfull approached Bodichon for a reference to an American woman who was a potential sponsor of a lecture she was then planning. Bodichon consulted Davies, who found the request 'vexing' and suggested that she might explain diplomatically that Faithfull was not a friend, but should provide the reference. 'I should not like [to] make such an adroit manager of people our active enemy.' ED to BB, 16 January 1872, *EDCL*, 366.

SPEW, and in 1866 she would launch a new magazine, *The Englishwoman's Review: A Journal of Woman's Work*, which effectively took the place of the *English Woman's Journal* and monitored and reported on developments. She seems to have remained friendly with everyone, and would join in their efforts as and when she saw fit, but essentially followed her own course.

The one alliance that continued, and that would be critical for future developments, was that between Barbara Bodichon and Emily Davies. It was never a friendship of the kind that had held together Langham Place. Although Davies visited Bodichon in Sussex most Septembers, they never became intimate. There was always a formality in their correspondence, as between friendly acquaintances rather than close friends. Bodichon was still, at this stage, the acknowledged leader of the women's movement, but she was also a professional artist, tied up with friends and family (though to her sorrow she had been unable to have children herself), and spending much of her time out of the country. She looked to Davies to put her ideas into practice. For Davies, the question of *how* those ideas should be put into practice was almost more important than the ideas themselves. Although she tended to credit herself with ideas that had almost certainly come through Bodichon, her real skills were as a campaigner and organizer. In those respects, she felt, the Langham Place group had taken a wrong turning, and even while working within that group as an editor, she had embarked on a parallel course. The movement was moving on.

7

From Educating Women to Examining Girls

By the time Emily Davies moved to London, Elizabeth Garrett had been accepted as a candidate by the Society of Apothecaries, which required no degree, but she hadn't entirely given up on a university qualification. Encouraged by both Davies and John Chapman to exhaust all possibilities, she applied in early 1862 to take the matriculation examinations of the University of London, writing at the same time to each member of the senate, and calling on those to whom she could secure good introductions. In an effort to avoid the hostility of the doctors on the senate, no mention was made of medicine.[1]

The chances of success were small. Some years earlier the university had rejected an application from a woman, Barbara Bodichon's friend Jessie White, and had both precedent and legal advice to fall back on. It so happened, however, that the university's charter was coming up for revision so as to enable it to offer degrees in surgery, and this provided a lobbying opportunity. As expected, the application was referred to the senate, which met and voted on the matter in early April. The vote was, in essence, no more than a straw poll. Even if they had supported the application in principle, they had no power under the charter to admit women. But it was encouragingly close, the application being rejected by just seven votes to six, with both the chancellor and the vice-chancellor in the minority.[2] Immediately after the vote, Newson Garrett submitted a memorial to the university on behalf of his daughter and himself, proposing that a clause be inserted in the new charter, removing the legal objection to his daughter's admission and opening the university to women:[3]

> It appears to us very desirable to raise the standard of female education, and that this object can in no way be more effectually furthered than by affording to women an opportunity of testing their attainments in the more solid branches of learning.... [A]s the University requires no residence, and the examinations

---

[1] FC, 226; Manton, 125–6; ED to BB, 3 December 1862, *EDCL*, 7–10.

[2] Willson, 92; FC, 250a. William Carpenter, the registrar of the university, who was himself by no means set against women being admitted, later recalled Elizabeth Garrett as being a 'bumptious self asserting girl': Willson, 89. Supporting her admission were the chancellor and vice-chancellor, James Heywood, Edward Ryan, E. T. B. Twiselton, and Lord Wodehouse: Willson, 93.

[3] Emily Davies, 'The influence of university degrees on the education of women', *Victoria Magazine*, 1 (July 1863), 260–71, in *Thoughts*, 41–62: 45–6.

Emily Davies and the Mid-Victorian Women's Movement. John Hendry, Oxford University Press. © John Hendry 2024.
DOI: 10.1093/oso/9780198910237.003.0007

FROM EDUCATING WOMEN TO EXAMINING GIRLS 109

involve nothing which could in the slightest degree infringe upon feminine reserve, we believe that by acceding to our wishes you would be conferring an unmixed benefit.

Meanwhile, Davies took charge of a support campaign, mobilizing connections through Langham Place and her brother to send out 1500 letters to members of the university and influential men and women, seeking their support.[4] (These were signed S. E. Davies, after Llewelyn suggested that use of her Christian name would conjure up an image of a 'horrid woman in spectacles'.) She then had printed and circulated some of the positive responses received, including from Mary Somerville, F. D. Maurice, Russell Gurney, William Gladstone, and Henry Alford, dean of Canterbury.[5]

The matter came to a vote almost immediately, with a proposal in support of the change by the vice-chancellor, George Grote.[6] Davies recalled that her brother had been quite sanguine about the chances of reform: 'Oh, you'll get it,' he said. 'These men are all advanced Liberals.'[7] Once again, however, it was a close defeat, with ten votes each way and the question decided on the casting vote of the chancellor, Lord Granville. Granville seems himself to have been in favour, but decided quite properly, and after consultation, that in such circumstances he should go with the status quo.[8] If the vote was encouraging, however, the division was not. Support came mainly from those senators recruited from politics and government, whilst opposition came mainly from the professions, the lawyers, and especially the doctors, five out of six of the latter voting against. For reforms to go through the support would be needed of convocation, the wider body of university graduates, in which the professions were dominant.[9]

A letter to Newson Garrett explained, rather ingenuously, that there was a general concurrence in favour of the proposal that women should have an opportunity of testing themselves in the more solid branches of learning, but that the majority view was that the charter should not be changed to effect that.[10]

Encouraged again by Chapman, Elizabeth Garrett next tried her luck in Scotland, where she found a warm welcome from some of the professors but was again refused admission to the universities and their courses.[11] Davies, meanwhile, signed up to help Isa Craig with the administration of that year's Social Science Association congress, which was to take place in London in June. Brought forward to fall within the London season, this was a great affair, lasting for nine days and featuring a soirée for eight thousand people in the Palace of Westminster.

---

[4] FC, 251, 251a–e; Stephen, 73.
[5] FC, 252 ff., 254a–d; and see also Girton GCPP Davies 2/7.
[6] Grote's wife, Harriet, was among those lending her name, and also wrote a supporting letter to the *Times* (8 May): Willson, 95.
[7] FC, 247.   [8] Willson, 97.   [9] Willson, 95–7; FC, 255–6.
[10] Davies, 'The influence of university degrees on the education of women', in *Thoughts*, 46–7.
[11] Manton, 141.

110 DAVIES AND THE MID-VICTORIAN WOMEN'S MOVEMENT

Almost anyone in London possessed of a white tie and tails or ball gown must have been there. It was an opportunity for Davies to meet people and make connections, and to work with potential male allies including George Hastings, the secretary; John Westlake, the international secretary (also a Christian Socialist and close associate of her brother); and Joshua Fitch, a noted educationist and secretary of the education section.[12]

In an attempt to win over the London University doctors, Davies also contributed a paper of her own, read for her by Russell Gurney, on 'Medicine as a profession for women'. This bent over backwards to appease male vanity and pride (there could be no threat to men's pre-eminence as the leaders of the profession) but suggested modestly that there was a demand for women doctors from those women who could not afford the *best* doctors; and that medicine appeared especially suitable as a profession for ladies, should they wish to work. That appearance might not be born out by reality, but the only way to find out was to make the experiment. If it failed, it failed. There could be no question, naturally, of mixed medical schools or any such horror, and doctors being reasonable men the only real obstacle was uninformed public opinion.[13]

The congress also provided an opportunity to discuss the question of university admissions in the wake of the London University experience, and this happened in two forums. One was a fringe meeting arranged by William Shaen, clerk to convocation. The other was a paper by Frances Power Cobbe, delivered to great applause, on 'Female education, and how it would be affected by university examinations'.[14]

It would be interesting to know how much advance notice, if any, Davies had of Cobbe's paper. She certainly knew of her work, which had been published in the *English Woman's Journal* and in pamphlet form by Emily Faithfull, as well as in the elite magazines. But Cobbe was in Italy while the campaign for London University matriculation was under way, and while this provided the hook for the paper they may well not have met before the congress.

Frances Power Cobbe came from a well-to-do family of Irish gentry. An only daughter in a family of sons, she was ever at odds with her father, who disapproved first of her tomboy ways and later of her unorthodox religion and 'female friendships'.[15] After her mother got ill and died, however, she was obliged to spend much of her twenties and thirties looking after him and running the household, escaping only when he died in 1857. Before that, her only escape was through books. She had taught herself from her father's library and from books

---

[12] Lawrence Goldman, *Science, Reform and Politics in Victorian Britain: The Social Science Association, 1857–1886* (Cambridge University Press, 2002), 74–5. FC, 257.

[13] Emily Davies, 'Medicine as a profession for women', in *Thoughts*, 34–40.

[14] Frances Power Cobbe, *Female Education and How It Would Be Affected by University Examinations* (Emily Faithfull, 1862); reprinted in her *Essays on the Pursuits of Women* (Emily Faithfull, 1863), 216–39.

[15] Mitchell, 61.

bought with her allowance and had written two substantial and learned volumes of deist theology. After her father's death, she had travelled in the Middle East, spent time with the artistic communities of Florence and Rome, where she met her life partner, the sculptor Mary Lloyd, and worked for a year with Mary Carpenter at one of her reformatory schools, before embarking on a career as a journalist.

It seems that people didn't quite know what to make of Cobbe. She was now a single woman of forty, who had recently written in *Fraser's* of the pleasures of being such, of running cheerily about 'untrammelled by husband or children',[16] and rejoicing in her true and tender friendships with other women; a woman of independent views and acknowledged learning and intellect and, more than that, a rational deist; a woman, surely, as strong-minded as any. But she was also a woman who had been, to all appearances, a dutiful daughter, and had devoted herself to philanthropic work with destitute children, a round and cheery figure with a twinkle in her eye, assured yet unthreatening. Her paper, combining clear argument with gentle wit, was a sensation, attracting summaries in all of the daily papers, and comments in most.

Should university exams be open to women? Cobbe's concern, she said, was with the aimless and profitless lives of so many single women and childless wives, deprived through no fault of their own of all the rewards of motherhood. Did they not deserve their share of human happiness? Whether they were women of independent means and too much leisure, or needing to support themselves by intelligent labour (the reference to the middle classes was implicit but clear), it had to be admitted that they were sadly in need of improvement in their condition.

There was, she admitted, a common prejudice that too much education, or the wrong sort of education (maths and classics), would be harmful to women, but as Sydney Smith, the renowned wit and cleric, had said: 'A woman's love for her off-spring hardly depends on her ignorance of Greek, nor need we apprehend that she will forsake an infant for a quadratic equation.' Look at Mary Somerville, the most eminent female intellectual living, but 'whose home [where she had stayed] was the happiest I ever saw'; or at Mary Carpenter, the most perfect philanthropist, who had taught Homer and Virgil in her father's school.[17]

The next objection sometimes made was that a university education for women would obliterate the difference between the sexes, but, said Cobbe, the very essence of education was to bring out people's nature, not suppress it (the clue was in the etymology) and woman's nature was God-given. The *same* education would inevitably bring out *different* qualities in men and women. Truths were truths,

---

[16] Frances Power Cobbe, 'Celibacy vs. marriage', *Fraser's Magazine*, 65 (February 1862), 228–35: 233.

[17] Cobbe, *Female Education and How It Would be Affected by University Examinations*, in her *Essays on the Pursuits of Women*, 222–3.

but men and women would naturally assimilate them differently, and anyway, to make women only what men were *not* was nonsensical, like forbidding them beef because men ate it.

The final objection made was that even if Greek and maths were harmless to women they would be useless to them, and any higher education should embrace a different course of studies. But 'who is to decide what is fit for a woman's brain save the owner of the brain herself', asked Cobbe. 'The proof of this particular description of pudding lies exclusively in the eating!'[18] It was a big mistake to assume that what was judged a proper pursuit for women in general (no doubt quite rightly) was a proper one for each woman in particular. '[B]*ecause* few women rise to the love of abstract truth, *no* women are to be permitted to do so? This is utterly absurd.'[19] If people wanted to take on a particularly arduous task, let them try, and see what happens.

Cobbe then had one positive argument to make, which aimed straight at men's prejudices. It was generally recognized, she suggested, that whereas men tended to argue logically, women tended to resort to intuition. But how dangerous was this? Unchecked quickness of intuition was both a peril and a misfortune. Surely women, who were apt to jump to conclusions, needed the discipline of a university training far *more* than men, who were by nature more rational! It was generally recognized, too, that women were often satisfied with a state of knowledge that was often terribly inaccurate and superficial: again, education was needed, and if women were to be brought up to par it needed the tests and exams that a university offered. It didn't need women to graduate in numbers, and that wouldn't happen. But even bringing a few women up to a university standard would serve to raise standards generally. She finished with a word of reassurance: strong-minded women were every bit as distasteful to refined women as they were to men.

The coverage was mixed. The *Saturday Review* was predictably scathing. In one article, on the congress more generally, the SSA was described as Lord Brougham's 'modern *Ecclesiazusae*', revisiting the writer's earlier reference to Aristophanes' sex comedy.[20] Another, devoted mainly to Cobbe's paper, mocked her unmarried status—'An unmarried woman is only half a woman and therefore can only deliver half-truths'—and described her paper as a 'petulant appeal for man's place and work'. Its response was 'first, that woman cannot do it if she would, and next, that she would not be half so happy if she could.'[21] On the other hand, she was praised in the *Daily Telegraph* for her 'rare combination of wit and vigorous argument' and in the *Times* for her 'close and well-sustained' arguments.[22] In the *Spectator*, Richard Hutton—himself a member of the university's annual

---

[18] Ibid., 227–8. [19] Ibid., 229.
[20] 'The Social Science Association', *Saturday Review*, 13 (14 June 1862), 668.
[21] 'Ladies at the Guildhall', *Saturday Review*, 13 (14 June 1862), 680–1: 681.
[22] Mitchell, 127.

FROM EDUCATING WOMEN TO EXAMINING GIRLS   113

committee of convocation, a small working committee of the full convocation—
took a middle line. While open to a university-level education for women, he suggested that the most appropriate education for women was unlikely to be the
same as that for men; and that while a (different) university-level education would
be appropriate for a small number of exceptional women, no case had been made
for opening up University of London degrees to women in general.[23]

Described by his opponents as a man 'bristling with eccentricities',[24] William
Shaen was a secular Unitarian, graduate of University College London, and lawyer to the most prominent Unitarian families.[25] He would be a consistent supporter of women's causes and had already responded to Davies's circular letter of
April (which he, like others, took to be from a man), suggesting that if the university were to be won over the endorsement of convocation would be needed, and
offering to give what help he could.[26] As part of the London congress he arranged
an evening meeting with some of those who had supported the admission of
women on the senate to discuss ways forward. He was not optimistic. The doctors
were evidently opposed, but of greater concern was the hostility of convocation,
whose representatives on the senate had voted solidly against the proposed reform.

One of those present at the discussion was the chairman of convocation,
Charles Foster, who had backed a change to the charter but now suggested that
'the ladies who desired to be admitted to the universities did not want to take the
same degrees as were given to men', but rather some equivalent. This opened the
way to other speakers suggesting that the senate had not been against higher education for women at all. On the contrary. But called on to say that the same course
of education stipulated for men, with the same severity of examinations, would
also be the best calculated to suit young women, they could not agree.[27] This was
essentially the line pressed by Hutton in the *Spectator*, and was to be a continuing
bugbear.[28] The implication, of course, was that while women might get some kind
of higher qualification, might even get degrees, they would not be the degrees
men got, so be no threat to the professions.

Despite the poor prospects of success, the campaign continued. Davies set up a
'fund' for the purpose and donations were received from James Heywood, a
Unitarian reformer who had supported the case on the senate; Peter Taylor, the
Radical MP and husband of Mentia; Thomas Jess-Blake, father of Sophia; and
Louisa, Lady Goldsmid, wife (and cousin) of the Jewish barrister, MP, and philanthropist Sir Francis Goldsmid, who had been one of those women present at the
launch of the SSA and agreed to be treasurer of the fund.[29] The following spring,

---

[23] 'Miss Cobbe on degrees for women', *Spectator*, 35 (14 June 1862), 655–6.
[24] *Lancet*, 27 November 1858.
[25] See M. J. Shaen, *William Shaen: A Brief Sketch* (Longmans, 1912).
[26] FC, 251–3; Willson, 61.   [27] *TNAPSS*, 6 (1862), 339–42; Willson, 98; FC, 260–1.
[28] 'Girl graduates', *Spectator*, 35 (5 June 1862), 377; 'Miss Cobbe on degrees for women', *Spectator*,
35 (14 June 1862), 655–6.
[29] FC, 261.

Shaen manoeuvred the annual committee of convocation into securing a discussion of the topic at the meeting of convocation in May. On his suggestion, Davies put together a short paper, 'Reasons for the admission of women to university examinations', and a thousand copies were circulated to members of convocation and others on behalf of a 'Committee for obtaining the admission of women to university examinations'—actually another committee (see below) renamed for the occasion. The paper included reference to Cobbe's paper, a summary of the SSA discussions, reference to the (occasional and exceptional) granting of degrees to women in France and Italy, and a list of those who had earlier given their support, around 150 names in all, including about fifty MPs.[30]

Convocation was not to be moved, but Shaen had also made another suggestion, namely that it might be politic, before pressing the University of London any further, to 'try to get something from the old Universities'. He said, recalled Davies later, that 'the University of London [meaning, presumably the graduates, jealous of their privileges] did not like being treated as a *corpus vile*, on which all experiments were to be tried'.[31] The statutory and cultural constraints at Oxford and Cambridge were more severe than those at London—the admission of women seemed literally unthinkable—and admission was by personal introduction rather than examination. But both universities had, for the past few years, set examinations more or less equivalent to the London matriculation examinations. Barbara Bodichon had noted in an SSA paper, reprinted in the *EWJ*, that the examination papers seemed as suitable for girls as for boys, and in the wake of the discussions at the London SSA congress, Davies looked at them herself and came to the same conclusion.[32] She wrote to Anna Richardson that while getting girls accepted might not be worth much in itself—her focus was still on the university education needed to qualify as a doctor—it might be a useful step towards gaining admission to the University of London.[33]

The Oxford and Cambridge Local Examinations, also known as the Middle-Class Examinations, were effectively nationwide school-leaving examinations for boys, precursors of today's GCSEs and A levels. They were designed for boys from the eight hundred or so endowed grammar schools (historically schools that taught Latin grammar) and a smattering of private boarding schools that taught boys up to the age of seventeen or eighteen but possessed neither the academic reputations nor the Oxbridge connections of the elite 'public schools', and whose pupils were thought to be discriminated against when it came to Oxford and Cambridge entry.

The examinations were not open to girls, but then girls' secondary schools very rarely taught to anywhere near their level. The two London ladies' colleges,

---

[30] WS to ED, 23 April 1863, FC 291–2; FC, 292–3, to which 'Reasons' is attached.
[31] FC, 263; ED to AR, 12 July 1862, *EDCL*, 3–4.
[32] Barbara Bodichon, 'Middle Class Schools for girls', *EWJ*, 5 (November 1860), 168–76.
[33] ED to AR, 12 July 1862, *EDCL*, 3–4.

Queen's and Bedford, Dorothea Beale's Cheltenham Ladies College, Frances Buss's North London Collegiate School, and a handful of mainly Quaker or Unitarian schools around the country aimed to provide a rigorous academic education, but even they offered nothing like the same education as boys' schools in the traditional boys' elite subjects of mathematics and classics. The vast majority of girls' secondary schools were effectively 'finishing' schools. They took middle-class girls who had been taught at home up to the age of around fourteen (the elementary schools were considered to be for the working classes) and prepared them for the marriage market: English literature (carefully chosen), history (by rote), French conversation, music, art, dancing, needlework. The best of these schools taught the more academic subjects with reasonable rigour, but the great majority didn't. That was neither what their teachers were trained for nor what their clients wanted.

The campaign that followed was typical of Davies. Whereas Bodichon had argued for the admission of girls in principle, Davies focused on the practical task of getting them admitted. She began by writing politely to the secretaries of the local examination syndicates at both Oxford and Cambridge, enquiring about the administration of the exams and the prospects for having girls examined. She also began to gather the names of schoolteachers and governesses who might sign a memorial requesting admission on behalf of their pupils.[34] Nothing more could be done during the long vacation, though she presumably discussed her plans with Barbara Bodichon, Anna Richardson, Elizabeth Garrett, and Annie Austin, all of whom she visited in September.[35] Back in London in October, however, she set up a Committee for the Proposed Admission of Girls to University Local Examinations, and promptly wrote, as secretary of that committee, to each of the local committees responsible for administering the exams at centres around the country.[36] She explained to the secretary of the syndicate at Cambridge that she had been instructed to do so by her committee, as it had been suggested that the universities would be reluctant to impose an innovation on their local committees, and any proposal should probably come through them.[37] Who had suggested this, she didn't say. It may have been her own idea; it may have come from her brother Llewelyn, who was a member of the London Local Committee for Cambridge and could hope to influence their response. It was, anyway, a key move, pre-empting any attempt by the universities to stop the campaign at source.

Davies's committee was by design a roughly equal mixture of well-respected men and women, with herself as secretary, the main purpose of which was simply to legitimize her campaigning. She determined the objectives and dictated the strategy and tactics for achieving them, looking to the committee members for support when needed. For this committee she co-opted three men: Russell Gurney,

---

[34] ED to AR, 12 July 1862, *EDCL*, 3–4.   [35] FC, 269.
[36] FC, 270–2.   [37] ED to GL, 11 November 1862, *EDCL*, 5.

116 DAVIES AND THE MID-VICTORIAN WOMEN'S MOVEMENT

George Hastings, and James Heywood, who had all supported her attempts to gain admission for women to London University, and who all brought valuable connections. Alongside these were three women: Barbara Bodichon, Isa Craig, and Eliza Bostock, a trustee of Bedford College who had already taken an interest in Elizabeth Garrett's efforts to train as a doctor.[38] Lady Goldsmid was again treasurer.

The responses from Oxford were deeply frustrating. Through the secretary of the Exeter local committee, Davies was put in touch with Thomas Dyke Acland, one of the originators of the examinations, who was unfailingly courteous and helpful, and in the end very supportive, but only on the condition that any girls' examinations should be different from the boys'. He was worried that overworking girls and submitting them to public examinations would ill serve their development as women, and that neither the examinations nor the examiners were suited to judge girls' knowledge and ability. An experiment should certainly be made, but with separate papers: the idea of competition between the sexes was repugnant.[39]

This insistence on separate curricula and examinations for boys and girls, men and women, reflected some of the more sympathetic responses in respect of the University of London matriculation examinations, and was to be the bane of Davies's life. She knew, and said, that separate girls' examinations would be considered inferior.

Meanwhile, Davies was also in communication with the secretary to the delegacy, John Griffiths, who suggested she should put forward a memorial to the delegates but expressed strong doubts as to its prospects. His initial thought was that it would end up with the senate, which would consider the examination of young ladies 'a matter altogether beyond its sphere of duty'.[40] When Davies visited Oxford the following June, however, staying with Sir Benjamin and Lady Brodie (he part of a broad church network, she a friend of Bodichon's), she discovered that it had never got that far. The delegates were of the view that admitting girls to any examination was not within their power and would need a change of statutes.

Despite this, Griffiths encouraged Davies to put forward some formal proposals, and Acland too continued to encourage her, whilst assuring her that a proposal for girls to take the existing examination would fail. Towards the end of the year, she gracefully withdrew.[41] The whole process had got nowhere,

---

[38] FC, 206; Sophie Badham, 'Bostock, Elizabeth Anne', ODNB/52743.

[39] FC, 279; TDA to ED, 14 January 1863, 28 January 1863, 2 February 1863, 8 May 1863, 13 May 1863, FC, 280–3, 287–8, 293–5, 295–6; ED to TDA, 19 January 1863, 30 January 1863, *EDCL*, 34–6, 38–9.

[40] JG to ED, 19 July 1862, FC, 265–7: 266.

[41] FC, 330–5; ED to TDA, 9 May 1863, 28 October 1863, 2 November 1863, 14 November 1863, 20 November 1863, 30 November 1863, *EDCL*, 34–6, 38, 47–8, 61, 63–4, 68–9, 71–2, 78; ED to JG, 24 November 1863, *EDCL*, 75.

FROM EDUCATING WOMEN TO EXAMINING GIRLS   117

foundering in the end on the deeply engrained belief that what was good for boys was by definition inappropriate for girls; but it was a valuable experience.

At Cambridge, the secretary to the local examinations syndicate, George Liveing, was no more encouraging than his Oxford counterpart.[42] Davies did, however, receive much more positive responses from two of the secretaries of local committees, and between them they were in a position to help. One was Robert Potts, secretary of the local committee at Cambridge, who seems to have served in a coordinating role in respect of the examinations. The other was Henry Tomkinson, secretary of the local committee in London, of which Llewelyn Davies was a member. Tomkinson turned out to be immensely helpful, and would act as Davies's main comrade in arms both in this venture and in her later establishment of Girton College. So who was he?

Henry Tomkinson came from a prosperous Cheshire family, his ordained father holding one of the local livings. There were three sons, Henry being the youngest, and two daughters. The sons all went to Rugby, where their father had been a pupil under Thomas Arnold and where their brother-in-law George Cotton was their housemaster.[43] The eldest, Edward, had acquired a commission in the Hussars and served in Crimea, leading a squadron in the Charge of the Light Brigade and surviving, though his horse did not and he never again saw active service.[44] The second son, Francis, had died in his early thirties. Henry had gone from Rugby to Trinity College, where he gained first-class honours in mathematics, rowed in the university boat race, and played cricket for the university against the MCC. After graduating in 1853 he read for the Bar, but was soon recruited by Cotton, who had become master of Marlborough College, to be assistant master and bursar. Cotton had found the school in a financial mess and Tomkinson, as bursar, is credited with having saved it from disaster.[45]

In 1858, Cotton was installed as Bishop of Calcutta, and Tomkinson became managing director of the Sun Fire Insurance Office in London. He also took on the secretaryship of the London Local Committee for the new Cambridge local examinations. We know nothing directly of his religious or political persuasions, but he was brought up in a thoroughly Arnoldian mould, his brother-in-law Cotton identified as broad church, and he seems to have shared Davies's liberal

---

[42] GL to ED, 22 July 1862, 16 August 1862, FC, 267–8, 268–9.

[43] Cotton married after the older boys had left school but for Henry's last years at school his sister was also his housemaster's wife.

[44] Edward was one of the witnesses for the dire state of supplies and equipment in the Crimea. He wrote from Sebastopol that the tents were unfit to live in: 'They let in water to such an extent that in heavy rains the ground beneath them is flooded and the men are obliged to stand up round the pole during a whole night.' WO 28/162, quoted in Orlando Figes, *Crimea: The Last Crusade* (Allen Lane, 2010), 281.

[45] *AC*, Pt. 2, Vol. 6, 203; P. G. M. Dickson, *The Sun Insurance Office, 1710–1960* (Oxford University Press, 1960), 120, 285–6; Census for 1851, 1871, 1881; *Rugby School Register*; *Military List* for 1863, 1865; Family tree at www.thornber.net/cheshire/htmlfiles/tomkinson.html; A. J. Arbuthnot and Gerald W. Savage, 'Cotton, George Edward Lynch', ODNB/6412.

118 DAVIES AND THE MID-VICTORIAN WOMEN'S MOVEMENT

conservatism. A general good egg, avoiding controversy and not particularly ambitious, he was greatly liked, trusted, and respected by everyone who knew him. He seems not to have met Emily Davies prior to their correspondence, but he must have known Llewelyn Davies quite well from Trinity, through the local committee, and through the Vaughan brothers, the Christian Socialist David Vaughan being Davies's best friend and the prominent broad churchman Charles Vaughan, sometime master of Harrow, being Cotton's.[46] It turned out, too, that Henry's mother subscribed to the *English Woman's Journal*, which Davies was then editing, sending it on to his sister in Calcutta.[47]

Tomkinson immediately offered to consult his committee, and at the beginning of 1863 he sent a summary of the responses, which were mixed. Some thought it would be injurious to the existing examinations; some that it would be injurious to the girls taking part; some thought the examinations not suited to female education, some that the university was not the proper body to get involved in female education. One suggested a preliminary examination in needlework, cookery, and child care. All in all, however, Tomkinson thought that while time would be needed for the idea to sink into people's minds the case was far from hopeless.[48] He was enthusiastic enough to get into a discussion of the practicalities and by May 1863 he had been recruited onto Davies's committee.[49]

Meanwhile in Cambridge Potts had reached a similar conclusion. 'As might be expected', he reported, 'some laughed & others looked grave, & some considered that the subject was not unworthy of serious consideration.'[50] The idea needed time to sink in and such innovations should generally not be pushed 'until the minds of the resident members of the Senate have either become favourable or indifferent to the new questions.' But he was generally positive and suggested that as a first step Davies's committee might seek to bring the girls' schools under university inspection.[51]

This reflected one of Potts's own enthusiasms, for a scheme of university inspection of the middle-class schools, and was not what Davies wanted at all. As she explained, the education of girls and its oversight should generally be in the hands of women. In marking examination papers, however, it should make no difference whether they were written by girls or boys.[52] Instead she put up the

---

[46] For Charles Vaughan's life and sudden departure from Harrow, accused of sexual impropriety with one of the boys, see Trevor Park, '*Nolo Episcopari': A Life of C. J. Vaughan* (St. Bega, 2013). See also John Roach, 'Vaughan, Charles John', ODNB/28124; Boyd Hilton, 'Manliness, masculinity and the mid-Victorian temperament', in Lawrence Goldman, ed., *The Blind Victorian: Henry Fawcett and British Liberalism* (Cambridge University Press, 1989), 60–70.

[47] ED to BB, 14 January 1863, *EDCL*, 29–33.

[48] ED to BB, 14 January 1863, *EDCL*, 29–33; FC, 272, 278–9.

[49] ED to HRT, 26 November 1862, 31 December 1862, 18 May 1863, *EDCL*, 6, 19–20, 40; ED to RP, 18 May 1863, *EDCL*, 48–9.

[50] RP to ED, 5 January 1863, FC, 276–7.

[51] Ibid., 277.   [52] ED to RP, 23 January 1863, 27 January 1863, *EDCL*, 36–7.

FROM EDUCATING WOMEN TO EXAMINING GIRLS 119

idea, which she attributed to Acland, of an experiment. If the examiners were willing to cooperate, the London committee might allow a small number of girls to informally take the examinations in December, thus testing the viability of her proposal. Of course, she stressed, they would not receive certificates.[53]

By May, this had become a definite objective. Liveing was deeply sceptical, envisaging opposition all round, but his role on the syndicate had now been taken on by Charles Gray, who was distinctly more sympathetic. Tomkinson asked whether it might be possible to print additional examination papers for girls and make private arrangements with the examiners to assess their answers, and talked the London Local Committee into cooperating. Davies pressed Potts to drum up support for the proposal.[54] In late September, after the long vacation, a formal application from Davies's committee, backed up by a suitably worded resolution from the London Local Committee, went in to the syndicate and a month later they agreed to the request. It would be up to Davies's committee to reach private arrangements with the examiners to have the papers assessed, but the syndicate agreed to extra papers being printed and released. With just seven weeks remaining until the examinations were to be held, the challenge now was to drum up candidates and make the necessary arrangements for rooms and examiners.[55]

The next few weeks were hectic. The experiment could only work if girls were presented, so Davies wrote round all the schoolmistresses whose addresses she had and pushed her friends to do the same. A particular concern was to get a good bunch of candidates from Queen's College and she delegated this to Charlotte Manning, now added to her committee. It is not clear what Manning's connections with Queen's were. She wrote to Edward Plumptre, the dean (he was also a professor of theology and chaplain of King's College), but Plumptre was a broad churchman, brother-in-law to F. D. Maurice, with whom Davies had more obvious connections. It may just have been a question of all hands to the pump.[56] Also added to the committee at this time were William Ballantyne Hodgson, one of the founders of the College of Preceptors (a professional body for teachers), a longstanding champion of girls' education and SSA stalwart;[57] and Fanny, wife of Hensleigh Wedgwood of the pottery family, who was a friend of both Maurice

---

[53] ED to RP, 11 February 1863, *EDCL*, 39.

[54] ED to RP, 18 May 1863, 10 June 1863, 17 June 1863, 20 June 1863, 23 July 1863, *EDCL*, 48, 50–4; ED to HRT, 18 May 1863, 10 June 1863, 20 June 1863, *EDCL*, 49–50, 54; ED to AR, 13 June 1863, *EDCL*, 51–2; HRT to ED, 8 July 1863, in FC, 305–6; GL to HRT, June 1863, in FC, 301–2; FC, 298, 300, 305a–306.

[55] ED to CG, 26 September 1863, *EDCL*, 57; CG to ED, 23 October 1863, CG to HRT, 23 October 1863, in FC, 318a, 318b.

[56] ED to CM, 24 October 1863, 31 October 1863, *EDCL*, 58–9, 62–3; ED to AR, 26 October 1863, *EDCL*, 59–60; ED to HRT, 30 October 1863, *EDCL*, 61–2.

[57] A prolific lecturer, sometime school principal, and friend and supporter of Frances Buss, Hodgson had been a champion of girls' education since the 1840s. See Jane Martin and Joyce Goodman, *Women and Education, 1800–1980* (Macmillan, 2003); Alexander Gordon, 'Hodgson, William Ballantyne', ODNB/13448.

120 DAVIES AND THE MID-VICTORIAN WOMEN'S MOVEMENT

and Emilia Gurney, and centre of a wide social and literary circle. Barbara Bodichon, wintering in Algeria, dropped off.[58]

As well as candidates, the examiners also had to be secured. Gray at first offered to see to that, but when it became apparent that there might be as many as one hundred girls to be examined he got cold feet. Davies ended up writing to the examiners herself, asking them to take on the extra work, adding a note from her brother to those he knew personally. In the end eighty-three girls took the examination, with around five hundred boys. All the examiners agreed to cooperate and the conducting examiner, Alfred Chalker, was friendly and helpful. The only slight hiccough concerned John Norris, an inspector of schools who had professed some interest in the question and was persuaded to act as conducting examiner for the girls. Having complained that the examinations did not include needlework, he began questioning the girls on their knowledge of shirt making, to the great annoyance of the schoolmistresses present, though fortunately more to the amusement than the discomfort of the girls themselves.[59]

When the results came out in March, only thirty-three girls had passed, most of them failing in arithmetic, and both Gray and Thomas Markby, a fellow of Trinity Hall who was examining in English, expressed the view that the standard in arithmetic was higher than was needed or appropriate for girls. It was noticeable, however, that where the teaching was good, so were the results: amongst those passing were no less than fifteen pupils of Frances Buss's North London Collegiate School, although even in her case ten students failed: something not to be repeated as she focused on raising standards further.[60] 'No doubt you are blissfully ignorant of the change,' she wrote to Davies as her girls were prepared for the examinations the following year. 'You are not an unfortunate schoolmistress with a reputation to maintain....And our girls! We sometimes think they have taken leave of their senses. Either we have taken up too much, or they are hopelessly stupid.' She feared the latter, but they excelled.[61]

Chalker, in his report on the London examination, stressed that he saw no reason why the girls should not, if properly instructed, come up to the mark, and very much hoped that the standard would not be reduced. Teachers were encouraged and impressed by the impact on their pupils, and Davies turned the failure, which was hardly unexpected, into an argument for the examinations. It showed up just how bad the teaching of girls was in the absence of an objective standard at which to aim. 'I am charged to impress upon "the Cambridge people"',

---

[58] The committee members are listed on the circular sent to schoolmistresses: FC, 323b.

[59] ED to RP, 19 November 1863, 21 November 1863, 23 November 1863, 26 November 1863, 12 December 1863, 9 January 1864, 12 January 1864, EDCL, 70–3, 76, 81–2, 88–90, 94–5; ED to HRT, 28 November 1863, 5 December 1863, EDCL, 77, 80–1; FC, 325–30.

[60] The full report is attached to FC at 346a, and at Girton GCPP Davies 8/168. For Buss's results see Kamm, 66.

[61] FB to ED, 2 December 1865, in Annie Ridley, Frances Mary Buss and Her Work for Education (Longmans, Green & Co, 1896), 254.

she wrote to Potts, 'that we do not want [a lower standard for girls].... The girls must be brought up to the mark, not the standard brought down to them.'[62]

The next step was to persuade the university senate to formally endorse the admission of girls to the examinations. In principle this was just a question of submitting a memorial, but Davies was by now wise to the need for careful tactical planning. Potts was for moving straight away, but she was mindful of his earlier advice, to give members time to get used to the idea, if only to become indifferent.[63] She was also mindful of having to steer a path between three groups: those who were opposed on principle; those whose support might do more harm than good; and those who were supportive of girls' examinations but wanted them to be different from boys'. Potts himself fell into two of these groups. He had a clear preference for separate examinations, and he had a reputation in Cambridge as an oddball—indeed as something of a lunatic.[64]

To keep Potts happy, Davies prepared a memorial and got it approved by her committee. Eliza Bostock, who hadn't worked with her before, tried rewriting it completely, but Isa Craig restored it more or less to the original. It made clear, of course, that the examinations for boys and girls had to be the same.[65] As Davies had explained to Potts, in the present state of public opinion separate examinations for girls would be assumed to be of a lower standard, even if they were not.[66] He seems to have agreed.[67] Before the memorial could be submitted, however, the ground had to be prepared, and Davies initiated action on three fronts.

The first challenge was to give the memorial weight by assembling an impressive list of signatories. Davies wanted to show that the proposal came with the support of girls' teachers, and not just a group of people claiming to speak on their behalf. She also wanted to demonstrate the support of a large body of distinguished men and women: it should not appear to come just from the girls' teachers, in a culture in which they were not highly regarded.

There was no complete register of girls' schools, and none at all of governesses, so Davies drew on all her friends and contacts to circulate the memorial amongst schoolteachers and governesses in their regions. She also put a lot of effort into getting the support of the professors at the two London ladies' colleges, Bedford and Queen's, eventually getting the signatures of all but two in each.[68] In all, she gathered 999 signatures of teachers and governesses. This accomplished she set

---

[62] ED to RP, 12 March 1864, *EDCL*, 105–6; For a range of responses to the results see FC, 338–45.

[63] ED to RP, 2 December 1863, 12 December 1863, *EDCL*, 79–82; ED to HRT, 30 November 1863, *EDCL*, 79.

[64] ED to RP, 2 January 1864, 9 January 1864, *EDCL*, 87–90; ED to HRT, 14 December 1864, *EDCL*, 137.

[65] ED to JC, 23 January 1864, *EDCL*, 96–8; ED to RP, 26 January 1864, *EDCL*, 98–9.

[66] ED to RP, 9 January 1864, *EDCL*, 88–90.

[67] ED to RP, 28 January 1864, 4 February 1864, *EDCL*, 101–3.

[68] ED to CM, 12 February 1864, *EDCL*, 103–4; ED to RP, 23 March 1864, *EDCL*, 108.

about doing something 'in the Rank and Influence direction',[69] starting with the lady visitors at the London colleges—effectively chaperones, who might be committed to the colleges, simply curious, or using it as way to pick up some learning themselves. She soon secured the support of, amongst others, the Duchess of Argyll and Lady Stanley of Alderley.[70] She then set Lady Goldsmid, Emilia Gurney, and Charlotte Manning onto working their own connections, eventually gathering the signatures of 120 eminent individuals, men and women.[71]

She also boosted her committee by engaging Henry Alford, dean of Canterbury, as its chair. A supporter of Maurice and the Christian Socialists, noted *New Testament* scholar, poet, and editor, Alford had put his name to the proposal that women be admitted to the University of London. He was known for his amiability, and was liked, it seems, by everyone—a perfect chair.[72] On being asked to take on the role, he expressed a reservation, apart from being extremely busy, that the committee might seek 'degrees for ladies. Much as I shd wish to deepen the foundation of female education & furnish ladies with the elements of sound knowledge, I should deprecate introducing anything like competition or personal public designation into the characteristics of female society in England.'[73] The reference to degrees is curious, given his earlier support, but it seems to have been the notion of public competition that worried him.[74] Davies was able to reassure him, but it was a worry that would repeatedly return to baulk her efforts. Society looked on competition as unfeminine, and as a danger to girls' health. Lurking underneath this was a fear on the part of men that competition from girls and women might reveal that they were not as inferior as commonly, and conveniently, held. But women also shared the concern. Dorothea Beale, principal of Cheltenham Ladies College, which was possibly the most academic of all the non-dissenting girls' secondary schools, would refuse to put her pupils into the locals. The rivalry would be 'most undesirable', the desire for distinction unwomanly. The object of a woman's education was to cultivate, through rigorous study, obedience to duty, self-restraint, and humility.[75]

For Beale and some of the other schoolmistresses, rivalry with boys was not the only issue. One of the features of girls' schools was their fine class distinctions. Beale thought her pupils, whose brothers would typically go to public schools, of a higher class than the boys who took the locals. Others would have reservations about their pupils (or daughters) competing against those in a lower segment of the middle classes.[76]

---

[69] ED to HRT, May 1864, *EDCL*, 120; RP to ED, 8 May 1864, FC, 360–2: 361.
[70] Emily Davies was herself a lady visitor at both Bedford and Queen's colleges.
[71] The memorial with a full list of signatories is attached to the FC at 385a.
[72] W. H. Freemantle and Roger T. Stearn, 'Alford, Henry', ODNB/341.
[73] HA to ED, 22 July 1864, FC, 367–8: 367.   [74] HA to ED, 23 July 1864, FC, 368.
[75] Dorothea Beale, 'On the education of girls', paper read to 1865 SSA congress, published as A. Utopian, 'On the education of girls', *Fraser's Magazine*, 74 (October 1866), 509–24.
[76] Sara Delamont, 'The domestic ideology and women's education', in Sara Delamont and Lorna Duffin, eds., *The Nineteenth-Century Woman: Her Cultural and Physical World* (Routledge, 2014), 164–88: 177.

The second challenge was to raise support amongst the Cambridge dons. Here Davies was on less sure ground. Her brother still wielded a little influence, but he had been away for many years, as had most of his Christian Socialist colleagues. Maurice had not yet returned. Kingsley was now Regius Professor of Modern History, but had shown little interest in the education of women or, indeed, in his fellow dons. John Westlake, who had resigned his fellowship to marry only a few years before, was rapidly gaining in eminence, but Davies was concerned that he spoke badly. The best person to lead the campaign, in her view, would be the new Professor of Political Economy, Henry Fawcett.

Fawcett was a larger-than-life character.[77] Six foot three and a powerful athlete, he had been totally blinded in a game-shooting accident in 1858, when he was twenty-five (his father shot him by mistake), but hadn't let it interfere with his life. In economics and politics he was a Radical, and a disciple of John Stuart Mill. Davies will have heard him speak at the SSA and almost certainly knew him, either through Bessie Parkes, to whom he had once proposed, or through Elizabeth Garrett, to whom he also proposed (he eventually married her sister Millicent). As she wrote to Potts, he spoke well and was 'sure to be willing to do all he can for us'.[78]

Unfortunately we know virtually nothing of the discussions that took place in Cambridge. Fawcett will certainly have supported the reform. He always supported reform, both in the university and in women's rights. But he had only narrowly been elected to his chair and had a reputation—of which Davies might not have been fully aware—as an 'infidel radical'. His friend Leslie Stephen described his religion as that of an 'attached member of the Church of England...who doesn't believe in any of the Thirty-nine Articles, except perhaps that which suggests a Christian may swear'.[79]

Davies's third challenge was to engage the wider public, familiarizing people with the idea so as to make it less frightening and building support. Her aim here was not only to influence the Cambridge insiders but also to impact the many MAs who would get to vote if the matter got as far as the senate.

Here she recruited Joshua Fitch, the inspector of schools with whom she had worked on the administration of the 1862 SSA congress. Fitch wrote an article describing, from his professional perspective, the dire state of girls' education and setting out the advantages to be gained from bringing them into the scheme of local examinations.[80] This was published in the *Victoria*, which Davies was still editing, and subsequently distributed in pamphlet form round Cambridge and to the press.[81]

The next move was to arrange for an open meeting to be held in London under the auspices of the SSA, whose secretary, Hastings, and his assistant Craig were

---

[77] See Lawrence Goldman, 'Introduction: an advanced Liberal: Henry Fawcett, 1833–1884', in Lawrence Goldman, *The Blind Victorian* (Cambridge University Press, 1989), 1–40.
[78] ED to RP, 12 January 1864, *EDCL*, 94–5: 94. [79] Goldman, 'An advanced Liberal', 19.
[80] *Victoria Magazine*, 2 (March 1864), 432–53. [81] ED to RP, 24 January 1865, *EDCL*, 145.

124   DAVIES AND THE MID-VICTORIAN WOMEN'S MOVEMENT

both on Davies's committee. This was fixed for late April and George Lyttelton, 4th Baron Lyttelton, was persuaded to preside. Lyttelton was a rare combination of contrasts. A distinguished scholar (joint first classic with Charles Vaughan at Cambridge), moderate high church and liberally inclined land-owing peer, then in his forties, he was both pleasure-loving and deeply conscientious. A confirmed member of the Conservative aristocracy, he was nevertheless a close friend of Gladstone (they married sisters) and an indefatigable supporter of working men's interests, and especially of their education.[82] He had been an early proponent of the local examinations and now brought establishment respectability to Davies's campaign.[83] To emphasize the respectability and avoid the impression that might be created by some of their 'strong-minded looking' supporters, Davies got Craig to position 'three lovely girls for the front row'—Alice Hare, soon to be Mrs John Westlake, and two of her sisters.[84]

The purpose of such a meeting was to emphasize support for the proposal while downplaying any opposition. Hardline opponents were unlikely to attend, and the report of the discussion, printed for circulation, would suggest a genuine debate while being weighted to one side.[85] The speakers in support included Hodgson ('erratic'), Maurice ('characteristic'), Plumptre ('good'), and the physiologist Samuel Solly, one of Charlotte Manning's brothers. Between them they could attest with authority to the educational benefits of the proposal and the absence of any religious, moral, or health risks. It also became known just before the meeting that Edinburgh University was to introduce its own version of the local examinations for Scotland, including girls from the beginning. 'If only people wd. always do things in that reasonable way,' wrote Davies to Tomkinson, 'it wd. save a great deal of trouble & fuss.'[86]

The main note of dissent came from one of those involved in the local examinations in Cambridge, Henry Roby, who was supportive of girls being examined but put the by now familiar case for a different set of examinations, better suited to girls' schools: more modern languages, music, needlework; less classics and higher mathematics.[87]

---

[82] Betty Askwith, *The Lytteltons*; *The Times*, 26 April 1876.

[83] See 'Lord Lyttelton on Middle Class Examinations', *Saturday Review*, 6 (25 September 1858), 297–8. Lyttelton's daughter Lucy married Lord Frederick Cavendish and is commemorated today in the name of Lucy Cavendish College, Cambridge, founded as a college for mature women. She seems, however, to have taken no interest in the education of women at least until after her husband's murder, at the hands of Irish republicans, in 1882, devoting herself instead to church missions amongst the poor.

[84] FC, 359; ED to HRT, 9 May 1864, *EDCL*, 118.

[85] *Report of a Discussion of the Proposed Admission of Girls to the University Local Examinations* (Emily Faithfull, 1864).

[86] ED to HRT, 18 April 1864, *EDCL*, 111.

[87] ED to AM, 30 April 1864, *EDCL*, 115; *Report of a Discussion of the Proposed Admission of Girls to the University Local Examinations*, 17–18. See FC, 359a.

One thing that Davies was rapidly discovering was that in a tactical battle her best friends, if out of her control, could also be her worst enemies. Shortly after the SSA meeting Hodgson published a greatly expanded, 'scholarly' version of his contribution in which he argued first that the education of women should be extended to the highest level, including degrees; and second that one of the reasons for admitting girls to the local examinations was to show up the inadequacies of boys' education.[88] Davies agreed with the first, but she had taken great pains to play down such ambitions, which could only be counter-productive for the present campaign. The second just muddied the waters. And sure enough, the *Saturday Review* responded with a belated review of the SSA meeting under the provocative heading 'Feminine wranglers'.[89]

This article was in fact a satire upon a recent vogue for examinations more generally, including for entrance to the civil service (Sir Edward Ryan, who was implementing these, has been amongst Garrett's supporters on the London University senate). But the opportunity to attack the 'busybodies who compose the Social Science Association' was irresistible,[90] and the idea of 'submitting young ladies to Local University Examinations' made for a good joke. 'Do Mr Hastings and his brother philanthropists...imagine that the young men of England prefer an examined to an unexamined wife?', asked the writer. Considering that there was 'a strong and ineradicable male instinct, that a learned, or even an over-accomplished young woman is one of the most intolerable masters in creation', this seemed unlikely. However, the marriage market as it stood, controlled by personal influence and connections, was evidently rotten to the core, so when a man wanted a wife let him communicate with the Civil Service Commission and have it put out to competition. The local examinations will furnish the necessary machinery.

Fortunately, the article was funny enough to do little damage and had probably been forgotten by the time of the next public airing of the proposal at the SSA congress in York in September. Here Hodgson presented a version of his pamphlet and Davies herself contributed a paper, read for her by Fitch, in which she focused on the inadequacy of girls' schooling.[91] This skirted round the question of whether their examinations should be the same or different, simply asking that, through admission to the locals, their education should at least be *encouraged*.

Others, inevitably, did not skirt round it. John Norris, the inspector of schools who had conducted the experimental exam and questioned the girls about needlework, argued that even the remotest suggestion of competition between boys and girls should be avoided at any cost; and that if they were to be examined,

---

[88] William Hodgson, *On the Education of Girls; and the Employment of Women of the Upper Classes Educationally Considered*, 2nd ed. (Trübner & Co, 1869).
[89] 'Feminine wranglers', *Saturday Review*, 18 (14 June 1864), 111–12.
[90] *Saturday Review*, 6 (25 September, 9 October 1858), 297–8, 344–5.
[91] 'On secondary instruction relating to girls', in *Thoughts*, 63–83.

126   DAVIES AND THE MID-VICTORIAN WOMEN'S MOVEMENT

even in written examinations, it should be by older married men, not bachelor fellows.[92] The Archbishop of York, chairing the session, repeated the view that it was great mistake to assume that what was suited to boys would also suit the purposes of girls.[93] Soon after the congress there was also discouraging news from Liverpool where the Cambridge Local Committee adopted a resolution expressing doubts that the examination of girls would be beneficial and a strong opinion that it would tend to lower the character of the local examinations in the estimation of the public. The exams would be too exciting for girls, and the girls' inclusion might expose those exams to ridicule, and lead to their being spurned by the most promising boys.[94] The latter point had been mentioned by one of the Liverpool committee, John Howson, to Davies's sister-in-law, Mary. Howson was one of the few men to have argued for the improved education of girls, and had indeed set up a girls' school in association with the Liverpool Collegiate Institute, of which he was principal, but he seems to have shared the objection.[95]

Similar objections had also been raised at the syndicate, prompting Markby to suggest that it might be politic to proceed for the time being on the existing, informal basis, rather than pushing the university towards something formal.[96] Davies decided, however, that having gathered signatures for the memorial it would not do to hold it back any longer. In mid-October it was formally submitted to the council,[97] who considered the matter without taking fright and appointed a special syndicate to consider it further and report.[98] In an encouraging move it appointed Markby as chair.

Davies's main concern was that despite Markby's support the syndicate might recommend separate examinations for girls. She again found herself in correspondence with Acland, who was arguing for something along those lines in Oxford, still thinking he was helping her cause, and who interpreted boys and girls taking the same exams as 'a neck & neck race between the sexes on the same course'.[99] Such a race would, responded Davies, be 'repugnant to one's taste & feelings', but there was no danger that it would be brought about. She didn't want to prove girls equal to boys, she protested to Anna Richardson, just to give them the freedom to do what they wanted.[100] But not everyone was convinced, and to smooth matters in Cambridge she wrote a short pamphlet, which carefully made

---

[92] John Norris to ED, 10 September 1863, FC, 371–3; ED to RP, 22 September 1864, 26 September 1864, EDCL, 125; ED to HRT, 16 September 1864, EDCL, 124. Norris didn't attend the congress himself, having his paper read for him: FC, 370.

[93] Spectator, 37 (1 October 1864), 1132–3; ED to RP, 25 November 1864, EDCL, 134.

[94] FC, 368–9; ED to RP, 13 October 1864, EDCL, 128–9.

[95] J. S. Howson, 'On schools for girls of the middle class', TNAPSS (1859), 308–16; ED to RP, 14 November 1864, in EDCL, 133.

[96] TM to ED, 31 August 1863, FC, 369–70.

[97] The memorial with a full list of signatories is attached to FC at 385a.

[98] ED to RP, 13 October 1864, 19 October 1864, 25 November 1864, EDCL, 128–30, 134. For membership of the syndicate see Grace 1 of 24 November 1864, annexed to FC, 385b.

[99] TDA to ED, 22 December 1864, FC, 391–2: 391.

[100] ED to TDA, 28 December 1864, EDCL, 138–9; ED to HRT, 3 January 1865, EDCL, 141.

FROM EDUCATING WOMEN TO EXAMINING GIRLS   127

the point that having different exams for girls would make no sense at all. Nobody had suggested restricting girls to feminine grammars and dictionaries, or producing textbooks on arithmetic or geography specially adapted to the female mind. The textbooks and the lessons were exactly the same for boys and girls, so a common examination seemed to follow 'as a matter of course'.[101] With Potts's help, she got this pamphlet and Fitch's circulated in Cambridge and also distributed copies to influential journalists.[102]

The syndicate reported in February. The exams should be open to girls, initially on a three-year trial, but to prevent the appearance of competition the girls' results would not be published. A discussion in the senate seems to have gone reasonably well. There was opposition from Edward Perowne, emerging as leader of the conservative faction in the university, and several others, but strong support from Liveing, Fawcett, and Markby. Potts, curiously, sat on the fence, though speaking 'at some length'.[103] The most challenging step of the process, however, was the last one: a vote open to the full body of MAs. This was a deeply conservative body, which routinely elected two Conservative MPs to Parliament.[104] In times past, very few would have turned up for such a vote, but that had changed with the growing convenience of the railways and there was no telling who might come, especially when, as now, an innovation faced opposition.

The *Saturday Review* (whose owner Alexander Beresford Hope was one of the MPs elected by the MAs) waded in again, not so much shocked as amused, but pointing to the grounds on which people might be shocked.[105] Hutton in the *Spectator*, on the other hand, was supportive.[106] On 8 March, the day before the vote took place, Markby telegrammed Davies: 'Send up all you can tomorrow, voting at 12, opposition organised.'[107] She was then at dinner with the Gurneys, and among the guests was Leslie Stephen. Would he go up and vote, asked Emilia? No, he had actually been the one arguing against them in the *Saturday Review*![108]

The vote was very close, the recommendation squeaking through by fifty-five to fifty-one, Markby claiming credit for drumming up last-minute support.[109] He didn't think to communicate the result, however, and Davies heard the news

---

[101] Emily Davies, 'Reasons for the extension of the University Local Examinations to girls' (1864), Girton GCPP Davies 8/173: 3.

[102] Davies, 'Reasons', ibid.; ED to MA, 23 December 1864, *EDCL*, 137–8; ED to AR, 3 January 1865, *EDCL*, 141. ED to RP, 24 January 1865, *EDCL*, 145.

[103] 'The proposed examination for girls', *Cambridge Chronicle*, 4 March 1865, copy in FC, 409–12; RP to ED, 9 March 1865, FC, 416–17.

[104] The body of MAs formed the electorate for the constituency of the University of Cambridge; similarly at Oxford.

[105] 'Ladies and examiners', *Saturday Review*, 19 (25 February 1865), 220–1.

[106] 'Women "associates" at Cambridge', *Spectator*, 38 (25 February 1865), 208–9.

[107] FC, 413, 413a.

[108] FC, 413. Was Stephen also the author of 'Feminine wranglers' and other of the *Saturday*'s satirical attacks on the SSA and the women's movement? It seems he had no strong views on the matter, but simply wrote what he thought would make for a good read. See ED to HT, 16 June 1866, *EDCL*, 177–8.

[109] TM to ED, 23 February 1865, March 1865, FC, 408–9, 415.

through Frances Buss, who had been telegrammed by an undergraduate. It was a victory, however, and a party at the Westlakes in the evening provided an opportunity to celebrate. As Elizabeth Garrett remarked, in response to a note, 'This will be the stepping stone to so much more.'[110]

Eleven days later, Davies's memorial was also considered by the Council of the University of Oxford, who decided by ten votes to eight to take the matter no further, but no effort had been put into its support, and opposition was expected.[111] After three years, the admission of girls to the Cambridge local examinations would be made permanent, and that was enough for now.

[110] FC, 414; EG to ED, 9 March 1865, FC, 414.
[111] ED to JG, 4 January 1865, 7 January 1865, 13 January 1865, *EDCL*, 142–4.

8

The Education of Girls

'Not a "Woman's Question"'

The focus of Davies's 1864 SSA paper was not on the local examinations, mentioned only very briefly at the end, but on the general state of girls' secondary education.[1] It was prompted by the establishment of a Royal Commission to look at the country's endowed schools, typically boys' grammar schools, of the kind whose pupils sat the locals. Its purpose was to persuade the commissioners to include girls' schools in their remit, and its dominant theme was that the secondary education of boys and that of girls were inextricably linked.

Davies's personal experience of girls' schools was almost non-existent. She knew from Elizabeth Garrett, however, what passed for an education at a well-respected girls' boarding school, and from Anna Richardson what might be taught in a good Quaker school. She was familiar with Queen's College and Bedford College and had come to know, through her campaign for the locals, some of the more progressive schoolmistresses, including Frances Buss, whose North London Collegiate School provided her with a prototype or model: a large girls' day school, run on Church of England principles, with an academic curriculum. She was certainly familiar with what had been written on the subject over the past ten years by Bessie Parkes, Jessie Boucherett, and Barbara Bodichon.[2] Whether she knew of the earlier writing of Emily Shirreff and Maria Grey, or of the very rare contributions by men such as John Howson is not clear.[3]

There was still no systematic survey of how middle-class girls were schooled— that would come with the work of the Royal Commission—but the general picture would have been familiar and reflected the highly gendered structure of middle-class Victorian society with its broadly separate spheres.[4] Boys would typically attend school from the age of eight to sixteen or eighteen, before going on to business, a profession, or university. Girls would be taught at home—or *not*

---

[1] Emily Davies, 'On secondary instruction relating to girls', in *Thoughts*, 63–83.

[2] Bessie Rayner Parkes, *Remarks on the Education of Girls, with Reference to the Social, Legal, and Industrial Position of Women in the Present Day* (John Chapman, 1854); Jessie Boucherett, 'On the education of girls, with reference to their future position', *EWJ*, 6 (December 1860), 217–24; Barbara Bodichon, 'Middle class schools for girls', *EWJ*, 6 (November 1860), 168–77.

[3] Emily Shirreff, *Intellectual Education and Its Influence on the Character and Happiness of Women* (J. W. Parker, 1858); Maria Grey and Emily Shirreff, *Thoughts on Self Culture Addressed to Women* (Edward Moxon, 1850); J. S. Howson, 'On schools for girls of the middle class', *TNAPSS* (1859), 308–16.

[4] Carol Dyhouse, *Girls Growing up in Late Victorian England* (Routledge & Kegan Paul, 1981).

Emily Davies and the Mid-Victorian Women's Movement. John Hendry, Oxford University Press. © John Hendry 2024.
DOI: 10.1093/oso/9780198910237.003.0008

taught at home—by their mothers or by governesses until they were about ten. They might then spend a couple of years at a day school, or continue with a governess, before spending a few years in their teens at a boarding school; or they might spend four or five years at a day school, finishing their education at fourteen or fifteen; or they might just stay at home, as Davies had, with what could be taught by their parents supplemented by visiting teachers.[5]

If they were lucky enough to go to a good Quaker or Unitarian school, or to one of the kinds of school run by Frances Buss in Camden or Anne Clough in Ambleside, middle-class girls might get quite a good education. But in other cases they might well end up less educated than their working-class contemporaries attending the national elementary schools, from which they were effectively barred by their parents' class consciousness. This was a concern even in the case of boys. It was less of a concern in the case of girls, since a girl's education was less highly valued, but a much more likely prospect. Somewhere in the middle was the education provided in the literally thousands, maybe as many as ten thousand small private girls schools, most with between five and twenty-five pupils.[6] In most cases these schools must have been constrained by limits of accommodation, but their small size was also seen as a virtue. The Sewell sisters, whose well-regarded school was limited to about seven girls, could have taken many more, but intentionally preserved the character of a home: they were referred to as 'aunt'. Hannah Pipe, another very successful schoolmistress, was known as 'school mother' and her charges as 'school daughters'.[7]

Catering to the demands of parents, these schools typically presented themselves as providing a Christian home from home in which girls were both academically and socially prepared for the marriage market. Finely graded on class lines (if the girls were boarding they would inevitably mix socially, so could only be prevented from mixing with their 'inferiors' if there were no inferiors), they typically made no attempt to separate girls by age or ability. They taught English language and (selected) literature, French, some history, geography, general knowledge, religion, music, dancing, and fine needlework. At one end of the scale the French might be no more than basic conversation; at the other end it would aim for fluency, and be complemented by German or Italian. Mathematics might be limited to the addition and subtraction needed for household accounts. Latin, the foundation of a boy's grammar school education, was almost unheard of.[8]

[5] *SIC Report*, Vol. 9, 823 ff.; Dyhouse, *Girls Growing Up*, 40 ff.

[6] The numbers are guesswork, but James Bryce estimated there were around five hundred in Lancashire. See Dyhouse, *Girls Growing Up*, 46.

[7] Ibid., 46–7. Elizabeth Sewell, *Principles of Education, Drawn from Nature and Revelation and Applied to Female Education in the Upper Classes* (Longman, Green et al., 1865).

[8] *SIC Report*, Vol. 1, 549–51. Daniel Fearon, 'Girls' grammar schools', *Contemporary Review*, 11 (August 1869), 333–54.

With such small numbers these schools were expensive, but according to their critics they taught little, and they taught it badly. The emphasis was on 'accomplishments', and on display over substance. The teachers were often ignorant themselves, pretending to knowledge they didn't have. Much of the learning was by rote. Memory was valued, imagination discouraged, reason ignored. Where girls were taught at home, by governesses, much the same applied.

The reality was perhaps more varied than the critics claimed.[9] The popular image of a Victorian governess or schoolmistress (women moved between the two, according to preference, connections, and financial circumstances) is of an orphaned and destitute middle-class lady, obliged to earn her living in the only way considered respectable (if slightly demeaning) in middle-class culture. As the Royal Commission would discover, this was sometimes the case: many women were driven to teaching by domestic misfortunes.[10] But many middle- and upper-middle-class families were far from wealthy and had not the means to support unmarried daughters, even if the father were alive. Lawyers and doctors often failed to prosper as they had hoped, as did men of business. Clergymen had poor livings or low stipends. Officers on half pay had modest incomes. If they were blessed with a profusion of daughters rather than sons, embarrassment loomed. It was therefore quite common for well brought up ladies not only to look to education as a means of earning an income but also to be prepared for it, through their own education.[11]

If they were lucky they might find the capital to start a school, or a governess position amongst family or friends. If not, they might start as an assistant teacher, or enter the governess's marketplace. Many schoolmistresses were in effect entrepreneurs, with little interest in a school other than as a respectable business. Many traded on gentility and religious observance rather than on education. But some were serious educators. They might study teaching methods at the national teacher training colleges for elementary teachers (though class considerations would prevent them becoming elementary teachers), or as Anne Clough did at the Home and Colonial School Society, which taught Pestalozzian methods. They might attend public lectures, or take the College of Preceptors's examinations in the theory and practice of education. They might study for a year in France, learning both French and French teaching methods.

Since any training in teaching methods was anathema to most grammar school masters (the College of Preceptors was set up to provide substitute qualifications

---

[9] Joyce Pedersen, *The Reform of Girls' Secondary Education in Victorian England: A Study of Elites and Educational Change* (Routledge, 2017), offers a view close to that of the critics, but Christina de Bellaigue, 'The development of teaching as a profession for women before 1870', *The Historical Journal*, 44 (2001), 963–88, presents a richer and more complicated picture.

[10] *SIC Report*, Vol. 1, 562.

[11] de Bellaigue, 'The development of teaching', 966 ff.; and see also her *Educating Women: Schooling and Identity in England and France 1800–67* (Oxford University Press, 2007).

for non-university men), girls might in some cases get a rather more professional education than their brothers. They would also get much more personal attention. What they would not get, however, was any mathematics, beyond very simple arithmetic, or classics, the staples of a boy's education. And whilst they might be none the worse for a lack of Latin, what they missed out on was the intellectual rigour associated with these subjects: a training in reasoning and, through classics, the use of the imagination. Women were supposed to be weak reasoners, so were not trained (and could not be trained, by most of their teachers) in reasoning. They were supposed to be easily misled by their feelings and imagination, so those had to be kept down, which left only the discipline of memory. Whereas boys were sent to school to have their minds and bodies trained for the rough and tumble of the world of business and public affairs, girls' schooling was designed to protect them from that world. The school was a protective second home, the schoolmistress a surrogate mother, performing the function a mother would, were she not required by class conventions to be a lady of leisure. The education was designed to make the girls pleasing and attractive, but subservient to the men who might court them.

Apart from those associated with the women's movement, a few dedicated schoolmistresses, and the very odd man, few people seem to have been perturbed by the state of girls' schooling. The parents got what they asked for and the politicians and political commentators just didn't think it very important. The state of boys' schooling, however, was considered important, and there was widespread concern that it was not what it should be, that many of the country's grammar schools were badly governed or incompetently run, and that owing to the historic circumstances of school endowments there was a very serious lack of provision in the large industrial towns. It was on middle-class men, and especially on those who might enter industry, that the prosperity of the country depended, and there was a concern that they were not being properly prepared.

In 1861, a Royal Commission had been established under George Villiers, 4th Earl of Clarendon, to look into the governance of the nine leading 'public' schools, in the wake of concerns about financial mismanagement at Eton.[12] Since these were the schools attended by the leading statesmen and politicians of the age they were naturally considered the most important, but when the commission reported, early in 1864, the question arose as to what should be done about the much larger number of lesser proprietary schools and endowed grammar schools: the middle-class boys' schools for which the local examinations had been designed. The failings of these schools had been a regular theme of discussion at the Social Science Association, which now pressed the prime minister,

---

[12] The nine schools were Eton, Harrow, Charterhouse, Rugby, Shrewsbury, Westminster, Winchester, St Paul's, and Merchant Taylors'.

Palmerston, for an inquiry.[13] The government's response was to set up another Royal Commission, under the chairmanship of Henry Labouchere, 1st Baron Taunton. Sometimes referred to as the Taunton Commission, or the Endowed Schools Commission, this was generally known as the Schools Inquiry Commission. Twelve commissioners were appointed, including Lord Lyttelton, Lord Stanley, Thomas Dyke Acland, and Frederick Temple, then master of Rugby, who had been another of those behind the original local examinations initiative.[14] The bulk of the work was done by the secretary, who was Henry Roby, and eight assistant commissioners, investigating different parts of the country, one of whom was Joshua Fitch. Matthew Arnold, who had recently published a series of essays on secondary schools and universities in France and Germany, was commissioned to prepare a comparative report on schools in continental Europe.

From the time the commission was first proposed, in the summer of 1864, one of Davies's main concerns was that it should include girls in its remit. This was partly a matter of principle, but also a matter of practice. It had become clear through the local examinations experiment that even if girls were to be admitted in principle to the universities, their prior education generally fell far short of what would be needed. Very few girls' schools taught to anything like the standard of the better boys' schools and even they struggled. A proper investigation would lay bare the state of things and could not but be beneficial. If the commission were to look at girls' schools as well as boys', it would be hard not to apply similar standards to both and the quality of girls' schools—and thus the prospects for degrees and graduate careers—could only be enhanced.[15]

At first, there was little Davies could do. Writing to Lord Brougham in connection with the memorial to Cambridge University calling for the formalization of girls' admission to the locals, she urged him to use his influence, but at that stage the commissioners had not been appointed.[16] She could, however, make the case for the inclusion of girls' schools, and this was the object of her Social Science Association paper.

In this paper, Davies offered no comment on the current syllabi or teaching methods of girls' schools, or on what they should be. If female education were only deemed worthy of investigation by the commission, the questions of what and how would sort themselves out. Instead she started from a characterization of the products of girl's secondary schools, which had the great advantage of being incontestable. Critics might lament the situation, conservatives might accept it as only natural, given the nature of womanhood, but there was a general consensus

---

[13] Sheila Fletcher, *Feminists and Bureaucrats: A Study in the Development of Girls' Education in the Nineteenth Century* (Cambridge University Press, 1980), 17.

[14] Lyttelton was apparently offered the chairmanship but declined: Betty Askwith, *The Lytteltons: A Family Chronicle of the Nineteenth Century* (Chatto & Windus, 1975), 152–3.

[15] ED to Lord Brougham, 30 July 1864, *EDCL*, 121.   [16] Ibid.

134 DAVIES AND THE MID-VICTORIAN WOMEN'S MOVEMENT

that the great mass of younger middle-class women of the age, the products of these schools, were poorly informed, incapable of sound reasoning, and mentally and physically weak.

The next stage of the argument was characteristic of Davies's writings on education, and also reflected the writings of her brother and other broad churchmen on religion. In the past, school would have been followed by a training for life, in the case of young women for the life, in general, of a wife, mother, and household manager. That this was the life for which their education should prepare, Davies accepted completely, if perhaps slightly tongue in cheek: 'I take the commonly received theory that except as wives, mothers, daughters, or sisters, women have no raison d'être at all.'[17] But the world had changed. The chores that occupied the minds and bodies of an earlier generation were increasingly taken over by machinery and factory work. It was cheaper to buy than to make.

This had two consequences. One was that while a boy's secondary education was a preparation for the training for life he would receive at a university or business or professional apprenticeship, a girl's secondary education now *was* her training for life. There was nothing of substance to follow. The other was that there was a void that had to be filled. The married middle-class woman of the present had time on her hands, which was typically filled by 'women's talk' (the duties of visiting etc.), but with no knowledge on which to base that talk. She knew nothing of literature, of current affairs, or indeed of anything to which her mind might turn. The not-yet-married woman, meanwhile, had no training to occupy her, and only the options of being idle or else active in inappropriate ways. These women were condemned to a life of dullness, and while men tended to think of this as a pleasant state of calm, 'if they had ever tried being a young lady, they would know better.'[18] (One imagines Davies speaking from the heart here.) The male ideal of the middle-class female might be an amiable and inoffensive lady, ready to give pleasure and be pleased, but what could be more stupefying? And what could be more harmful to men?

One further argument completed the case, for which she drew on one of Matthew Arnold's recent essays.[19] (With Richard Hutton, he was one of her two favourite writers: as she wrote to Adelaide Manning in respect of this article, 'his writing *stirs* me more than almost anybody's.'[20]) Arnold had condemned the present generation of English upper- and upper-middle-class male youth for their intellectual slackness, their preference for amusement over fine culture, while he had seen in the middle classes great potential but potential that was as yet unrealized. Given the state of girls' education, argued Davies, it would remain that way.

---

[17] Emily Davies, 'Secondary instruction as relating to girls', reprinted in *Thoughts*, 63–83: 70.
[18] Ibid., 70.
[19] Matthew Arnold, 'A French Eton: Part III', *Macmillan's Magazine*, 10 (May 1864), 83–96.
[20] ED to AM, May 1864, *EDCL*, 116.

Since their wives knew nothing of literature or politics or any of the things to which their own, more educated, minds might turn, home became a bore for husbands too. Just as middle-class women were pushed down the route of trifling elegance (or, in the lower ranks, trifling without the elegance), middle-class men were pushed down the route of mere providers, devoting themselves to earning money. Everything that their own education had supposedly prepared them for, in terms of culture and public service, was lost. Their sons, meanwhile, learnt from their mothers and sisters only the virtue of idleness. In two respects the education of middle-class girls was emphatically 'not a "woman's question"'.[21] It impacted directly on men. And it was in the hands of men—in particular, should they so choose, the soon to be appointed commissioners.

This was a strong and well-crafted paper, which avoided the main areas of contention bedevilling discussions of women's education. It said nothing about how girls' education should relate to boys', and it explicitly adopted the received view that in the vast majority of cases the principal 'profession' of a lady should be that of a daughter, sister, wife, and mother. There was no hint of competition and consistent with Davies's Millian principles the benefit sought was for men as much as for women. The paper also caught, for her purposes, a good tone: amusing without being mocking, serious without being heavy-handed, and entirely unthreatening.

Davies's was not the only appeal of its kind. Harriet Martineau published an article in the November *Cornhill Magazine* (unsigned but probably recognizable) lamenting the state of girls' education in England as compared with France and America, calling for the commissioners to address the imbalance of endowments between boys and girls, and calling specifically for a classical education for girls as well as boys.[22] Davies must have agreed with everything, but she would not have thought it productive to say so.

By the time Davies's paper was delivered, the commission had been formally set up and the commissioners appointed. The list of names offered some small grounds for optimism. The appointment of Roby as secretary promised well. He may not have agreed with Davies in respect of the content of girls' education, but he recognized its importance; she had evidently come to know and like him and could work with him. Lyttelton had supported her in the locals and Stanley had voted for the admission of women to London University. Acland had been as much of a nuisance as a help in respect of the locals, and would continue to take a patronizing line in respect of the relationship between the sexes. When Davies pressed for the inclusion of women on the governing bodies of girls' schools, he

---

[21] *Thoughts*, 81.
[22] Harriet Martineau, 'Middle class education in England: girls', *Cornhill Magazine*, 10 (November 1864), 549–68.

136 DAVIES AND THE MID-VICTORIAN WOMEN'S MOVEMENT

suggested that an advisory ladies' committee would surely be more appropriate.[23] Like Roby, however, he recognized the importance of girls' education and was unlikely to argue against the consideration of girls if others argued for it. Amongst the assistant commissioners, Fitch was already a strong supporter and may well have been able to assure Davies of the sympathies of others, such as Daniel Fearon, James Bryce, and Lemprière Hammond. Neither the secretary nor the assistant commissioners would have any say in the matter, however. One commissioner, John Storrar, had voted against admitting women to London University and the views of the chairman and the majority of the commissioners were unknown.

In the months following the SSA congress, Davies was heavily occupied with putting together the memorial for the Cambridge locals, but she soon started making enquiries and lobbying where she could. Immediately after the congress, Lyttelton responded to her enquiry by stating that he had 'no doubt girls are to be included in our Commission'. The remit was middle-class education and boys were not specified. On her request, though, he mentioned the matter to Lord Granville, Lord President of the Council.[24] Arnold took the opposite view. The commission (which was in his view badly unbalanced anyway) would have too much on its hands with the boys to be willing to take on girls as well.[25] Reports reached her from other sources to similar effect.[26] Acland assured her that the matter would be carefully considered, but given his past record that was no comfort.[27]

The issue could not be decided until the commission met, by when it would be too late to start lobbying, so Davies resorted to the usual recourse of a memorial, urging the commissioners to include girls' education as falling within the scope of their inquiry. With the help of Eliza Bostock she gathered the signatures of just over one hundred names.[28] This was fewer than those just garnered for the Cambridge memorial, but more selective. It also included some significant new names, including Arthur Stanley, the broad church leader, now dean of Westminster, and his wife Lady Augusta ('Lady' by virtue of being the daughter of the Earl of Elgin). Lady Stanley of Alderley was on both lists, as a visitor of Queen's College. So too, amongst the more prominent teachers, were Anne Clough, sister of the poet Arthur, who ran a school in Ambleside, and Elizabeth Wolstenholme, a committed feminist with a school in Salford. Davies would have

---

[23] Carol Dyhouse, 'Miss Buss and Miss Beale: gender and authority in the history of education', in Felicity Hunt, ed., *Lessons for Life: The Schooling of Girls and Women 1850–1950* (Basil Blackwell, 1987), 2–39: 33.

[24] LL to ED, 11 October 1864, GCPP Davies, 6/2; PRO 30/29/18/12, no. 11, Granville Papers, in Fletcher, 19.

[25] MA to ED, 28 December 1864, GCPP Davies, 6/5.

[26] ED to MA, 23 December 1864, *EDCL*, 137–8.

[27] TDA to ED, 31 December 1864, CGPP Davies, 6/3.

[28] The memorial is at Girton GCPP Davies 6/8, and in FC, 418a.

'NOT A "WOMAN'S QUESTION"' 137

known of Clough both through Barbara Bodichon, one of whose cousins was her sister-in-law, and through Anna Richardson, who lived in the next village. She probably met Wolstenholme at Langham Place and at this stage, unaware of her more radical tendencies, appears to have treated her as a good friend. Besides their shared interests their brothers were exact Cambridge contemporaries, so there would have been a ready basis for friendship.

In the event, the commissioners were sympathetic, and by late February they had agreed to include girls' schools in their remit.[29] From then on Roby and Davies were in constant communication, and despite his earlier reservations he would be unfailingly supportive.[30] As the work of the commission gradually ramped up over the next year he sought her advice on what questions the commissioners should be addressing and on whom they should call as witnesses in respect of girls' schools. He shared the evidence with her and he put her in touch with those assistant commissioners who would be visiting girl's schools: something that proved to be no easy matter, given that so many schoolmistresses treated their schools as homes and resented any invasion of their privacy.[31] James Bryce, assistant commissioner for Lancashire, entered into a long and detailed correspondence with her, asking what to look for in girls' schools, what questions to ask, and so on, and both he and Daniel Fearon became, through the process, prominent advocates of girls' grammar schools.[32]

Apart from the evidence collected by the assistant commissioners, most of the evidence on girls' schools came, not surprisingly, from the advanced schoolmistresses (many proposed by Davies) and the advocates of improved girls' education. William Hodgson was the first to be interviewed on the subject, and this was followed by 'a gathering [of schoolmistresses] to meet some of the commission people', at which it was apparent that the assistant commissioners were fully engaged with the issue of girls' schools, not only gathering evidence but also, through their enquiries, 'stirring up & encouraging the schoolmistresses'. At around the same time Davies herself gave evidence alongside—at her suggestion—Frances Buss, and found the commissioners 'favourably disposed towards women generally'.[33] Others followed, including Anne Clough, Elizabeth Wolstenholme, Dorothea Beale of Cheltenham Ladies College, Eleanor Smith from Oxford, and Mary Porter, then running a school in Tiverton.[34]

---

[29] LID to ED, 22 February 1865, GCPP Davies, 6/10; HR to ED, 28 February 1865, GCPP Davies, 6/9.

[30] HR to ED, 18 March 1865; HR to EB, 28 February 1865, FC, 418, 418b. FC, 418 ff.

[31] Fletcher, 23; ED to HR, 8 November 1865, *EDCL*, 158–9. Some of the correspondence from Roby is at GCPP Davies 6/11, 13, 15.

[32] For Davies's correspondence with Bryce see FC, 429–32, 446–7, 452–3.

[33] ED to BB, [December 1864], *EDCL*, 166–8.

[34] Beale's submission was perhaps the most straightforwardly effective. If girls were better educated they would be less likely to marry, since less likely to marry unwisely, but likely to marry better and to be better for it whether they married or not. See A. Utopian [Dorothea Beale], 'On the education of girls', *Fraser's Magazine*, 74 (October 1866), 509–24.

138 DAVIES AND THE MID-VICTORIAN WOMEN'S MOVEMENT

When the report came to be written, it seems to have been Roby and, amongst the commissioners, Lyttelton whose views dominated. Both were, of course, sympathizers and Lyttelton undertook to write the chapter on girls' schools. It had, he wrote in a note to his family, 'a strong likeness in features and deportment to its parents. It is uproarious—squalls incessantly—and hopes to make much noise in the world.'[35] It was indeed forthright in its condemnation of the existing state of girls' secondary education:[36]

> The general deficiency in girls' education is stated with the utmost confidence, and with entire agreement, with whatever difference of words, by many witnesses of authority. Want of thoroughness and foundation; want of system; slovenliness and showy superficiality; inattention to rudiments; undue time given to accomplishments, and those not taught intelligently or in any scientific manner; want of organisation.

What was to be done? On the extensive evidence collected by the commission, Lyttelton observed, there could be little doubt that the essential capacity for learning of the two sexes was the same, or nearly so. In practice, however, some witnesses had spoken of differences between the sexes, and suggested that while their secondary education should be similar it should not be carried so high in the case of girls. Lyttelton prevaricated, noting only a 'probable' conclusion that boys' and girls' education should not be completely assimilated; but he went on to use the experience of the Cambridge locals to argue, in effect, that the girls were every bit as capable as the boys.[37] He also followed Davies's line on other matters. The inadequacies of teachers were blamed not on their lack of teacher training, as some suggested, but on their lack of a good liberal higher education: 'Miss Davies', he noted approvingly, 'thinks special Training Institutions very undesirable.'[38] And he supported in general terms her call for women's higher education.

When Davies was interviewed by the commissioners, she asked to be questioned on two items specifically.[39] One was post-school education, i.e. university admission. This was not strictly within their purview, but Lyttelton's report nevertheless addressed the issue, coming out strongly in favour of women's higher education and in support of the various initiatives that had taken place in the years during which the commission was operating. This included the establishment of 'Colleges for young women to carry on their studies, after school, into higher

---

[35] Quoted by Askwith, *The Lytteltons*, 154–5, and Fletcher, 40.   [36] SIC *Report*, Vol. 1, 548–9.

[37] *SIC Report*, Vol. 1, 553–4. Dyhouse, *Girls Growing Up*, 44, reads the report as recommending that girls should not be educated so highly as boys, but that was referred to merely as an opinion Lyttelton felt bound to recognize.

[38] *SIC Report*, Vol. 1, 562.

[39] HR to ED, 16 November 1865, FC, 442; ED to HR, 18 November 1865, *EDCL*, 162–3. For the evidence session itself, which proved traumatic to Buss, see FC, 444 and Kamm, 74 ff.

'NOT A "WOMAN'S QUESTION"' 139

regions, when able and desirous to do so'.[40] From Davies's perspective, this would be something of a two-edged sword. On one hand, support for the higher education of women from such an august body was clearly to be welcomed. On the other hand, Lyttelton was careful not to favour any particular scheme, giving equal support to lecture courses for young women, implicitly assumed to be different from those given to young men.[41]

The other issue was that of endowments. The question of endowments generally was central to the commission's work, and the specific question of endowments for girls' schools had been raised before by both Bodichon and Boucherett.[42] It had also been raised in the context of elementary schools by the first in the series of Royal Commissions on education, the Newcastle Commission on the state of popular education, which reported in 1861.[43] The endowed grammar schools catered almost exclusively for boys. Out of over eight hundred endowed schools identified by the commission, only ten seem to have offered any secondary education for girls.[44] Davies knew something from a growing friendship with Frances Buss, whose North London Collegiate School was the closest she had seen to providing a rigorous academic education for girls, of the difficulties of funding proprietary schools,[45] and she realized that recommendations from the commission would be of little practical use if there were not funds to implement them. She had already suggested in her 1864 SSA paper that some of the existing endowments might, 'without much divergence from the intentions of the original donors, be used for the foundation of a few first-rate girls' schools, or in some other way be made available for the advancement of female education'.[46] For the 1865 congress, in Sheffield, she wrote a paper specifically on the subject, arguing that many of the endowments were originally intended for 'children', without distinction of sex, and proposing that at least half of them might in principle be thrown open to girls.[47]

The commissioners were not persuaded of this argument, but only because they took a more robust line still. Endowments, they argued, were for the living, not the dead, and the wording of ancient endowments in almost all respects should be viewed as of antiquarian interest only. On the issue of endowments for girls' schools, they concluded that 'the testimony may be called unanimous, and

[40] *SIC Report*, Vol. 1, 568.   [41] Ibid., 569.
[42] Jessie Boucherett, 'On the education of girls, with reference to their future position', *EWJ*, 6 (December 1860), 217–24; Bodichon, 'Middle class schools for girls'.
[43] *Report of the Commissioners Appointed to Inquire into the State of Popular Education in England*, Vol. 1 (1861), 456 ff.
[44] See table in *SIC Report*, Vol. 1, 565.   [45] See ED to BB, 19 February 1866, *EDCL*, 168–9.
[46] *Thoughts*, 83.
[47] Emily Davies, *The Application of Funds to the Education of Girls* (Longman, Green etc., 1865); copies at FC, 421a, Girton GCPP Davies 11/6. She was not, of course, suggesting that the boys and girls be taught together, which she would have found every bit as objectionable as anyone else: FC, 428–9.

Mr Fearon sums it up, not too strongly, in saying that "appropriation of almost all the Educational Endowments of the country to the education of boys is felt by a large and increasing number, both of men and women, to be a cruel injustice".[48] On the more general question, the central plank of their recommendations, justified in two key chapters of the report, both written by Roby, was that the existing endowments should be carefully reviewed and, barring any strong reasons to the contrary in specific cases, reassigned so as to meet present needs.[49]

This process would have to await a new commission, and would prove immensely difficult to implement, but establishing the principle was a strong gain for the women's movement, and while it could not have happened without the efforts and commitment of Lyttelton and Roby, Fitch and Fearon, Davies could claim much credit.

When Davies later recalled her main achievements, her contribution to the Schools Inquiry Commission was not among them, and it's not hard to see why. She took the lead in ensuring that girls' schools were included in the remit, and as Arnold had suggested it would have been all too easy, without her lobbying, for commissioners to have restricted themselves to boys. Sheila Fletcher, in her detailed account of the work that resulted, saw her contribution as critical.[50] Her influence over Lyttelton and Roby, the main authors of the resulting report, was also exceptional. Her role was, however, essentially a supporting role, and supporting roles didn't come naturally to her. She took much more pride in something that followed on from the commission and in which she took the lead, the London Association of Schoolmistresses.

Both the local examinations campaign and the commission brought Davies into close contact with schoolteachers, especially those who put up students for the locals and those who, on her recommendation, were interviewed by the commission. Late in 1865, Wolstenholme set up a Manchester Board of Schoolmistresses,[51] and early the next year, following their appearance before the commissioners, Davies and Buss created a London equivalent, the London Association of Schoolmistresses.[52] This was very much Davies's baby, and as with her other committees was created as an authoritative body through which she, as honorary secretary (and not herself a schoolmistress) could act. Its formal object was 'to promote the higher education of women'—a phrase intended to cover both secondary and university education. Besides Buss, early members included Eliza Bostock; Octavia Hill; Elizabeth (Whitehead) Malleson, who had taught in Barbara Bodichon's school and since gone on with her husband to found a working women's college on the model of Maurice's Working Men's College; Mary

---

[48] *SIC Report*, Vol. 1, 567. See also Fearon, 'Girls' grammar schools'.   [49] Fletcher, 38.

[50] FB to ED, 5 December 1865, GCPP Davies, 6/17; Fletcher, 19.

[51] FB to ED, 5 December 1865, FC, 444–5; Wright, 60.

[52] FC, 455, 455a, b; Crawford, 117–18; Margaret Bryant, *The London Experience of Secondary Education* (Athlone Press, 1986), 326–8.

'NOT A "WOMAN'S QUESTION"' 141

Porter; Hannah Pipe; and Fanny Metcalfe, who with her sister and mother ran an academically advanced school in Hendon. Visiting schoolmistresses from round the country also participated, and some went on to set up similar associations in their own towns. Adelaide Manning, Charlotte's stepdaughter, with whom Davies had become close friends, was co-opted as 'Auditor'.[53]

The evidence collected by the commission, much of which Roby had shared with Davies, had raised a number of issues with respect to girls' schools and their teaching, on which the opinions of the schoolmistresses themselves clearly differed. Amongst these were the question of training; of syllabus; of physical education; and of the optimum size and structure of schools. The association provided a forum in which these could be debated, through which good practice could be promoted, and through which Davies could promote her own views.

Two issues in particular proved contentious, on both of which Davies found herself in a minority. One was the question of training. The (male) establishment view was that the appropriate 'training' for a teacher of the middle class and above was a good liberal education. This view was firmly held in the case of boys, and in the case of girls and young women taught by men. Queen's College was originally established for the education of governesses and at that point included lectures on the theory and practice of education. There was always resistance to the idea of training, however, and within a few years those had been dropped. Training, it was deemed by the men in charge, was for elementary teachers.[54] The case of women teachers was more complicated, since taking the same line might imply that they should receive a higher, even perhaps a university, education. Both Lyttelton and Roby (both, as it happened, first classicists in their Cambridge years) were, however, firm supporters of a liberal education. Witnesses had conveniently argued that women were natural teachers anyway and the report concluded that while some training might be appropriate on top of a general liberal education, it was that education that really mattered.

The leading schoolmistresses, on the other hand, were generally in favour of trained teachers. Both Buss and Wolstenholme were members of the College of Preceptors, and Buss would be appointed to its council.[55] Beale had resigned a tutoring role at Queen's when the pedagogical lectures were dropped.[56] Both Buss and Clough recruited from the Home and Colonial School Society and in their evidence to the commission, Buss, Wolstenholme, Clough, and Porter all spoke in favour of training colleges for girls' schools teachers.[57]

---

[53] FC, 455a, b; ED to BB, 19 February 1866, *EDCL*, 168–9. The minute books are at Girton GCPP Davies 9/1–3.

[54] de Bellaigue, 'The development of teaching as a profession for women', 974.

[55] Ibid., 973, 975.

[56] Ibid., 978. See also Elaine Kaye, *A History of Queen's College, London, 1848–1972* (Chatto & Windus, 1972), 737.

[57] *SIC Report*, Vol. 1, 562.

On this issue, Davies was on the side of the establishment. She was a firm believer in a classical liberal education but much more importantly she was opposed to any distinction being drawn between what was suitable for women teaching girls and what was suitable for men teaching boys. The normal qualification for a master in a good boys' school was a university degree, and to endorse training colleges for their female equivalents would be to open the way for parallel but different forms of higher education, and potentially close the way for women to get university degrees.

The other contentious issue related to the appropriate size, style, and culture of a girls' secondary school. Here Davies and Buss were in general agreement. The girls should be taught the same syllabus as boys, and take the same examinations, in schools large enough to provide proficient teaching across the range of subjects, and with no class distinctions. While both believed in religious teaching according to the Church of England, moreover (Buss's two ordained brothers were closely involved in her schools), they also thought there should be no religious distinctions. Many of the leading schoolmistresses, however, including Clough, Beale, and Pipe, saw things differently. The syllabus and examinations (if there were any) should be adapted to the special needs of girls. Competition should be avoided. The emphasis should be on a homely, caring environment.[58] Beale put religion at the heart of her instruction, and refused to admit the daughters of men in trade.[59]

Neither of these issues seems to have split the association. Rather it provided a forum in which they could be discussed, and in the context of which informed decisions could be taken, especially when in the early 1870s a raft of new girls' high schools came to be founded. For over twenty years the association would serve a valuable function in promoting good practice amongst the London girls' schools, exploring educational innovations and generally raising educational standards. Meeting roughly once a quarter it also both broadened and cemented Davies's relationships with the more enlightened London schoolmistresses and kept her in touch with developments such as that of the Girls' Public Day School Company.

Davies's first educational campaigns, for admission to the Cambridge locals and the reform of girls' secondary education, were both distinctive and different from what had gone before. Like other feminists of her generation and earlier she was guided by strong principles, but she was also intensely practical. She had a strong strategic sense of what might be achievable. She didn't push for too much too soon, and she focused on issues that could be decided at the institutional

---

[58] de Bellaigue, 'The development of teaching as a profession for women', 979–80; K. M. Reynolds, 'The school and its place in girls' education', in *The North London Collegiate School, 1850–1950* (Oxford University Press, 1950), 106–38.
[59] Martha Vicinus, *Independent Women: Work and Community for Single Women 1850–1920* (Virago, 1985), 167.

rather than the political level. She was tactically astute, working out how best to achieve her objectives and working to a plan rather than just relying on their intrinsic merit. She was also careful to work with men rather than against them, and where possible with men who, whilst liberal in their views, were respectable members of the establishment. Few in the women's movement would have recognized the value (the immense value, as it turned out) of a political conservative like Lord Lyttelton.

While some of the men with whom she worked on the locals were Unitarians, like Shaen or Heywood, Davies was helped considerably in this by both her broad church connections and her own commitment to the established church. In the context of the locals, men like her brother, Maurice, Alford, and Hutton (her principal target when addressing the press) were well known and well respected. Whereas political Radicals claimed the high ground of rationality as against religion, the broad churchmen were by this time the representatives of reasonableness and thoughtful compromise. In the cases of both Cambridge University and the Schools Inquiry Commission, the men she had to deal with were solidly Church of England, and both they and the schoolmistresses with whom she worked most closely placed the education of girls firmly within a religious and Church of England context. Lyttelton came to believe, through the work of the commission, that endowed schools should generally be open to dissenters and religious instruction not compulsory, but he remained a high churchman himself, his faith at the centre of his life.

Others within the women's movement, with their Unitarian or anti-religious backgrounds, took a very different view, but if proposed reforms to girls' secondary education were to carry weight with the establishment they had to be set within this context. Davies's position at the intersection between the women's movement and established religion, combined with her commitment to broad church reasonableness, and her fusion of Millian rationalism with Burkean conservatism and respect of institutions, made for a rare and powerful combination.

9

Votes for Women?

In the spring of 1865, Emily Davies, Charlotte Manning, and Isa Craig set up a women's discussion group under the name of the Kensington Society: it met in Manning's Kensington house. Manning was president, Davies secretary, and Craig made up a small committee, who invited members from both London and further afield. Davies recalled it as a way of keeping in touch after the local examinations campaign, but its origins seem rather to have been in the Ladies London Emancipation Society (LLES). This had been set up by Mentia Taylor in 1863, after she was refused admission as a woman to the London Anti-Slavery Society and in response to an appeal from Harriet Beecher Stowe, to support the North in the American Civil War. This was now nearing its end. All three had been involved, Manning as one the founders, Craig as a writer of tracts, and Davies on the committee.

Although their circles of support overlapped considerably, Davies and Mentia Taylor had very different styles and approaches, and Davies seems from the beginning to have been uneasy with Taylor's assertive radicalism. Taking part in an LLES reception for the Italian nationalist hero and abolitionist Giuseppe Garibaldi, in 1864, she had felt greatly honoured (he was widely regarded, especially by the English working classes, as a hero), but remarked to Anna Richardson that 'We were a disreputable set of people (except myself & one other lady.) & our address was a most inflammatory production.'[1]

The discussion topics chosen by the committee for the first meeting of the new society in May were unlikely to inflame anyone: the national characteristics of English dress; sentimentality; and the basis and limits of parental authority. The last was the main one discussed, with papers from Cobbe and Wolstenholme.[2] One of the topics chosen at that meeting for the next, however, in November, was much more incendiary: 'Is the extension of the Parliamentary suffrage to women desirable, and, if so, under what conditions?'[3]

The context here was that a general election was due, the last having been in 1859. John Stuart Mill had been persuaded by his political friends to stand for Parliament and had committed himself, if elected, to pressing for female suffrage. In a letter to the *Times* he had declared himself in favour of opening the suffrage to 'all grown persons, both men and women, who can read, write, and perform a

---

[1] ED to AR, 19 April 1864, *EDCL*, 112. [2] FC, 424. Girton GCPP Davies 10/6.
[3] FC, 423d, 424.

Emily Davies and the Mid-Victorian Women's Movement. John Hendry, Oxford University Press. © John Hendry 2024.
DOI: 10.1093/oso/9780198910237.003.0009

VOTES FOR WOMEN? 145

sum in the rule of three, and who have not, within some small number of years, received parish relief'.[4]

For two of those at the May meeting, in particular, this was an opportunity not to be missed. One was Helen Taylor, Mill's stepdaughter, who had been introduced to the Kensington Society through Alice Westlake.[5] For her, the female franchise would have been the fulfilment of her mother's dreams. The other was Barbara Bodichon, who had long advocated votes for women and had been disappointed that the *English Woman's Journal* had not done more to advance this cause. In the run up to the election, in July, she energetically joined Mill's campaign, driving her carriage through Westminster plastered with posters and taking with her Bessie Parkes, Isa Craig, and Emily Davies. All three had reservations. Parkes had had enough of campaigning and wanted a quieter life. Craig was not particularly interested in female suffrage. Davies was, but must have disliked the flamboyance of the campaign, and feared that it might backfire. Bodichon on the march, however, was a force of nature. None felt able to refuse.[6]

In the event the Liberals under Palmerston were returned with an increased majority and Mill was elected on a Radical ticket, as was Henry Fawcett. Russell Gurney was also elected, as a Conservative. For the Kensington Society meeting, both Bodichon and Helen Taylor were out of the country, but both submitted papers, strongly in favour of votes for women. Three other papers were opposed, but a resolution in favour of women's suffrage was carried by a large majority.[7]

Even before the discussion, there were moves for political engagement and activism. Bodichon suggested a committee be formed to lead a campaign and others evidently had similar thoughts. From Davies's perspective, this was not good news. She was committed to female suffrage in principle, but convinced that in practice now was not the time. Strategically, it was far too soon. The ground had not been laid and she was concerned that agitation for the vote would just stir up fierce opposition, doing more harm than good and hindering her more modest claims to women's education. Sending Henry Tomkinson a copy of Bodichon's paper, she expressed her concern:[8]

> Some people are inclined to begin a subdued kind of agitation for the Franchise. I have rather tried to stifle it, & they are willing to be stifled if there seemed to be any risk of their damaging other things by it....I don't see much use in talking about the Franchise till first principles have made more way. The scoffers don't

---

[4] *Times*, 21 April 1865.
[5] Ann Dingsdale, '"Generous and lofty sympathies": the Kensington Society, the 1866 women's suffrage petition and the development of mid-Victorian feminism', University of Greenwich PhD thesis (1995), 90.
[6] FC, 427; Hirsch, 216.   [7] HT to ED, 2 December 1865, FC, 448.
[8] ED to HRT, 10 November 1865, *EDCL*, 159–60: 160.

see how much is involved in improved education, but they are wide awake about the Franchise.

She strongly disagreed with the robust language, and the language of rights, in which both Bodichon's and Taylor's papers were couched, and which Tomkinson seems to have endorsed. Even in the 'extreme case of Slavery', she argued,[9]

> It would surely be better that the right of freedom should be restored by the people who have stolen it [i.e. out of duty], than that it should be extorted by an insurrection of the slaves. As to the suffrage, my view is that, the object of representation being, not to confer privileges but to get the best possible government, women should be politely invited to contribute their share of intelligence in the selection of the legislative body. As to their 'asserting their rights successfully & irresistibly,' the idea is, if I may say so, rather revolting to my mind. It goes against me to think of it.

She was also worried about the kind of people likely to get involved in any campaign, and the harm *they* might do. Writing to Bodichon, she threw cold water on the proposed committee. 'I have taken further advice, & it is all against. If we could have a perfect Committee, it might do good, but I doubt whether the sort of people who can really help us would join, yet, & wild people might do great harm.' To Tomkinson she expressed her doubt whether a 'safe' committee could be formed—'& if wild people got upon it, who would insist on jumping like kangaroos. (the simile is not flattering.) they would do harm'.[10]

No names were mentioned, but it must have been apparent that the greatest enthusiasts for the fight were likely to come from Radical MPs and the Radical wing of the women's movement. Even if they didn't, the chances of a committee being formed that Davies could effectively control must have looked slim. People like Mentia Taylor, Frances Cobbe, Jessie Boucherett, and Elizabeth Wolstenholme, all of whom were to get involved, weren't going to do her or any one else's bidding.

As it turned out, Elizabeth Wolstenholme, who was just a visitor in London, had already set up her own committee in Manchester, with the Radical politician Jacob Bright, soon to be a local MP, and his wife Ursula.[11] In London, with both Bodichon and Taylor abroad for the winter, nothing happened until the following spring. In March 1866, however, Lord Russell, who had become prime minister once more following Palmerston's death the previous October, introduced through William Gladstone, his leader in the House of Commons, a new Reform Bill. His aim was to significantly extend the male suffrage, something he had long

---

[9] ED to HRT, 14 November 1865, *EDCL*, 161–2: 162.
[10] ED to HRT, 14 November 1865, *EDCL*, 161–2: 161. [11] Wright, 59.

wanted to achieve, but a new bill also represented an opportunity for promoting votes for women. Bodichon immediately set about putting together a committee and a petition, enlisting Helen Taylor's support, and with it her father's.[12]

The petition proved straightforward. Taylor drafted something, Bodichon cut and redrafted. The end product was short and straightforward, asking for women property holders to be enfranchised on the same basis as men. 'No idea is so universally accepted and acceptable in England', wrote Taylor, 'as that taxation and representation ought to go together, and people in general will be much more willing to listen to the assertion that single women and widows of property have been overlooked and left out from the privileges to which their property entitles them, than to the much more startling general proposition that sex is not a proper ground for distinction in political rights.'[13] Boucherett and Helen Taylor contributed funds. Bodichon marshalled the troops—Davies, Garrett, Crow, Parkes, Boucherett, Cobbe, and Mentia Taylor all seem to have been involved at this stage, as well as Wolstenholme in Manchester—and within a few weeks 1,499 signatures had been collected.

On 7 June, Davies and Garrett (Bodichon being indisposed) met Fawcett in Westminster Hall. He sent for Mill and the petition was handed over and duly presented to the House that same day.[14] There had been some hope that Gurney would join him. But while Gurney, a political Conservative, was to prove a strong and consistent supporter of the women's movement, he ultimately thought it impolitic—or at least premature, in his parliamentary career—to take such a prominent role.[15]

The committee proved to be much less straightforward, as Davies, Helen Taylor, and Mentia Taylor each sought to take control. The first reference to a 'committee' is to the informal group coordinating the gathering of signatures, which was effectively the remnants of Bodichon's Langham Place circle, but once the petition had been submitted Bodichon proposed to Helen Taylor a more formal committee of five: herself, Helen Taylor, Mentia Taylor or Jessie Boucherett, Craig (now Mrs Knox) as secretary, and Davies if she felt able, given her commitments to education. Taylor responded that five was the right number, and 'if Miss Davies does not herself think that being on our committee will be injurious to her more special work of education, she would be the best fifth person'.[16]

---

[12] BB to HT, 9 May 1866, LSE MILL-TAYLOR 12/40.

[13] HT to BB, 8 May 1866, LSE 7BMC/B/1.

[14] FC, 483–7. HT to BB, 6 June 1866, cited in Hirsch, 218. The presentation of petitions was part of the routine business of the house: twenty-eight were recorded in the *Times* as being presented that day. Both the size of the petition and its topic marked this one out as special, however.

[15] HT to BB, 7 June 1866, LSE 7BMC/B/4.

[16] HT to BB, 9 June 1866, LSE 7BMC/B/5, quoted in entry of 'London Provisional Petition Committee' in Elizabeth Crawford, *The Women's Suffrage Movement: A Reference Guide, 1866-1928* (Routledge, 2000).

They had evidently discussed Davies's reservations. Bodichon will certainly have known of these, but will have been mindful too of her campaigning skills and her value as an ally and indefatigable worker. They must also have discussed her views on the merits of women working with men. Taylor reported that her father had suggested a structure including a large general committee of around a hundred 'names', and a much larger paying membership, the whole forming a society. This, she proposed, should be formally constituted with fixed rules, fixed meeting times, 'financial exactitude', and plans submitted to and approved by the wider membership. She was insistent, however, that the executive committee should comprise women only:[17]

> To admit men into the governing body is merely to give over the whole credit into their hands—all the women concerned will merely be considered to take their usual and proper subordinate position.

Immediately, Davies tried to take control. Might there not, she suggested to Taylor, be two secretaries, the unmarried Adelaide Manning (who happened to be her trusted friend) making a perfect complement to Craig? Lady Goldsmid (whom she again trusted) would be excellent as treasurer, if one were needed. And even if the *officers* were to be all women, could there not also be men on the committee? They could be really useful, and some of those with whom she'd worked on education would be happy to join.[18]

Taylor also wished to control things. She would have no men, and one secretary was enough.[19] Davies suggested meeting on Thursday to discuss everything, with just the two of them, Bodichon, Knox, and Manning. She knew Mentia Taylor, a strong political Radical, from other committees, and clearly wanted to keep her out of things. (Boucherett was out of town.) Taylor suggested Wednesday, without Manning, and at Mentia Taylor's home: she had already sent out the invitations. I doubt if Davies ever cursed but if she did, she might have then. They did meet on Wednesday, at Mentia Taylor's, and without Manning (who was conveniently indisposed), and decided, presumably because they couldn't agree otherwise, not to form a society or association at all, and not for the present to have a formal committee. It was agreed, however, that Davies would continue the work, already started, of seeking positive press coverage and reprinting and circulating anything useful.[20]

As things turned out, the extension of the franchise to women was never even considered at this stage. Even without it, the Russell–Gladstone Reform Bill was

---

[17] LSE 7/BMC/B6, quoted in Hirsch, 220.

[18] ED to HT 6 June 1866, *EDCL*, 174; Hirsch, 219.

[19] HT to BB, 10 June 1866, LSE 7BMC/B/6.

[20] HT to BB, 21 August 1866, LSE 7BMC/B/8; ED to HT, 9 June 1866, 17 June 1866, *EDCL*, 176–7, 179–81; EDCL,178.

too radical for some of their own MPs.[21] On 18 June the government was defeated on an amendment and a week later Russell resigned. Disraeli, the Conservative leader in the Commons, was unable to command a majority and the result, for the third time in fifteen years, was a minority Conservative government led by the Earl of Derby, with Disraeli leading in the Commons. There was immediately speculation that Disraeli might introduce a Reform Bill of his own, and he was on record as supposedly favouring votes for women. In a commons debate at the end of April he had noted in passing that 'if there is to be universal suffrage, women have as much right to vote as men. And more than that—a woman having property ought to have a vote in a country, in which she may hold manorial courts and sometimes elects churchwardens.'[22] This was met by laughter, and some thought it satirical, a form of *reductio ad absurdum*, but others took it seriously and Davies continued her work.[23] Then on 17 July, Mill made a speech in Parliament in support of women's suffrage, arguing in effect that if women—in particular women householders, who might be supposed to be amongst the most capable and responsible of women—had the ability to contribute to the common good in this way, society should avail itself of this benefit.

This was not going to be the ground on which the matter was decided. As the *Saturday Review* promptly noted, it wasn't a question of talent but of fitness: they might indeed make a contribution but at the far too great expense of decency and modesty.[24] It was the kind of argument of which Davies approved, however, and whatever her reservations as to how a suffrage campaign might turn out one now looked to be inevitable. She decided to take the initiative. The next day she sent copies of the petition to all the weeklies and wrote to Taylor praising her father and asking for her thoughts, in particular on local petitions and on how best to handle the case of married women. A month later, she informed her that the time had now come to formalize the committee that had met earlier so that there was a body in place to direct the process and hold the substantial funds that would be needed for a campaign, and with a secretary authorized to act. Knox was already doing part of the secretary's role keeping accounts and records, and she was happy to keep doing the press work. With Bodichon, Mentia Taylor, Adelaide Manning, and Helen Taylor herself, that made a practical committee.[25]

Though presented as a committee of five plus secretary, this was not, of course, the committee originally proposed, but that plus Manning, who could be relied upon to do Davies's bidding. Taylor, as she reported to Bodichon, was not pleased. For one thing, Manning had been gratuitously added. For another, there was not yet, on her understanding, any committee, formal or otherwise, and could not be

---

[21] This group of conservative Liberals, led by Robert Lowe, were christened the Adullamites, in reference to the biblical cave of Adullam.

[22] *Times*, 28 April 1866.   [23] ED to HT, 7 July 1866, *EDCL*, 179–81.

[24] 'Mr Mill and the ladies', *Saturday Review*, 22 (21 July 1866), 73–4.

[25] ED to HT, 18 July 1866, 4 August 1866, 6 August 1866, *EDCL*, 182–90.

one without a society, with members, fixed rules, times, and objectives. And what was Knox doing keeping accounts, if there was no society? She couldn't put her name to something she didn't know what it was, or for what.[26]

This suited Davies well. In a long, friendly, and no doubt deeply irritating response (her letters to Helen Taylor were always friendly, almost fawning) she detailed how she had made use of a committee in her education campaigns and the advantages it conferred: clarifying objectives, pulling in people and money, coordinating activities. It seemed to her that a committee was necessary in this case too, and a permanent one at that, not restricted to just one petition, so she had set one up![27] And with Taylor out of the country for the winter, she proceeded without her. By October she had put together a 'provisional' Suffrage Committee comprising herself, Bodichon, Parkes, Boucherett, Knox, Garrett, Mentia Taylor, Cobbe, and Mary Lloyd, Cobbe's partner.[28] The first 'official' meeting followed three weeks later, by when she had assembled a general committee comprising five men and eight women, as well as a smaller all-female executive committee. The men were Dean Alford, George Hastings, James Heywood, and Walter Clay, secretary for that year's SSA congress, all presumably chosen by Davies, and a prominent Irish political economist, John Elliott Cairnes, who seems to have been proposed by Cobbe.[29] The female members were now Davies, Boucherett, Knox, Lady Goldsmid, and Adelaide Manning, with Mentia Taylor as treasurer, Louie Garrett Smith as 'nominal secretary', providing a conveniently anonymous address, and Harriet Cook assisting Davies in the actual secretarial duties. Parkes had retired. Bodichon excused herself as being abroad, providing a justification for Helen Taylor's exclusion. Cobbe and Lloyd had withdrawn. Elizabeth Garrett was now fully occupied with her medical work.[30] Cook, who had met Garrett in Edinburgh, was staying with her and Crow in London and devoting herself to the campaign.[31]

This was Davies's committee, dominated and controlled by her nominees, and constructed with complete disregard for Helen Taylor's views. She would have preferred not to have Mentia Taylor on it, but she had volunteered as treasurer and to resist proved impracticable.[32]

---

[26] HT to BB, 21 August 1866, LSE 7BMC/B/8.   [27] ED to HT, 28 August 1866, *EDCL*, 196–9.
[28] ED to HT, 6 August 1866, 16 August 1866, *EDCL*, 187–90, 192–3; ED to BB, 10 August 1866, 16 August 1866, *EDCL* 190–1, 193–4. See also BB to HT, n.d. (summer 1866), LSE MILL-TAYLOR 12/51–4. On Mentia's Taylor's earlier support see Crawford, 114.
[29] Cairnes was best known at this time for his economic analysis of slavery, *The Slave Power* (Carleton, 1862), which condemned slavery as unjustifiable economically, as well as on moral grounds.
[30] ED to HT, 31 October 1866, 26 November 1866, 15 December 1866, *EDCL*, 211–16; ED to AM, autumn 1866, in Stephen, 116; Mitchell, 164–5; *EDCL*, 213.
[31] FC, 507. Crow had moved in with Garrett, partly to help run the household as Garrett's medical practice grew.
[32] ED to HT, 16 August 1866, *EDCL*, 192–3; ED to BB, 10 August 1866, *EDCL* 190–1.

Davies's objections to Mentia Taylor were partly based on her general Radical sympathies, but were heightened at this time by her outspoken support for the Reform League. The Reform League had been established in early 1865 by a group of trade unionists and other reformers to campaign for working-class (male) suffrage. Its language was one of rights. Respectable working men, defined in practice as those of fixed abode, had a constitutional right, it was claimed, to representation. The Radical MPs John Bright and Peter Taylor, Mentia's husband, were amongst its supporters and Taylor was one of its main funders.[33] Davies recalled later that 'Mrs Peter Taylor... belonged to the extreme Left of the Liberal Party, & looked at matters from a different point of view from other members of the Committee. This difference was the more embarrassing as she was by far the most zealous & active member.'[34]

Following the failure of Gladstone's Reform Bill and the fall of the Liberal administration, the Reform League organized a series of demonstrations, one of which, at Hyde Park on 23 July, was declared illegal by the government. A large procession of maybe 200,000 was met by lines of police and railings round the park. The railings were pulled down, the military called in. The affair ended peacefully, but this was not the kind of thing with which Davies wished to be associated in any way.

From Davies's perspective, Mentia Taylor's radicalism posed one kind of problem. She wanted and, in respect of other campaigns, needed her committee to appear utterly respectable. Mill's radicalism posed a rather different problem.

On a philosophical level, Davies was a committed follower of Mill. She not only held him in high esteem, she modelled her arguments closely on his. On a personal level, too, she was an admirer. She had visited his home in Blackheath twice in the early summer of 1866 and was impressed not just by the conversation ('"society" in a very delightful form') but by the 'simple goodness' of father and daughter, and what struck her as their moderate agnosticism. 'I fancy too that they are a good deal nearer to us as to religious belief [this to Adelaide Manning, a fellow Christian] than I had thought.'[35]

Mill the politician, however, proved to be very different from Mill the philosopher or Mill the man, as indeed the *Manchester Guardian* (liberal high church) noted in August and the *Contemporary Review* (broad church) in September. Mill the MP was associating himself with positions far more radical and far less defensible than those carefully argued in his writings, and was thought to be

---

[33] For an account of the league sensitive to its male exclusivity see Keith McClelland, 'England's greatness', in Catherine Hall, Keith McClelland, and Jane Rendall, eds., *Defining the Victorian Nation: Class, Race, Gender and the British Reform Act of 1867* (Cambridge University Press, 2000), 71–118.

[34] FC, 509.

[35] ED to AM, 26 June 1866, in Stephen, 112, and see HT to ED, 18 June 1866, FC, 480–1.

losing support.[36] This was only the third volume of the *Contemporary*, which in its first year would come out in favour of both women's education and female suffrage. Edited by Alford and taking a consistently broad church line, it would have been required reading for Davies.

Part of the problem was Mill's strong support of the Reform League and near-universal male suffrage, which would, according to moderate opinion, put government in the control of those least equipped to judge on political questions. This was the concern referenced in the *Contemporary*, and it took on new and dangerous connotations after the Hyde Park protests. The other part of the problem was his leading role on the Jamaica Committee.

In Jamaica in 1865, as a result partly of economic problems, partly of a draconian government, and partly, according to some, of incitement by Baptist missionaries, tensions between the white planters and the Black population were running high. In October, protests in Morant Bay against the vindictive trial of a Black man turned violent. The local militia opened fire and by the end of the day twenty-five people (on both sides) had been killed. In response the governor, Edward Eyre, imposed martial law and ordered reprisals. 439 Black people were killed indiscriminately and others hanged after cursory martial trials. The latter included George Gordon, a wealthy mixed-race businessman and one of the very few non-whites to sit in the House of Assembly, who had no direct connection with the protests but was a long-standing critic of Eyre.

When reports reached England, opinion was divided, with the rival camps led by the country's two most famous intellectuals: Thomas Carlyle, who was unapologetically racist as well as misogynist in his views and defended Eyre, and Mill, who condemned him. A Jamaica Committee, calling for his trial on a charge of mass murder, included an array of liberal intellectuals, moderate, radical, and non-political, and was led in the House of Commons by Mill. Carlyle set up a Governor Eyre Defence and Aid Committee, with its own list of prominent intellectuals. A Royal Commission was set up and reported the following spring, to the effect that the use of martial law had been excessive, but that no action should be taken against Eyre. After the Liberal government was defeated, however, the Jamaica Committee began pressing for a private prosecution.[37]

Davies's personal views on the issue are not known, but the issue is one that would have been much discussed amongst family and friends. The Christian Socialist MP Tom Hughes, whose family was very close to her brother's, was

---

[36] ED to BB, 10 August 1866, *EDCL*, 190–1; An Ex-MP, 'The extension of the franchise', *Contemporary Review*, 3 (September 1866), 435–52.

[37] For full detail and a reading in terms of race and gender see Catherine Hall, 'The nation within and without', in Hall, McClelland, and Rendall, eds., *Defining the Victorian Nation*, 179–233; 'Competing masculinities: Thomas Carlyle, John Stuart Mill and the case of Governor Eyre', in Catherine Hall, *White, Male and Middle Class: Explorations in Feminism and History* (Polity, 1992), 255–95; and for background *Civilising Subjects: Metropole and Colony in the English Imagination 1830–1867* (Polity, 2002).

amongst those representing the Jamaica Committee in Parliament, whilst another of the Christian Socialists, Charles Kingsley, was on Carlyle's committee. Amongst the many other big names involved, Huxley, Darwin, Fawcett, and Leslie Stephen were with Mill; Tennyson and Ruskin with Carlyle. Russell Gurney was one of the commissioners, and he went out to Jamaica to investigate, accompanied by Emilia, who would no doubt have been quizzed on her return.

Davies's sympathies, like those of other members of the women's movement, would almost certainly have been with those massacred and their families, but the issue was far from straightforward. Most of the middle classes would either have sided with Eyre or have gone along with the Royal Commission. Even if they condemned the massacre, they would have felt some sympathy with Eyre and would have viewed those who continued to press against him, even after the commission reported, as dangerous radicals. Not only were Mill and the Reform League urging on potentially violent working-class demonstrators in Hyde Park, which was bad enough, they were defending Black violence in the colonies, at a time when the Indian Rebellion of 1857 was still strong in people's memories. Carlyle's utter contempt for both women and Black people was extreme, and for the broad church community and other progressives the ideal of a physically dominant masculinity underlying them would have seemed outdated. Manliness was now to be associated, following Arnold, with more kindly and caring qualities. But the idea that Black people were essentially inferior to white people, physically and mentally less vigorous yet at the same time savage and prone to outbreaks of violence, was commonplace. Indeed, with abolition achieved, racial prejudice seems to have become more acceptable, amongst liberals as well as conservatives. The new science of anthropology (not yet very scientific) endorsed it, and events in Jamaica seemed to confirm it.[38]

It is interesting, in this context, to read the travel journal of Emilia Gurney. She mainly commented on other people's views rather than her own, but she described the experience as like going indignantly to take the part of an ill-treated wife and, when she got there, finding her sympathy ebbing away.[39] The response had been far too harsh, and the case against Gordon not strictly proven, but there were 'extenuating circumstances'. She thought Gordon a persistent troublemaker, and found most of the atrocities to have been committed by Maroons (descendants of escaped slaves from the Spanish era) rather than by British troops.

There was a complex dynamic here. Mill and others had habitually identified the subjection of women with that of enslaved Black people, but to mainstream opinion this was a nonsense. The enslaved were forcibly deprived of both liberty and personhood. English women retained their liberty and gave up personhood

---

[38] See for example Christine Bolt, *Victorian Attitudes to Race* (Routledge 1971, reprinted 2007), chapter 3.

[39] See Ellen Gurney, *Letters of Emilia Russell Gurney* (James Nisbet, 1902), 286–327: 326.

only partially, if at all, and willingly, in marriage. For the vast majority of people in England, moreover, with no direct experience of slavery, their perceptions will have been moulded above all by Harriet Beecher Stowe's novel *Uncle Tom's Cabin*. At least 1.5 million copies had been sold in England within a few years of its publication in 1852,[40] and at the time of the American Civil War it must have been widely read and reread. The work has a strong Christian evangelical tone, and what comes out most forcefully, apart from the sheer brutality, is the way enslaved women were deprived of the chance to marry and build a stable home—deprived, indeed, of the very status to which radical feminists objected.

Where the dominant ideology of the period did link women and Black people (free Black people) was in treating both as naturally subordinate, to be cared for or controlled, depending on one's persuasion; and as both physically and intellectually weak, and incapable of the judgement needed for political representation. The scientific authorities of the time endorsed this view: whether physiologically or through the experience of centuries, both women and Black people were deemed in general (individual cases excepted) inferior, and Black men were typically cast as 'feminine': simple-minded, affectionate, naturally subservient.[41] It was generally agreed, moreover, that while slavery might be an abomination, the suffrage should definitely not be extended to Black subjects of the empire, whether in India or in the West Indies. In this context, any connection in the public mind between women and Black people in the context of reform could only be harmful to the women's case.

Catherine Hall has argued that the debates over reform in 1866–7 brought out these issues, as discussions of citizenship brought out distinctions between the ideal citizen—white, male, English—and others: especially Black people, women, and, in the context of growing Fenian agitation, Irish.[42] (The term 'citizen' was generally associated with revolutionary French politics rather than Britain, where all people were 'subjects', but it was the preferred language of the Reform League.) It is hard to read how this impacted on the women's movement, but it must surely have been a concern to Davies, a liberal in respect of women but a conservative in all else and certainly no radical. As the campaign for the suffrage grew through 1866 and into 1867 she was increasingly anxious to dissociate her campaign from Mill and his radical sympathies.[43] Pushing to get articles in the press, she did her best to dissuade people from writing in either the *Westminster Review*, a radical mouthpiece with long associations with Mill, or the recently launched *Fortnightly*

---

[40] Marianne Holohan, 'British illustrated editions of Uncle Tom's Cabin: race, working-class literacy, and transatlantic reprinting in the 1850s', *Resources for American Literary Study*, 36 (1), 27–65.

[41] Hall, *Civilising Subjects*, explores this at length in the context of Baptist missionaries. For a good discussion in the American context see Louis Menand, *The Metaphysical Club* (HarperCollins, 2001), 102 ff.

[42] Hall, 'The nation within and without'.   [43] ED to BB, 10 August 1866, *EDCL*, 190–1.

Review.[44] Edited initially by George Lewes, George Eliot's partner, and then by John Morley, this attracted writers across the liberal spectrum from moderates to extreme radicals, but the early issues were noted for two articles by the young Radical MP, Viscount Amberley, son of Lord Russell, who made his mark by arguing that the Church of England should not merely be broad but should, as a national church, embrace all theologies equally. Amberley was, with Mill, a supporter of female suffrage, but it was the kind of support Davies could do without: the last thing she wanted was to have her campaign associated with 'Atheism and Democracy'.[45]

Apart from controlling any committee, keeping the campaign respectable, and protecting her own campaigns in the field of education, Davies faced two practical challenges. One was to optimize the press coverage. The other was to ensure that any further petitions were worded so as to cast no hostages to fortune.

With regard to the press, she was on familiar ground but found that she could make little headway. Both Bodichon and Cobbe were willing to write articles, but getting something into non-radical elite periodicals proved at this stage impossible. Davies hoped that the editor of *Macmillan's*, David Masson, might have taken something, but the proprietor, Alexander Macmillan, seems to have been resistant, his excuse being that he already had in hand an article (on women and criticism) by Helen Taylor. *Fraser's* published an article in favour of Mill and reform, but without addressing the question of women, and was publishing regular articles on other subjects by Cobbe, and the editor, James Froude, seems likewise to have considered that enough.[46] The article in the *Contemporary Review* criticizing Mill the politician expressed support for modest and lasting reform, but again didn't address the question of women, though Alford would later solicit an article in support.[47] The impression is that these moderate liberal, broad church outlets took much the same view as Davies herself, that while female suffrage might be desirable, now was not the time.

Thanks to Davies's persistence, three articles by Bodichon were eventually published, all heavily edited by Davies so as to conform to her view of the correct tone and argument, but none of them in elite publications. A version of her original paper to the Kensington Society came out in a new and short-lived journal associated with the SSA.[48] Another paper, which must in the end have been as much Davies's as Bodichon's, was read to the 1866 SSA congress in Manchester. Davies managed to get involved in the planning of the congress, with Hastings

---

[44] ED to BB, 16 August 1866, 21 August 1866, August/September 1866, *EDCL*, 193–5, 199–200.

[45] Viscount Amberley, 'Liberals, Conservatives and the Church', *Fortnightly Review*, 2 (6 September 1865), 161–8; 'The Church of England as a religious body', ibid., 6 (1 December 1866), 769–90. See also his *An Analysis of Religious Belief* (Trübner & Co, 1876). ED to BB, 21 August 1866, *EDCL*, 194–5: 195.

[46] Mitchell, 161–2.   [47] ED to HT, 15 December 1866, *EDCL*, 215–16.

[48] Barbara Bodichon, 'The enfranchisement of female free-holders and householders', *Journal of Social Science* (October 1866), 613–20.

156 DAVIES AND THE MID-VICTORIAN WOMEN'S MOVEMENT

and Clay, and ensured that Bodichon's paper was puffed, so that it was reported at length in the *Guardian*, and printed as a pamphlet.[49] A follow-up article, which again seems to have been drafted by Davies on Bodichon's behalf, then appeared in a new review launched by Jessie Boucherett as a substitute for the defunct *English Woman's Journal*.[50]

Meanwhile, there was forthright opposition to contend with, in particular from the *Saturday Review* and *Blackwood's*. The *Saturday's* mocking was both predictable and relatively harmless. Its main objection was the 'unfitness and impropriety of allowing women an active share in public affairs'.[51] Women voting would be 'anomalous, indecorous and offensive'. But this was presented as simply self-evident and while coming down hard on female suffrage it admitted that in other respects, such as education, women's opportunities did need improving.

Blackwood's set its stall against reform generally, Mill more specifically (a particular bogeyman, he was the subject of two comic ballads) and his views on the female franchise especially ('mere clap-trap').[52] Then in September it published an article by 'A woman', actually Margaret Oliphant, defending the status quo, rejecting the call for the franchise, and, in the process, grossly understating the number of signatories to the petition.[53] Mill's proposals, Oliphant accepted, were perfectly logical. He was a great logician, after all, and no doubt our greatest thinker. But he evidently had no knowledge or understanding of women, and in the real world his proposals were quite absurd. Excitable young things might want the vote, but women of property, typically more mature, did not. They were quite happy as they were, thank you, and did not want equality with men, or indeed to be compared with men in any way. There might be a few exceptions. The mere twenty rather unusual women who signed the petition (a misreading of a short notice penned by Cobbe for the *Pall Mall Gazette*, which listed a few of the more famous signatories) might represent two hundred in all, but they did not represent the women for whom the vote was sought. If they got the vote, moreover,

---

[49] Barbara Bodichon, *Reasons for the Enfranchisement of Women* (National Association for the Promotion of Social Science, 1866); ED to HT, 15 October 1866, *EDCL*, 207–10. ED to HT, 7 July 1866, *EDCL*, 179–81; ED to BB, 16 August 1866, *EDCL*, 193–4; ED to BB, 21 August 1866, *EDCL*, 194–5. ED to BB, 6 September 1866, *EDCL*, 200–1.

[50] ED to BB, 22 August 1866, August/September 1866, 6 September 1866, 17 September 1866, *EDCL*, 196, 199–201, 202–3: 199; ED to HT, 28 August 1866, *EDCL*, 196–9; 'Authorities and precedents for giving the suffrage to qualified women', *Englishwoman's Review* (January 1867), 63–75. A further version of Bodichon's arguments under the title *Reasons for and against the Enfranchisement of Women*, incorporating much of her SSA paper, was published in 1869 by the National Society of Women's Suffrage.

[51] 'Women's rights', *Saturday Review*, 21 (16 June 1866), 715–16; 'Mr Mill and the ladies', 74; 'Female suffrage', *Saturday Review*, 23 (30 March and 25 May 1867), 385–6 and 647–8. ED to HT, 16 June 1866, 7 July 1866, *EDCL*, 177–81: 177.

[52] *Blackwood's Magazine*, 99 (January, February, and May 1866), 28–45, 257–9, 668; 100 (August 1866), 245.

[53] ED to BB, 17 September 1866, *EDCL*, 202–3; 'The great unrepresented', *Blackwood's Magazine*, 100 (September 1866), 367–79. Hirsch, 220.

they would not stop there, but seek to be politicians themselves and so on. And if married women were to be given the vote—admittedly Mill had not suggested that, but... heaven forbid!

This was not the first time Oliphant had criticized Bodichon and it wouldn't be the last time she laid into Mill.[54] In each case her argument distinguished between the theoretical and legal on one hand and the practical and moral on the other. It was essentially the same line of argument as suggested by the *Saturday Review*, but presented, as in Oliphant's articles of the late 1850s, in a reasonable and well-reasoned way, by one who could claim to speak for the very class of women she opposed. It was an argument thoroughly in sympathy with contemporary values, and one that gave the politicians the easiest of ways out. To make matters worse, the article was excerpted elsewhere and the inaccuracy at least had to be addressed, but the best Davies could do was to get Bodichon to write a short pamphlet, ten thousand copies of which, together with ten thousand copies of her SSA paper, were distributed by Davies on behalf of her committee.

The most interesting press response, from Davies's point of view, was that from Richard Hutton, who had become her regular sparring partner, in the *Spectator*. Hutton had already printed a letter in March (anonymously) from Cobbe, asking why the same arguments treated as unanswerable when applied to bricklayers should be treated with contempt if applied to women.[55] He had somewhat compromised the seriousness of her argument with the heading 'Class representation for petticoats', but it was a witty piece of writing that foreshadowed her famous article in *Fraser's* a couple of years later, 'Criminals, idiots, women and minors'.[56] 'What, then,' she wrote in March, 'is this class which is thus excluded from the franchise.... Possibly I may be an alien... or a criminal... or, at all events, a member of a class so small and inconsiderate that it has been overlooked by our legislators. None of these hypotheses will apply.'

When Hutton addressed the issue himself in June, his conclusion was that the proposal was premature. Women must show a glimpse of political capacity, diffused throughout their population, before talking of political rights, and this was unlikely to happen for a couple of generations at least. American women pushing the case talked a lot of inflated and empty nonsense. But there was praise for the petition itself, as a businesslike and politically able document, showing wise political and intellectual reserve.[57] He also published further letters by Cobbe, signed this time, and Helen Taylor,[58] and in later articles, published as the

---

[54] For Bodichon see Chapter 1. Margaret Oliphant, 'Mill on the subjection of women', *Edinburgh Review*, 130 (October 1869), 572–602; reprinted in Pyle, 109–40.

[55] *Spectator*, 39 (24 March 1866), 325–6.

[56] *Fraser's Magazine*, 78 (December 1868), 777–94.

[57] 'Women's petition for the franchise', *Spectator*, 39 (16 June 1866), 628–30.

[58] *Spectator*, 39 (16 June 1866), 663; ED to HT, 18 July 1866, 6 August 1866, 16 August 1866, *EDCL*, 182–4, 187–90, 192–3; Mitchell, 161.

158 DAVIES AND THE MID-VICTORIAN WOMEN'S MOVEMENT

campaign progressed, he elaborated on his position. In regard to opportunities for employment, including the professions, he was firmly on the women's side. He could see no reason for excluding them on grounds other than those applicable to men. How successful they would be, no one could say, but they should be free to try. But he was still against opening up degrees to women, other than for professional qualifications, because he did not believe that boys' and girls' education generally should follow the same track. And he was against giving women the vote because their political interests and notions were in general far less developed than men's of the same class and income. Indeed, spinster householders were in his view the least politically informed class of women.[59] Davies disagreed, of course, but at least the debate was as it should be, in her view: measured, reasoned, respectful.

When it came to the wording of new petitions to Parliament, Davies and Helen Taylor almost inevitably disagreed. In this case it seemed essential to Davies to keep Mill's support, and thus his daughter's, so she was willing to compromise— but not to give way. Taylor's view was that the principle of equality was paramount. The vote for women should be sought on the same basis as that for men. For Davies the key thing was to avoid any suggestion that the vote might be given to married women, and if possible to discourage anyone from even asking the question. That was, of course, the long-term aim, but at this stage it could only excite male opposition: it was unachievable in itself, and claiming it risked stirring up opposition to the women's movement generally and her own objectives specifically. There were also complications. It was agreed that there should be one petition from female householders (widows and single women) and another, general petition,[60] but it transpired that the latter was not straightforward. In the first place, the way the law was worded, there were a few married women who managed property, albeit not in their own name, and were legally householders. In the second place, the 'householder' qualification applied to the boroughs only, and not to the county seats, where the basis of the franchise was different and the general inclusion of women would include some single women living with their parents. These complications could be overcome, but only by complicating the language of the claim, which Taylor was reluctant to do.[61]

Discussions between Davies and Taylor appear to have continued quite amicably into the autumn, but when Davies formed her new committee she made it clear that it (i.e. she) would have the final say on the wording, as indeed it did, signing off on it at the end of November.[62]

---

[59] 'Justice to women', *Spectator*, 40 (13 April 1867), 410–12; 'Mr Mill's case for women', ibid. (25 May 1867), 574–5.

[60] Davies initially favoured separate petitions from each borough, but was talked out of that.

[61] ED to HT, 18 July 1866, 4 August 1866, 6 August 1866, *EDCL*, 182–90.

[62] ED to BB, 17 September 1866, *EDCL*, 202–3; ED to HT, 15 October 1866, 31 October 1866, 26 November 1866, *EDCL*, 207–15; HT to ED, 26 October 1866, FC, 501–4; Mitchell, 165.

Davies had won her battle. Moderate liberal opinion appeared to be on her side, the committee was under her control, and the petition was worded as she preferred. When the petitions were circulated and funds raised for the purpose, Taylor took no part, effectively running her own campaign with an article in the *Westminster*, of which Davies would not have approved, arguing that it was the exclusion of women from the franchise that was anomalous, not their inclusion. A question of rights again.[63] When the London petition came to be presented to Parliament at the end of March, it was by the eminently respectable Gladstonian Liberal, Henry Bruce, soon to be home secretary and Lord Aberdare. Mill presented a more strongly worded petition from Elizabeth Wolstenholme's Manchester committee and Davies escaped any association with the Radicals.

Davies's London committee, her object achieved, soon fell apart. In February, Louie Garrett Smith died from appendicitis. Bodichon was nominally made secretary but was ill with typhoid fever. Davies continued doing the bulk of the work but her mind was very much on other things. She went through the motions and tried to maintain control but this wasn't her battle and it showed. Boucherett complained to Helen Taylor, who had presumably complained to her, that things were being poorly managed, and that this was because Davies 'knows so little of what is going on'. Taylor complained that she wasn't being consulted. Had her letters to Davies given offence? I can't see how, replied Boucherett: Davies had no excuse, and 'the waste of our petition is altogether her fault'. She herself would have preferred to do things as Taylor had originally suggested, but with Taylor out of the country had thought it best to let Davies get on with things. 'I believe I was mistaken.' Mentia Taylor complained, again to Helen Taylor, that she felt like a pariah, received no support or sympathy from the rest of the committee, and was regarded by them 'as a dangerous, go-a-head revolutionary person'. A new committee was needed. The day after writing this she dined with Fawcett, John Bright, and Frances Cobbe and shared her frustrations.[64]

Somehow the committee struggled on, but the rival camps could not agree on how to move forward. The old arguments about whether or not men should be included resurfaced, and when Mill's proposed amendment to the new reform bill, replacing the word 'men' by the word 'persons', failed, Davies withdrew.[65] As she wrote to Anna Richardson, 'It is a great relief to me to get away from uncongenial companionship and to abandon the vain effort to work with Radicals. Heaven protect me from trying it again!'[66] The committee disbanded and a new

---

[63] 'The ladies' petition', *Westminster Review*, n.s. 31 (January 1867), 63–79. ED to LB, 25 February 1867, *EDCL*, 229–30.

[64] Jessie Boucherett to HT, 9 April 1867, 14 April 1867, LSE MILL-TAYLOR 12/58, 60. MT to HT, 4 March 1867, LSE MILL-TAYLOR 13/264. See Crawford, *The Women's Suffrage Movement*, 207; Andrew Rosen, 'Emily Davies and the women's movement', *Journal of British Studies*, 19 (1979), 118–19. Mitchell, 167–71.

[65] ED to AR, 14 June 1867, *EDCL*, 530.   [66] ED to AR, n.d., in Stephen, 118–19.

one was promptly formed, comprising Helen Taylor, Mentia Taylor, Cobbe, and Millicent Garrett, since April Mrs Henry Fawcett:[67] a women-only committee, but one in which three of the four women acted alongside their menfolk, the Radical MPs John Stuart Mill, Peter Taylor, and Henry Fawcett. After some argument over naming, the London Society for Obtaining Political Representation for Women was formed with an executive committee including, alongside the four founders, Mary Lloyd, Katherine Hare (daughter of the political reformer Thomas Hare), Margaret Bright Lucas (sister of John and Jacob Bright), Carolyn Stansfield (wife of the Radical MP James Stansfield), and Jane Hampson (a friend of Cobbe). Radical women, all of them wives and daughters of Radical politicians, plus Cobbe and her friends, who were never really comfortable in that company and had resigned by the end of the year.[68]

With the exception of Millicent Fawcett, the sister of her best friend, Davies would not be seriously troubled again by the London Radicals, who were not greatly interested in her other projects. In the process of the suffrage campaign, however, she had inadvertently helped to create another women's group that would trouble her, in Manchester.

Although Davies almost certainly didn't know it at this stage, Elizabeth Wolstenholme was a socialist, secularist, and freethinker.[69] Like Davies, she preferred to work with men rather than against them, but she was also very happy to work with Radicals, and in particular with Jacob Bright. Through Davies, she also secured introductions to two other women in the north-west, who would go on to play major roles in the women's movement: Josephine Butler, wife of a liberal clergyman, and Lydia Becker, a single woman best known as an amateur botanist. Butler and Wolstenholme embraced such radically different morals that they were bound eventually to split, but meanwhile they evidently got on very well and agreed on many things, and all three women were to work together on a range of campaigns. In respect of the suffrage, however, it was Becker who immediately took the lead.

Lydia Becker appears to have known nothing about the women's movement when, aged thirty-nine, she chanced on Bodichon's paper at the 1866 SSA congress. She was academically minded, a regular at BAAS conferences, and when the SSA came to her home town she attended, heard Bodichon's paper, and threw herself into the work. Davies provided her with contacts and much advice and

---

[67] Manton, 180–2. Elizabeth Garrett's first response to the engagement was to suggest she get the opinion of someone who knew them both, like Barbara, to which Millicent responded tartly that 'judging from Dr Bodichon's appearance, I should say that it is improbable that we should agree in the choice of husbands', quoted in Strachey, 27. See also David Rubinstein, 'Victorian feminists: Henry and Millicent Garrett Fawcett', in Lawrence Goldman, ed., *The Blind Victorian: Henry Fawcett and British Liberalism* (Cambridge University Press, 1989), 71–92.

[68] ED to BB, 3 June 1867, *EDCL*, 240–1; FC, 509–10; Hirsch, 223; Stephen, 118; Mitchell, 171–4.

[69] Wright, *passim*; Laura Schwarz, *Infidel Feminism: Secularism, Religion and Women's Emancipation in England, 1830–1914* (Manchester University Press, 2013), 154 ff.

VOTES FOR WOMEN? 161

arranged with Alford for a paper she wrote (and Davies, of course, edited) to appear in the *Contemporary Review*, arguing that the main thing against the proposal of female suffrage was its sheer novelty, and that there were no grounds on equity (not equality) for it to be rejected.[70] Although more radical than Davies (she believed in universal suffrage and was, privately, a rationalist in religion), Becker shared both her commitment to respectability (dress, behaviour, established church) and her determination and administrative skills.[71]

The suffrage campaign was not successful. Mill's 1867 amendment was defeated by 196 votes to 73, a respectable minority but nowhere near enough to make any impact, or indeed to require the majority of MPs to bother voting at all. The whole debate, moreover, was accompanied by much laughter, many treating it as a joke, not even worth taking seriously.[72] Becker was not to be discouraged, however. Indeed, she seems to have believed that the campaign was nearly won.[73] For the next decade, she and Jacob Bright would lead a continuing campaign, both petitioning Parliament and encouraging women who would be eligible to vote if men to get themselves onto the electoral register.[74] Each year Jacob Bright introduced a new bill. Each year the troops were rallied and articles written: Mill, Bright, Fawcett, Cobbe, Becker, Faithfull, Millicent Fawcett, John Morley, Richard Pankhurst, Lady Amberley, Julia Wedgwood. Each year the *Saturday Review*, representing mainstream opinion, insisted that it wasn't actually that important but would nevertheless be disastrous. 1868: were it just a matter of a few thousand women voting, whose political education was of course incomplete, it would be no great matter. The only question is, what next? 'We are afraid that... suffrage in itself will not prove to be the boon which all human beings (artisans, women, niggers, and dockyard clerks) believe it to be.' (The word 'nigger' was already derogatory and offensive in the 1860s but it was widely used, especially in respect of emancipated Black people, both by frank racists, most notably Carlyle, and by those who wouldn't have thought themselves racists but took it for granted as scientifically established that Black people were biologically inferior.) 1869: the claim may be for the suffrage, but what is really at issue is the perfect and entire equality of the sexes. 1870: women constitute 'a sex which is invariably incapable of understanding that some things right in themselves cannot advantageously be

---

[70] Lydia Becker, 'Female suffrage', *Contemporary Review*, 4 (April 1867), 307–16. ED to LB, 3 January 1867, 7 January 1867, 12 January 1867, 14 January 1867, 17 January 1867, 19 January 1867, *EDCL*, 216–20; EDCL, 216; Wright, 60–3; Williams, 28 ff. Williams suggests that Davies acted as Becker's mentor.

[71] On Becker's political and religious commitments at this time see Williams, 19, 35. On her organizing ability see Jessie Boucherett to HT, 9 April 1867, LSE MILL-TAYLOR 12/58, and the memorial volume of the *Women's Suffrage Journal* (August 1890).

[72] As the *Saturday Review* had predicted: 23 (30 March 1867), 35, and as even Kate, Lady Amberley, like her husband a Radical protégée of Mill's, had to admit: *Amberley Papers*, Vol. 2, 36.

[73] Williams, 39.

[74] Jane Rendall, 'The citizenship of women and the Reform Act of 1867', in Hall, McClelland, and Rendall, eds., *Defining the Victorian Nation*, 119–78.

enforced.' 1871: The line between voting and not voting 'corresponds pretty fairly to that distinction between the proper functions of the two sexes which we have endeavoured to indicate'. 1872: 'To give the franchise to women would be not only to upset the basis of our present social system, but also to plunge the country in anarchy and confusion.' 1874: a bluebottle is a formidable antagonist; female suffrage is ridiculous, but by harping on year after year it gets (quite wrongly) to be taken seriously. And so on.[75] In 1870 hopes were raised when Jacob Bright's bill passed its second reading, albeit on a small turnout. This was, wrote Mill, 'enormous progress'; for Lydia Becker, 'a great advance in public opinion'.[76] But Gladstone was having none of it and at committee stage it was heavily defeated—as it was each year. And for the time being, at least, and for many years to come, Davies kept well out of it.

[75] *Saturday Review*, 26 (5 September 1868), 323-3: 323; 28 (24 July 1869), 107–8; 29 (2 April and 21 May 1870), 435–6, 662-3: 623; 31 (21 January and 6 May 1871), 71–2, 557–8: 557; 33 (3 February and 4 May 1872), 149–50, 550-1: 551; 35 (3 May 1873), 569–70; 37 (11 April 1874), 454-5. For a detailed account see Martin Pugh, *The March of the Women: A Revisionist Analysis of the Campaign for Women's Suffrage, 1866–1914* (Oxford University Press, 2002).

[76] Rendall, 'The citizenship of women', 119.

10

Towards the Higher Education of Women

When Jessie Boucherett and others complained in the spring of 1867 that Emily Davies was mismanaging the suffrage campaign, and knew 'so little of what is going on', they were almost certainly right. Davies was trying to keep control, but for several months her focus had been on other things. Part of her reason for taking over and trying to control the suffrage campaign had been to protect her own projects and, as she saw it, the women's movement generally, from reputational harm. In her view a radical, rights-based clamour could only excite opposition and set everything back. In respect of her own educational projects, the move was initially precautionary, but in early 1867 she embarked on a new project to establish, from scratch, a university-level college for women. That spring it was still in the ideas stage, but it must have dominated her thinking.

Looking at the challenges of the women's movement at that time—married women's property, the vote, divorce, prostitution—it would be easy to dismiss a new college as being of secondary importance. It could only impact directly on a minuscule sector of the population, and one that was already relatively advantaged. It required no change in the law, or even in university statutes. But it was to be of immense symbolic significance and would have enormous indirect consequences and repercussions. It would also be an extraordinary achievement. This was not a question of a rich philanthropist pursuing a pet project; or of the proprietors or governors of a secondary school expanding into tertiary education; or of a men's college or university branching out or spinning off something to cater for women; or of a programme of lectures for women establishing a residence or formalizing its qualifications. All of these would quickly follow and were comparatively straightforward. This was one woman with no formal educational herself, no teaching experience, no academic or intellectual reputation, and, above all, no source of funding, establishing the country's first university-level, university-examined institution open to women.

At some point in the winter or spring of 1865–6, Davies wrote a short book (effectively a very long article in book form) entitled *The Higher Education of Women*. As in the objectives of the London Association of Schoolmistresses, which she set up at this time, 'higher education' encompassed secondary education onwards. University education is only mentioned explicitly very briefly towards the end. This was part of the strategy, however. Emphasizing the distinction between school and university could only serve those who wished to preserve the latter for boys. Davies's approach was to ask what the most appropriate

Emily Davies and the Mid-Victorian Women's Movement. John Hendry, Oxford University Press. © John Hendry 2024.
DOI: 10.1093/oso/9780198910237.003.0010

164   DAVIES AND THE MID-VICTORIAN WOMEN'S MOVEMENT

education in preparing girls for womanhood would be, and to follow where that led.

The book was written at around the time Davies was presenting evidence to the Schools Inquiry Commission; discussing with Buss how girls' schools might be improved; and asking herself what the next step might be now that girls were being admitted to the local examinations. It followed a paper by Elizabeth Wolstenholme to the 1865 SSA congress in 1865, and a decision by London University to look again at examinations for women. Davies will also have been aware of growing interest in the topic more generally, and in particular of two recent articles by distinguished intellectuals.

Back in the spring of 1865, following the passing of the 13th Amendment, abolishing slavery in the United States, Thomas Huxley had written a curious article for the *Reader*.[1] This picked up on the analogy of the emancipation of enslaved people with the emancipation of women, but applied it to duties rather than rights. Huxley believed that, on the basis of current science, Black people were statistically—though not individually—inferior intellectually to whites. Though freed from slavery they would consequently lose out in the Darwinian competition of American society, and it was in his view a duty on the American government to address this. Where nature made humans unequal, men had a fundamental moral duty to alleviate that inequality, not to make it worse. He didn't think women inferior to men in the same way, but even if they were, that would in itself be a reason for improving their education, not constraining it, and in particular for admitting them to universities.[2]

> Let us have "sweet girl graduates" by all means. They will be none the less sweet for a little wisdom; and the "golden hair" will not curl less gracefully outside the head by reason of there being brains within. Nay, if obvious practical difficulties can be overcome, let those women who feel inclined to do so descend into the gladiatorial arena of life...Let them, if they so please, become merchants, barristers, politicians. Let them have a fair field, but let them understand, as the necessary correlative, that they are to have no favour. Let Nature alone sit high above the lists, "rain influence and judge the prize."

The other contribution had been a lecture by John Ruskin, 'Lilies: of queens' gardens', published in his small volume *Sesame and Lilies*.[3] Ruskin was at this time an opponent of Huxley in respect of the Eyre case, and he had a much lower view of Black people. He also had a lower view of women, and while he agreed with Davies that the existing girls' education was bad, and even wanted girls to be

---

[1] Thomas Huxley, 'Emancipation—black and white', *The Reader*, 5 (20 May 1865), 561–2; *Lay Sermons, Addresses and Reviews* (Macmillan, 1870), 23–30.

[2] Huxley, *Lay Sermons*, 28–9.   [3] John Ruskin, *Sesame and Lilies* (Smith, Elder & Co, 1865).

TOWARDS THE HIGHER EDUCATION OF WOMEN 165

taught the same as boys—with the exception of theology, which he thought dangerously beyond them—he was adamant that their education should nevertheless be very different:[4]

> All such knowledge should be given her as may enable her to understand, and even to aid, the work of men: and yet it should be given, not as knowledge,—not as if it were, or could be, for her an object to know; but only to feel, and to judge.... [A] girl's education should be nearly, in its course and material of study, the same as a boy's; but quite differently directed.... [S]peaking broadly, a man ought to know any language or science he learns, thoroughly—while a woman ought to know the same language, or science, only so far as may enable her to sympathise in her husband's pleasures, and in those of his best friends.

Huxley's paper will not have been widely read, though Davies will certainly have seen it, but Ruskin was extremely influential and hence dangerous.

In this context, Davies will have wanted to set out her own stall, both claiming for herself the territory of the higher education of women and setting out the kinds of arguments she thought might carry weight, not only with the converted but with the middle ground. Her specific recommendations were much the same as Wolstenholme's, and in line with the evidence they both gave to the Schools Inquiry Commission.[5] But the tone was much gentler. The whole book is calm, modest, and unthreatening, and while it is quite witty in places, the wit is very gentle and benign. More significantly, the framing of the argument is quite distinctive.

Despite its progressive conclusion—that the education of girls and boys should be essentially the same, and examinations at all levels open to them equally— Davies's book is socially conservative. The best education for a woman will be that which prepares her best to be a wife, mother, and mistress of a household. It should also prepare her to help her husband with his business where required, and to gain appropriate employment where necessary, but the family role takes priority.

In determining what the best outcomes should be, the book is also explicitly Christian. Men and women are assuredly different, but they are first and foremost children of God. Their natures overlap. More specifically, the ideal woman is primarily a child of God, and secondarily a wife and mother, not the other way around. This chimes with what Davies's brother, Llewelyn, was writing at the same time in his commentaries on St Paul, and with broad church teaching more

---

[4] Ibid., 155, 160–1.
[5] Elizabeth Wolstenholme, 'What better provision ought to be made for the education of girls of the upper and middle-classes', *TNAPSS*, 9 (1865), 287–91; and see also 'The education of girls, its present and its future', in Josephine Butler, ed., *Women's Work and Women's Culture* (Macmillan, 1869), 290–330.

166 DAVIES AND THE MID-VICTORIAN WOMEN'S MOVEMENT

generally.[6] Quoting from the baptismal service and catechisms, Davies argued that the primary purpose of education from a Christian perspective was to help one lead a Christian life, follow the example of Christ, glorify God, and so on—and that this recognized no distinction of sex. Both men and women were created in God's image, and while they might serve different roles their fundamental duties were the same. Teaching women to think of family claims as embracing their whole duty—to serve man rather than God—would be harmful not only to their own lives but also to those of the men they served.

Combining the progressive, the socially conservative, and the Christian in Davies's form of Liberal Conservatism is an approach wholly characteristic of the broad church: a fundamental but adaptive Christianity, maintaining its Christian values but adapting these to a changing world. A central feature of Davies's argument is that with servants and new technologies, the task of household management has changed. In past times, the years after a girl's schooling might have been considered as a training in household management, much as the years after a boy's schooling were seen as an education (through university, apprenticeship, or training) in the business of life. It was productive. The management of a household nowadays, however, and other household duties (kitchen, nursery, needlework) took up very little time. Between school and marriage, the very years in which an adult's character was formed, a girl lived a life of leisure and idleness, and while she might turn to pastimes, to be satisfied with mere vanities was neither Christian nor virtuous. If a young woman had energy she needed direction. If not, she needed a stimulus: surely the time should be used as it used to be, productively.

What, then, were the skills needed to manage a household? If it were to correspond to the English ideal of a harmonious, well-ordered home, the requirements were for imagination, combined with sensitivity and refinement, to recognize what was wanting; and prudence, foresight, judgement, and careful decision-making, to ensure that that was what was delivered. The ideal training for this? A liberal education, first and foremost, combined with some training in practical judgement, perhaps through experience of business or a profession.

Beyond this, if a lady was well provided for by her husband or father, what was called for seemed to be something corresponding to the education given to young men by the universities. This ought to mean the highest and finest culture of the time, together with the accurate habits of thought associated with intellectual scholarship. Quite apart from what this would bring to social intercourse and the tone of society, the duties of a lady typically required both varied and extensive knowledge and a disciplined mind. She was expected to act herself and guide others on difficult matters of ethics; to make difficult judgements on the treatment of paupers and the management of hospitals, workhouses, prisons,

---

[6] J. Llewelyn Davies, *The Epistles of St Paul to the Ephesians, the Colossians, and Philemon* (Macmillan, 1866), 58, 72–3.

reformatories, and charitable organizations; to put into practice in church schools policies on national education, and so on. In all of these a well-trained mind and a body of knowledge based on a large and liberal culture, combined with practical judgement, would surely be a more reliable resource than mere feminine instinct and gushing benevolence.

The same kind of education would also provide the appropriate basis for women who might work in the arts, and especially for those who might become teachers themselves. If a woman had to engage in other lines of work, to assist her husband or earn her own living, the education appropriate would depend on the work: book-keeping, farming, the supervision of women labourers or nurses (Davies was careful to stick mainly to traditional female employment roles), plus of course medicine, would each require their own training.

All this seemed to suggest that the content of female education should be essentially the same as that of male education. There was, Davies noted, a widespread view that they should be different, but no clear view on how they should differ, or even on what the content of a boy's education should be. The current situation was, in her word, 'whimsical', as boys who travelled on business learned classics while girls learnt conversational French and German that they might never use. Men, expected to play a part in political life, learnt maths, while girls, forbidden from doing so, learnt history. There was, however, a common ground in English literature, and to a large extent men and women read the same books, magazines, and newspapers. And what mattered, anyway, was less what was taught than how and, allowing for variety in both, what general improvement could be made.

Onto this structure, Davies added responses to some of the common objections. Were men and women not complementary? Yes, but with a strong core of common values. A man with no female qualities would be monstrous and vice versa. Might not so similar an education lead to an unwelcome similarity between men and women? No: having one group knowledgeable and the other ignorant hardly made for welcome diversity. The difference between men and women lay not in different knowledge or values but in different approaches to the same knowledge and values. Might not over-educated women lose interest in their husbands' concerns? On the contrary, they would understand them much better, and an active mind must always make for a better partner than a dead one. Why should fathers pay for their daughters' education, knowing that they would probably be married? If they married money it wouldn't matter; if they didn't it would be a valuable investment.

The book was published by Alexander Strahan, proprietor of the *Contemporary Review*, in the summer of 1866. Cobbe and Helen Taylor professed themselves delighted, the former particular enjoying the 'quiet sarcasm'.[7] The reviews when

---

[7] FPC to ED, n.d., FC, 479–80. HT to ED, 18 June 1866, FC, 480–1.

168 DAVIES AND THE MID-VICTORIAN WOMEN'S MOVEMENT

they came were generally encouraging, albeit mainly in what Davies termed 'dubious sources', with thoroughly positive notices in the *Contemporary* (unsurprisingly) and *Westminster*.[8] The first responses in print, however, and the most interesting from Davies's perspective, were by Richard Hutton, writing in both the *Spectator* and the *Economist* in early July.

The immediate context was a new move by London University, where Hutton was a member of the annual committee of convocation and, from 1866, of the senate. On the initiative of Joshua Fitch and Ebenezer Charles, the university had set up a subcommittee of the annual committee to look at examinations for women. This had met in early 1866, with Charles taking upon himself the task of advancing the women's case, and liaising on this with Davies.[9] The resulting report was agreed by the convocation in May and by the senate in June, and it was not what Davies would have wanted. The recommendation was that the university should institute examinations for women at the level of the university's matriculation exams, but that these should be 'special examinations', neither the same as those for men nor acting as matriculation examinations.[10] An amendment proposed by Grote as vice-chancellor would have omitted the words 'special in nature', but this was narrowly defeated.[11]

This was by now a familiar problem: arbitrary limits imposed on women without any evidence to justify them, and exams which, being for women only, would not be taken seriously. Davies wrote to Grote before the final vote to say that special examinations for women were not desirable (as shown by his amendment he was sympathetic), and rather tartly to Hutton: 'the people who are interested in improving the education of women are a thankless crew. Instead of accepting as a great boon, the admission of women to the London University Exmns. 'in the manner proposed', they have come to the conclusion that they do not consider a special examn. any boon at all, & will have nothing to do with it.'[12]

Hutton responded equally tartly: 'I think you are thankless, & I think moreover that you will have no choice in the matter. What is proposed we did not propose

---

[8] ED to HRT, 28 September 1866, *EDCL*, 205–7: 207; ED to BB, 17 September 1866, *EDCL*, 202–3; 'Woman's work', *Manchester Guardian* (supplement), 12 September 1866; 'The higher education of women', *Pall Mall Gazette*, 14 September 1866; *Nonconformist*, 12 September 1866; *Westminster Review*, n.s. 30 (October 1866), 487–9; *Contemporary Review*, 4 (January 1867), 286–7.

[9] EC to ED, 14 February 1866, FC, 453–4; ED to BB, December 1865, 19 February 1866, *EDCL*, 166–9; ED to RHH, spring 1866, *EDCL*, 171–3. Willson, 101. The editors of *EDCL* take this to be Albert Onesiphorus Charles, secretary of the Reformatory Union, but it was in fact Ebenezer Charles, a barrister on the annual committee: Willson, 101.

[10] Willson, 102–3. EC to ED, 25 April 1866, 9 May 1866, FC, 457–8, 459; WS to ED, 10 May 1866, FC, 459.

[11] FC, 460; *EDCL*, 170, Richard Hutton, 'Masculine monopolies', *Economist*, 24 (7 July 1866), 793–4; Willson, 104. This was not the end of the story, as in August the Crown law officers opined that the university's charter prevented even this. It was to be another year before a supplementary charter was approved, and May 1869 before the first of these special examinations, now called 'general examinations', was held. Willson, 105–9.

[12] ED to RHH, 2 June 1866, *EDCL*, 170–1.

TOWARDS THE HIGHER EDUCATION OF WOMEN 169

for you enlightened ladies but for girls, & if girls accept the boon how can you middlewomen come in & cut them off from what we propose? We did not, as far as I know, grant you anything. We offered something to girls in general & I shall be surprised if your influence proves so mischievously great as to prevent its being accepted.'[13] Like seeking the vote, her wishes were 'altogether premature'. When women were better educated, that might be the time to consider what their specific strengths and weaknesses were vis-à-vis those of men, and whether their education should be the same.

Hutton was both influential and representative of moderate liberal opinion generally, and he had been more supportive of the women's case for improvement than most, so this was an important debate. A further exchange followed and then Hutton put his views in print.[14] The *Economist* article covered both Davies's book and a meeting of the Female Medical Society, which offered courses for women midwives. The latter, he suggested, was an example of how educated women might fill valuable niche roles and he used the article:[15]

> to protest against those exclusive customs founded purely on prejudice which so often shut out women from the higher labour markets without even permitting them to try what they can do at all. It seems to us perfectly obvious that if women's powers are inadequate to various branches of professional labour in which they are ambitious to succeed, there is no means of proving it so good as letting them try, and fail; and if they are adequate either to the highest or, as is more likely, to some quieter side-branches of the professions hitherto inadequately attended to [e.g. midwifery], we shall get quite a new advantageous division of labour such as all the principles of true economy show to be the conditions of a great advance in productive industry.

Women might fill 'crevices' in the professions, but without actually entering them, or threatening male dominance.

Moving on to the London University vote, Hutton noted Davies's 'able and thoughtful' book but insisted that she had pushed her principles 'a step too far'. In practical pursuits, he argued, the test was success or failure and the experiment should be tried. But a degree examination effectively determined the channel which the education leading up to it would pursue. No doubt if the examination were offered, schools would prepare for it and women would pass it. But the consequence would be to submit them to a course of education that might well prove to be quite undesirable for girls, solely on the grounds that it was what had been

---

[13] RHH to ED, 4 June 1866 in FC, 462–3: 462; *EDCL*, 171.
[14] *Economist*, 24 (7 July 1866), 793–4; *Spectator*, 39 (7 July 1866), 751; RHH to ED, 7 July 1866, in FC, 475, and ED to RHH, July 1866, *EDCL*, 181–2.
[15] *Economist*, 24 (7 July 1866), 793.

170 DAVIES AND THE MID-VICTORIAN WOMEN'S MOVEMENT

developed for boys. If higher education were to be developed for girls it should be designed for girls, and should be carefully thought through and prepared for. The same point was made, more briefly, in the *Spectator* review. The familiar objection to competition between boys and girls wasn't raised explicitly but was clearly implicit, at least in the *Economist* article.

Davies signed off her exchange with Hutton by claiming that[16]

> we expect to get from Cambridge examns. for the [London women's] Colleges...The same papers with the same standard as those for the University examn. will be used. Only College students will be allowed to go in & the final Certificates will certify the having passed thro' a prescribed course of instruction & discipline, which seems to me a better thing than a mere certificate of knowledge. It will be equivalent to a Cambridge Degree, but at first...without the title or the formal sanction of the University. The arrangements have not yet been made, but we are told that there is not likely to be any difficulty at Cambridge.

In reality she had no such expectations, or if she did they were unfounded. Back in April, on hearing from Edward Plumptre of the vacancy, she had applied for the post of assistant secretary at Queen's College. She recalled later that her idea was that she might lead the college into some sort of affiliation with Cambridge, and while this might not have been her initial reason for applying, it had probably become so by early May, when the news from London University came through.[17] She did not get the post, but the idea evidently lived on and while it came to nothing in itself it did set off a further train of events.

Davies's idea now was that the London girls' colleges might upgrade their teaching from secondary to tertiary level, following the Cambridge syllabus and taking the Cambridge degree examinations—informally at first—on the same basis as girls were now taking the local examinations. In September she wrote to Plumptre that she had been invited to give a talk to the Manchester Board of Schoolmistresses, chiefly about Queen's:[18]

> I find among the higher class of schoolmistresses in all parts of the country, a strong disposition to put themselves into friendly relations with the London Colleges. They wd. like their schools to be to the Colleges what the Public Schools are to the Universities, but with that view they want the Colleges to be really places of higher education than schools can be....I do not see how this can be got over excepting by raising the age of the College students & giving them some higher kind of examn. than any that is open to schools. I believe

---

[16] ED to RHH, July 1866, *EDCL*, 181–2.   [17] FC, 456.
[18] ED to EP, September 1866, *EDCL*, 203–5.

there wd. be no difficulty in getting these from Cambridge, if the Colleges are willing to accept what the University has to give, that is, the examns. for ordinary Degrees. Mr Markby thinks there wd. be no objection to holding examns. in the same papers, to be judged by the same standard, simultaneously with the examn. at Cambridge. . . . It wd. have to be done informally at first, as an experiment. If it were to be made permanent on the part of the University, some guarantee wd. probably be required as to the discipline of the College. It seems to me that this kind of affiliation to Cambridge wd., in the case of Queen's College, be much more satisfactory than anything we are likely to get from the London University, & I am sure it wd. make the College much more popular with the schools & more looked up to in the country generally than it now is.

Anything attributed to others is almost certainly a cover for her own views, though Markby had presumably been consulted.

Plumptre, not surprisingly, disagreed. He saw no reasons for changing the way the college operated, and several reasons why such a change would be undesirable. Bedford College appears to have given a similar response, except that in their case their secular constitution effectively ruled out a link with Cambridge.[19]

The Manchester meeting was timed to coincide with that year's SSA congress in the same city, attended as usual by many members of the women's movement. Bodichon gave her paper on the franchise, Garrett one on the professionalization of nursing superintendence. Davies went up via Leeds, where Fitch was addressing a local meeting of schoolmistresses on the local examinations, and via visits to friends in the north. She didn't give an SSA paper, but delivered her talk to the Manchester schoolmistresses and came out of it with a new plan, which she relayed in a letter to Helen Taylor—perhaps seeking to counter the impression that Taylor was being frozen out of the suffrage campaign by involving her on other matters. 'Two facts were distinctly brought up' at the schoolmistresses' meeting, she reported: '1. That the schools want a place of higher education for which to prepare their pupils, which should be to them what the Universities are to boys' schools. and 2. that the existing ladies' Colleges do not supply the want.'[20] They had, of course, been brought up by herself. Her response was a new plan:[21]

The only resource seems to be to found a new College. If we could start a College on a broad Church basis, accepting the University examns. as they are, and accepting as much control as the University might desire, but with a Conscience clause effectively securing that religion should not be forced upon anybody that

---

[19] EP to ED, 29 September 1866, *EDCL*, 205; ED to HT, 15 October 1866, *EDCL*, 207–10; FC, 494.
[20] ED to HT, 15 October 1866, *EDCL*, 207–10: 209.
[21] Ibid., 210. The letter was phrased as seeking Taylor's support, but as Davies must surely have foreseen, Taylor, an atheist, was not going to support an explicitly church venture.

172 DAVIES AND THE MID-VICTORIAN WOMEN'S MOVEMENT

did not want it, I believe we might get affiliated to Cambridge, & that by so doing we should not only get the direct advantages of having one College connected with one of the old Universities, but should also shame the University of London into opening its exams. We should be able to say, "Here are Churchwomen able to get a University examn., & Dissenters are excluded from what professes to be their own University."

Ten days later, in a letter to Anna Richardson, Davies added physical substance to the idea:[22]

I am very glad you like the idea of the College—people take to it so kindly that I have great hopes of seeing it done some day. Mrs Bodichon is quite fired by the vision of it.... It is to be as beautiful as the Assize Courts at Manchester and with gardens and grounds and everything that is good for body, soul and spirit. I don't think I told you how intensely we enjoyed the beauty of the Assize Courts. I have seen no modern building to be compared with it, and the delight we felt in it made one realize how much one's happiness may be influenced by external objects. If Mr Waterhouse will build us a college as noble and beautiful, Mrs. — shall have a high place in it as a reward.

Alfred Waterhouse's Assize Courts, which did indeed become the model for Girton College, were the venue for several Social Science Association social events during the congress, but it reads as though Davies, and perhaps Bodichon too, had also had a private visit arranged by 'Mrs —'.[23]

Two questions immediately come to mind. First, on what basis if any was Davies confident that Cambridge would go along with her scheme, had Queen's College been persuaded? She seems to have had some exchange with Markby, then the secretary of the Local Examinations Syndicate, but the correspondence is no longer extant and this was not a matter of local examinations but, so to speak, the real thing, degree examinations. Presumably she wrote to him over the summer, outlining her proposal, and he gave some kind of positive or at least non-committal reply, on which she could draw as 'evidence' that the proposal would be workable. He was certainly a supporter of both women's education and

---

[22] ED to AR, 25 October 1866, in Stephen, 149.

[23] The original letter, no longer extant, presumably named the lady. Crawford, 120, suggests that it may have been Hannah Ford, who was then one of Waterhouse's clients. Ford was from a prominent Quaker family, would almost certainly have been known to Anna Richardson, and as an active supporter of women's education quite probably met Davies at the meeting of schoolmistresses in Leeds. Her daughters, Emily and Isabella, were still teenagers, but would themselves become important figures in the women's movement. John Ford, who seems to have been her brother-in-law, was headmaster of Bootham School and a prominent Quaker who was certainly known to Richardson. Se Richardson, 143, 177.

TOWARDS THE HIGHER EDUCATION OF WOMEN   173

the university's role in it. But Markby was neither important nor influential in the university, and she would surely have known that.

The second question is, what exactly prompted the thought of a new college? Here we are reliant on memories, both conflicted and unreliable. Many years later, in late 1882, Bodichon objected to seeing Davies described, in relation to her portrait, as 'originator' of the college. Davies explained that this had arisen only because she had herself objected to being described as 'the founder'. She would have preferred 'one of the founders', but had suggested 'originator' as an accurate alternative, should that have been thought preferable. Constance Jones (later to be mistress), who was in charge of the matter, had preferred it and she had 'let it go'.[24] At the outset of the college, Bodichon, writing to Helen Taylor, had in fact disclaimed the label originator herself:[25]

I do not think that I deserve to be called the originator of the College for though ever since my brother went to Cambridge I have always intended to aim at the establishment of a college where women could have the same education as men if they wished it, I certainly could not have carried out the plan as Miss Davies has done. I am not strong enough, or orthodox enough.

Feeling grumpy about other matters, however, she had now demurred and a few weeks later Davies wrote again, staking her claim:[26]

As to the early history of the College, I think from something said in a letter from Amy Moore [Bodichon's niece], that you must be under a mistake about dates. I understand you to be under the impression that the beginning of the College dates from my visit to you at Scalands in August, 1867. That is not the case. The idea of starting a new College suggested itself to me on Oct. 6th, 1866, after a meeting of Schoolmistresses at Manchester. By February 1867, I had arrived at the printed Programme. In sending this to Mr Plumptre...I wrote as follows. "The project [grew out of a meeting of Schoolmistresses...]" You see, these preliminary steps were being taken while you were at Algiers or somewhere abroad; so that it must be a mistake to speak of conversations at your house 'which led to the issue thence of the first letters on the scheme.'

In her Family Chronicle, Davies located her conception of the idea still more specifically, on the drive back to her Manchester hosts after the schoolmistresses' meeting. She shared it with Isa Knox and George Hastings, who came to dinner,

---

[24] ED to BB, 21 December 1882, Girton GCPP Bodichon 1/197.
[25] BB to HT, 1 August 1869, LSE MILL-TAYLOR 12/50.
[26] ED to BB, 14 January 1883, Girton GCPP Bodichon 1/199 and see also ED to BB, 3 January 1883, Girton GCPP 1/198. See also Crawford, 119; Hirsch, 306.

174 DAVIES AND THE MID-VICTORIAN WOMEN'S MOVEMENT

and presumably soon after with Bodichon, who had also been in Manchester, though they may not have seen each other again until they returned to London.[27] Indeed, the language in which Davies wrote to Richardson ('with gardens and grounds and everything that is good for body, soul and spirit') is strongly suggestive of Bodichon's way of talking about things, and the suggestion is that the vision was one they discussed, either in Manchester or more likely in London after the congress and before Bodichon left for the winter. If the latter, then this might have got confused in Moore's account with the conversations in Sussex the following year. The idea of a women's college akin to the men's colleges was familiar to anyone who had read Tennyson's poem *The Princess*, a poem that had enthused Bodichon and Parkes in their youth, and Bodichon had no doubt raised the possibility herself many a time. She may well have felt that Davies's new idea was in some ways a joint one. But the particular conception was undoubtedly Davies's and its place and time Manchester that early October.

The new college was a bold project, to put it mildly. A grand Waterhouse building would not be cheap: Plumptre, startled at the magnitude of the enterprise, had suggested that at least £30,000 would be needed—not much had they been raising money for a boys' school, but a daunting figure for girls.[28] And the proposed link with Cambridge raised all sorts of issues. Admitting girls to the locals was one thing, but they were an external activity. Degrees were the core business of the university, and they were earned as much by residence as by examination. They were also intimately connected to the university's role as seminary for the Church of England priesthood, and the content—primarily mathematics, classics, and theology—raised the question of how far women's education should match that of men in an especially acute form. Undaunted, Davies circulated her ideas amongst friends and colleagues. Elisabeth Wolstenholme approved, as did Henry Roby and Mark Pattison, the broad church rector of Lincoln College, Oxford, whom she met on a visit to the Brodies.[29] All the Cambridge men with whom she had spoken, she reported to Anna Richardson, seemed to take to the idea.[30]

How many Cambridge men she had consulted she didn't say, but her acquaintance there was slight. Indeed, it seems to have been restricted mainly to those with whom she'd worked on the locals: Potts, Markby, and Liveing, none of whom carried much influence. Suitably encouraged, though, in February 1867 she had a

---

[27] FC, 500.

[28] ED to EP, February 1867, *EDCL*, 223; EP to ED, 14 February 1867, FC, 512; ED to BB, 29 January 1866, *EDCL*, 221–2; ED to AR, 4 February 1867, *EDCL*, 224–5.

[29] FC, 510, noting responses from Wolstenholme and Roby; ED to BB, 29 January 1867, *EDCL*, 220–2; ED to AR, 4 February 1867, EDCL, 224–5. The rather dry Pattison, author of a biography of Isaac Casaubon, and his wife Emilia (later Lady Dilke), a reviewer and art historian, are mostly remembered as originals of George Eliot's unhappy couple in Middlemarch, Edward and Dorothea Casaubon. But while his marriage could not be called successful, he was a consistent supporter of women and their causes.

[30] ED to AR, 29 December 1866, in Stephen, 149.

version of her proposal printed up and circulated to friends and colleagues. The challenge, she wrote, was to supply the want of education for women, higher than that currently provided:[31]

> In the hope of supplying the want which has been indicated, it is proposed to establish a College, in which the instruction and discipline will be expressly adapted to advanced students, and the results tested by sufficiently stringent examinations. It is intended to place the College in a healthy locality, about equidistant between London and Cambridge, thus putting it within reach of the best teaching in all the subjects of the College course. The religious instruction will be in accordance with the principles of the Church of England; but in cases where conscientious objections are entertained, such instruction will not be obligatory.

There would be 'University Examinations of an advanced character, open to, but not enforced upon, all students'. Summing up, 'the projected institution is designed to be, in relation to the higher class of girls' schools and home teaching, what the Universities are to the public schools for boys'.

Amongst the comments received, two issues were raised that would continue to be contentious. One was in respect of religion. Several of Davies's supporters were Unitarians, and Lady Goldsmid was Jewish. She sought to deal with this through a conscientious objection clause, but not everyone was happy with this. Moreover, as John Westlake pointed out, the very notion of religious 'instruction' was inappropriate. Cambridge undergraduates were not required to attend anything that could be called religious instruction, unless candidates for orders. There might be religious services, but that was another matter—and raised problems of its own. Westlake also asked pointedly who had promised university examinations of an advanced character, thus raising the question of exactly what examinations the women would take.[32]

In a revised version of the programme sent out a few months later, Davies stuck to her guns on religion but added some detail on the last point. 'Application will be made to the University of Cambridge to hold Examinations at the College in the subjects prescribed for the Ordinary (or Poll) Degree.' In case this arrangement should be found impracticable, it was proposed to hold equivalent examinations under the direction of the Local Examinations Syndicate. Periodical examinations would also be provided by the college in the range of subjects to be taught, including modern languages, music, drawing, and other subjects which

---

[31] FC, 516a.
[32] FC, 516, 516a. Samuel Steinthal, who will have been shown the programme by Elizabeth Wolstenholme or James Bryce, wrote with objections to the religious element.

176 DAVIES AND THE MID-VICTORIAN WOMEN'S MOVEMENT

'usually form part of the education of an English lady'. Students would be admitted from the age of sixteen upwards.[33]

The early age of entry, the inclusion of provisional girls' subjects, and college examinations were concessions to public opinion. The hope was presumably that girls might be admitted as if to a residential version of Queen's College but then progress to higher learning. The reference to the Local Examinations Syndicate was a long stop to appease doubters. Davies wanted degree examinations, not 'special' examinations such as that body might conceivably offer. The specification of examinations for the ordinary degree only, and not honours degrees, is curious. It may have been suggested as a suitably modest beginning, but many Cambridge men—including Davies's brother, Llewelyn, who would surely have enlightened her on the subject had she chosen to listen—thought the ordinary degree far too easy, far too narrow, and badly in need of reform.

The proposed location is also curious at first sight. Was Davies dreaming of a college like that of Tennyson's Lilia, were she a princess, 'far off from men', in Waterhouse gothic and wholesome air? The truth seems to be that she was worried about proprieties. Her college would be residential, on the Cambridge model, and must provide a safe and secure home from home, away from the distractions of the city, of young men, or, as she would later insist, of non-scholarly female society.

At the same time as developing her prospectus, Davies had also been looking at putting together a committee and raising funds, but neither at first made much progress. Her first call on funding was to Bodichon, but she was ill with typhoid fever and in no state to respond. Roby sounded out Lyttelton on chairing a general committee of the great and good, but seems at this stage to have got no further.[34] Then in April Davies's local examinations committee met and, having dealt with the normal business of the committee, she raised the question of 'the College project'.[35] Opinion was deeply divided. Lady Goldsmith, who was not present, had written to say she thought it premature: better to wait until the 'ferment about the Franchise was over'. Russell Gurney had also written suggesting Davies hold fire until she could say more about the domestic arrangements and pastoral care. In the meeting itself Fanny Wedgwood was also hesitant, worried about breaking the young women's ties with their homes. Hastings, Tomkinson, and Henry Clay, now on the committee, were strongly in support, but Bostock was strongly against, arguing that whatever might be needed Bedford College would offer. '[W]e were rather embarrassed in replying,' reported Emily, 'as it was awkward to insist that the people we expect to get have either never heard of Bedford College

---

[33] FC, 519a.

[34] ED to BB, 29 January 1867, 9 March 1867, *EDCL*, 220–2, 232; HR to ED, 27 February 1867, FC, 516–17; ED to EG, 30 March 1867, *EDCL*, 237. Lyttelton did eventually join a 'General Committee' for the new college.

[35] ED to BB, 6 April 1867, *EDCL*, 237–9.

TOWARDS THE HIGHER EDUCATION OF WOMEN 177

or despise it & won't think of going near it'—which would, of course, have been the case for Anglican families.[36]

In terms of the details, both Tomkinson and Clay thought the ordinary degree not worth going for: they should aim for honours. Davies seems to have treated this as humorous banter, but it was a serious point: insistence on an examination which Davies's most natural supporters in Cambridge—the liberal reformers—thought worthless might be counterproductive. What was apparent was that the details needed to be worked out more fully, and a wholly sympathetic executive committee assembled. At the beginning of June she circulated a revised version of the programme to friends and supporters, with a view to gathering feedback before beginning planning proper in the autumn. As she explained to Tomkinson, she wanted to know who amongst them would support her, and 'to hear everything that is to be said against the scheme. Please let me know the worst.'[37] It would in fact be November before a working committee was put together, but meanwhile one piece of feedback led to some frenetic activity, in the form of a memorial to the Schools Inquiry Commission.

This was instigated by James Bryce, a historian and lawyer, fellow of Oriel College, Oxford. Still in his twenties, Bryce was both a distinguished scholar and a political activist. (He would be elected Regius Professor of Civil Law in Oxford in 1870 and would go on to a distinguished political career.) He was also involved in a campaign for a new university in Manchester. He had corresponded at length with Davies while visiting schools in Lancashire for the Schools Inquiry Commission and she had sent him her programme drafts. In early June he responded enthusiastically, suggesting that a memorial be submitted to the commission requesting a grant for the proposed college.[38] Nothing came of this request, and Davies probably didn't expect anything to come from it, but she saw the memorial as a way of demonstrating support for her project, especially amongst the schoolmistresses. Having consulted Roby, Anne Clough, and her London Association of Schoolmistresses, she set things in motion. The memorial was submitted on 9 July, signed by 521 schoolmistresses and 175 distinguished supporters, ranging from the scientists Huxley, Tyndall, and Lyell to the poets Tennyson and Browning and, encouragingly, a number of Cambridge dons.[39]

Bryce also made some important observations on the programme. He didn't like Davies's solution to the religious difficulty (though he admitted he could see no alternative), and like Tomkinson and Clay he was scathing about the

---

[36] Ibid., 238. Barbara Bodichon, the recipient of the report, had studied at Bedford College herself, so one wonders what she would have made of this comment.

[37] ED to HRT, 1 June 1867, *EDCL*, 240; see also ED to BB, 28 May 1867, *EDCL*, 239; FC, 519. The local examinations committee decided *not* to take the project on themselves, and Davies's request for feedback was strictly supererogatory to that committee's work.

[38] JB to ED, 4 June 1867, FC, 519–21.

[39] FC, 525–9, 428a; ED to AR, 18 July 1867, *EDCL*, 242–3.

178 DAVIES AND THE MID-VICTORIAN WOMEN'S MOVEMENT

examinations for the ordinary degree, which he deemed 'really very bad & quite unworthy of a University....contemptibly low'. It would be much better, he suggested, to have new examinations of a higher standard, with the subjects better chosen and of more educational value.[40] The honours examinations were better, but he doubted whether they were as good as they could be, or (a warning sign for Davies) the 'fittest for a ladies' College'.

A week later he wrote again. He had been in Cambridge and had shown Davies's programme to Henry Sidgwick, a fellow of Trinity, who was an 'earnest sympathiser' but who also thought it a mistake to start with the ordinary degree examinations, which were of too low a standard to be really useful. Since the mathematical and classical triposes, for honours, were probably of too high a standard in the short term (not too high for girls, he stressed, but too far beyond what the girls' schools were teaching), it would be better to start with a new examination.[41] Two months later another Cambridge don, John Seeley, wrote in support of the project but arguing against copying Cambridge too closely, which he thought in a very bad state. He didn't mention the examinations specifically, but suggested that the German universities would be a much better model to follow.[42]

Bryce, Sigwick, and Seeley were to be important figures in what was to follow, and Sidgwick and Seeley especially so. Sidgwick was still in his late twenties but was influential beyond his years and already a leader of liberal reform in Cambridge. Seeley, a fellow of Christ's (and from 1869 Regius Professor of Modern History), was another Cambridge reformer, best known as the author of *Ecce Homo*, a recent historical study of Jesus the man and the impacts of his moral teaching, controversial in its complete avoidance of any mention of Jesus's divinity.[43] Like Sidgwick and others he was open to the higher education of women on terms equal to that of men, but strongly opposed to the existing Cambridge regime for men, and anything that reinforced it.

With the SIC memorial submitted and the arguments over the suffrage committee resolved, the summer passed relatively quietly. Davies was exhausted. Her mother, now into her late sixties, was unwell, 'pulled down by a kind of nervous prostration', perhaps as a result of living with Davies's stress levels. Barbara Bodichon was also still very weak, the effects of the typhoid fever exacerbated by domestic worries. She had failed to have the children she badly wanted; her husband was refusing to live in England or even learn English; and he and her sister Nannie, living next door in Algiers, were at loggerheads. Her most intimate friend, Bessie Parkes, had become engaged to a Frenchman, Louis Belloc, and would shortly be moving to France.[44]

---

[40] JB to ED, 4 June 1867, FC, 519–21, in Stephen, 155.
[41] JB to ED, 12–14 June 1867, FC, 522–4. [42] JS to ED, 15 August 1867, FC, 536–7.
[43] John Seeley, *Ecce Homo: A Survey of the Life and Work of Jesus Christ* (Macmillan, 1865). By 1866 this was already into its fifth edition.
[44] ED to AR, 18 July 1867, (24) August 1867, *EDCL*, 242–5 (Stephen, 162, cites a different version of the latter); Hirsch, 227 ff.

TOWARDS THE HIGHER EDUCATION OF WOMEN 179

In early August, Davies left her mother in the care of Annie Austin, now widowed and living immediately opposite in Cunningham Place (a house presumably found for her by Llewelyn Davies), and Lizzie Garrett, and went down to Bodichon's house in Sussex, where she spent nearly a month. This was part rest and recuperation, part planning. Davies and Bodichon had probably not seen each other for nearly a year, and had never spent this long together. The idea of a women's college was a dream for both of them, and Davies badly needed Bodichon's support, if only for her money and connections. But their dreams were not quite the same. Davies wanted a female equivalent of the men's colleges, with ladylike elements attached but with a wholly academic emphasis. Bodichon's vision was more embracing, closer to the ideal portrayed in *The Princess*. She was not at all interested in the Cambridge examinations, which were not, in her view, in any way ennobling. She had always described herself as a sanitarian and she *was* interested, passionately, in physical and moral education, and wanted to see those given a high place. She wanted, in particular, a professor of hygiene, ideally her friend Elizabeth Blackwell, and when pressed for financial support she initially offered £1,000 on condition that Blackwell be appointed.[45]

They also disagreed on the religious question. For Davies, the new college had to be, like the Cambridge men's colleges, a Church of England foundation. This was her strong personal preference, but it would also be a necessary condition, in her view, for both the respectability and the formal relationship with the university she hoped to achieve. Bodichon, from a dissenting background and at most a theist herself, could not agree. Davies insisted that anyone joining her college committee would have to sign up to a set of aims that included a commitment to a Church of England institution, and Bodichon would not join on those terms, so it was agreed she should not, her illness providing a good cover for their differences.[46]

Davies still needed Bodichon to commit her money, and here Bodichon brought in two of her friends to act as intermediaries. First Emily Blackwell, Elizabeth Blackwell's sister, suggested a compromise whereby Bodichon's initial condition be replaced by two others: a promise to provide for teaching in hygiene; and a condition that the £1,000, while pledged, would not be paid until the whole £30,000 had been raised. When Davies still resisted, she received an invitation from Mrs Lewes, aka Marian Evans aka George Eliot, at Bodichon's instigation, to pay her a visit and discuss the project.[47] Although Evans now lived just a few hundred yards away from Cunningham Place and was a close friend of Bodichon, it seems Davies had not yet met her, though she had met George Lewes. Evans didn't go out much, and many people would not visit on principle. Consulting her

---

[45] BB to ED, 31 October 1867, FC 540–1, in Hirsch, 247–8; ED to BB, 20 November 1867, *EDCL*, 246–8.

[46] Hirsch, 248.

[47] GE to ED, 16 November 1867, FC, 541–2 and Girton GCPP Davies 4/3.

180 DAVIES AND THE MID-VICTORIAN WOMEN'S MOVEMENT

friends, Davies found that both Emilia Gurney and Charlotte Manning took the view that it was alright to visit but not when others (including Lewes) were there, and Davies seems to have followed this guidance. Having once visited she could not stay away, and went back repeatedly, but she always made sure to catch Mrs Lewes alone.[48]

The outcome was that Davies agreed on the first condition, that the £1,000 should be a pledge, not an immediate donation. Teaching in hygiene was more difficult, Davies and Evans apparently agreeing that it was not so much teaching that was wanted as the formation of good habits under the guidance of ladies who would act as resident authorities. Davies agreed to bring in some wording to achieve this, but felt she could go no further and urged Bodichon to commit her money now, on trust, 'because this is the only way, as you will not be on the Committee, that you can be counted among the founders of the College. If you wait to see whether we do things in the proper manner, we shall not be able to reckon you among the believing few, who walk by faith and not by sight. It is quite clear to me that if the thing is to be done at all, there must be, not only faith in the idea, but trust in the people who are to carry it out.' Cold-blooded blackmail? Perhaps, but it worked. Barbara wrote back two days later that 'you can say you have my £1000 promised'.[49]

It was now late November, and Davies was also in the process of putting together a committee. Lyttelton declined to chair, explaining that as SIC commissioner in receipt of the memorial requesting funding he would be compromised,[50] but she hoped instead to get Henrietta, Lady Stanley of Alderley, and set down her hoped-for committee members, with the 'peculiar walk' she associated with each:[51]

Lady Stanley of Alderley.
Lady Goldsmid.   economy
Lady Hobart   sweetness
The Dean of Canterbury [Alford]   Gr[eek] Divinity
James Bryce, Esq.
Mrs [Emilia] Russell Gurney.   Drawing[52]
James Heywood, Esq.   Business
G. W. Hastings, Esq.   The World

---

[48] ED to CM, 25 November 1867, *EDCL*, 248–9; FC, 542.

[49] ED to BB, 20 November 1867, EDCL, 246–8: 247; BB to ED, 22 November 1867, FC, 552–3: 553.

[50] Lord Lyttelton to ED, 11 November 1867, FC 544.

[51] FC, 518; Girton GCPP Davies 15/1/1/3. Stephen, 161, following its location in the FC, dates this to early 1867, but the inclusion of Sedley Taylor dates it to November onwards.

[52] We know Emilia Gurney to have been a proficient pianist; she may also have been a watercolourist. Her real value, though, was in emotional support, of which she had enormous quantities to give. 'May you be strong in body soul & spirit for your great "Campaign",' she wrote when asked to join the committee: ERG to ED, 22 November 1867, in FC, 551–2: 552.

Mrs [Charlotte] Manning   Domestic morals
H. J. Roby, Esq.   Latin
H. R. Tomkinson, Esq.   Conciliation
Rev. Sedley Taylor   Music & Mathematics
E. D.   principles.

Two aspects of this list are immediately striking. One is the absence of the more prominent members of the women's movement. Davies recalled later that 'the list includes no one especially known as advocating the Rights of Women. It was felt to be important to put forward only such names as wd. be likely to win the confidence of ordinary people.'[53] The other is the absence of almost anyone from Cambridge. Tomkinson had responded to an earlier draft that, given that Cambridge degrees were sought: 'Shd. not some distinctly Cambridge names of the day be got for it?'[54] Davies had replied that Cambridge residents would not be able conveniently to attend meetings in London, that she hoped to set up a local committee there, and that she would be more open to young Cambridge men (for she supposed that they would all be young men) if she could get a few more old ladies to balance youth with experience. It happened that on receiving Tomkinson's letter she was away from home and that a fellow guest in the house was Sedley Taylor, then a fellow of Trinity, who had agreed there and then to join the committee, but he was the only one.[55] Of the others only Roby and Alford had held Cambridge positions, and not for seven and thirty years respectively.

Lady Stanley was the wife of the Liberal politician Lord Stanley (not to be confused with the liberal Conservative politician Lord Stanley). An intelligent, sometimes acerbic woman, descendant of both Charles II and James II, she was kept down by her husband, spending much of her time in Cheshire with her children (nine of whom survived infancy) while he did the political rounds. Often described as a lady from an earlier era, intelligent, rationalist, forthright (and on her son-in-law, Bertrand Russell's account, assured of her own superiority), she was passionate about education, giving her daughters a good liberal, if idiosyncratic, education at home. When in London, she attended Maurice's services, and through him became a visitor at Queen's College.[56] She signed Davies's educational memorials. Davies seems to have met her in the summer of 1866 through her daughter Kate Amberley, a strong feminist who became a patient and supporter of Elizabeth Garrett. Invited to join her weekly salons, she initially felt uncomfortable at mixing with the aristocracy but seems

---

[53] FC, 519.   [54] HRT to ED, 12 November 1867, FC 545–7: 546.

[55] ED to HRT, 15 November 1867, *EDCL*, 246.

[56] Josephine Kamm, *Indicative Past: A Hundred Years of the Girls' Public Day School Trust* (George Allen & Unwin, 1971), 21–4. Bertrand Russell, *Autobiography of Bertrand Russell*, Vol. 1 (Chatto & Windus, 1967), 32–4. Russell remembered her mainly for her caustic tongue, but he was not keen on the Stanleys generally and his sketches are gross caricatures.

182 DAVIES AND THE MID-VICTORIAN WOMEN'S MOVEMENT

to have persisted and sought her support.[57] At this stage Lady Amberley was much more interested in women's education than her mother, and had recently written to Davies with her observations of Vassar College, a higher education college for women founded in 1861 in New York State.[58] Whilst Davies had very much liked her on meeting, however, she was not only far too young to be considered for the committee, but was also fast acquiring a reputation as a political Radical.[59] She offered her services the following year, but noted that '[Miss Davies] did not wish to have my name on the Committee as she thought it was a very dangerous name.'[60]

In the event, Lady Stanley was 'prevented by her husband from joining us (dislikes publicity.).'[61] She was, however, keen to help privately. Her many children having all left home, her energies needed an outlet and she would eventually join the committee in 1872, after her husband's death. The other 'Lady' on the list, Lady Hobart, was the wife of the colonial administrator Vere Hobart, heir to the earldom of Buckinghamshire, and daughter of a former Bishop of Bombay. How and where they met we don't know—indeed, we know very little about her, other than that she served on Davies's college committee and was both diligent and compliant—excellent qualities in Davies's book.[62]

Bryce, who continued to disagree with Davies both in respect of the educational value of the Cambridge examinations and in respect of her insistence on the religious standing of the college, also withdrew.[63] Heywood, a Unitarian, also objected to the religious proposals but was persuaded to join the committee on the understanding that they might not actually be followed.[64] To 'represent the schoolmistresses' Davies recruited Fanny Metcalfe, headmistress of Highfields, a progressive girls' boarding school in Hendon.[65] On 5 December a college committee was formally instituted and Davies's programme was formally agreed together with four resolutions incorporating the principles she required all committee members to accept and a list of the initial members. It was also agreed

---

[57] ED to AM, summer 1866, and n.d., Stephen, 110; FC, 478.

[58] Stephen, 161–2; Amberley Papers, Vol. 2, 52. She also visited Oberlin, the Calvinist teaching of which repelled her, but which was noted not only for admitting Black students on equal terms to white but also for taking both men and women. Different courses were put on for the different sexes, but women could take the men's course and take degrees. Ibid., 62.

[59] ED to AM, n.d., Stephen, 110; Amberley Papers, Vol. 2, 37–9. In 1870, in a diatribe against women's rights, Queen Victoria observed that 'Lady Amberley ought to get a good whipping.' Victoria Regina to Theodore Martin, 29 May 1870, in Theodore Martin, Queen Victoria as I Knew Her (William Blackwood & Sons, 1901), 69–70.

[60] Amberley Papers, Vol. 2, 268.

[61] ED to BB, 9 December 1867, EDCL, 251–2. She wrote that 'it is not liked to see my name before the public': HS to ED, 28 November 1867, FC, 557.

[62] She wrote a 'cordial note' in respect of the memorial to the SIC, but of prior contact we know nothing. ED to AR, August 1867, EDCL, 244–5.

[63] JB to ED, 20 November 1867, 26 November 1867, FC, 549–51, 554–5.

[64] JH to ED, 9 October 1867, FC, 537–8.   [65] FC, 559.

to solicit names for a general committee of prominent men and women to confer authority and aid fundraising. The four resolutions were as follows:[66]

(1) That the following ladies and gentlemen, with power to add to their number, form a Committee for the purpose of founding a College for the higher education of women: Lady Hobart, Lady Goldsmid, the Very Rev. the Dean of Canterbury, Mrs Russell Gurney, G.W. Hastings Esq., James Heywood Esq., Mrs Manning, Miss F. Metcalfe, H.J. Roby Esq., Reverend Sedley Taylor, H.R. Tomkinson Esq., Hon. Sec. Miss Davies.
(2) That the College shall be, if possible, connected with the University of Cambridge, and that efforts shall be made to obtain the admission of students, under suitable regulations, to the Examinations for Degrees of that University.
(3) That the religious services and instruction shall be in accordance with the principles of the Church of England, but that where conscientious objections are entertained, attendance at such services and instruction shall not be obligatory.
(4) That the resident authorities shall be women.

By the time of its first full meeting in February 1868, the committee had been augmented by another lady and another Cambridge don. The lady was Lady Augusta Stanley, a friend of Davies's brother, wife of the dean of Westminster and daughter (hence her title) of the Earl of Elgin.[67] The don was John Seeley, still critical of Cambridge degrees but prepared to get involved.

---

[66] Minutes of First Meeting of College Committee [now lost], in Stephen, 163–4; *EDCL*, 252.
[67] FC, 559.

11

Rival Projects

Davies did found a college, against all the odds. It began operations, in 1869, half-way between Cambridge and London, just as she had intended. Four years later it moved to a greenfield site at Girton, just outside Cambridge, which was not part of her original plan, but the new buildings were designed, just as she had hoped they would be, by Waterhouse. Her religious preferences also prevailed. There were no restrictions on admission, but services were conducted by a Church of England priest. After thirty-five years (and long resistance by Lady Stanley of Alderley, who thought the money better spent on education) a chapel was constructed (Waterhouse again), dedicated though not consecrated for Church of England services. From the beginning, the students took the Cambridge degree papers, including not only those for the reviled ordinary degree but also those for the even more reviled little-go, a compulsory preliminary examination in mathematics and classics considered by Cambridge reformers to be completely worthless.

To achieve all this, Davies had, as in the suffrage campaign, to struggle as much against her friends as against her enemies. There were enemies, of course, both in Cambridge and amongst the wider public. Many commentators continued to see the higher education of women along the same lines as men as either unnecessary or inappropriate or both. Many continued to think the same of their education along any lines. But it was the friends who caused the trouble. These could be divided, roughly speaking, into two groups. First there were the Cambridge reformers, led by Henry Sidgwick and including in their number both of the Cambridge men on Davies's committee, Sedley Taylor and John Seeley. They were generally very much in favour of the higher education of women, but very strongly against the existing Cambridge degree structure and content. They supported equal opportunities for women, but they thought educational values more important than the degrees that went with them, whereas Davies's priorities were the other way round. Most would have identified as broad church Christians, but some were moving towards agnosticism or theism, and some were politically radical, and Davies distrusted them on both counts.

The second group comprised a network of women activists from the northwest of England, the most prominent of whom were Elizabeth Wolstenholme, Lydia Becker, Josephine Butler, and Anne Clough. After the fragmentation of the suffrage campaign in London, Becker and Wolstenholme were now the de facto leaders of the women's movement as a political force. Radicals both, their main

---

Emily Davies and the Mid-Victorian Women's Movement. John Hendry, Oxford University Press. © John Hendry 2024.
DOI: 10.1093/oso/9780198910237.003.0011

RIVAL PROJECTS   185

focus was on legislative change: on votes for women; on changing the married women's property laws; and on repealing the Contagious Diseases Acts. With the first two campaigns running from early 1868, and the third from 1869, education was a secondary concern for Becker, but Wolstenholme was still running her school and very much engaged with educational matters.

Butler was also one of the leaders of the campaigns for married women's property rights and the repeal of the Contagious Diseases Acts, and would take a leading role, too, in promoting the higher education of women, but she came from a very different background and perspective. Born into the aristocratic Grey family, the deeply religious, evangelical wife of a liberal clergyman, she was a strong feminist (as was her husband—it was an explicitly equal marriage) but her main concern was with the protection and care of women, rather than with equality or rights.[1] She had recently set up a house of rest for diseased and dying prostitutes and had a particular concern for the suffering of children thrown into prostitution. Her concern with property rights was with working-class wives mistreated by their husbands. In education her main concern was with the education of teachers and governesses, so as to provide better for the children under their care.

Clough wasn't really part of the women's movement at all but a teacher who wanted, rather like Frances Buss, to improve the secondary education of girls. The daughter of a Liverpool cotton merchant, she had been tutored at home by her brother, the poet Arthur Hugh Clough, and had established a school in the Lake District. She had given up her school after Arthur's death to live with her sister-in-law, who happened to be a cousin of Barbara Bodichon. Introduced by Bodichon, she had joined Davies's London Association of Schoolmistresses and submitted a paper to the SIC (published in *Macmillan's*) making much the same arguments as Davies and Buss.[2] She had then developed a proposal of her own for replicating something like the London girls' colleges in Liverpool and other large towns, and had put this to George Butler, then headmaster of Liverpool College. This already had a girls' secondary school attached, founded in 1855 by Butler's predecessor, John Howson, one of the very few men to have made the case for a rigorous female education.[3] Butler was strongly supportive and Clough had quickly become friends with Josephine and, through her, with Wolstenholme.

Clough's proposal was for a programme of lectures in the largest towns, delivered by university men, ideally overseen by some government, municipal, or university board and open to the older pupils from across the schools in the area. Even as an experiment this would create amongst the brighter girls a taste for

---

[1] Helen Matthews, 'The evangelical spirituality of a Victorian feminist: Josephine Butler, 1828–1906', *Journal of Ecclesiastical History*, 52 (2001), 282–312, makes the case for Butler's evangelical inner self, but also notes her practical ecumenicalism.

[2] Anne Clough, 'Hints on the organization of girls' schools', *Macmillan's Magazine*, 14 (October 1866), 435–9.

[3] J. S. Howson, 'On schools for girls of the middle class', *TNAPSS* (1859), 308–16.

higher study; engage the universities, with their resources and authority, in the practical problems of girls' education; and provide valuable stimulus and assistance to teachers. If the experiment were successful, it might subsequently be extended beyond the range of subjects taught at the London colleges, opening the way to higher levels of education, but the primary aim was to enhance girls' secondary education, and in particular to improve the education of those who might go on to be teachers and governesses. Clough had no particular interest, at this stage, in giving women a university-level education or university degrees, which would only appeal to a small elite. And she had no interest in matching the syllabuses of boys' education. The course of instruction should be that which was most useful to the girls concerned.

From early 1867, then, there were two projects in development, involving most of those then active in the women's movement. One was Davies's project for an elite residential college for women, following the existing Cambridge University syllabus and preparing women for its degree examinations under the same terms and conditions as men with a view, eventually, to incorporation within the university. The other was Clough's project for a large programme of lectures tailored specifically for girls and young women, similar to those given at the London colleges. A third scheme, of lectures for young women in Oxford, was also launched around this time, initiated by Mark Pattison and managed by Eleanor Smith, but seems to have been much more modest in its ambitions.[4]

The rival projects were in many ways complementary, and both gathered strong broad church support, both at the personal level and through articles in broad church mouthpieces such as *Macmillan's Magazine*, *Fraser's Magazine*, and the *Contemporary Review*. From Davies's perspective, however, Clough's project was a harmful distraction, drawing away potential supporters (and with them the funding that her own project needed but the other didn't), and playing into the hands of those who insisted that women's education and examinations should be different from men's, either because women were intellectually inferior or because the same syllabus and examinations might damage their femininity. As she struggled to progress her own project, moreover, Davies found, ironically, that the women of the north-west were able to work together with the men from Cambridge in a way that she, despite her principles on the matter, was not. Indeed, the only man with whom she found she could work effectively as her project progressed was Tomkinson, and that only because, while giving advice, he always let her have the final say.

Clough's project was the first to bear fruit, spearheaded by the Butlers, who shifted the emphasis from replicating the teaching of the London colleges to going beyond them and providing some kind of truly higher education. Almost

---

[4] *SIC Report*, Vol. 1, 569.

immediately, they engaged Frederick Myers, a fellow of Trinity College, Cambridge, a former pupil of Butler and son of a close friend, to deliver a course of twelve lectures in Liverpool, the first eight on modern Italian history.[5] Although a prospectus was issued, nothing came of this first attempt, but Clough gave a talk on her proposals to both the London Association of Schoolmistresses and the Manchester Board of Schoolmistresses.[6] Wolstenholme got involved and spread the idea to colleagues in other towns and by early summer there was a concerted campaign to set up a system of lectures across the north of England.

As Clough and her friends looked around for teachers for the proposed courses, their top priority was to find someone who might lecture on educational theory.[7] Middle-class girls looking for something beyond what the schools were offering were mostly headed for work as schoolmistresses or governesses so this would be directly relevant, and if some of their teachers attended the lectures as well there would be a double benefit. In the event, however, the person with whom they came into contact was James Stuart, another recently appointed fellow of Trinity, and he wanted to teach something more substantial.[8]

Stuart had been involved with the Schools Inquiry Commission, writing up the report of one of the assistant commissioners, Lemprière Hammond, when he had been indisposed. Stuck himself at home in Scotland following his father's illness and death, he had come up with two plans for the improvement of education.

One was for a programme of intercollegiate lectures at Cambridge, on the Scottish university model, the teaching up to then having been conducted mainly within the colleges. The other was for a university extension programme taught by non-resident peripatetic lecturers.[9] He would in due course play the leading the role in bringing both about, but meanwhile he jumped at the opportunity of the proposed lecture scheme—as he did also at opportunities to lecture to working men and co-operative societies. He had no particular interest in the teaching of women, but he was a gifted and enthusiastic teacher and passionately interested in furthering his project of a university extension programme.

Asked if he would give lectures to women on 'educational theory' he willingly agreed to lecture but insisted that his lectures should be on what he saw as a proper subject. What mattered, he stressed, was that students should learn the discipline entailed in gaining and transmitting knowledge, rather than any particular knowledge.[10] For this purpose he proposed a course in one of his own interests, physical astronomy. (He would be appointed in 1875 Professor of Mechanism and Applied Mechanics.) Young women would be perfectly able to cope with such a subject, he argued, if properly taught. The lectures were

---

[5] Crawford, 129.   [6] Clough, 117.   [7] Jordan, 87.
[8] The contact was probably through Myers and Sidgwick. See Clough, 118, 120; Rita McWilliams Tulberg, *Women at Cambridge*, 1st ed. (Gollancz, 1975), 52.
[9] Stuart, 152 ff. See also ODNB 38025.   [10] Crawford, 129; Stuart, 157–8.

delivered in Manchester, Liverpool, Leeds, and Sheffield, beginning in Manchester on 9 October 1867. Each course was introduced by George Butler, who gave a speech on 'The higher education of women' promising future courses in mathematics, natural history, English history and literature, and a range of other subjects. The take-up was extraordinary, with a total of 550 women attending the four series.[11]

Meanwhile, work had been under way to create an association to oversee and coordinate a more substantial programme of lectures for the future. The North of England Council for Promoting the Higher Education of Women met for the first time in November in Leeds, with members drawn from Liverpool, Manchester, Leeds, and Sheffield. The two Liverpool representatives, Anne Clough and Josephine Butler, acted as secretary and president, respectively, and James Bryce, Joshua Fitch, Thomas Markby, and Samuel Steinthal were co-opted as expert consultants.[12] In the spring of 1868, two lecturers gave courses in five towns, and the following autumn three lecturers gave courses in nine towns. By 1870 a substantial group of Cambridge dons would be delivering lectures for women in twenty-three centres around the country.

Davies's initial response to the lecture scheme was positive. 'I am glad there is a prospect of its being tried,' she wrote to Anna Richardson in August.[13] Then the following February: 'I think we ought not only to accept, but to <u>desire</u> the introduction of the Lectures into every large town, with a view to their growing into local Colleges, or as Mr Bryce puts it, institutions like the Scotch Universities.'[14] The North of England Council, in turn, expressed support for Davies's college.[15] But there were tensions. One was around competition for resources. Early on, Clough and Butler asked Davies to refrain from promoting either the college or the Locals in Liverpool, so that the lecture programme could get off the ground. 'The amount of cold water Miss Clough has thrown upon me', she complained, 'is such that I cannot <u>think</u> of her without a shudder.'[16] In theory the lectures should pave the way for the college, but Davies's fear—also with respect to Edinburgh, where a similar programme of lectures was under way—was that given two options for higher education, one easy and doable from home, the other difficult and requiring residence, young women and their parents would naturally opt for the former.[17]

---

[11] Jordan, 87; Wright, 64; Clough, 118.

[12] Clough, 120; Stuart, 157; Jordan, 86; Wright, 64. Gillian Sutherland, 'Anne Jemima Clough and Blanche Athena Clough: creating educational institutions for women', in Mary Hilton and Pam Hirsch, eds., *Practical Visionaries: Women, Education and Social Progress 1790–1930* (Longman, 2000), 101–14.

[13] ED to AR, August 1867, *EDCL*, 244–5: 245.

[14] ED to AR, 21 February 1868, *EDCL*, 262–4: 262 (this is cited by Stephen as 4 February 1868).

[15] Clough, 132.   [16] ED to AR, 21 February 1868, *EDCL*, 262–4: 262.

[17] ED to AR, 17 December 1867, 30 December 1867, 21 February 1868, *EDCL*, 254, 255–7, 262–4. For Edinburgh see Katherine Burton, *A Memoir of Mrs. Crudelius* (privately printed, 1879; Forgotten Books, 2018).

RIVAL PROJECTS   189

Another tension was around examinations. Clough's one reservation with respect to the college was her belief—all too familiar to Davies—that the Cambridge degree examinations were not well suited to the circumstances of women.[18] This Davies could live with. More serious was a proposal that the lecture scheme should be examined, by a university examination specifically for women.

The idea that the lectures should be tested probably came from Stuart, who wanted to introduce as much discipline as possible to his courses, but both Clough and Wolstenholme, looking at the education of teachers, were interested in certificating the learning. Bryce was also enthusiastic, suggesting rather ingenuously to Davies that by stimulating education and awakening public interest the proposed examination would help pave the way for the college.[19] Of course, he responded to her reply, the more examinations for boys and girls were assimilated, the better for both,[20] and in a subsequent meeting with Davies he seems to have bent over backwards to show support for her project, and distance himself from the proposed examination, but he was evidently trying to keep both sides happy.[21]

The initial proposal was for examination by a 'Voluntary Board' drawn from the faculties of both Oxford and Cambridge, but the intention was evidently to prepare the way for something more formal. In February 1868, Josephine Butler visited Cambridge to sound out opinion, and in an open letter to Bryce she reported much enthusiasm for the scheme. Within weeks a flysheet was circulating in the university signed not only by Stuart, Myers, and Sidgwick and Fawcett, but by others to whom Davies might naturally have looked for support, such as Maurice, Fawcett, Markby, and Liveing. Headed by the vice-chancellor, it included no fewer than eight professors.[22]

The support was in fact so strong that the need for a voluntary arrangement was coming into question. Davies visited Cambridge herself at this time, staying with the Liveings, and was told that Myers was proposing a formal university examination 'to get rid of the female stamp', such as the little-go modified only slightly by making German an optional alternative to Greek—a compromise she felt she might accept.[23] What was actually being proposed, however, was an entirely different university examination for women. In mid-March, Myers wrote to Wolstenholme with instructions for getting up a memorial, to be signed by

---

[18] Anne Clough manuscript notes, Newnham College archives, quoted by Crawford, 131.
[19] Stuart, 161–2; FC, 543; JB to ED, 20 November 1867, FC, 549–51.
[20] JB to ED, 26 November 1867, FC, 554–5: 554.
[21] ED to AR, 21 February 1868, *EDCL*, 262–4: 263; Willson, 108–9. For Bryce's simultaneous correspondence with Clough see Sutherland, 'Anne Jemima Clough'.
[22] Davies was presumably well aware of this, as she kept a copy: FC 583a, b.
[23] ED to AR, 28 February 1868, *EDCL*, 265–6: 266.

schoolmistresses, governesses, and others, asking the university to set up advanced examinations for women.[24]

A few days later, Stuart also wrote to Wolstenholme, encouraging the North of England Council to apply to the university for an examination specifically for women, and setting aside any concerns she might have about opposition arising from Davies's project.[25] He was quite sure that Davies's suggestion that women be admitted to the same examinations as men would not even 'for a moment be listened to in the University'. Even if it were, 'it would be speedily overturned.... Miss Davies does not influence the university.'

To settle the matter, Myers wrote round to all those involved in the discussions, soliciting their views, either in writing or at a meeting of the North of England Council, as to whether the examinations sought should be special examinations, as had been proposed, or the same examinations as for men, as urged by Davies. The response was unanimous. Bryce, Fitch, Markby, Venn, Maurice, Burn, Bonney, and Lightfoot all sent in letters arguing strongly for special examinations for women, and those present at the meeting agreed. Some urged, as a practical consideration, that the senate just wouldn't accept women sitting the men's examinations. But all argued that the Cambridge syllabi were 'unsuitable' or 'totally inappropriate' for women. Even if men and women were intellectually equal, they were not the same, and the lives for which they were being prepared were not the same.[26]

A flysheet in support of the special examinations was signed by no fewer than seventy-four resident members of the senate, with two of the four columns headed by Maurice and Kingsley, the other two by prominent conservatives, Henry Luard and Edward Perowne.[27] The memorial put together by the North of England Council, presented personally to the senate by Josephine Butler, was signed by 550 teachers and 300 ladies of standing.[28] A syndicate was set up to consider the matter and in October the senate approved the setting up of women's examinations, on a three-year trial basis, to be operated on essentially the same model as the existing local examinations. The first of these examinations were held in June 1869, with thirty-six women presenting themselves at three centres, and three years later they were made permanent.[29]

---

[24] ED to AR, 17 March 1868, *EDCL*, 269; ED to BB, 18 March 1868, *EDCL*, 152–3 (incorrectly dated there as 18 March 1865). Davies interpreted this as Myers calling the shots, but he was probably just filling in Wolstenholme on developments.

[25] JS to EW, 20 March 1868, Newnham College archives, quoted by Crawford, 131–2.

[26] *Report of the 2nd Meeting of the North of England Council for Promoting the Higher Education of Women, 15th and 16th April 1868*, with associated papers: in bound collection of pamphlets at LSE Women's Library, 371.822 WOM.

[27] Stuart, 181; Crawford, 132–3. The memorial and flysheet were reprinted in the *Victoria Magazine*, 11 (July 1868), 269–70.

[28] Clough, 129; Jordan, 95.

[29] Crawford, 133; Menella B. Smedley, 'The English girl's education', *Contemporary Review*, 14 (April 1870), 29–41: 29 lists the local secretaries.

RIVAL PROJECTS 191

Rather ironically, these examinations would within a few years be made open to men and renamed the higher local examinations. Meanwhile, however, the whole process left Davies deeply uncomfortable.

Her main practical concern was that the new examinations would play into the hands of those who had always argued for separate examinations for men and women, both in the university and more widely. Parents would see the lectures and special examinations as a safe option as well as an easy one. Her supporters in the university, being supporters of women's education, would all want to get involved in the lecture scheme and, once involved, would come to think it the best possible. Indeed, this was already happening: the strength of opinion in favour of women's education might be encouraging, but the strength of opinion against women taking the men's examinations was alarming. Stuart's claims in his letter to Wolstenholme, if she heard of them, would have been even more so. The stark prospect was that the university would respond to her own appeal for access to degree examinations by rejecting it out of hand. 'They will offer us a Myers Examn. instead.'[30] She had relied throughout her campaigning on broad church support, but with both Maurice and Kingsley to the fore in support of separate women's examinations that ground looked to be taken from her.

Davies didn't want to get involved in arguing the case publicly, which she felt would only create discord to no effect,[31] but she couldn't resist writing an article, for the *London Student*, arguing against the principle of separate educational schemes, and especially separate examinations, for men and women.[32] This refrained from any mention of Cambridge, focusing on developments in London and making the point that by some 'curious coincidence' the subjects prescribed for the new London University examinations for women turned out to be almost identical to those prescribed for the men's matriculation examination, absent only some books of Euclid. She also determined, at a meeting for her local examinations committee, that anyone seeking a qualification as preparation for entry to her new college should look to the new London examinations rather than those proposed for Cambridge.[33]

Besides these practical concerns, the lecture scheme and its examination also led to personal differences, which Davies could have done without. She remained friendly with the freethinking, socialist Wolstenholme, who had earlier shared

[30] ED to AR, 27 March 1868, 23 May 1868, *EDCL*, 270–2, 279–80: 280.

[31] ED to AR, 23 March 1868, *EDCL*, 269–70.

[32] ED to BB, 9 September 1868, EDCL, 289–90; Emily Davies, 'Special systems of education for women', *London Student* (June 1868), in *Thoughts*, 118–37. This short-lived monthly magazine was produced in connection with University College London from April to August 1868. A paper in the May number, 'On the influence upon girls' schools of external examinations', ibid., 108–17, is reprinted as Davies's in *Thoughts*, but as the editors of *EDCL* point out (p. xiv) this article is actually by Wolstenholme. Originally a talk to the London Association of Schoolmistresses, it was presumably submitted by Davies, hence the confusion.

[33] FC, 597.

her opposition to female-only examinations. Both misreading and underestimating her, she considered her to have been 'captured' by the opposition.[34] Relations with Clough were more difficult. Bodichon and other mutual friends tried to mediate, but to little effect. Clough was as convinced of the need for special examinations for women as Davies was of their inappropriateness.[35] At first Davies looked on Clough as being at least honest and straightforward, but a misunderstanding over the context of some letters circulated by the North of England Council in support of its memorial, which Davies thought attributed one of Myers's proposals to herself, set them more seriously at odds.[36]

While Davies granted that Clough was at least honest (and that the affair of the letters was probably not her fault), she was not prepared to say the same of either Myers or Josephine Butler. Myers was for her the chief architect of the piece and just not to be trusted. Butler, she seems just not to have liked. They met in London at the time of a meeting on the proposed voluntary board, to discuss a book project. Albert Rutson, who had edited a volume entitled *Essays on Reform* for Macmillan,[37] had suggested they jointly edit a volume of essays on women's issues. With very different approaches to the subject, they didn't see eye to eye at all and agreed to split the project, editing a volume each.[38] Then when Butler circulated her open letter to Bryce, reporting enthusiasm in Cambridge for the examination scheme, Davies was disgusted.[39]

> I do not like [Mrs Butler's letter] because I feel it is not quite true.... I have found her not strictly truthful & it makes me shrink from having more to do with her than is necessary. I do not mean that she is not a genuinely good Christian woman. I am sure she is. And I believe her "inaccuracies" are a good deal caused by a kind of looseness & slipperiness of mind. But all the same, by means of them she conveys false impressions, & the task of correcting her statements is very invidious & disagreeable.

Nobody else would accuse Butler of falseness, though it is fair to say she tended to be ruled by her heart rather than her head, but Davies had presumably heard exactly the opposite feedback on her own visit to Cambridge. Her hosts will have been courteous to a fault, and she will have heard what she wanted to hear.

A few months later, Butler wrote to Rutson, expressing sympathy for Davies, who was she thought 'depressed about the possible failure of her College'. She

[34] FC, 543; ED to AR, 23 March 1868, *EDCL*, 269–70.
[35] ED to AR, 27 March 1868, 29 April 1868, *EDCL*, 270–4.
[36] ED to AC, 29 April 1868, 1 May 1868, *EDCL*, 274–7: 276; ED to AR, 29 April 1868, *EDCL*, 273–4; ED to ST, 16 May 1868, *EDCL*, 278–9.
[37] Albert Rutson, ed., *Essays on Reform* (Macmillan, 1867).
[38] Josephine Butler, *Woman's Work and Woman's Culture* (Macmillan, 1869). Davies didn't pursue the idea.
[39] ED to AR, 22 February 1868, *EDCL*, 264–5.

RIVAL PROJECTS 193

knew 'only too well' what it was like when the object of one's life was lost, she wished the college well, would grieve for it if it went down, and would write to Davies and comfort her were it not for fear of a snub. Which, we may judge, she would surely receive. In this, as in all her causes, Butler's concern was for women as women: for their aid and protection in a cruel and unfeeling male-dominated society. She had no interest in equality of opportunity, either for itself or for the betterment of society, and saw Davies's insistence on equality as 'masculine aiming'. It would be doomed, because men were not sympathetic to such women, but just as Davies saw the special examinations as threatening her plans, Butler saw Davies's plans as threatening hers. 'I dread their failure,' she wrote, 'because it clogs the wheels and blocks up the path of us who are driving towards a different and a higher goal. I pray for Miss Davies constantly, and for all like her, that a wise heart may be granted them in time, and that God may gently turn them back from error.'[40] Two leaders of the women's movement, both committed Christians, both with the very best of intentions, yet so, so far apart.

By this time, Davies was coming to realize that Butler's earlier report of Cambridge opinion had not been so far off the mark after all, but that didn't help relations and it did lead her to be less trustful of the Cambridge men. 'The sweetness and light here is in the highest degree refreshing,' she had reported during her February visit. 'I am amazed, bewildered, almost stupefied by the reception of the College idea.'[41] By the summer she must have been more doubtful.

Further developments added further confusion. In April, Millicent Garrett Fawcett, Elizabeth Garrett's sister, published an article in *Macmillan's* in which she suggested, quite simply, that Cambridge University should—and could, with perfect propriety—admit women.[42] The only conditions the university imposed on students before passing their examinations (apart, of course, from being men, but she didn't need to say that) were keeping terms of residence and attending professors' lectures. Some of the professors, including her husband, had already begun to admit ladies to their lectures, and the residence regulations had recently been changed to allow, with special permission, residence in the house of a Master of Arts that had been licensed as a 'hostel'. So all that was needed was for a respectable married MA to obtain the necessary licence from the vice-chancellor and the residence issue too would be solved.[43]

---

[40] JB to Albert Rutson, 23 May 1868, LSE 3JBL/02/26a–c. Butler's reference to loss was to the accidental death of a daughter. Her view of men was tainted by her experience of misogyny among Oxford dons.

[41] ED to AR, 28 February 1868, *EDCL*, 265–6.

[42] Millicent Garrett Fawcett, 'The education of women of the middle and upper classes', *Macmillan's*, 17 (April 1868), 511–17.

[43] This change, which was designed partly to reduce costs and partly to assist dissenters wishing to study, had been pressed on the university by government-appointed commissioners since the 1850s but was only instituted in 1869.

194 DAVIES AND THE MID-VICTORIAN WOMEN'S MOVEMENT

Fawcett was still only twenty, and as Davies noted the idea was 'utterly untenable'. In itself, it was not to be taken too seriously, but it did suggest the presence of a radical feminism in Cambridge that might stir up opposition to her own more modest proposals.[44] Then a few months later, Fawcett published another paper, in the *Fortnightly*, in which she took up Hutton's earlier pairing of Davies's proposals with the Ladies Medical College and accused both of perpetuating and stereotyping the separation already existing between the education of men and women, effectively condemning women to a second-class education and status.[45] Cambridge would be more open, she suggested, to admitting women than to recognizing a college outside its boundaries, and it was evident that the educational opportunities that could be provided by the universities, with their libraries, museums, and established routines of study, were far greater than those that could be provided in a new and distant college.

Around the same time, Lydia Becker gave a paper to the British Association for the Advancement of Science arguing on biological grounds that all educational establishments, and all professions, should be equally open to men and women. Such a wild proposal within the male establishment setting of the BAAS was widely noticed, and some of the responses were not unhelpful. The *Times* suggested that it wouldn't happen because the men wouldn't allow it, but saw no objection to women studying to university level, provided they didn't mix with men, which would be 'condemned by the existing code of moral norms and inconvenient under any', a sympathetic line also pursued by *Fraser's* in response to Fawcett's first article. For Davies, who was as horrified as anyone at the idea of young men and women freely associating as undergraduates, this was positive. An article in the *Quarterly*, however, responded with 'unmitigated disgust', and took the opportunity to condemn Davies's college proposal as well: what was needed was a true college for women, devoted to the training of governesses and teachers.[46] Even in the normally supportive *Contemporary Review*, an article by Joseph Mayor took the opportunity to stress that the education of men and women should be different. If the new college could help train up some teachers it might have some use, but there was no need for a university-level education for ladies.[47]

---

[44] ED to BB, 18 March 1868, *EDCL*, 152–3 (incorrectly dated there as 18 March 1865) and see AR to ED, 16 April 1868, in Richardson, 223. In neither case do we have the other side of the correspondence. David Rubinstein, *A Different World for Women: The Life of Millicent Garrett Fawcett* (Harvester, 1991), 80.

[45] Millicent Garrett Fawcett, 'The medical and general education of women', *Fortnightly Review*, 10 (October 1868), 554–71.

[46] 'Women's education', *Fraser's Magazine*, 79 (May 1869), 537–52; 'The suppressed sex', *Westminster Review*, 90 (October, 1868), 437–62; 'Female emancipation', *Saturday Review*, 26 (5 September 1868), 322–3; *Times*, 27 August 1868; *Quarterly Review*, 126 (April 1869), 448–79.

[47] J. B. Mayor, 'The cry of the women', *Contemporary Review*, 11 (1869), 196–215.

RIVAL PROJECTS 195

While all this was going on, Henry Sidgwick, who was genuinely supportive of Davies's project as well as the lecture scheme and special examinations, suggested that a house might be taken in Cambridge for the women who might be the resident authorities of Davies's college, so that they could gain experience of Cambridge teaching methods, attending lectures and learning from tutors. Unfortunately he accompanied this with the suggestion that the house might be placed under the superintendence of a competent lady. It was intended to be reassuring, but Davies was insulted. Anyone in the position envisaged would be a mature woman, not a girl, and quite able to manage things by herself.[48]

While the lecture scheme gathered pace quickly, Davies's college project was slow to take off. She had planned for a large general committee of big names to raise funds, but although she persuaded a few people to join it doesn't seem to have materialized until the college was well under way and was only ever intended as a publicity tool. For practical purposes she worked best with a very small committee, which she could keep under tight control, and with support from friends.[49] Jane Crow and Annie Austin helped on the administrative and domestic sides, respectively, and Adelaide Manning and Anna Richardson acted as sounding boards. Emilia Gurney gave emotional and spiritual support. 'I have thought so much of you since I saw you,' she wrote when the special examinations were mooted, '& all the worry that you must have had about that business. It must have been annoying & disagreeable to little tender parts of your being...I see how often this kind of experience is the fate of pioneers.'[50]

Barbara Bodichon, tired of Algiers and missing her friend Bessie, now married and procreating, was also around and offering support. Although she had committed her money, she was still not convinced of the project—either of the value of Cambridge degrees or of the wisdom, if going for those degrees, of the proposed location, halfway between Cambridge and London. She would defend Davies's plans against her critics. 'Miss Davies ought to be helped & not too much hampered with criticism,'[51] she wrote to Helen Taylor, whilst fully agreeing with Taylor's criticisms of the Cambridge education. But she easily grew despondent at the challenges faced and kept urging Davies to do things differently.[52]

In order to launch the project and raise funds, Davies's college committee decided on a 'semi-public' meeting, to be held in London at the end of March. Alford took the chair and about two hundred people attended, including friends,

[48] ED to AR, 25 June 1868, *EDCL*, 282–3; ED to ST, 19 June 1868, *EDCL*, 281–2.
[49] ED to AR, 17 December 1867, 28 December 1867, 4 February 1868, 18 February 1868, 23 May 1868, *EDCL*, 254–5, 260–1, 279–80; AR to ED, 23 December 1867, FC, 563–4, in Richardson, 218; ED to BB, September/October 1868, *EDCL*, 291–2.
[50] ERG to ED, 29 May 1868, FC, 612–13: 613.
[51] BD to HT, 1 August 1869, LSE MILL-TAYLOR, 12/50. See also HT to BB, 4 August 1869, LSE 9/02/031.
[52] ED to BB, (15) March 1868, 23 November 1868, *EDCL*, 267–9, 294–5; ED to AR, 6 March 1868, *EDCL*, 266–7.

196 DAVIES AND THE MID-VICTORIAN WOMEN'S MOVEMENT

supporters, a gaggle of distinguished ladies (assembled by Bodichon and Gurney), and what Davies now saw as the rival camp: Anne Clough, Millicent Fawcett, Albert Rutson, and Henry Jackson of Trinity College, who had become one of the prime movers in respect of the ladies' examinations.[53]

The speakers included Seeley, Roby, Hastings, and Tomkinson, from the committee, as well as Llewelyn Davies and Joseph Lightfoot, the Hulsean Professor of Divinity. Lightfoot was an old friend of Llewelyn's who had been enlisted as a potentially influential supporter, but he was also a supporter of the female examinations and had not apparently been warned that he would be asked to speak. To address the issues arising from the competition of the lectures, Hastings read a letter from Wolstenholme on the need for some provision for exceptionally clever young women. Seeley and Roby discoursed on the advantages of a residential college in a country location, as giving greater privacy and freedom than was possible in town, to which Lightfoot added the need for solitude and quiet for effective study. Seeley stressed, 'to laughter & applause', that while study for the ordinary degree examination might be a beginning, of course the students would not be expected to stop at that.[54]

Davies was pleased. She was especially pleased that her committee members managed to toe the line and not contradict her principles: 'I expected every minute that somebody wd. be offering to sacrifice some vital principle, but nobody did.'[55] The meeting also received some broadly favourable reviews, along with the inevitable mocking ones, which she circulated as a pamphlet.[56] But it brought forth little in the way of financial contributions. By mid-July the fund, excluding Bodichon's pledge, stood at just £1,000.[57]

The campaign continued. In June, *Macmillan's* published an article by Llewelyn Davies, using Millicent Fawcett's paper (arguing simply for the admission of women to Cambridge) as a hook for proposing something more practical, in the form of the college.[58] Extolling the benefits of college life as its main advantage, he pleaded common sense in respect of the subjects taught and carefully avoided the question of degree examinations. Besides the general publicity afforded by the paper, the emphasis on college life seems to have made its mark on Hutton, who in September came out with his latest thoughts on female education. He now

[53] A partial list of names collected by Annie Austin is at FC, 607a.

[54] Annie Austin to AR, 31 March 1868, Girton GCPP Davies 15/1/1/5, copied in FC, 602–7. There was also a full report in the *Victoria Magazine*, 11 (July 1868), 74–8.

[55] ED to HRT, April 1868, *EDCL*, 272.

[56] 'Proposed new college for women', Girton GCPP Davies 15/2/2/2. The accounts reproduced were from *The Jewish Chronicle*, 10 July 1868, *The Queen*, 11 July 1868, *The Literary Churchman*, 11 July 1868, *The Economist*, 18 July 1868, and *The Express*, 19 September 1868.

[57] Stephen, 173; ED to HRT, April 1868, *EDCL*, 262. Contributors included Charlotte Manning, Henry Tomkinson, Lady Goldsmid, George Eliot, Lizzie Garrett, and Anna Richardson's brother. The only significant contribution from outside the immediate circle was £100 from Leonard Courtney, the London examiner of the Cambridge local examinations.

[58] J. Llewelyn Davies, 'A new college for women', *Macmillan's Magazine*, 18 (June 1868), 168–75.

distinguished between the 'nonsense' of women's rights, especially as pursued in America, and the sensible claims as to women's need for education and the necessity, in particular, of the higher education of women. Unlike other proposals (such as the admission of women to London University degrees, which he was still resisting) Davies's college offered women the possibility of tutored independent study. The proposal would be discussed at the forthcoming SSA congress, and it deserved support. The outcome might be uncertain but the trial should be made.[59]

At the SSA congress, held in October that year in Birmingham, Emily Davies praised the lecture scheme (on which Myers was speaking),[60] but observed that it could only reach the big towns, whereas the great majority of middle-class young women lived in country villages and small towns.[61] Appealing to the conservative values of traditional England ('The Hall and the Rectory are the centres of light for a whole parish'), she presented the proposed college and the intellectual discipline and training it would provide as a preparation for the duties of life. It would be a stepping stone from the restraints of childhood to the responsibilities of adulthood—in a woman's case, typically, the responsibilities of wifehood, motherhood, or philanthropy—such as the universities provided for boys. She finished, on Roby's suggestion,[62] with a short account of college life, designed to appeal to both parents and daughters. For parents there was reassurance: excursions would be strictly controlled, their daughters would not be mixing in any way in society, there would be daily prayers. For the daughters there was the promise of a room of their own: 'Each student will have a small sitting room of her own, where she will be free to study undisturbed, and to enjoy at her discretion the companionship of friends of her own choice.'[63]

There were still doubts, even amongst supporters, as to whether girls had the intellectual capacity or physical strength for university study, but Lyttelton, in the chair, and the *Times*, reporting on the paper, agreed with Hutton that the trial should be made.[64] The *Times* writer did note with amusement Davies's comment

---

[59] 'Women's needs and women's rights', *Spectator*, 41 (19 September 1868), 1095–7. By 1871, Hutton had become a strong supporter of the college: 'The higher education for women', *Spectator*, 44 (14 October 1871), 1235–6.

[60] Myers's paper was published as 'Local lectures for women', *Macmillan's Magazine*, 19 (December 1868), 159–63. See ED to BB, 9 September 1868, *EDCL*, 289–90.

[61] An expanded version was published as Emily Davies, 'Some account of a proposed college for women', *Contemporary Review*, 9 (December 1868), 540–69. The greater part of the article, but omitting bits on college life and the call for students and funds, was reprinted as a pamphlet in 1872 and in *Thoughts*, 84–107.

[62] ED to AR, 1 August 1868, *EDCL*, 284–5; ED to HRT, 5 August 1868, *EDCL*, 531. Pushed by Bodichon, Davies was also getting support from Marian Evans and had detailed suggestions on her paper from both her and George Lewes, but rejected them all. GE to ED, 11 August 1868, 10 September 1868, FC, 635–40.

[63] Emily Davies, 'Some account of a proposed college for women', *Contemporary Review*, 9 (December 1868), 540–69: 553.

[64] ED to BB, September/October 1868, *EDCL*, 290–1; Stephen, 176–7. *Times*, 10 October 1868, quoted in Stephen, 177–8.

198 DAVIES AND THE MID-VICTORIAN WOMEN'S MOVEMENT

that her college would 'aim at no higher position than, say, that of Trinity College'. 'Such a degree of humility', they observed, 'will not be considered excessive.'[65] Still, it was publicity, and not wholly damning: '[it] will do some good, I hope'.[66]

Alongside the campaigning, Davies had set in motion three processes, what would now be called work streams. In February she had set up a subcommittee of studies. This included most of the college committee, but in practice the work devolved onto Seeley, who began by preparing a syllabus for entrance examinations and ended up, under pressure from Davies, producing an entire draft syllabus for the college.[67] Unfortunately—and almost inevitably, given Seeley's reformist educational views—it was not what Davies had in mind. A compromise was reached by which some subjects outside the university syllabus might be taught and internally certificated, but Davies insisted on strict adherence to the Cambridge examinations and Seeley had little option but to concede.[68]

In July, another subcommittee was set up, following advice from William Shaen, to look at the college's corporate status.[69] The members were Taylor, Roby, and Tomkinson (who took over at some point from Lady Goldsmid as treasurer), and they too got it wrong. 'I am all the more obliged to you for letting me know the direction in which you are tending,' wrote Davies, 'as it is not exactly the line in which I am inclined to follow....I am sorry to send you such a cross letter (& such a long one) but when you go so terribly astray, what can I do?'[70] The letter was indeed a long one, full of objections. A second version was better but still not what she wanted, but by February 1869 a constitution had been agreed and sent off for enactment.[71] The key point was that the college should aim, in the longer term, at incorporation within the university, not affiliation with it. It 'should, as far as might be practicable, occupy the same position in relation to the U. of C. as the existing Colleges'.

The third process was finding a site. Though she said nothing in public, Davies had quickly settled on Hitchin as being the only place to satisfactorily combine country air with good communications with both Cambridge and London.[72] One of Llewelyn's broad church Cambridge friends, Fenton Hort, also held a village

---

[65] *Times*, 10 October 1868, quoted in Stephen, 175.

[66] ED to BB, September/October 1868, *EDCL*, 291–2: 291.

[67] ED to AR, 23 May 1868, 1 August 1868, 15 August 1868, *EDCL*, 279–80, 284–6; ED to BB, September/October 1868, *EDCL*, 291–2.

[68] JS to ED, 13 January 1869, 20 January 1869, 4 March 1869, Girton GCPP Davies, 15/1/3/4, 6, 8.

[69] ED to HRT, 5 December 1868, *EDCL*, 296.

[70] ED to HRT, 6 January 1869, *EDCL*, 297–300: 297, 299.

[71] HR to HRT, 13 January 1869, 4 February 1869, 8 February 1869; ST to ED, 6 February 1869; ST to HR, 6 February 1869; HRT to ED, 8 February 1869, Girton GCPP Davies, 15/1/4/6, 7, 12, 10, 11, 13. ED to ST, January 1869, and January/February 1869, *EDCL*, 302–4; ED to HT, 5 February 1869, 18 February 1869, *EDCL*, 305–7; ED to AM, 1 February 1869, *EDCL*, 532; ED to BB, 16 February 1869, *EDCL*, 306.

[72] ED to AR, 27 March 1868, *EDCL*, 270–2. One of Joshua Fitch's brothers was head of a boys' school at Hitchin.

RIVAL PROJECTS 199

living close by and might, she thought, provide some valuable teaching.[73] By late May she had engaged two local residents to search out a site,[74] and a month later her committee appointed Waterhouse as architect.[75] The money didn't come in, however, and by November she was looking at the possibility of starting in a rented house. Emilia Gurney had apparently persuaded, or half persuaded, Charlotte Manning to rent and supervise one for the purpose, at least for a year, and this might make it possible to finance the venture initially from fees alone, while using the limited funds raised to buy a site (if Bodichon would release her pledge) and draw up plans for a building, which could be displayed so as to attract further funding.[76]

Bodichon, however, had misgivings, and so did Davies's Cambridge supporters, who couldn't understand why, given her longer-term aims, she should insist on building her college 30 miles away. At some point Taylor had set up a Cambridge committee of sympathetic academics to advise the college committee, with a membership of John Couch Adams, Professor of Astronomy; George Liveing, Professor of Chemistry; Joseph Lightfoot, Professor of Divinity; Thomas Bonney, geologist and tutor at St John's; and Robert Burn (classicist) and Henry Sigwick, tutors at Trinity. With the exception of Lightfoot, all signed a motion arguing for a location in Cambridge and against Hitchin.[77]

Bodichon also thought that the college should be in Cambridge, and didn't want her donation spent on a site in Hitchin. She argued, too, that spending money on temporary accommodation and teaching for what would likely be very small numbers would be a waste of money. As a matter of principle she would never actually have stopped Davies doing things her own way, but she was evidently uneasy, and since the release of her donation was critical to Davies's plans she had to be appeased.

In making her case against a Cambridge site, Davies put forward several arguments. There was no suitable house. It would stir up local opposition. And the more she heard of Cambridge society, the less she regretted the impossibility of going there: 'the social influence of the place would be not helpful, but very injurious'.[78] This third reason was presented as a kind of supplement to the other two, but seems to have been her main one. Llewelyn, recalling his own undergraduate life, had suggested that the discipline in a Cambridge location would need to be very strict and restrictive,[79] but she may have been less concerned for the students

[73] ED to AR, 23 April 1868, in Stephen, 204; ED to AR, 23 May 1868, *EDCL*, 279–80.
[74] ED to AR, 23 May 1868, *EDCL*, 279–80.
[75] ED to ST, 19 June 1868, *EDCL*, 281–2; ED to AR, 25 June 1868, *EDCL*, 282–3.
[76] ED to AM, 29 October 1868, *EDCL*, 531; ED to BB, 14 November 1868, *EDCL* 292–3.
[77] Stephen, 206. ED to ST, January 1869, *EDCL*, 302–4. Writing to Tomkinson, Davies suggested that the future time at which the college moved to Cambridge might be around 1900: ED to HRT, 5 February 1869, *EDCL*, 305–6.
[78] ED to BB, 23 November 1868, *EDCL*, 294–5: 295.
[79] ED to AR, 4 February 1868, *EDCL*, 260.

200 DAVIES AND THE MID-VICTORIAN WOMEN'S MOVEMENT

than for their parents. She was convinced that if parents were to risk sending their daughters to her college the utmost propriety was essential, so anything in Cambridge had not only to be well protected but very visibly so.

Bodichon, who was still convalescent, depressed, and inclined to pessimism about the whole project, was not convinced, especially as by February 1868, by when Davies had identified a possible house for rent and wanted to publicly announce the opening of the college, only five women had expressed an interest in attending.[80] How many students would there be? How much would the temporary house cost?[81] Davies couldn't exactly say, and she admitted to Tomkinson that her decision to start slowly was a product of patience acquired under the influence of despair.[82] But where Bodichon saw the lack of progress as a reason to delay, for Davies it was a reason to plunge ahead, for it was evident that just waiting would achieve nothing. And the way to kindle faith, she insisted, was to show it. If those committed to the project were not prepared to take the risk of getting it off the ground, how could they expect anyone else to take the risk of supporting it?

Bodichon was appeased. An announcement was made that the College for Women would open that October, in Hitchin, with fees set at £35 a term (100 guineas a year).[83] The house initially identified didn't work out but another was found.[84] A house committee of Emilia Gurney, Lizzie Garret, and Annie Austin was set up to oversee domestic arrangements.[85] After some active campaigning by Gurney and Adelaide Manning, Charlotte Manning had already agreed in late 1868 to be the first mistress (the title chosen for the resident authority), albeit only for one term, and this was now formally approved.[86] The role of mistress at this stage was a curious one, having much more in common with the lady of a house than with the master of a college, in charge of the servants and the menus, reading daily prayers, and acting where necessary as a mother substitute. It was not a role that particularly appealed, and Manning, who was now in her midsixties and in not particularly good health, seems to have taken it on purely out of friendship.[87]

The other requirement was for tutors, prepared to make the relatively long journey to Hitchin (about an hour and a half each way from the centre of

---

[80] ED to BB, 20 February 1869, *EDCL*, 307–8; ED to AM, 26 February 1869, *EDCL*, 532–3.

[81] ED to BB, 2 March 1869, 11 March 1869, *EDCL*, 309, 311–13.

[82] ED to HRT, 13 March 1869, in Stephen, 208.

[83] ED to MB, 1 March 1869, 9 March 1869, *EDCL*, 308, 310; ED to BB, March 1869, *EDCL*, 311; *Athenaeum* (6 March 1869), 345. This was a small paragraph in amongst the 'weekly gossip'. The same number also included an advertisement for a lecture by Emily Faithfull on the condition and claims of women with special reference to higher education: ibid., 325. The fact that she had been completely cut by Davies did not prevent her from promoting the cause.

[84] ED to BB, ? May 1869, 4 June 1869, 29 June 1869, 13 July 1869, *EDCL*, 315–16, 318–19.

[85] Stephen, 218.

[86] ED to AM, 29 October 1868, *EDCL*, 531; ED to BB, 14 November 1868, *EDCL*, 292–3; ED to CM, 16 April 1869, *EDCL*, 533; ED to MB, 1 May 1869, *EDCL*, 314–15.

[87] She died in April 1871.

Cambridge). Davies evidently paid well enough, however, for she quickly assembled a strong team. For the core Cambridge subjects she engaged John Venn, James Stuart, Edwin Clark, and Fenton Hort. Venn, a mathematician later famous for his Venn diagram, was a cousin of Emilia Gurney. He had recently married and resigned his fellowship but was still lecturing in Cambridge.[88] Clark, engaged to teach Greek and Latin, was another married former fellow, shortly to become Regius Professor of Civil Law. Hort, a distinguished biblical scholar, would teach theology and the Greek New Testament. Also on the books for subsidiary subjects, should they be wanted, were Seeley, Liveing, and two London teachers for modern languages.[89]

That left the project wanting only students—or parents willing to send their students. It had always been intended that candidates should sit an entrance examination, and by the time this took place, in London on 16 July, eighteen candidates presented themselves, while another one, known to be strong, asked to be examined in October.[90] Two full scholarships were offered, for three years each, funded by Emilia Gurney, Lady Marian Alford (wife of the dean), and four other ladies.[91] Even Bodichon was encouraged.[92] Thirteen of the candidates passed, and meeting them individually Davies was impressed. All were twenty or older, good natured, and prepared to put up with the inevitable limitations of a hired house.[93] 'There is not one', she wrote to Bodichon, 'as to whom there need be the least fear that she will do anything foolish.'[94] For Davies, acutely conscious of reputation, that was probably their most important quality.

[88] JS to ED, 4 March 1869, GCPP Davies 15/1/3/8; ED to MB, 9 March 1869, *EDCL*, 310.
[89] *EDCL*, 327; ED to MB, 9 March 1869, *EDCL*, 310; ED to AM, 2 June 1869, in Stephen, 198–9; ED to HRT, 16 March 1869, in Stephen, 208–9.
[90] ED to BB, 4 April 1869, 13 July 1869, *EDCL*, 316–17, 319.   [91] Stephen, 214.
[92] ED to BB, 29 June 1869, 21 July 1869, 2 August 1869, August 1869, *EDCL*, 318–21.
[93] ED to BB, 2 July 1869, 21 July 1869, *EDCL*, 533, 319; Stephen, 213.
[94] ED to BB, 2 August 1869, *EDCL*, 320.

12

Girton and Newnham

In October 1869, the College for Women in Hitchin opened its doors to the first intake of five students (a sixth was delayed by illness and joined in January). By this time Davies had recruited a general committee of thirty-six names, including Acland and Bryce, Lyttelton and Maurice, the bishops of Peterborough and St David's, and the deans of Chichester and Ely. The college committee was now described formally as an executive committee (though it would still be referred to under its old name), comprising Lady Augusta Stanley, Lady Goldsmid, Dean Alford, Barbara Bodichon, Emilia Gurney, George Hastings, James Heywood, Charlotte Manning, Fanny Metcalfe, Henry Roby, John Seeley, and Sedley Taylor, with Henry Tomkinson as treasurer and Emily Davies as secretary.[1]

Two months later, in early December, Henry Sidgwick co-opted the Fawcetts' drawing room for a tea party launch of a programme of lectures for women in Cambridge. These were tailored to the new examinations, but the Cambridge reformers were more interested in opening up university-level education to women, as Davies was trying to do, than in providing certificated learning for teachers and governesses. They differed from her only in their disapproval of the existing examination structure and their belief that the work could best be done in Cambridge.

Cambridge in 1869–70 was a university in the process of change. John Maynard Keynes would later pinpoint the late 1860s and early 1870s as a 'great change-over', the 'critical moment at which Christian dogma fell away from the serious philosophical world'.[2] It was already very different from the university Llewelyn Davies had attended twenty years earlier, and in some ways quite different from what Emily Davies seems to have imagined.[3]

One of the changes was academic: it had become intellectually much broader. Mathematics was still central. All degree candidates had to pass papers in elementary mathematics and all honours candidates had to pass more advanced papers, but the requirements on candidates for honours outside mathematics had been gradually loosened. Moreover, the two new tripos examinations introduced in 1859, in natural sciences and moral sciences, which had at first grown very slowly,

---

[1] College Report, November 1869, Girton GCCP 1/1/1pt.
[2] A. C. Pigou, ed., *Memorials of Alfred Marshall* (Macmillan, 1925), 7–8.
[3] Peter Searby, *A History of the University of Cambridge*, Vol. 3: *1750–1870* (Cambridge University Press, 1997), 507 ff.

Emily Davies and the Mid-Victorian Women's Movement. John Hendry, Oxford University Press. © John Hendry 2024.
DOI: 10.1093/oso/9780198910237.003.0012

were rapidly gaining ground. Colleges were employing lecturers to teach them and they were no longer considered easy options.

A second change was religious. The university was still in effect a Church of England institution and some of the colleges were church foundations, but under the influence of internal, broad church pressures on one hand and parliamentary pressures on the other it had opened up considerably. Since 1856, dissenters had been able to take the BA degree and from 1871, following the Universities Tests Act, they would also be able to take their MAs and be members of the senate. The same Act would loosen the religious requirements on fellowships, most of which had traditionally required ordination, while the Clerical Subscription Act of 1865 had already loosened the requirements on ordained clergymen, responding to broad church pressure by requiring only 'general' assent to the 39 articles.

A third change of importance in the present context was what Sidgwick described as a movement against celibacy—an acceptance of marriage and with it a general loosening of social and sexual boundaries that brought women more into contact with the university.[4] The university had traditionally comprised three groups of men: masters or heads of house, who were the only people allowed to combine a college position with marriage and were at the top of the hierarchy; resident fellows, who formed the main body of the community, including salaried tutors and college officers together with single men who found it convenient to live in college, perhaps taking private students, but without any formal obligations; and professors, who could either be married or attached to a college but not both. As the new triposes had gained ground, the professors, whose expertise covered a much wider range than the subjects traditionally taught, had become more involved with the rest of the university. In the course of the 1860s, some of the colleges had amended their statues so as to allow professors and a very few others to hold fellowships, even though married. Meanwhile, fellows who married and had on that account to give up their fellowships were increasingly continuing to live and pursue their academic work in the city, often with some other kind of college appointment.

Amongst the reformers at this time was Henry Sidgwick. A classicist and moral philosopher (his book *The Methods of Ethics*, which he was writing at this time, is often considered the greatest work of philosophy in the English language), he had been a fellow of Trinity since 1859 and had campaigned ceaselessly both for a widening of the curriculum to reflect contemporary intellectual developments and for revisions to the existing classical and moral sciences triposes to make them intellectually more rigorous.[5] John Peile later wrote of him, 'He was at no time the leader of the party. But he often led the leaders: and he always had wide influence on those who were not leaders.'[6]

[4] HS to Oscar Browning, 7 June 1871, in Sidgwick, 247.
[5] Bart Schultz, *Henry Sidgwick: Eye of the Universe* (Cambridge University Press, 2004).
[6] Sidgwick, 204.

In June 1869, feeling unable to subscribe to the Apostle's Creed and the religious commitments he had entered into as a fellow, Sidgwick had after much agonizing resigned his fellowship, but not his faith.[7] He would eventually come to concede that he could not strictly consider himself a Christian—he would describe himself rather as a religious theist—but for the present he remained firmly in communion with the church. And as all around him recognized, he was deeply religious. His main influences were F. D. Maurice and Arthur Clough, Anne's deceased brother, who had tormented himself with religious doubt. He identified particularly with Clough's religious trials and wrote to Myers in 1870 that 'If Clough had not lived and written I should probably be now exactly what he was.'[8] But through reading Clough he saved himself the same torment, and although he drifted away, always questioning, from Christianity towards theism he always remained close in spirit to Maurice. At this time he considered himself a broad church Maurician, the only question being—as for many of his Cambridge colleagues—how broad the Christian church could be while still being Christian.[9]

On resigning his fellowship, Sidgwick was immediately appointed to a well-paid college lectureship, and it was widely thought that it was his resignation, above all, that prompted the 1871 Universities Tests Act. Meanwhile, as well as becoming a friend and colleague of Maurice, working together on the moral sciences tripos, he had also become a close colleague of Henry Fawcett, both being strong advocates of Mill's philosophy, and a close friend of Arthur Clough's widow and, through her, of Anne Clough.[10] With these multiple connections, and as the university's leading reformer, it was natural that he should take the lead in the move towards educating women at Cambridge.

According to Millicent Fawcett, 'the object of the tea', at her house on 2 December, 'was to collect ladies whom I thought would be interested in a lecture scheme that has just been started here for women'.[11] A committee was formed with Sidgwick and Markby as joint secretaries and a mixture of Cambridge dons and their wives and daughters. According to Fawcett, writing to Helen Taylor, 'All the promoters of this scheme feel that it will very probably be the means of ultimately admitting women to the University'. They didn't say so publicly, only 'because it would frighten so many excellent people who are now willing to help'.[12]

---

[7] Sidgwick, 188–9.

[8] HS to FWHM, 26 October 1870, in Sidgwick, 227.

[9] A few years earlier, Leslie Stephen, another Cambridge disciple of Maurice, had come to the conclusion that its breadth was limited and that Maurice was really an agnostic, and had resigned his college tutorship but had remained for a time a fellow and in holy orders. Noel Annan, *Leslie Stephen: The Godless Victorian* (University of Chicago Press, 1986), 45–6.

[10] Sidgwick, 141, 192–3, 197.

[11] MG to Louise Garrett, 3 December 1869, Anderson Family Papers, quoted in Crawford, 133–4.

[12] MFG to HT, 4 December 1869, Johns Hopkins University, J. S. Mill letters, quoted in David Rubinstein, 'Victorian feminists: Henry and Millicent Garrett Fawcett', in Lawrence Goldman, ed., *The Blind Victorian: Henry Fawcett and British Liberalism* (Cambridge University Press, 1989), 71–92: 80,

GIRTON AND NEWNHAM   205

Whether that was really the case, or whether at this stage it was just the Fawcetts, Sidgwick, and a few others who shared that ambition, is hard to say, but the first step was to get up some lectures and this happened almost immediately. About eighty women attended courses in the Lent term, all of which seem to have been at the level of the new examinations. There was also talk of arrangements by which women outside Cambridge might attend the lectures and the following October, at Markby's instigation, three young women who had performed particularly well in the local examinations, one of them a niece of Wolstenholme's, took up residence in a girls' boarding school in order to do so.[13]

Both Sidgwick and Millicent Fawcett had earlier suggested hostels for women wishing to study in Cambridge, Sidgwick for the 'resident authorities' of the College for Women, Fawcett for women undergraduates. Wolstenholme, visiting her niece and brother during the winter of 1870–1, urged Sidgwick on and in January he reported to his mother that the responsibility for finding suitable accommodation had fallen on his shoulders. Two months later he wrote to Anne Clough saying that he had engaged to open a boarding house for women staying in Cambridge to attend the lectures; that he needed someone to take charge of it; that if she weren't so occupied with her own work he would press her to do it; and could she think of anyone else?[14]

By October 1871 Sidgwick had rented a house in Regent Street and Clough had moved into residence with five students, one of whom was in receipt of an exhibition donated by John Stuart Mill and Helen Taylor. Three others soon joined them.[15] A year later the house was moved to Merton Hall, a larger building on St John's College land, taken initially on a two-year lease. Ostensibly at least the purpose was still to accommodate young women attending the Cambridge lectures, but by the following year it was being suggested to several of them that they might study for the tripos examinations, receiving private tutoring from their lecturers. Four of the original eight did just that, three of them taking and passing the tripos examinations in 1874 and one in 1875.[16] Meanwhile, Merton Hall ceasing to be available, a fundraising campaign led to the building and opening, in 1875, of Newnham Hall, which would later become Newnham College.[17]

By the time those taking the Cambridge lectures began work on the tripos at Merton Hall, Emily Davies had long since secured the agreement of enough of the university degree examiners to also examine her own students, in a private capacity and without charge, both for the little-go and for the tripos, and the first

and see David Rubinstein, *A Different World for Women: The Life of Millicent Garrett Fawcett* (Harvester, 1991), 26–7.

[13] Menella B. Smedley, 'The English girl's education', *Contemporary Review*, 14 (April 1870), 29–41: 38. Ann Phillips, ed., *A Newnham Anthology*, 2nd ed. (Newnham College, 1988), 2.

[14] Wright, 86; HS to Mary Sidgwick, 15 January 1871, in Sidgwick, 242; HS to AC, 18 March 1871, Sidgwick, 244.

[15] HS to FWHM, May/June 1870, in Sidgwick, 246; Crawford, 136.

[16] Phillips, ed., *A Newnham Anthology*, 3; Sidgwick, 210.   [17] Clough, 156–62.

were about to sit their final examinations.[18] In that sense Sidgwick was following in her footsteps. The conditions under which the two groups of students worked were, however, quite different. Davies stuck to the prescribed regime for men: the little-go, which took up the first four terms of study, was compulsory, and the whole was to be completed within the prescribed terms of residence. The Merton Hall students were under no such restrictions. They were not required to take the little-go, and they could if they wished study at their leisure. And for Davies, Sidgwick was not so much a fellow innovator as a thorn in the side, his scheme 'a serpent gnawing at our vitals'.[19]

In his own eyes, and in those of the world at large, Sidgwick was a supporter of the College for Women. In January 1869 he wrote an article for Hutton's *Spectator*, putting the case for the special examinations and also setting out the relationship between the two projects:[20]

> Whatever may be said in favour of a different school education for the two sexes, the present exclusion of women from the higher studies of the University is perfectly indefensible in principle, and must sooner or later give way. When this barrier is broken down, whatever special examinations for women may still be retained will be very different from any that we now institute. At present we have two distinct classes to consider: students who wish for guidance and support in their studies, and professional teachers who wish to obtain proof of adequate capacity. The first class will be composed of specially intellectual girls, and all these will try to obtain honours. It is only the inferior portion of the second class who will try merely to pass. In their case we shall be distinguishing the competent from the incompetent by examining them in the few subjects which they will certainly profess and be required to teach. We cannot expect parents in general suddenly to alter their views of what girls are to be taught; and we shall probably have more immediate effect in improving education by raising the quality of what is demanded, than by attempting to supply something else.

In June 1871, by when there was talk of Davies building outside Cambridge, he wrote to his friend Oscar Browning that 'we shall have two systems of Higher Education of Women going on side by side. However, we are accustomed in Cambridge to a complexity of systems, and there are plenty of fine old arguments to prove that it is rather a help than a hindrance.'[21] Dealing with Davies was, how-

---

[18] ED to HRT, 25 November 1870, *EDCL*, 353; W. M. Gunson to ED, 18 November 1872, in Stephen, 273.

[19] ED to HS, 19 May 1871, *EDCL*, 543.

[20] *Spectator*, 42 (16 January 1869), 42, reproduced in Sidgwick, 189.

[21] HS to Oscar Browning, 7 June 1871, in Sidgwick, 247. He went on to say: 'The work takes up my time rather, but is very entertaining. And I am growing fond of women. I like working with them. I begin to sympathise with the pleasures of the mild parson.'

ever, a struggle. 'I am forced more and more into involuntary antagonism with Miss Davies,' he declared to Myers.[22] Others felt the same. Clough wrote to her sister-in-law: 'If it is possible, Miss D will out general us. She is a most formidable and skilful antagonist.'[23] But Sidgwick maintained his position: 'I find it hard to get my friends here to sympathise with my extreme disinclination to hinder in any way the success of [Davies's] efforts,' he wrote, again to Blanche Clough. 'However, I trust in the strong breeze that is at present carrying on all movements in this direction.'[24]

Davies, for her part, seems to have been convinced that he and his party were trying to sink her: 'I am sure', she had written to him prior to the letters just mentioned, 'that it is generous inconsistency and not cruel mockery that makes you say you are willing to help us, when your scheme is the serpent which is gnawing at our vitals. It glides in everywhere. As soon as any interest is awakened, people are told there is something else, as good or better, and which does not ask for money. I daresay it does not end in their doing much for the Lectures, but it is enough to hold them back from doing anything for the College.'[25]

Davies was clearly frustrated by her own lack of progress in fundraising, but she also had a view of Sidgwick and the Cambridge reformers that must have revived her earlier hostility to the radicals in the women's movement. Hearing of the tea party at which the Cambridge lectures were launched (either via Elizabeth Garrett from her sister or via Bodichon from Elizabeth Blackwell, who was visiting Cambridge and attended), she referred, in a letter to Bodichon, to the possibility that 'the ultras [i.e. the Sidgwick–Fawcett faction] may start a small secular female place at Cambridge, with lectures given by University men'.[26] A month later she wrote to Anna Richardson that 'One reason why I am not anxious to join hands with the ultras is that I do not care to have a set of lawless young Radicals, thinking it clever to disbelieve, and setting aside Christian teachers as narrow old fogies, not to be listened to.'[27]

The Fawcetts were certainly 'young Radicals', and Millicent had probably set aside her early adherence to Maurice and joined her husband as a 'disbeliever'. But even they were perfectly lawful and, as applied to Sidgwick and those involved in the Cambridge lectures more generally, the criticism was wholly unfounded. Sidgwick was, as noted above, deeply religious and still much influenced by Maurice. He would question Christian teachers—he was a profound philosopher who would *question* all authorities—but he would never disrespect them or set them aside. Of those involved with the lectures, whether on the executive committee, the wider general committee or as lecturers, some were indeed young

[22] HS to FWHM, May/June 1871, in Sidgwick, 247.
[23] AC to Blanche Clough, n.d., Newnham College archives, quoted in Sutherland, 81.
[24] HS to Blanche Clough, 9 December 1871, in Sidgwick, 255.
[25] ED to HS, 19 May 1871, *EDCL*, 543.   [26] Ibid.
[27] ED to AR, 12th day 1870, in *EDCL*, 537–8: 538.

men, others older, established academics. All were liberal reformers. But almost all were committed members of the Church of England, and several were in orders, Maurice amongst them. They were certainly no more radical and no less Christian than Davies's own college committee, which included both James Heywood, a Unitarian who had been at the forefront of the reform movement in the late 1840s, and Sedley Taylor, another reformer who like Sidgwick resigned his Trinity fellowship, and in his case also left holy orders, in 1869, but like Sidgwick remained both resident in Trinity, with a college appointment, and in communion with the church.[28] Whilst Merton Hall would be 'secular', moreover, in the sense of having no specifically Christian commitments (and allowing its students to omit the study of theology required for the little-go), it would never be actively opposed to Christian teaching.

While Davies was railing at Sidgwick and his colleagues over the Cambridge lecture programme, she was also tussling with her own committee over a location for her college. The house at Hitchin had been taken for three years, eventually extended to four, but it could only ever be a temporary solution. The house itself could only accommodate six students, and even with the gardener's cottage and a 'tin tabernacle' in the garden—a functional temporary building of tin-clad iron—it could only accommodate thirteen. A site on which to build was needed. The question was, where?

Davies was still set on Hitchin and insisted, in writing to Bodichon, that '5-sixths of the Committee & nine-tenths of our supporters all over the country' were not only with her but would 'withdraw altogether' if they were to move to Cambridge. Citing Emilia Gurney, Lady Augusta Stanley, '&c. &c.', she insisted that 'It would be breaking faith with the public generally, & more directly with a large number of people who have been & are, working for us on the distinct understanding that the College is *not* to be at Cambridge.'[29] Bodichon, on the other hand, was still set on Cambridge. So was Sedley Taylor and so, when they were eventually consulted, were the Cambridge committee, who resolved unanimously 'that it would be far more advantageous for the College to be established in Cambridge or its suburbs, rather than at a distance exceeding three miles from it.'[30]

The 'distance exceeding three miles' seems to have arisen from Tomkinson, the 'conciliator' on the College committee, who had declared himself 'wishing simply that Hitchin were within half an hour, from door to door, of Cambridge...Until Cambridge becomes Cornell in many respects I shall wish us to be anywhere rather than actually at it. Half an hour off we should be safe from its evils and sure

[28] Stuart, 180. For Heywood's past engagement in university reform see Searby, *A History of the University*, 518–20.

[29] ED to BB, 5 December 1869, *EDCL*, 329–31: 330.

[30] Resolution of 15 November 1870, in Stephen, 250.

GIRTON AND NEWNHAM   209

of its advantages.'[31] Cornell University, which had taken its first students in 1868, was a 'land grant' foundation, occupying a campus built on open farmland in New York State. It would very soon become one of the first universities to admit women, but was evidently a place for serious study, away from the distractions of a university town like Cambridge, which catered for the idle poll degree men as well as serious scholars.

The arguments for being in Cambridge were obvious and powerful. As Sidgwick pleaded, the college would benefit from the professors' lectures, museums, and other resources. The teaching would be cheaper and more readily available, and the teaching in the newer tripos subjects, where teachers were still few but very enthusiastic, would be much more readily available than at a distance.[32] From Davies's perspective, of course, Sidgwick was not to be trusted, the new tripos subjects were easy options, and what Sidgwick saw as a strong positive, the possibility of perhaps bringing the two projects together under the aegis of the college, was to her a strong negative. But the core case was irrefutable. Still, as Tomkinson recognized, she was simply not going to accept a move to Cambridge itself, so some compromise was needed, and in the course of correspondence with Charlotte Burbury, she had talked herself round to the 'not less than three miles.'[33]

Burbury was the daughter of Benjamin Kennedy, then Regius Professor of Greek at Cambridge but for many years earlier the esteemed headmaster of Shrewsbury and the well-known author of Kennedy's *Latin Primer*. Following the death of her husband she had become involved in the women's movement. She was on the committee of SPEW and from 1871 would be secretary to the London suffrage committee. In the process, she had become friendly with Davies and was someone Davies felt she could look to for guidance on Cambridge, where both her father and her sister, Marion Kennedy, were closely involved in the lecture series (as they would be in the creation of Newnham).[34]

Why was Davies so set against being in Cambridge? Her initial objection seems to have been to the male undergraduates, many of whom were not serious scholars. As she wrote to Bodichon, 'Without actually seeing something of College and University life, you can scarcely understand how disturbing it would be to have 2,000 undergraduates, most of them idle and pleasure loving, close to your doors.'[35] But she had no experience of that herself, and when her Cambridge committee argued for being in Cambridge Sedley Taylor made the point on their behalf that 'The moral objections seem to be imaginary. There has never been the

---

[31] HRT to ED, 22 July 1870, in Stephen, 249.
[32] Stephen, 250, and see ED to HS, 31 December 1870, *EDCL*, 540–2.
[33] ED to CB, 2 August 1870, 23 August 1870, *EDCL*, 339–40.
[34] Davies had asked her serve on the house committee for Hitchin, but she had declined: ED to CB, 18 March 1869, *EDCL*, 313–14.
[35] ED to AR, 12th day 1870, *EDCL*, 537–8: 537.

slightest difficulty with the ladies' lectures, though many of those who attend are young girls.' 'With regard to our fitness for judging such a question,' he added, 'I may ask you to remind the Executive Committee that four of those who have signed our Resolution are married men.'[36]

The argument that moving to Cambridge would lose all the support gained signally failed to hold up against the fact that very little support—and very little money—had been gained. The argument that it would stir up opposition in Cambridge was also unpersuasive. Davies ended up by protesting, in a long letter to Sidgwick, 'the impossibility for women to carry on a free, healthy, undisturbed student-life in a town at all, and especially in a University town.'[37] It was not the undergraduates she now dreaded, but the female society: 'the morning calls and the dropping in and the servants coming with notes to wait for an answer, and the general victimisation by idle ladies.'[38] Some would succumb, others would resist, but even those resisting would expend worry and nerves upon it. If anything, this was even less convincing than her other arguments, but she was not to be moved.

Informed by the College committee that they would not be building in Cambridge, the Cambridge committee disbanded in despair.[39] When a suitable site was eventually found, on the Huntingdon Road near the turn-off to Girton village, it was only just over two miles from the centre of town and university. The story usually told is that the site was chosen as being close enough for the lecturers to get out, but far enough away to prevent the students going in. There was something of that, but it was basically as close as Davies could be persuaded to accept, in the absence of anything suitable further out. And behind all the rationalizations, the most persuasive explanation of her resistance would have to centre on two factors. One is her innate conservatism: a fear that like the suffrage movement it would be pushing too far too soon, and through association with atheists and radicals would set back the women's movement rather than advancing it. The other is her fear of losing control: outside Cambridge she would be in control of her own venture, her own empire; inside she would be in danger of being overwhelmed. As in the case of the suffrage, the two factors seem impossible to separate.

Davies must have already felt that she was losing control. The college was her project and her committee were not going to force her to move into Cambridge, but they were clearly divided on this and on other matters. By the late spring of 1871 she wrote to Tomkinson that she was 'seriously considering the propriety of shutting up, but it looks almost as difficult as going on.'[40] Emilia Gurney reflected what must have been her own concerns in a letter of sympathy:[41]

---

[36] ST to ED, n.d., in Stephen, 250.

[37] ED to HS, 31 December 1870, *EDCL*, 540–2. [38] Ibid., 541.

[39] ED to HRT, 22 December 1870, in Stephen, 254; Stephen, 255. See also ED to George Reyner, 18 February 1871, *EDCL*, 356.

[40] ED to HRT 17 May 1871, in Stephen, 258. [41] ERG to ED, 30 May 1871, in Stephen, 259.

GIRTON AND NEWNHAM   211

I own the lukewarmness of <u>friends</u> of the scheme and the division of their sympathies are more discouraging to me than the opposition of enemies—first, the strong feeling of many in favour of Cambridge—secondly, the dislike of many with Professor Lightfoot and J. Venn to our taking the Cambridge examinations rather than those they have agreed upon for women—then the desire for the Lecture system, and boarding out at Cambridge...

I own I have serious doubts whether we are a sufficiently warm-hearted <u>united</u> body to carry it on. Each one of the Committee seems to have a different view,—the Cambridge question rends us in half, yet we are neither half strong enough to do without the other.

Divided support and as yet no money. Only £4,000 had been raised, including Bodichon's £1,000 pledge, and about £2,000 of that had been spent at Hitchin.[42] A fundraising campaign had been launched that spring, with a target of £10,000, and Davies's despair followed the first of what was intended to be a series of fund-raising meetings. 'If I were quite candid,' she wrote to Tomkinson, 'I should confess that it gave me a sense of failure, but I am not sure whether it was because I was cold, and the outer chill penetrated within. The meeting did not strike me as one from which much could be expected to follow, nor that people who came sceptical would go away enthusiastic.'[43]

It is not clear who put together the panel for the meeting, but it looks as though Skelton Anderson, a businessman who had recently married Lizzie Garrett, may well have been involved. The speakers were Garrett Anderson herself; Lyttelton and Fitch, both now familiar faces in the context of women's education; William Connor Magee, the Bishop of Peterborough, who was on the College's general committee; and two men who had no prior record of any interest or involvement in the area: Sir Wilfrid Lawson, the Radical MP for Carlisle, and Henry Winterbotham, the young dissenting Liberal MP for Stroud. With Lyttelton and Magee both sitting on the Conservative benches in the Lords, there was a political balance, but the presence of Lawson is nevertheless striking, given Davies's own political views. Lawson was not merely a Radical but on the extreme and extremely vocal wing of the Radicals: the very last person she would want to be associated with. Winterbotham, who held a junior office in the Gladstone administration, was a moderate Liberal, but a strong supporter of the women's movement. His constituency had been the base for Kate Amberley's recent launch of

[42] A printed prospectus of February 1871 lists donations to date. Other than Bodichon's pledge, about half had come from committee members, typically contributing £100, and the other half in small donations of £10 or £25. Prospectus in bound copy of pamphlets, Women's Library, LSE, at 371.822 WOM, and see also ED to BB, 2 September 1869, *EDCL*, 323–4.
[43] ED to HRT, 15 May 1871, in Stephen, 258.

212 DAVIES AND THE MID-VICTORIAN WOMEN'S MOVEMENT

her own radical feminist campaign,[44] and he had become known for his parliamentary efforts to direct the commission set up to re-purpose school endowments in the wake of the Schools Inquiry Commission, which was chaired by Lyttelton, to allot endowments 'equally' to boys and girls. in this he failed—even Fitch and Bryce thought it impractical—but he did ensure that the Act made specific mention of girls, and stated that they should share in endowments 'as far as conveniently may be'.[45]

The two main speeches were delivered by Garrett Anderson and Magee. Garrett Anderson, by now quite famous and a name to be reckoned with, spoke of the health benefits of both a higher education and, specifically, a college education. Magee, a charismatic orator known to the public mainly as a passionate defender of the established church in Ireland, spoke as a family man, for whom the family came before everything else, and he argued that women should have the highest possible education for one main object: that they should succeed in the 'profession of a matron'. This 'profession' covered all of a woman's domestic responsibilities, but especially the bringing up of children, from their earliest education and training through the awakening of their intellects to winning their confidence and elevating their instincts as they grew into adulthood.

This had always been part of Davies's argument, but it had always been a subsidiary part. The higher education of women, both enabling and ennobling, would *also* benefit those going on to be wives and mothers. Magee made it into the main argument, and coming from a father and bishop, rather than from a spinster, it was much more convincing. The *Saturday Review* remained unconvinced as to the benefits of such an education but was sufficiently impressed by Magee's speech to concede that, if the experiment were to be tried, 'it could not be in better hands than those of the promoters of Hitchin College'.[46]

The meeting resulted in pledges of £600, and in Skelton Anderson being added to the College committee.[47] Though she liked him, and thoroughly approved of her friend's marriage, Davies had doubts. He was an ardent Liberal, committed amongst other things to the separation of state education from the church, and the question was 'whether he could, without outraging his convictions, accept Liberal-Conservative solutions of such questions as are likely to arise in the government of the College'.[48] The reference was to religious status, and this would indeed prove a sticking point, but for now Davies was persuaded that his

---

[44] This was in a speech at Stroud, later published as Viscountess Amberley, 'The claims of women', *Fortnightly Review*, n.s. 9 (January 1871), 95–110. It included a plug for Davies's college, but was received with such disgust that Davies probably wished it hadn't.

[45] Sheila Fletcher, *Feminists and Bureaucrats: A Study in the Development of Girls' Education in the Nineteenth Century* (Cambridge University Press, 1980), 3, 25–9.

[46] 'The profession of an English matron', *Saturday Review*, 31 (20 May 1871), 626–8: 627.

[47] ED to BB, 4 June 1871, *EDCL*, 357–8.

[48] ED to HRT, 17 May 1871, in Stephen, 258.

GIRTON AND NEWNHAM   213

enthusiasm, connections, and abilities were too great to forego—and persuaded also to continue the fight.[49]

A series of less formal fundraising events round the country, set up primarily by Davies herself, with the help of local supporters, followed.[50] A meeting at Leeds was even promoted by Hutton in the *Spectator*, his readers being urged to contribute financially.[51] By early 1872 the campaign had raised over £3,000 on top of the £2,000 plus carried over from earlier,[52] enough to purchase the Girton site and engage Waterhouse to produce some plans. Further funds for the building itself were then raised in the form of a loan, secured by personal guarantees from some of the more wealthy supporters.[53] Meanwhile, with the question of location settled and the tension between them eased, Davies and Bodichon had started working together on the specification for the building and grounds.[54] Davies then worked with Waterhouse and by April 1872 they were ready to start building.[55]

The ability to borrow rather than relying solely on cash in hand was made possible by a decision in late 1871 to incorporate the college as a limited company, registered with the Board of Trade under the 1862 Companies Act. For this purpose the college's aims and purpose had to be written into the memorandum and articles, which again raised two issues of earlier contention. Davies wanted the wording of the memorandum of association to be taken from the existing trust deed for the College for Women, which in turn reflected her original position: that the ultimate aim of the college was incorporation in the University of Cambridge, not merely association with it; and that there were to be religious services and instruction 'in accordance with the principles of the Church of England as by law established'. She insisted, moreover, that the latter wording be incorporated into the memorandum—which was legally binding on the company and could only be changed by Act of Parliament—rather than in the articles of association, which could be modified from time to time as circumstances changed.

Given that the existing men's colleges were all Church of England establishments, the two requirements, in Davies's view, went hand in hand. From her supporters' perspectives, however, they were very different. The aim of incorporation

---

[49] ED to BB, 4 June 1871, *EDCL*, 357–8; Stephen, 258.

[50] Stephen, 261; ED to BB, November/December 1871, 12 December 1871, 20 December 1871, *EDCL*, 362–4.

[51] 'The higher education for women', *Spectator*, 44 (14 October 1871), 1235–6. Apart from pressing the need for a cadre of highly educated women, Hutton emphasized the advantage of an education that was both systematized and, especially, tutorially supported. He supported the college again a few years later, noting that Girton was the only place properly equipped to teach the teachers of the rapidly expanding system of girls' secondary schools, and that it desperately needed funds for building: 'Women's colleges', *Spectator*, 48 (4 December 1875), 1513.

[52] Stephen, 262; ED to BB, 2 February 1872, *EDCL*, 367–8; WS to BB, 10 January 1872, Girton GCPP Bodichon 3/8.

[53] Stephen, 263; ED to BB, 15 January 1872, *EDCL*, 365–6.

[54] ED to AR, 27 September 1871, *EDCL*, 543–4.

[55] ED to BB, 16 January 1872, 21 January 1872, 21 April 1871, *EDCL*, 366–7, 371; John Westlake to BB, 27 March 1872, Girton GCPP Bodichon 3/10.

was shared by the more radical of the Cambridge reformers, including Sidgwick and the Fawcetts, whom Davies saw as her enemies. But for most it was a step too far. Using the resources of the university to advance the higher education of women was one thing. Admitting them into the thoroughly male preserve of the university itself was quite another. Twenty-five years later, the distinguished economist Alfred Marshall, who had been one the very first contributors to the ladies' lectures, who had encouraged his students to sit for the tripos, and who had gone on to marry one of them, led the opposition to awarding them degrees.[56] Even seventy-five years later, they were still to be admitted as members of the university. And for now Davies's insistence on 'incorporation' lost her the support of one of her committee members, Lightfoot, who professed himself utterly opposed to 'anything like a mixed University'.[57]

The religious requirement, on the other hand, was widely seen as too conservative in the context of a university that was increasingly opening itself up to dissenters. This was the case both for the Cambridge reformers and for members of Davies's own college committee, several of whom urged her, as did the Board of Trade officials, to at least put it into the articles rather than the memorandum. Davies was not to be moved, and most bowed to her will, but it did lose her Skelton Anderson, despite his wife's attempts to keep him on board.[58]

The memorandum and articles were formally adopted on 15 May 1872, at which point Girton College came formally into existence. The members of the college committee became members of the college and after various additions and subtractions there were now seventeen of them, the most striking feature of the list being that only two were academics (Bryce and Taylor) and only one was either resident in Cambridge or employed in the university or colleges. That one, moreover, Sedley Taylor, was a constant thorn in Davies's side. She wanted to keep him, if only for appearance's sake,[59] but he had repeatedly disagreed with her, and would grow further apart as the college developed. A year after the college was incorporated, when he was again causing her problems, she complained to Bodichon, 'I think it rather too bad of people who never come to a meeting & do nothing at all for the College, to take advantage of their position on the Committee to worry those who are doing the work.'[60] 'I wonder', she wrote of him a few weeks later, 'it does not seem to occur to people who do nothing that they have no right to bother.'[61]

---

[56] See the reminiscences of John Maynard Keynes and Francis Edgeworth in Pigou, ed., *Memorials of Alfred Marshall*, 55, 72.

[57] Stephen, 263.

[58] ED to W. H. Crosskey, November 1871, *EDCL*, 544–5. EGA to JSA, 6 November 1871, in Stephen, 265; Stephen, 265. Elizabeth Garrett Anderson seems not to have seen it as a big issue. Standing for the London School Board she had declared herself against secular education at elementary level. Anderson was for it. It didn't stop them marrying. EG to ED, 24 October 1870, GCPP Davies 5/1/6.

[59] ED to ST, 28 November 1871, *EDCL*, 361.

[60] ED to BB, 18 February 1873, *EDCL*, 394–5.

[61] ED to BB, 11 March 1874, *EDCL*, 398–9: 399.

GIRTON AND NEWNHAM   215

Of the other fifteen, Tomkinson, Roby, and Heywood were at least Cambridge graduates (though Heywood, as a Unitarian, had been unable to take his degree), but the largest constituency was 'ladies': Lady Goldsmid, Lady Augusta Stanley, Lady Stanley of Alderley (who had joined the committee after her husband had died),[62] Lady Rich (Tomkinson's cousin, widow of a baronet), Mary Ponsonby (wife of the Queen's private secretary, whom Davies had met on another committee), and Emilia Gurney.[63] This reflected Davies's continuing belief that the top priority in respect of establishing the college was to persuade mothers that it was a safe place for their daughters, that social respectability counted for more than reforming zeal. It should not be allowed to obscure the fact, however, that the college was very much a product of the women's movement. Besides Davies herself, Bodichon, Gurney, and Goldsmid were all long-standing members of the movement and Bodichon, who might be called the founder of the movement in its current form, was a key player. Garrett Anderson was a constant presence in the background, as were Davies's longstanding aides Jane Crow and Annie Austin. At the more radical end, Wolstenholme, Butler, Fawcett, and more tangentially Becker and Helen Taylor had all been involved in the parallel development of Merton Hall/Newnham. In the grander scheme of women's rights and opportunities, two colleges in Cambridge, neither formally connected with the university, might seem a minor matter, but they engaged a large part of the women's movement of the 1860s and early 1870s.

While all this was going on, the college at Hitchin was moving forward in fits and starts, as start-up ventures often do. Davies spent as much time there as she could spare from her many committees, campaigning, and family obligations. In those early years it was a curious amalgam of college, domestic household, and finishing school. Davies had always insisted that her students would be responsible young woman, not girls, and several of the early students were well into their twenties, but she nevertheless imposed school-like constraints: a fixed regime with roll calls three times a day, prayers, and early gate hours; strict rules on going out or on visitors coming in; written permission to be excused prayers or church.[64] She insisted on chaperoning the students in their lectures—to James Stuart's amusement and amazement—and insisted on some resident authority—the mistress, herself, or one of the lady members—being in the building at all times, day and night.[65] A famous event occurred in early 1871 when the students, engaging

---

[62] He had died in 1869 but she had first to sort out her family affairs and joined the committee a year later. It turned out that her eldest son and successor to the title and estates had secretly married a Roman Catholic Spanish woman, of uncertain provenance (and who turned out to be already married under another name), and that he had himself converted to Islam.

[63] Lady Hobart's husband had been appointed governor of Madras, taking her out of the country.

[64] Stephen, 220; Louisa Lumsden, *Yellow Leaves: Memories of a Long Life* (Blackwood, 1933), 46–7; 'Daily schedule', Girton GCPP Davies 15/2/21, part in *EDCL*, 327.

[65] Stuart, 179; ED to BB, 5 December 1869, 13 December 1869, *EDCL*, 329–32; Stephen, 230; Lumsden, *Yellow Leaves*, 49; Crawford, 130.

in amateur dramatics, put on a performance for staff and visitors (Davies, Annie Austin, Julia Wedgwood, lecturers, and servants) and those in male roles dressed in men's clothes. Davies was horrified and wanted disciplinary action. She felt, she recalled later, that the whole future of the college was at stake.[66] Bodichon and Tomkinson were called in and managed to reduce the temperature. Bodichon reported to Davies afterwards that she had never met such a spirit of revolt and self-confidence and had probably made little impression, but in private she evidently sympathized with the students and used her natural warmth to smooth things over, so that the whole matter could be quietly dropped.[67]

The peculiar nature of the college was reflected in the job description of the mistress. Charlotte Manning took on the role for only a term, to get the enterprise up and running. Thanks to contacts made through Emilia Gurney and Fanny Wedgwood, she was succeeded in January 1870 by Emily Shirreff, with Fanny's daughter, Julia ('Snow') Wedgwood, also joining temporarily as a tutor.[68] Wedgwood, Darwin's niece, a novelist, writer, and intellectual, disciple of Maurice and intimate friend of Gurney, was already active in the women's movement.[69] The daughter of an admiral, Shirreff was not personally known to Davies. She had mixed in intellectual circles and was for a time a close friend and confidant of the historian Henry Buckle.[70] Back in the 1850s she had written two books (one with her sister Maria Grey) on girls' education, arguing strongly that women should be educated as the equals of men and not as their subordinates.[71] She had also written a pamphlet for the Ladies London Emancipation Society, but she had spent much of the previous decade either sick herself or caring for family and friends. She had recently returned from nine months in France and Italy, caring for a friend (and getting ill herself), and while she recalled that 'a proposition to go as a missionary to Fiji' would have caused less amazement to her friends, she accepted the offer.[72]

---

[66] Stephen, 241–4.

[67] ED to HRT, 8 March 1871, *EDCL*, 452–3; 17 March 1871, 24 March 1871, in Stephen, 242–4; ED to AM, 17 March 1871, in Stephen, 243.

[68] ED to BB, 5 December 1869, 31 January 1870, *EDCL*, 329–31, 333–4; ED to AR, 30 December 1869, *EDCL*, 536–7; ED to HRT, 8 March 1871, *EDCL*, 542–3; Stephen, 229, 241.

[69] Julia Wedgwood, 'Female suffrage, considered chiefly with regard to its indirect results', in Josephine Butler, ed., *Woman's Work and Woman's Culture* (Macmillan, 1869), 247–89. See also her 'Female suffrage in its influence on moral life', *Contemporary Review*, 20 (August 1872), 360–70; and Sue Brown, *Julia Wedgwood, the Unexpected Victorian; The Life and Writing of a Remarkable Female Intellectual* (Anthem Press, 2023).

[70] Edward Ellsworth, *Liberators of the Female Mind: The Shirreff Sisters, Educational Reform and the Women's Movement* (Greenwood Press, 1979); ED to AR, 30 December 1869, *EDCL*, 536–7: 536.

[71] Emily Shirreff, *Intellectual Education and Its Influence on the Character and Happiness of Women* (J. W. Parker, 1858); Maria Grey and Emily Shirreff, *Thoughts on Self Culture Addressed to Women* (Edward Moxon, 1850).

[72] Quoted in Josephine Kamm, *Indicative Past: A Hundred Years of the Girls' Public Day School Trust* (George Allen & Unwin, 1971), 32; Ellsworth, *Liberators of the Female Mind*, 23.

Shirreff seemed to Davies a perfect choice for mistress: a highly respectable upper-middle-class lady in her fifties who was also extremely able intellectually. 'In some respects', she wrote to Anna Richardson, 'I like her better than anyone else that has been thought of. She has a Stoical way of talking which attracts me. Her view of coming here is simply that if she is wanted, and can do it, she ought. She takes a modest view of her duties, and undertakes them simply, without any grand air of self-sacrifice. It is a spirited thing to do, from mere interest in the idea, at her age.'[73] This was before she started, however. Once in place, her view of her duties, which were nowhere clearly defined, evolved in ways not quite to Davies's liking. In particular, she wished, quite reasonably, both to take charge of the direction of studies and to sit on the executive committee, neither of which Davies would allow.[74]

The situation was eventually resolved by Shirreff resigning as mistress after just two terms and joining the executive committee instead, and she remained a strong and public supporter of the college.[75] Davies produced various rationalizations for her views on the matter,[76] but her main reason for resisting Shirreff's claims was evidently that, like many innovators, she was frightened of losing control. This was reflected in her next appointment as mistress, Annie Austin. She would have preferred a distinguished lady (preferably a 'Lady'), but the position was unlikely to appeal to anyone of that kind. Austin had no obvious qualifications, in terms of either distinction or academe, but she was old enough and respectable enough to pass (a widow in her late thirties with a comfortable income and a teenage son) and could be trusted to do Davies's bidding.[77]

Austin served formally as mistress for two years, but in February 1872 she fell ill, and while she recovered fully she felt either unable or unwilling to resume this duty.[78] At first Davies boxed and coxed with Bodichon and Lady Stanley. At Easter she took over, reluctantly, as acting mistress.[79] By June, having tried everyone she knew and could trust, and unwilling to risk a stranger, she had conceded that the least risky option might be to do the job herself. 'Mrs Gurney asks in her last note,' she wrote to Tomkinson, ' "Shall you not be <u>driven</u> into being Mistress at last?" I begin to think of it as inevitable.'[80] She continued to prevaricate, but her closest colleagues were evidently of the view that if she couldn't agree to anyone

---

[73] ED to AR, 10 December 1869, *EDCL*, 536.

[74] ED to CM, 28 February 1870, in Stephen, 234; 2 March 1870, *EDCL*, 538.

[75] Ellsworth, *Liberators of the Female Mind*, 23; ES to BB, 7 May 1870, Girton GCPP Bodichon 3/6; ED to CM, 28 February 1870, in Stephen, 234; 2 March 1870, *EDCL*, 538. Emily Shirreff, 'College education for women', *Contemporary Review*, 15 (August 1870), 55–66; 'The schools of the future', *Contemporary Review*, 17 (June 1871), 443–60; 'Girton College', *Fortnightly Review*, n.s. 14 (July 1873), 87–93.

[76] ED to CM, 2 March 1870, *EDCL*, 538.

[77] ED to CM, 19 March 1870, in Stephen, 236.

[78] ED to CB, 26 March 1872, *EDCL*, 369.

[79] Stephen, 269–70.

[80] ED to HRT, 10 June 1872, in Stephen, 270.

else taking the role, which she couldn't, then she would have to take it herself. By early August she had been appointed.[81]

The practicalities were horrendous. She was heavily weighed down with London School Board work. She was still heavily committed to the London Association of Schoolmistresses and other activities in respect of girls' secondary education. There was building work at Girton that she would need to oversee. And there was her mother to look after. Mary Davies had two servants in the house and her brother and his family close by, but as she grew older the main responsibility must have fallen on her daughter. Jane Crow now moved in with her, however, and Davies was released.

The role of mistress was not one she really wanted, nor one to which she was well suited. She didn't have the natural authority of Bodichon (whom the students found warm, encouraging, and interested) or Lady Stanley (strict, dogmatic, but great fun and with no formality). Indeed, her natural tendency, rather than dealing with a problem herself, was to refer it upwards to the executive committee and then make sure it was decided how she wanted, but without appearing personally responsible for the decision. As secretary, behind the mask of her committee, she had been able to rub along with the students, more or less. As mistress, she was more obviously calling the shots, and remained somewhat distant.[82]

She was remembered by the students as kind and genial, plucky and courageous, but stiff and reserved and not strong.[83] (Given her other commitments at this time she must have been exhausted.) With rare exceptions she maintained an air of formality and seems to have taken little interest in the students personally.[84] Louisa Lumsden, one of the older students, recalled that the individual student was in some ways 'a mere cog in the wheel of her great scheme. There was a fine element in this, a total indifference to popularity, but…it was plain that we counted for little or nothing, except as we furthered her plans.'[85] This was perhaps biased (they crossed swords more than once), but Davies was certainly more interested in the project than the individual. Marian Evans had responded to the low initial intake by writing that 'I care so much about individual happiness that I think it is a great thing to work for, only to make half-a-dozen lives better than they might otherwise be.'[86] Davies wasn't really interested in half a dozen lives. Her mission was to use the college to change the world for women, and her main concern was with the things she felt might threaten that project. She needed the students to do well in the approved examinations, and she needed them above all

---

[81] Stephen, 270–2.

[82] Recollections of Constance Maynard, Girton GCPP Stephen 3.

[83] Recollections of Frances Dove, Girton GCPP Stephen 2. Barbara Stephen, *Girton College, 1869-1932* (Cambridge University Press, 1933), 63.

[84] Recollections of Constance Maynard, Girton GCPP Stephen 3.

[85] Stephen, 232, quoting from Louisa Lumsden, 'The ancient history of Girton College', *Girton Review* (Michaelmas Term, 1907).

[86] GE to ED, 19 November 1869, GCPP Davies 4/3, in Stephen, 227.

GIRTON AND NEWNHAM 219

to be respectable, to show by their appearance and behaviour what a highly educated woman could be. She was pained by those who didn't work or dropped out, and ever alert to the slightest transgression of the rigid rules she had set for the place. She was sorely tried.

Of the initial intake of six students, one left after a year and two were in Davies's terms 'eccentric'. Isabella Townshend failed the little-go in mathematics twice, so on Davies's rules was unable to sit any degree examinations; but holding a scholarship she stayed on. Emily Gibson really wanted to study moral sciences rather than mathematics or classics, and that not being available she left off her study, eventually left the college a term before finals, and got engaged to Townshend's brother. Their set of friends was, in Davies's view, thoroughly disreputable (she heard reports of Gibson's sister wearing a dress 'unpleasantly low'), and they were troublemakers.[87]

Subsequent intakes appeared to be more respectable: younger (the first intake had included women of twenty-eight and thirty-two) and so more suited to Davies's regime, regulars at daily prayers, more studious, and more churchgoing.[88] But they still struggled with Davies's insistence that mathematics and classics were the only proper degree subjects, and with a system in which the compulsory little-go took far more work than it would for a young man from a good boys' school, taking away time from higher studies. They weren't going to get a degree anyway, and to have their education dictated by degree requirements must have been very frustrating. In February 1873, all thirteen students then in residence signed a memorial to the executive committee requesting that the rules be changed so that students be allowed to take the tripos examinations without having taken the little-go, and that they be allowed more than the stipulated ten terms.[89]

Davies, who put the blame on the original intake, the survivors of which had just completed their finals,[90] was disgusted. It was like undergraduates daring to petition the master of a men's college, or Miss Buss's pupils petitioning to take the local examinations without sticking by the rules set for those.[91] It was, of course, not at all the same, but Davies was fiercely opposed to 'the unreasonableness & almost baseness of grasping at men's honours on women's terms', or 'getting men's Honours on cheap terms for women'.[92] She also believed that whatever its merits or otherwise, the little-go served an essential purpose for her students. If they

[87] ED to ECC, 15 March 1873, *EDCL*, 399–401; ED to BB, 25 May 1873, 12 June 1874, *EDCL*, 402–3: 403; 425–9; Stephen, 231.
[88] ED to Mrs Oliver, 22 November 1872, *EDCL*, 381–2.
[89] ED to BB, 8 February 1873, 18 February 1873, *EDCL*, 388–9, 394–5; Girton GCPP Bodichon 3/13.
[90] ED to BB, 8 February 1873, *EDCL*, 388–9; ED to ECC, 15 March 1873, *EDCL*, 399–401. One of the first intake, who acted as spokesperson for the students, had upset Davies the previous term by systematically absenting herself from the compulsory morning register.
[91] ED to BB, early February 1873, 18 February 1873, *EDCL*, 390–2; 394–5.
[92] ED to BB, 5 March 1873, *EDCL*, 396–7; 13 February 1873, *EDCL*, 392–3: 392.

were able to move straight to the tripos, she thought their choice would probably be moral sciences, which, she explained to Bodichon, 'would be the worst they could make. It is not the kind of reading for young persons from 18 to 21 to give their whole strength to during the whole of their College course.'[93] It was, in fact, precisely the kind of reading that Bodichon had given her whole strength to at that age, but that will probably not have crossed Davies's mind.

In practical terms, she treated the matter badly. First, she dissuaded the students from circulating the memorial to the executive committee, assuring them that the matter would not be decided immediately but would be referred to a subcommittee of studies. She then tabled the memorial (outside the agenda) at an executive committee meeting with a very small attendance, which referred some minor issues to the subcommittee, but simply rejected the requests to omit the little-go or extend the period of residence.[94] The situation quickly escalated, as the students heard one thing from Davies, another from members of the executive committee.[95] The lecturers were then involved. Most had long thought the little-go 'not only irksome, but comparatively useless',[96] and would have much preferred to teach to the special examinations for women instead. Sedley Taylor and at least one other objected strongly to how the matter had been handled, and a month later seven lecturers came out with a printed statement in the students' support.[97]

Most of the executive committee probably sympathized with the students as well, but they knew that Davies would not be moved and rallied round. The rules remained unchanged and the affair blew over. For Davies, the lesson seems to have been that, like it or not, she would have to remain mistress over the move to Girton, where the students would inevitably come into contact with those at Merton Hall and a firm hand would be needed.

---

[93] ED to BB, 13 February 1873, *EDCL*, 392–3: 392; ED to ECC, 15 March 1873, *EDCL*, 399–40.
[94] ED to BB, 8 February 1873, *EDCL*, 388–9, and see ED to BB, 11 February 1873, *EDCL*, 389–90.
[95] ED to BB, 8 February 1873, *EDCL*, 388–9.
[96] Statement by lecturers, Girton GCPP Bodichon, 3/14, cited in Stephen, 277.
[97] ED to BB, 11 February 1873, 18 February 1873, *EDCL*, 389–90, 394–5; ED to ECC, 15 March 1873, *EDCL*, 399–401.

13

Property, Prostitutes, and Public Service

> There has been, perhaps, a greater change of opinion in England on a greater variety of subjects—social, political, and religious—during the last ten years than had taken place in the whole period which had elapsed since Europe was convulsed by the Reformation. Whether the change has been for the better or the worse will be, of course, estimated differently by different minds, but the fact itself will hardly be disputed.

So opened an article in the *Contemporary Review* for July 1870 by the novelist and journalist Frances Parthenope Verney, sister of Florence Nightingale.[1] The article was a review of current debates about women's rights and related issues, but it set these in the context of a wider sense of change. In politics, the 1867 Reform Act had given the vote for the first time to working-class men, something that would have been unthinkable a decade earlier. So too the disestablishment of the Irish Church in 1869, whilst the claims of *Essays and Reviews*, condemned just ten years earlier as heresy, were now seen as commonplace. The question of women's 'rights' and 'wrongs' was being 'discussed in a manner which contrasts very remarkably with the tone of even a few years back'.[2]

This was partly a reflection on how much had changed during the 1860s, and with how little violence. It was also a reflection of what felt in many ways like a new age: more peaceful, more progressive, more temperate. There was the odd colonial skirmish but the empire was more or less quiet. The American Civil War and the economic disruption that resulted were well past. France and Prussia were at odds and, from July 1870, at war, but despite some occasional posturing there was no danger of Britain being sucked in. The Emperor Napoleon III was no longer seen as a threat. Italian unification had been largely achieved and would soon be completed with the fall of papal Rome.

In Britain itself, the age of Palmerston, Derby, and Russell was past, with Palmerston having died in 1865 and Derby in 1869. Russell still lived but was in his late seventies and had finally resigned from active politics. The Radical leader, John Bright, was still going strong, but politics were now dominated, and would

---

[1] Frances P. Verney, 'The powers of women, and how to use them', *Contemporary Review*, 14 (July 1870), 521–41: 521.

[2] Ibid., 522.

Emily Davies and the Mid-Victorian Women's Movement. John Hendry, Oxford University Press. © John Hendry 2024.
DOI: 10.1093/oso/9780198910237.003.0013

remain dominated for many years, by Gladstone and Disraeli, undisputed leaders of the Liberals and Conservatives, respectively, and leading from the House of Commons, not the Lords.

The Church of England still had its divisions, but in 1869 Frederick Temple, one of the writers of *Essays and Reviews*, was appointed to a bishopric. Amongst the other broad church leaders, Maurice and Kingsley held Cambridge chairs, Jowett was master of Balliol College, Oxford, and Stanley dean of Westminster. Archibald Tait, the only one of the bishops to have equivocated over *Essays and Reviews* rather than condemning it outright, was Archbishop of Canterbury. With the low-leaning Tait and the high-leaning Gladstone both seeking to conciliate and unite the church rather than divide it, it had become in practice, if not in name, a broad church.

This spirit of enlightened brotherhood, with opponents engaged in friendly debate rather than vicious dissent, prevailed not only in the established church, but across the religious spectrum. The Metaphysical Society, set up in 1869, brought together an extraordinary array of thinkers, of all shades of belief and none: high church, low church, broad church, Roman Catholic, Unitarian, theist, agnostic, spiritualist, and atheist. These men (they were, of course, all men—not *that* much had changed) were not only happy to belong to the same society but prepared to debate their differences in a calm and friendly way. '[B]y frank and close debate and unreserved communication of dissent and objection', recalled Henry Sidgwick later, the core aim was 'to attain…a diminution of mutual misunderstanding'.[3]

In science the theories of biological and geological evolution that had not so long ago been condemned on theological grounds were now judged by their scientific merits, and their authors—Darwin, Huxley, Lyell—honoured and respected. In letters, too, there was a change of the guard. The old poets, Tennyson and Browning, still reigned supreme, but Thackeray was dead and Dickens dying. The towering intellects of their generation, Carlyle and Mill, were retired from public life, their place being taken by younger writers like Matthew Arnold and Herbert Spencer.

The new spirit of the age was most obviously captured in the policies of a new government: Gladstone's first, reforming, administration. Gladstone came to power in the elections of December 1868, the undisputed leader of a Liberal party with a large majority. His first priority, he was reported as saying, was 'to pacify Ireland', and his first major piece of legislation was the disestablishment of the Anglican Church there. In a predominantly Roman Catholic country in which the Church of England had considerable wealth but few members, this was a long overdue measure. It was followed by some modest Irish land reforms, again

---

[3] Sidgwick, 220.

PROPERTY, PROSTITUTES, AND PUBLIC SERVICE   223

arguably well overdue. On the mainland, the legislation of 1869–71 followed a similar pattern: a series of modernizing measures of reform, mainly modest in scope, for which the time, in terms of public opinion, was deemed ripe. These included a reorganization of the civil service with an extension of recruitment entrance examinations; the legal recognition of trades unions; and a series of army measures including the abolition of flogging in peacetime, shorter periods of enlistment, and formal changes to the line of command.

These were largely symbolic rather than material changes, laying the ground for further modernization. In practice, not much changed, and none of it was relevant to someone like Emily Davies. Other measures were, however. They included in 1869 the Endowed Schools Act, the Municipal Corporations (Elections) Act, and the Contagious Diseases Act; in 1870 the Married Women's Property Act and the Elementary Education Act; and in 1871 the Universities Tests Act.

A reforming government both created opportunities for women and created an environment in which they were encouraged to seek further opportunities. For the next few years the concerns of the women's movement featured strongly in public debate, especially in the more liberal of the elite periodicals. There were four main foci of attention: the franchise; married women's property laws; education, medicine, and the professions; and the laws relating to prostitution.

The campaign for votes for women had continued after the 1867 Reform Act, with Lydia Becker and Jacob Bright taking the lead. As Emily Davies recognized, its chances of success were minimal and would remain so for many years, indeed for many decades, but it came to the forefront of attention following the eventual publication, in 1869, of Mill's *The Subjection of Women*. This work was marked by two main characteristics. First, it not only compared the disabilities of sex to those of slavery but asserted that wives were in important respects worse off than the enslaved. They might in practice be treated much better, but 'no slave is a slave to the same lengths, and in so full a sense of the word, as a wife is'.[4] Second, it treated all of the legal and institutional disabilities of women as consequent upon the marriage laws. If marriage were to be recast as a union of 'perfect equals', with no power or privilege on one side, no requirement of obedience on the other, and either party able to legally separate with good cause, then, according to Mill, a woman's property rights, voting rights, access to the universities and the professions would all follow.

Though welcome to radicals like Mentia Taylor, this went too far even for the leader of the suffrage campaign, Lydia Becker, whose campaigning would remain

---

[4] John Stuart Mill, *The Subjection of Women* (Longmans, Green et al., 1869), 57. It should be noted that Mill's conception of slavery as an institution was both global and historical: his reference here was to its multiple forms and manifestations over the centuries, not to the chattel slavery of the United States or the West Indies.

focused on securing the vote for property-holding widows and single women. But it inevitably coloured that campaign and others.

The book was well argued and received some positive reviews. The *Westminster Review* was predictably positive, as was Millicent Fawcett in the *Fortnightly Review*. Kingsley in *Macmillan's* was positively glowing: Mill's was a 'textbook of truths'.[5] Outside the mainstream, Cobbe in the Unitarian *Theological Review* was warmly appreciative, though she thought the problem might lie more with men than with the law.[6] For most people, however, it went far too far. There was already, from Mill's time in Parliament, a distinction being made between Mill the rational philosopher and logician, widely revered, and Mill the politician, supposedly misled by devotion to the prejudices of his deceased wife. Following the publication of his *Autobiography* a few years later, Goldwin Smith, a Liberal in politics but an opponent of women's education and rights, would blame his views on 'his hallucination (for it can surely be called nothing less) as to the unparalleled genius of his wife'.[7]

Meanwhile, *The Subjection of Women* served mainly to stir up conservative opposition. It was widely conceded that the current situation was in some ways unfair, but what was the alternative? Women were purer than men, they should not be spoiled by contamination with public life.[8] Women were physically weaker than men, they needed their protection: equality would only give men unfettered power.[9] Women were intellectually weaker than men: they were more open to bribery—and more numerous![10] Women were not now, nor ever would be, 'fit for independence': in marriage, in politics, in the professions, or in public service.[11] The last was from Sir Henry Taylor, a stalwart of the Colonial Office, who held much the same views about Her Majesty's subjects overseas, as indeed did Goldwin Smith. The links between attitudes to race, empire, and gender in this period are complex and yet to be fully explored, but there can be little doubt that for many conservatives Mill's leadership of the campaign against Eyre would have coloured their reception of his ideas on women.[12]

---

[5] Charles Kingsley, 'Women and politics', *Macmillan's Magazine*, 20 (October 1869), 552–61.

[6] 'The subjection of women', *Westminster Review*, 93 (January 1870), 63–89, in Pyle, 141–72; Millicent Garrett Fawcett, 'The electoral disabilities of women', *Fortnightly Review*, 13 (May 1870), 622–32, in Pyle, 223–35; Frances Power Cobbe, 'The subjection of women', *Theological Review*, 6 (July 1869), 355–75, in Pyle, 54–74.

[7] Goldwin Smith, 'Female suffrage', *Macmillan's Magazine*, 30 (June 1874), 139–50, in Pyle, 266–85: 268.

[8] 'The subjection of women', *Saturday Review*, 27 (19 June 1869), 811–13, in Pyle, 37–45.

[9] 'Mill on the condition of women', *Christian Observer*, 69 (August 1869), 618–29, in Pyle, 75–88.

[10] Matthew Browne [pen name of William Rands], 'The subjection of women', *Contemporary Review*, 14 (May 1870), 273–86, in Pyle, 207–22.

[11] Henry Taylor, 'Mr Mill on the subjection of women', *Fraser's Magazine*, 81 (February 1870), 143–65, in Pyle, 173–206. 'Mill on the condition of women', *Christian Observer*, 69 (August 1869), 618–29, in Pyle, 75–88.

[12] See Catherine Hall, 'The nation within and without', in Catherine Hall, Keith McClelland, and Jane Rendall, eds., *Defining the Victorian Nation: Class, Race, Gender and the British Reform Act of 1867* (Cambridge University Press, 2000), 179–233.

PROPERTY, PROSTITUTES, AND PUBLIC SERVICE 225

More sophisticated responses from the conservative side focused on the distinction between the legal and the moral. William Dixon in the *Athenaeum* and Anne Mozley in *Blackwood's* both drew a distinction between legal equality and moral justice, or equity. For Mozley this was a side issue: she thought Mill ignorant of the basic facts of life.[13] But for Dixon it was central. Yes, some modest reforms were needed, but by and large women weren't treated as slaves, didn't see themselves as slaves, and were happy with their lot. So long as men behaved responsibly, the law worked well enough, and if they didn't a change in the law would have little effect.[14] Margaret Oliphant, in the *Edinburgh Review*, put the same argument rather better, repeating more or less what she had written at the time of the first campaign for married women's property rights, over a decade earlier. The law in respect of women was, admittedly, unjust. But what mattered was not the law of the land, which would always be a compromise in such situations, but the laws of nature, of love, and of morality. In practice, the grievances of which women complained were relatively minor. The moral effects of the changes they sought, on the other hand, were potentially massive, and largely unpredictable.[15]

This was, broadly speaking, a conservative argument, but it was one that appealed across the political spectrum. For middle-class Victorians generally, moral virtues were very, very important, and much more important than legal provisions or institutional arrangements.[16] As Samuel Smiles, here echoing Burke, put it in *Self-Help*,[17]

> Morals and manners, which give colour to life, are of much greater importance than laws, which are but their manifestations. The law touches us here and there, but manners are about us everywhere, pervading society like the air we breathe.

This was partly a question of reputation, of character (as in a 'character reference'), of respectability. It was partly a question of personal virtue, of kindness, courtesy, honesty, honour. Both mattered deeply, across the social spectrum. For the working classes and the poor, the laws and institutions might seem deeply unjust, but there was nothing they could do about them. For the middle classes, they might also seem, on reflection, to be unjust, but just not that important.

---

[13] Anne Mozley, 'Mr Mill on the subjection of women', *Blackwood's Magazine*, 106 (September 1869), 309–21, in Pyle, 89–108.

[14] 'The subjection of women', *Athenaeum* (June 1869), 819–20, in Pyle, 46–53.

[15] Margaret Oliphant, 'Mill on the subjection of women', *Edinburgh Review*, 130 (October 1869), 572–602, in Pyle, 109–40.

[16] As Himmelfarb notes, this wasn't just a middle-class imposition. Morality mattered deeply throughout society. But it is the middle classes that concern us here. Gertrude Himmelfarb, *The De-Moralization of Society* (Institute of Economic Affairs, 1995).

[17] Samuel Smiles, *Self-Help: With Illustrations of Character and Conduct* (John Murray, 1859), 323.

George Orwell, in a classic essay on Dickens, noted that what concerned him in his novels was always a question of morals and never one of institutions or structures or laws.[18] The same could be said of all the writers of the period, almost without exception. All wrote and all were read as moralists. All wrongs were a consequence of bad behaviour, and could be rectified only by good. Even where laws and institutions are explicitly challenged, as in Wilkie Collins's *No Name* (1862), for example, or Charles Reade's *Hard Cash* (1863), the focus is overwhelmingly on people's moral responses. The legal and institutional situation provides a setting in which people can act viciously or virtuously, and while great harm might be done virtue can still triumph.

One of Orwell's observations on Dickens was that although he was a political radical, supportive of the working classes and acutely aware of the plight of the poor, in his novels, at least, he wasn't generally that interested in them. Again the same could be said of most contemporary writers, and of most of the middle classes. It mattered a lot how one treated one's servants, or for that matter one's factory or estate workers. But that was a matter of one's own moral virtue, it had nothing really to do with them. (There's a parallel here with the widespread view of the time that slavery, while evil, did more harm to the enslaver than to the enslaved.) The class system was taken for granted and while one might pity the plight of the poor, it was not something in which one was likely to take a great interest. Similarly with questions about the status of women. Whilst the conservatively minded defended the legal and institutional framework as reflecting the natural state of things or preserving female purity, many of the more liberally minded just didn't see it as terribly important: certainly not important enough to justify the moral risks entailed, however modest they might be. Morals were what mattered, and straightforward, received morals at that. Even a close enquiry into what morality might entail risked perceptions of immorality and took people into distinctly uncomfortable, if not distasteful, territory.[19] It was also far from clear where such an enquiry would take you: much safer not to go there.

The morality of the period was, moreover, a morality of duties, not rights—something that was completely self-evident to people at the time but tends to get forgotten now. Men were not generally claiming rights over their wives' property, for example: to make such a claim would be considered immoral. They were invoking a duty to care, protect, oversee, and, as the stronger party, govern. Their authority was conceived almost entirely in terms of a woman's duties of obedience, matched by duties of care on the man's part. In this context any claims made by women could only be conceived in terms of the duties they referenced, and in most cases there were none, or at least none that were obvious.

---

[18] George Orwell, 'Charles Dickens', in *Shooting an Elephant and Other Essays* (Penguin, 2003), 49–114.

[19] See Michael Mason, *The Making of Victorian Sexual Attitudes* (Oxford University Press, 1994).

Conservative though she was, Emily Davies would not have gone along with Oliphant's argument, but she did share the deep respect for moral values and the view that these took the form of duties, not rights. She would also almost certainly have agreed with a more modest version of the argument: that the law was a reflection of moral values, not the other way around. Changing the law in respect of the franchise or marriage, for example, might or might not have the dire consequences predicted, but it would not in itself change the attitudes of men, or indeed women. The way to go about things, in her view, was to change attitudes first. Changes in the law would follow.

She also remained deeply conventional, and as horrified as ever by radical women, and she was far from being alone in this. Kingsley's article in *Macmillan's* was one of the strongest statements of support for feminism by a man to appear in this period, but it was written in a fit of enthusiasm for Mill (and perhaps regret for his stand on the Eyre case, where he had been strongly influenced by his brother) and when he came into contact with the suffrage campaigners he drew back. He was a consistent supporter of education for women, and of women doctors, but like Davies he was socially conservative. In 1870 he wrote to Clementia Taylor:[20]

> If I, who has the movement at heart more intensely than I choose to tell any one, and also as one who is not unacquainted with the general public opinion of England, might dare to give advice, it would be, not in the direction of increased activity, but in that of increased passivity. Foolish persons have 'set up the British Lion's back,' with just fears and suspicions. Right-minded, but inexperienced persons, have set up his back with unjust (though pardonable) fears and suspicions. I do not hesitate to say, that a great deal which has been said and done by women, and those who wish to support women's rights, during the last six months, has thrown back our cause.

Davies would have agreed, and so would almost all of her supporters and most of those likely to support the more modest changes for which she was fighting.

The renewed interest in married women's property rights followed on naturally from the suffrage campaign of 1866–7. Radicals looked to equal property rights as paving the way for equal votes, whilst moderates looked to the possibility of more modest, but more realistic, gains. George Hastings, who as secretary of the Law Amendment Society had been closely involved in the 1850s campaign, started things off with a paper to the 1867 SSA congress.[21] Elizabeth Wolstenholme and Jessie Boucherett, helped by Josephine Butler and Elizabeth Gloyne, then

---

[20] Charles Kingsley to Clementia Taylor, 27 May 1870, in Frances Kingsley, ed., *Charles Kingsley: His Letters and Memories of His Life* (Kegan Paul, 1878), 245.

[21] *TNAPSS*, 11 (1867), 292.

drew up a memorial for presentation to the SSA council, urging them to take up the case. The memorial was delivered, with over three hundred signatures, in early December and at the instigation of the SSA a bill was drawn up and brought before the House of Commons by Shaw-Lefevre the following April, with support from Gurney and Mill. By then a new Married Women's Property Committee had been formed, almost identical in membership to the Manchester National Society for Women's Suffrage, with Wolstenholme as secretary and Becker as slightly reluctant treasurer.[22]

For Becker, the possibility that opposition to women's property rights might stir up opposition to the franchise made the cause a potentially harmful distraction. Whilst acting on the new committee she played down the importance of a 'branch' issue and urged a clear separation between it and the main issue of the franchise.[23] Jessie Boucherett agreed but for the opposite reason: she thought supporters of property reform might be put off by Becker, who had become very much a public, and publicly mocked, figure.[24] For Wolstenholme, however, who led the campaigning (and who later claimed to have been unaware of Bodichon's earlier campaign),[25] there was no such problem and the issue was especially salient on two counts. First, it raised the fundamental question of equal rights in a form she thought stood some chance of success. She recalled later that she had resisted Mill's urging to campaign all out against the marriage laws as being unrealistic, but the principle of equal property rights was one she felt could be realistically fought for, and might in due course lead to a broader franchise. Second, it addressed issue of class as well as of gender.

It was by now recognized that the majority of working-class wives in the industrial towns had to work in order to make ends meet, and that in many cases their earnings ended up paying for their husbands' drinking rather than for household expenses. For Wolstenholme, who was moving towards political socialism, this drinking and the marital abuse that often accompanied it were themselves consequences of despondency brought about by poor pay and working conditions, which were in turn exacerbated by the desultory pay afforded to working women. Property rights reform was thus part of a two-pronged strategy by which she hoped the conditions of the working class might be improved: pay women a decent wage, and give them the right to control what they earned.[26]

Wolstenholme's socialism was still a rarity within the women's movement, but the concern for the suffering of abused working-class wives was widely shared,

---

[22] Lee Holcombe, *Wives and Property*; Wright, 75–81; and see also Mary Shanley, *Feminism, Marriage and the Law in Victorian England*.

[23] LB to EW, 8 June 1868, quoted in Wright, 78–9, and Williams, 146.

[24] Jessie Boucherett to HT, 18 May 1868, 1 August 1868, LSE MILL-TAYLOR 12, quoted in Williams, 142.

[25] Elizabeth Wolstenholme Elmy, *Report of the Married Women's Property Committee* (Manchester, 1882).

[26] Wright, 76–7, and see Elizabeth Wolstenholme Elmy and Rosamond Hervey, *Infant Mortality: Its Causes and Remedies* (A. Ireland & Co., 1871).

PROPERTY, PROSTITUTES, AND PUBLIC SERVICE 229

not only within the movement but beyond. It was what brought Butler into the campaign, and it was in the end what determined its fate.

The bill presented by Shaw-Lefevre was almost identical to that proposed a decade earlier and led to similar and unsurprising responses, with the *Times* thundering that 'unless all experience up to the present day is at fault, it is absolutely requisite to the peace of the family and to the happiness of all the members of it, that the authority of the husband and the subordination of the wife and children should be decidedly maintained'.[27] As in the response to the suffrage campaign the sanctity of the family—to most people the sanctity of a family obedient to the male patriarch—was to the fore. Any significant change in the power structure of the middle-class family on which that ideology was built was as yet out of the question. It was universally recognized, however, that the middle and upper classes almost always avoided the law anyway, through settlements, and this suggested to the more thoughtful that the proposals might not do the harm claimed. Indeed, the moderate *Spectator* suggested that, given the extent to which they were avoided, a more sweeping review of the marriage laws might be appropriate.[28] There was a perception, moreover, that working-class wives might need legal protection, even though this was perhaps a case in which a change in the law was unlikely to have much impact on behaviour. A select committee was set up and concluded that reforms were needed.[29]

Following the election of the Gladstone administration in December 1868, a new bill was introduced, and reporting on the debate that followed the *Spectator* observed a distinct change of tone. There was still opposition, but instead of ranting about the divine right of husbands it took the form of detailed questioning over the appropriate framing of legislation, the need for which was now broadly accepted.[30] As the bill moved towards enactment in 1870, Arthur Hobhouse in the *Fortnightly* made a similar point when he drew attention to its 'unusual' progress: from the wildest of dreams; to an impious and unholy attempt to loosen the bonds of marriage; to an idea promoted by dangerous and sinister revolutionaries; to 'there's something in what they say, there's a lot of cruelty and hardship in the present system'; to 'perhaps it doesn't have much to do with marriage after all—and English law is anyway peculiar and outdated'; to what we were all thinking all along.[31]

The Married Women's Property Act, passed in 1870, secured for women any real estate they inherited as next of kin of someone dying intestate, together with

[27] *Times*, 23 April 1868, quoted in 'Married women and their property', *Spectator*, 41 (25 April 1868), 488.

[28] 'Married women and their property', *Spectator*, 41 (25 April 1868), 488.

[29] *Special Report from the Select Committee on the Married Women's Property Bill*, *Parliamentary Papers*, 1867–8. See 'The property of married women', *Westminster Review*, 90 (October 1868), 374–99, for the course of events.

[30] 'The House of Commons on wives' property', *Spectator*, 42 (17 April 1869), 470–1.

[31] Arthur Hobhouse, 'Forfeiture of property by married women', *Fortnightly Review*, 13 (1 February 1870), 180–6: 180.

230 DAVIES AND THE MID-VICTORIAN WOMEN'S MOVEMENT

inherited money and personal property up to £200, and anything earned by their own labour while married. It was highly restrictive and not retroactive, applying only to property earned or inherited after the Act had passed. To Wolstenholme's disgust, moreover, its passing was not based on a recognition of the oppression of the working classes, but on a middle- and upper-class demonization of the working-class man.[32]

What Davies made of all this, we simply don't know—it is never mentioned in her surviving correspondence—but she is unlikely to have felt strongly one way or another. The concern for working-class wives was one that was widely shared within the broad church. In a sermon of 1870, for example, presumably connected to the new Act, Fenton Hort urged a rereading of St Paul that focused on the duties of husbands to serve their wives as well as the other way around.[33] If in Hitchin at the time, Davies would probably have heard it. She was deeply engaged in her educational projects, however, and in combatting those of her rivals. She had no apparent interest in the working classes, and the campaign contributed nothing to her own agenda of demonstrating the ability of (implicitly middle-class) women to demonstrate their capability for taking equal responsibilities, whether in the home or in public life.

A third area of engagement for part of the women's movement at this time was in response to the laws concerning prostitution. The Contagious Diseases Acts, the first of which was enacted in 1864, provided for the regular internal examination of prostitutes in the neighbourhoods of army camps and naval bases for genital disease; and the detention in lock hospitals of those found to be diseased, or of anyone suspected of being a prostitute who refused examination. They were administered by plain clothes policemen ('the spy police'), who were hated not only by the prostitutes but by working-class women generally, who were often accused of prostitution on the basis of nothing other than class and appearance. A second Act in 1866 extended the areas covered, and after pressure from parts of the medical community an 1869 Act extended the areas covered further and extended the maximum period of detention to nine months. The new Act was passed in the dying days of the parliamentary session with little debate, when many members of Parliament had already left town. The radical press had drawn attention to the proposed legislation and the danger that it might do serious harm without achieving its object,[34] but opposition only took shape after it had passed.

From the point of view of much of the medical profession it was a necessary and proportionate measure. But it also condemned women prostitutes while condoning their male clients, and took in many women who were not in fact

---

[32] Wright, 80; Ben Griffin, *The Politics of Gender in Victorian Britain: Masculinity, Political Culture and the Struggle for Women's Rights* (Cambridge University Press, 2012), 87–92. The restrictions were removed in the Married Women's Property Act of 1882, but this was not retroactive either.

[33] F. J. A. Hort, *Village Sermons in Outline* (Macmillan, 1900), 127 ff.

[34] 'Prostitution in relation to the national health', *Westminster Review*, 92 (July 1869), 179–234.

PROPERTY, PROSTITUTES, AND PUBLIC SERVICE 231

prostitutes at all and were faced with the cruel choice of either subjecting themselves to the pain and indignities of examination as if they were, or being incar-
cerated, again on the basis that they were. The measures might have been well
meant, but it's not at all clear that they were effective. As carried out in practice
they were a cruel violation of women and their rights, and a dramatic illustration
of a moral code that prescribed one set of norms for men and another, completely
different, for women. Prostitutes or merely suspected prostitutes, the women were
sinners. The men were just men. They had an absolute right to violate women's
bodies, whether as the clients of brothels or as examining doctors, but no one
ever suggested that they should be examined and tested themselves.

Back in the 1850s, reviewing the law as it related to women, Bodichon had
been persuaded by Matthew Davenport Hill to omit all reference to prostitution.
The *English Woman's Journal* had likewise been very cautious. Respectable women
were somehow not supposed even to know about prostitution, let alone speak or
write about it. Now too, many of those involved in the women's movement steered
clear, including not only Davies and Bodichon but also, amongst others, Becker,
Cobbe, Boucherett, and Fawcett.[35] Elizabeth Garrett felt that she had to give an
opinion, as a female doctor who saw frequent cases of venereal disease in the
working-class patients. As with women's property rights, however, it was
Wolstenholme who took the initial steps.

The issue was completely different in many respects from those which had so
far engaged the movement. It was not concerned with longstanding laws preventing women from voting, owning property, or entering university and the professions, but with a new law, passed by a reforming Liberal government. It was not
concerned with creating opportunities for respectable women, but with those
considered by society at large to be the least respectable of all. It did, however,
impinge on Wolstenholme's deepest concerns. First, by perpetuating and indeed
reinforcing the moral double standard, it was an outrageous attack on women's
rights. Second, it was an attack specifically on working-class women, and in particular on those most disadvantaged by the capitalist system.

The first opportunity for debate was the 1869 SSA congress, in Bristol. A discussion in the formal programme was closed to women, excepting only Elizabeth
Blackwell. Although the people affected were all women it was not considered
a proper subject, even by such a liberal organization, for their hearing.
Wolstenholme therefore organized a fringe meeting and followed this up by seeking support from friends and colleagues, in particular Josephine Butler. Butler,
the committed Christian, spent many sleepless nights of prayer and tears agonizing over whether this could really be God's work.[36] She was already deeply committed, however, to the care of destitute prostitutes and the rescue of girls forced

---

[35] Wright, 83.   [36] Jordan, 108–9.

232 DAVIES AND THE MID-VICTORIAN WOMEN'S MOVEMENT

into prostitution. As Wolstenholme pointed out, she was also a married woman—
and married, moreover, to a clergyman, who was prepared to support her. She
might get a hearing where a spinster would not. With friends and doctors also
seeking her support, she was persuaded to take the lead.[37]

The campaign to repeal the Contagious Diseases Acts ran for over fifteen years
and proved immensely divisive. It produced over 17,000 petitions to Parliament,
with over 2.6 million signatures, 900 public meetings, and 500 separate
publications.[38] The Social Science Association got itself in a tremendous twist and
ended up banning discussion of the subject.[39] A Royal Commission set up in 1870
and reporting in the summer of 1871 produced six conflicting reports, and while
the radical and conservative elements of the press stood up for and against repeal,
respectively, the moderate liberal elements were completely torn.[40] Among Davies's
close associates, Bodichon was in favour of repeal, as was Blackwell, in her case
on the moral ground that the Acts effectively legalized prostitution. Elizabeth
Garrett, who by now counted Josephine Butler amongst her clients, nevertheless
wrote in the Acts' defence.[41] Two thirds of the women suffering from venereal
disease caught it, in her experience, from their husbands, and awful as the Acts
were she could see no other practicable way of protecting those women. Davies
offered no opinion, expect to say that she was sorry that Bodichon was sorry
about Garrett's paper, which her brother had helped place.[42] She would almost
certainly have considered it a medical matter on which Garrett was equipped to
judge, as she and Bodichon were not.

Whilst others in the movement, and especially in the north of England, put
their efforts into the suffrage, married women's property, and Contagious Diseases
Acts repeal campaigns, Davies by this time was almost exclusively focused on
educational reform as a means of improving the lot of women and enabling their
contribution to society. Three of the Gladstone reforms concerned education, and
two of these impacted directly on her work.

---

[37] Jordan, 108 ff.; Wright, 83–4.

[38] E. M. Sigworth and T. J. Wyke, 'A study of Victorian prostitution and venereal disease', in Martha
Vicinus, ed., *Suffer and Be Still: Women in the Victorian Age* (Indiana University Press, 1972), 77.

[39] Goldman, 177 ff.

[40] See, for example, 'Prostitution in relation to the national health', *Westminster Review*, 92 (July
1869), 179–234; 'Prostitution: its sanitary superintendence by the state', ibid. (October 1869), 556–70;
'The Contagious Diseases Act', *Saturday Review*, 27 (1 May 1869), 580–1; ibid., 30 (23 July 1870),
107–8; 'The Contagious Diseases Act and the Ladies' Association', ibid., 29 (8 January 1870), 45–6;
John Morley, 'A short letter to some ladies', *Fortnightly Review*, 13 (March 1870), 372–6; Emilie
Venturi, 'A short answer to Mr Morley's short letter', ibid. (May 1870), 633–8; 'The Contagious
Diseases Act', *Spectator*, 43 (8 January 1870), 39.

[41] Elizabeth Garrett, 'An enquiry into the nature of the Contagious Diseases Acts', *Pall Mall
Magazine*, 11 (25 January 1870), 6; reprinted by the Association for Promoting the Extension of the
Contagious Diseases Act, 1870; ED to BB, 31 January 1870, *EDCL*, 333–4. Manton, 178–80. For Butler
on Garrett see JB to Albert Rutson, 22 February 1868, LSE 3JBL/02/07, in Crawford, 52.

[42] ED to BB, 31 January 1870, *EDCL*, 333–4.

The Endowed Schools Act of 1869 was a direct consequence of the Schools Inquiry Commission and aimed to bring about some of its key recommendations. It was guided through Parliament by William Forster, one of the original commissioners, and provided for the appointment of commissioners with far-reaching powers to restructure the governance and endowments of the existing endowed schools—effectively the grammar schools, since the seven elite 'public schools' had been the subject of earlier legislation and were excluded from this—so as to create a coherent national (i.e. English and Welsh) system of secondary education for the middle classes, explicitly including girls as well as boys. Three commissioners were appointed: Arthur Hobhouse, a charity commissioner; Canon Hugh Robinson, who had served as principal of a training college; and Lyttelton as chairman, with Roby as secretary. When Hobhouse left in 1872 to serve on the Viceroy's Executive Council in India, his place was taken by Roby. Five assistant commissioners carried over from the Schools Inquiry Commission.

Despite the demands of promoting and setting up her college, Davies had never relaxed her efforts in respect of girls' secondary education. She continued to coordinate the entries to the Cambridge local examinations, both in London and, through a network of local secretaries, across the country. She continued as an active secretary of the London Association of Schoolmistresses, now chaired by Frances Buss. And with all the arguments about what subjects girls should or should not be taught and examined in, she evidently thought a lot about the appropriate curriculum for a girls' secondary school. In early 1869, just as she was taking the plunge to open the college the following October and when still, as she wrote to Bodichon, exhausted from the worries of the previous year, she was being 'used up' writing a paper on 'The training of the imagination'.[43]

Delivered first, in March, to a meeting of the London Association of Schoolmistresses, and published in July in the *Contemporary Review*, this was completely different in kind from anything Davies had written before, or would write after. The stated aim was 'to discuss, from the point of view of the practical teacher, to what extent, and in what way, the training of the imagination ought to be directly aimed at in education'.[44] The context, presumably, was the widely acknowledged, lamentable state of education in girls' schools, which was largely restricted to rote learning and the acquisition of mechanical skills. Girls were taught to memorize dates without understanding the history behind them; to memorize poems without thinking about their meaning; to play the piano accurately but without any attempt at feeling or expression. Whereas the education of boys provided disciplined mental training in the form of mathematics and classical languages (the art of construing) and some understanding of human nature through history and classical literature, that of girls provided neither. Nowhere in

---

[43] ED to BB, 11 March 1869, in *EDCL*, 311–13: 313.
[44] Emily Davies, 'The training of the imagination', *Contemporary Review*, 9 (July 1869), 25–37: 25.

the paper, however, is this context mentioned, and there is precious little reference to education at all, outside the opening and closing sentences. It is a paper about the imagination, understood as seeing things in the mind's eye (or hearing them in the mind's ear etc.), and the part it plays in various activities, most of them not generally associated with it: in logical reasoning, the physical sciences, history, social and political sciences, and, above all, in practical affairs, domestic life, and human relationships. Whether reasoning through general principles, planning household expenditure, or simply hearing properly what someone is saying to you, the exercise of imagination is essential and the lack of imagination disabling.

There is nothing particularly original in the paper. There are evident drawings from Mill's *Logic* and elsewhere, and Davies may have been inspired by one of John Tyndall's popular lectures, published the following year in his *Essays on the Use and Limit of the Imagination in Science*.[45] She also draws on Arthur Helps's *Organization in Daily Life*.[46] The paper is, however, extraordinarily clear and clear-sighted, and can still be read with profit today.

When the endowed schools commissioners were announced, with Lyttelton chairing and Roby as secretary, and Fitch, Fearon, and Hammond, all of whom had been outspoken supporters of improvements to women's education, as assistant commissioners, Davies must have felt that she *had* to contribute. These were people she knew, in some cases very well. They were people she could work with, people who took girls' education seriously. And they had been given extraordinary powers, which they intended to use. With certain exceptions, where schools were attached to cathedrals or Oxbridge colleges, they could, subject to approval of a committee of council, unilaterally reassign endowments of over fifty years' standing, and more recent ones too, if they couldn't be easily separated out. They could change the governance of schools, and their aims and scope, using for example the endowment of a small free boys' school to support larger fee-paying schools for both boys and girls. All three commissioners were on the public record as supporting the large-scale repurposing of endowments to radically reform secondary education, and Lyttelton and the majority of the assistant commoners were committed to doing so to improve girls' education.[47]

For Davies *not* to take the opportunity to do everything she could to bring about improvements in girls' schools in this context would have been criminal. Two things dominated her agenda. One was the question of endowments, and how best to use them to support girls' education. The other was what curriculum

---

[45] John Tyndall, *Essays on the Use and Limit of the Imagination in Science* (Longmans, 1870).

[46] Arthur Helps, *Organization in Daily Life: An Essay* (Parker, Son and Bourn, 1862).

[47] Hugh Robinson, 'Suggestions for the improvement of middle class education', *TNAPSS* (1864), 367–79. For Lyttelton and Hobhouse see *TNAPSS* (1868), 38–74; *Journal of the Society of Arts* (16 July 1869), 683. See also Joshua Fitch, 'Educational endowments', *Fraser's Magazine*, 79 (January 1869), 1–15, and for general discussion Sheila Fletcher, *Feminists and Bureaucrats: A Study in the Development of Girls' Education in the Nineteenth Century* (Cambridge University Press, 1980), 30 ff.

PROPERTY, PROSTITUTES, AND PUBLIC SERVICE   235

girls' schools should follow. In February 1870, back in London after two weeks in Hitchin, she wrote to Bodichon that she had been busy with the schoolmistresses, and with Elinor Bonham Carter had been 'grinding at a paper of Suggestions about Endowments', presumably for submission to the commissioners.[48] Shortly afterwards she seems to have heard Roby discuss a first draft of their 'Scheme' for girls' schools—they had been instructed to prepare draft schemes of their plans for the schools and endowments coming within their remit, for consultation. At some point in early or mid-March she sent Lyttelton her criticisms of the Girls' School Scheme, prompting an exchange of letters.[49]

Davies's main concern here related back to her paper on imagination. It was that there should be some sort of prescribed curriculum, if only for guidance, for girls as there was for boys, and that the curriculum for girls should more or less match that for boys. She accepted that there was no consensus on what girls should ideally be taught, but there was no consensus on what boys should ideally be taught either, and in the face of all sorts of contrary advice the headmistresses really needed guidance. The commissioners had proposed to leave the problem to school governors, but that was to leave it to people who were typically quite unfit to solve it. In her submission she included a list of the subjects she thought might be taught, and this led to further differences. For all his own love of classics, Lyttelton saw no reason why girls *or* boys should be taught Greek, which he thought far too subtle for elementary study,[50] and he thought some subjects might be included which Davies thought, if taught at school, would only be taught superficially and to no effect. On Latin, though, they were agreed, both considering the kind of rigorous mental training considered essential for boys to be also appropriate for girls. Lyttelton was fully committed, as was Davies, to 'giving a liberal education to the women of this country'.[51]

It's not apparent that Davies's pleadings here had any impact, but she kept herself informed of developments and continued to give advice informally, especially in respect of the new girls' schools being established by the commissioners.[52] Their progress was slow. They had to take account of the views of trustees of the endowments they wished to repurpose, almost always opposed, and to get higher approval of the changes they wished to make. They inevitably made themselves unpopular, and when a new Conservative administration took office in 1874 they were disbanded and their work handed to the Charity Commission. Meanwhile, however, they established forty-seven new endowed girls' schools and set in

---

[48] ED to BB, 25 February 1870, *EDCL*, 334. Elinor Bonham Carter was a cousin of Barbara Bodichon who in 1872 married Alfred Venn Dicey: see Menella B. Smedley, 'The English girl's education', *Contemporary Review*, 14 (April 1870), 29–41: 38.

[49] Draft of criticisms of Girls School Scheme, Girton GCPP Davies 6/25; Lord Lyttelton to ED, 17 March 1870, Girton GCPP Davies 6/26; ED to Lord Lyttelton, March 1870, *EDCL*, 334–6.

[50] Fletcher, *Feminists and Bureaucrats*, 107–9.   [51] *Times*, 8 June 1872.

[52] See, for example, ED to MB, 17 September 1870, *EDCL*, 340–1.

motion the establishment of as many again under the new regime. These were very small in number compared with the boys' schools, and few of them corresponded to what the commissioners termed, in the case of boys, 'first grade' schools—leading schools in each geographic area preparing boys for university entrance. As Lyttelton explained to Maria Grey, however, there were still too few girls' schools to make such distinctions. What the commission achieved was a massive improvement on what had gone before.[53] It was also a massive stimulus for further development.

Maria Grey was the sister of Emily Shirreff. Married young into the aristocratic Grey family (Josephine Butler was a relation both through her husband and through an aunt), she had been widowed in 1864. The years that followed were largely spent nursing friends and family—years of sickness and sorrow—but she shared her sister's longstanding commitment to a liberal education for girls and the latter's stint as mistress of Girton, combined with the interest raised by the SIC report and the establishment of the Endowed Schools Commission, set her into action. A forceful woman, in some ways not unlike Davies, and with the advantage of wide society connections, she proved unstoppable.[54] Her first step was to stand for the Chelsea district of the London School Board, but having failed, perhaps fortuitously, in that, she launched herself into the issue of girls' secondary schooling.[55]

Her first step, in early 1871, was to get involved in fundraising for Frances Buss, a cause in which Davies was also deeply interested.[56] Buss was in the process of setting up a new school, the Camden School for Girls, to serve a wider need (at lower fees) than could be met by her North London Collegiate School, and asked Davies to act as a trustee. She had, from pressure of other work, to decline the request: 'I am quite willing to accept the honour...,' she replied, 'tho' I am afraid it will be of little use without work, which I cannot give.'[57] She could and did, however, give support and advice.[58] Buss was one of her strongest supporters on university matters, sharing her insistence that if any reforms were to be made to the degree they should be made for men and women equally, and directing her students to Girton rather than Newnham. They had become good friends as well as colleagues.[59]

---

[53] Fletcher, *Feminists and Bureaucrats*, 106 and, for much more detail, *passim*.

[54] Edward Ellsworth, *Liberators of the Female Mind: The Shirreff Sisters, Educational Reform and the Women's Movement* (Greenwood Press, 1979).

[55] She also wrote a pamphlet in support of the franchise: *Is the Exercise of the Suffrage Unfeminine?* (London National Society for Women's Suffrage, 1870). Her main argument was that until women got the vote, men would see no reason to educate them.

[56] *Times*, 28 March 1871.   [57] ED to FB, 5 January 1871, *EDCL*, 354–5: 354.

[58] Annie Ridley, *Frances Mary Buss and Her Work for Education* (Longmans, Green & Co, 1896), 105.

[59] See Sara Delamont, 'The domestic ideology and women's education', in Sara Delamont and Lorna Duffin, eds., *The Nineteenth-Century Woman: Her Cultural and Physical World* (Routledge, 2014), 173.

In order to set up the new school, and to grow the existing one, Buss needed funds, and not having them herself she set out to make both schools 'public', funded by endowments and controlled by trusts. Raising the money proved next to impossible, and the whole venture might well have failed had it not been for the Endowed Schools Commission. On Davies's recommendation, Buss had been the first schoolmistress to be interviewed by the Schools Inquiry Commission. She had been almost speechless with nerves, and Davies had to be recalled from the claret and biscuits with which she was provided after her own evidence, but she evidently impressed the commissioners, who came to see North London Collegiate as an exemplar.[60] Both Lyttelton and Fitch officiated at her prize-givings and the assistant commissioner charged with restructuring in the area (chosen as one of those in which the commission began operating), William Latham, was instructed to do what he could. The Brewers Company, who acted as trustees for a grammar school in Aldenham near Watford, had recently been enriched by the sale of land for the new St Pancras Station, and were persuaded to help. The process took a long time, as the headmaster of the Aldenham school raised a formal objection and the dissolution of the commission imposed delays. The wait was nerve-wracking, but by 1875 the schools had received a substantial endowment.[61]

Meanwhile, Grey was struck by the difficulty, it seemed almost the impossibility, of raising endowments for a large academic day school such as Buss's, which she took as a model of what was needed if girls were to be properly educated. At the end of May she read a paper to the Society of Arts, drawing heavily on the SIC report, as well as on Davies's book, in which she lamented the state of girls' education and proposed the establishment of an Educational Association based on an educational charter for women, maintaining 'the equal right of women to the education recognised as the best for human beings' and the equal right of girls to share equally in educational endowments, existing and proposed.[62] A few weeks later she delivered the same paper, at Josephine Butler's invitation, to the North of England Council.

This talk of 'rights' was the language of the suffrage movement, and Davies would not have approved, but in this context and from someone like Maria Grey it seems to have been forgiven. By November Grey had drummed up enough support to launch a National Union for the Education of Girls of all Classes. Lyttelton chaired the launch meeting. Lady Stanley agreed to be a vice-president alongside a bevy of broad churchmen (Stanley, Temple, Tait) and an assortment of peers,

---

[60] Kamm, 75; FC, 444. Carol Dyhouse, 'Miss Buss and Miss Beale: gender and authority in the history of education', in Felicity Hunt, ed., *Lessons for Life: The Schooling of Girls and Women 1850–1950* (Basil Blackwell, 1987), 2–39, suggests that the commissioners were also charmed by her femininity.

[61] Fletcher, *Feminists and Bureaucrats*, 53–9.

[62] Mrs William Grey, *On the Education of Women* (William Ridgway, 1871), 37–8. This is an expanded version of the paper with voluminous footnotes.

238 DAVIES AND THE MID-VICTORIAN WOMEN'S MOVEMENT

peeresses, and politicians. Six months later, the union backed a new initiative of Grey's, the Girls Public Day School Company. The idea here was that since endowments were so hard to raise, schools might be run as paying businesses, with money raised in the form of shareholdings. Lyttelton again presided over the launch, this time in the Albert Hall. The initial shareholders included Grey herself, Lady Stanley, Joseph Payne, and Sir James Kay-Shuttleworth, the latter both renowned educationists, as the main shareholders; Mary Gurney, a young woman who had joined forces with Grey; Frances Buss, Joshua Fitch, Anne Clough, and Dorothea Beale.[63] Modelled on Frances Buss's schools, the first GPDSC school, the first of many, opened in Chelsea the next year with Mary Porter as headmistress.[64]

One of the main reasons why Davies could not make a formal commitment to Buss's schools (or get involved in Grey's ventures, though that would have meant playing second fiddle, which she would not do anyway) stemmed from another piece of Gladstone legislation, which was to affect her life much more dramatically. In England and Wales in the 1860s there was no compulsory education and no comprehensive system of primary schools. Elementary education for the working classes was provided by a network of voluntary schools, the great majority of which were run by local parish churches, in many cases subsidized by the state. In some areas there were also nonconformist schools run by the various dissenting churches, but these received no state subsidy. A significant proportion of children received little or no schooling at all.

There was broad consensus that this was unsatisfactory and that something needed to be done about it. The franchise reforms of 1868 and concerns over Britain's economic competitiveness had highlighted the need for a better-educated working class. There was much less agreement, however, over what to do. The more radical elements of the Liberal party, in which dissenters dominated, had long argued for a national system of free, compulsory, and secular, or at least non-denominational ('unsectarian') elementary schools, and saw the Gladstone administration with its comfortable majority as an opportunity to bring that about. In 1869 the Birmingham-based National Education League was formed to campaign to this end. Not surprisingly, however, the established church was less keen on changes that would diminish its power and influence, and a National Education Union was set up, also in 1869, to defend the existing denominational system. Gladstone himself, while recognizing the need for reform, stood on this issue with the established church.

The result, in the form of the Elementary Education Act of 1870, was in religious terms a rather messy compromise. The existing church schools retained

---

[63] Josephine Kamm, *Indicative Past: A Hundred Years of the Girls' Public Day School Trust* (George Allen & Unwin, 1971), 42 ff. Mary Gurney was Russell Gurney's great niece.
[64] Ibid.

PROPERTY, PROSTITUTES, AND PUBLIC SERVICE 239

their denominational status and in some cases received additional public funds, either in the form of building loans or in the form of free places for the poorest children, paid for from the local or municipal rate (and thus in large part by dissenters). Where provision was deemed to be inadequate, school boards, also financed from local funds, were empowered to set up new 'board' schools, and these were in theory, though not always in practice, non-denominational. The boards were also empowered to bring in local bye-laws to make attendance compulsory.

While the religious issues remained contentious, the 1870 Act dramatically extended the provision of primary education. It also had another effect. In 1869 the Radical MP Jacob Bright had secured an amendment to the Municipal Corporations (Elections) Act, which allowed female ratepayers to vote in town council elections and serve as Poor Law guardians. This was secured, remarkably, without a vote, the home secretary accepting it as a correction of an anomaly whereby women, who had always been able to vote in parish vestries, had been excluded from voting in the corporations which replaced them under the 1835 Municipal Corporations Act. The wording of that Act was lifted from the 1832 Reform Act and specified 'male persons', leaving a single female ratepayer in Manchester, say, without a local government vote where her near neighbour in the unincorporated suburbs still had one. The assumption, made explicit in the House of Lords, was that all this had nothing to do with the parliamentary franchise. Local authorities dealt with 'domestic' issues such as public health, the nursing of paupers, and prison government, in which women had a natural interest.[65]

While the new Act was clear as to who could vote in local authority elections—single women ratepayers—the criteria determining who could stand for election varied in practice from one kind of body to another. Whether by accident or intention, the Elementary Education Act allowed any woman to stand for election, including married women, though only ratepayers could vote. Since elementary education was widely seen as the province of women (though men had always set the rules, women did the work), a woman, especially one with an appropriate track record, had some chance of being elected. And since the work was considered to be of national importance, there was prestige and public recognition attached, especially in London, the largest board by far and one which inevitably set standards for the rest of the country. It was precisely the kind of opportunity that Davies had always argued women should take up, to

---

[65] Jane Rendall, 'The citizenship of women and the Reform Act of 1867', in Hall, McClelland, and Rendall, eds., *Defining the Victorian Nation*, 151–3; Patricia Hollis, *Ladies Elect: Women in English Local Government, 1865–1914* (Oxford University Press, 1987), 31. Williams, 161, following Helen Blackburn, *Women's Suffrage: A Record of the Women's Suffrage Movement in the British Isles, with Biographical Sketches of Miss Becker* (Williams & Norgate, 1902), 94–5, sees Bright as acting on a suggestion by Becker, but this is not clear.

240 DAVIES AND THE MID-VICTORIAN WOMEN'S MOVEMENT

demonstrate to the public, and to the men alongside whom they would be working, that they had the ability—the intellectual and physical strength, the practical competence, the informed judgement—to undertake responsible public service roles. It was not something she would have chosen to do. The reform of elementary education was neither her particular interest nor, in her view, the most pressing need. But it was, nevertheless, important, and the opportunity was not something she could turn away from.

Others in the women's movement, including Elizabeth Garrett and Lydia Becker, felt the same.[66] The men who stood for election to school boards across the country were mainly local 'names'. Prominent clergy were to the fore, both established and dissenting, together with politicians, including a good number of MPs, businessmen, and local celebrities. Some had an established interest in elementary education, but most didn't. There were just ten women candidates across the country, and of these a majority had demonstrable educational interests, but they also stood because they could. Seven were active in the women's movement.

It was Garrett who received the first approach, from the Marylebone Working Men's Association, who wanted her to stand for election in the Marylebone district of the London School Board.[67] She was by now something of a heroine to the working people of the area, having run for four years a women and children's dispensary for the poor alongside her consulting practice. She was also famous. In 1869, following pressure from the British Ambassador and the personal intervention of the Empress Eugénie, Napoleon's wife, she had been permitted to take the examinations for the Paris MD, and by the spring of 1870 she could finally and legitimately call herself 'Doctor'. She was also busy, having taken an appointment at a new children's hospital at Shadwell, on the other side of London, alongside her Marylebone practice, and having got deeply involved in its management as well as in medical work. She was also in the process of falling in love with a member of the hospital board, Skelton Anderson, to whom she would be married within months. But Garrett was not one to resist challenges. Her idea of a holiday in the summer of 1870 had been to visit the battlefront of the Franco-Prussian War, with a younger brother and sister, to see the field hospitals.[68] She asked Davies, still her closest friend, for advice.[69]

Davies's response is not recorded, but within a few weeks she too had been pressed to stand, by Paul Tidman, the uncle of one of the new Hitchin students.[70]

---

[66] For a full account see Hollis, *Ladies Elect*, 71 ff.

[67] EG to ED, 12 October 1870, Girton GCPP Davies 5/1, in Stephen, 120.

[68] Manton, 185 ff.

[69] EG to ED, 12 October 1870, Girton GCPP Davies 5/1, in Stephen, 120. It is easy to lose sight of this friendship in the context of their separate enterprises, but they evidently spent leisure time together and in February 1871 Davies was the only non-family guest at Garrett's wedding.

[70] ED to HRT, 7 November 1870, *EDCL*, 345. PT to ED, 7 November 1870, Girton GCPP Davies 5/7/1, 2.

PROPERTY, PROSTITUTES, AND PUBLIC SERVICE   241

Tidman sat on a committee chaired by Sir John Lubbock, a banker and natural scientist who had been recently elected a Liberal MP. In the event, the committee declined to support Davies as one of their candidates, but Tidman, who was also a friend of John Stuart Mill, promptly set up a committee at Greenwich, Mill's own district, and invited her to stand there.[71]

Elementary education was not a high priority for either Davies or Garrett, but they both felt strongly that if an opportunity was given to women to play a part in public life they should take it. Some of the more radical had reservations about the provision made in the Act for non-denominational religious instruction. Mentia Taylor, for example, objected that any religious instruction couldn't fail to be sectarian, and declined to support Garrett on those grounds. But she still thought it 'of the greatest importance that women should avail themselves of this privilege'.[72] Others agreed. The only cause for hesitation was a concern that if women stood for election and were badly defeated they might become a laughing stock, doing their cause more harm than good.[73]

In Garrett's case there was no cause for concern. Her standing in the district was exceptionally high. She had extremely strong support from the working men, and from no less than three hundred of their wives who campaigned for her from door to door, covering every house in the constituency. Her committee numbered over 150, including two distinguished doctors, a judge, and other gentlemen of note, alongside a host of Cambridge and Oxford professors with homes in the constituency, Thomas Hare, John Morley, Robert Browning, and other familiar names. Frances Buss sent out five thousand leaflets. Skelton Anderson, in whom Garrett trusted implicitly, chaired her campaign. Llewelyn Davies seems to have been cautious at first, but enthusiastically joined her committee and gave her strong and influential support. Emily Davies reported that he 'was so excited all last week about Miss Garrett's candidature that he could not write his sermon & was obliged to preach an old one. (to which Miss G. and I found ourselves unable to listen.)'. He was as well known for work amongst the poor of the area as she was, and had indeed been a strong supporter of her dispensary. Garrett quickly got into public speaking and eventually secured the highest number of votes of any candidate in London, and almost four times as many as the second-placed candidate in her district, also elected, the famous Thomas Huxley.[74] When

---

[71] ED to HRT, 7 November 1870, 10 November 1870, 12 November 1870, 14 November 1870, *EDCL*, 345, 347–50; ED to City of London School Board (draft), *EDCL*, 346; ED to BB, 8 November 1870, *EDCL*, 347; ED to AM, 15 November 1870, *EDCL*, 350–1. PT to ED, 8 November 1870, *et seq.*, Girton GCPP 5/7/3, 4, 5/13/1, 2, 5/15, 17.

[72] MT to EG, 19 October 1870, GCPP Davies 5/1/5.

[73] EG to ED, 24 October 1870, GCPP Davies 5/1/6; ED to HRT, 7 November 1870, *EDCL*, 345.

[74] Manton, 203–8; Crawford, 153–6. Hollis, *Ladies Elect*, 71 ff. Each voter had multiple votes, which could all be given to a single candidate or spread amongst them, and Garrett benefitted from this, but she also secured the support of over twice as many voters as the next candidate. For Huxley's wife's

242 DAVIES AND THE MID-VICTORIAN WOMEN'S MOVEMENT

Huxley stood down, after serving for just a year, Llewelyn Davies was elected to replaced him.[75]

Emily Davies faced a more difficult situation, being put up for districts in which she was not personally known. She clearly wanted to stand, but her brother took the view that it would be 'too audacious to offer to stand for "the greatest constituency in the world"', i.e. the City, without a much stronger invitation than she had received or was likely to receive.[76] As so often in such situations, she turned to Tomkinson for advice, sending him a draft of an address to the electors for his critique but also asking for advice on whether to stand at all: 'Do please give me some advice directly about the City. It strikes me as preposterous to think of. But preposterous things sometimes get done.'[77]

Tomkinson was not encouraging. He disliked parts of her draft, and questioned her seeking 'a conspicuous place' on an issue that was not comparatively high on her own priorities, and had nothing to do with the college.[78] He evoked, however, a spirited reply:[79]

> Your letter made me feel for a minute as if I had been doing a base thing. Please let me explain....Of course I think elementary education a desirable thing. It does not seem to me the greatest & most pressing want at this moment. If it had, I should naturally have been working at that, for which there are plenty of opportunities in my brother's parish, instead of on anything else. But surely it is not necessary to regard a thing as of primary importance, to be able to work at it honestly at all. The question to my mind in such a case as this of the School Board is whether one is prepared to give a fair amount of time & thought to the specific objects, not the degree of interest (by comparison with other things) that one feels in one's inmost heart....
>
> I do not feel guilty of having 'sought a conspicuous place' in connection with elementary education. I should not have thought of standing for any constituency, least of all the City, except on the conditions proposed to me, that the people who asked me to stand would take all the trouble & expense.

She was clearly dissuaded, however. 'It will be a relief to me personally,' she wrote, 'tho' I shall be sorry on public grounds, when Mr Tidman reports that there is not enough encouragement to make it worth while to go on.'

---

account of the two campaigns see Adrian Desmond, *Huxley: From Devil's Disciple to Evolution's High Priest* (Penguin, 1998), 401–2.

[75] *Lloyds Weekly Newspaper*, 4 December 1870, 31 March 1872. See 'List of members of the London School Board', Wikipedia, collated from multiple sources. For Garrett's committee see Girton GCPP Davies 5/3.

[76] ED to HRT, 7 November 1870, *EDCL*, 345. [77] ED to HRT, 7 November 1870, *EDCL*, 345.

[78] HRT to ED, n.d., in Stephen, 122. [79] ED to HRT, 10 November 1870, *EDCL*, 347–8.

PROPERTY, PROSTITUTES, AND PUBLIC SERVICE   243

A couple of days later, Mr Tidman did so report, but he also suggested she should try at Greenwich. She immediately wrote to decline. She would be supported there by radicals, in opposition to those seeking to preserve the dominance of the Church of England influence, and that for her would be a false position.[80] Tidman persisted, however, insisting that what the Greenwich electors wanted was not a radical but 'to return a woman (what woman being a secondary consideration)' and that her supporters, apart from Mill, would be 'very respectable ladies, "Low-Church persons," (perhaps High Church too)'. To Adelaide Manning she explained that the electors 'are vehemently desirous of returning a woman & have fixed upon me'; that Tidman would take full responsibility for the campaign and expenses; and that her committee was to be chaired by a low church clergyman. Neither Tomkinson nor his mother (who lived with him) approved, but she was going to do it anyway.[81]

Davies had no connections in the Greenwich area, but Tidman did his work. Henry Roby, Dean Alford, and Tom Hughes all spoke on her behalf, as of course did Garrett (and vice versa).[82] Tomkinson showed his support, despite his disapproval, by turning up to one of her speeches—unfortunately, from her point of view, the wrong one: 'I cannot help wishing you had been at Greenwich instead of Blackheath.'[83] All in all she had to give speeches at ten meetings across the district, and while in Blackheath she was faced with 'rows of ladies with apathetic faces', the audiences were mostly enthusiastic.

When the elections came, on 30 November, both Davies and Garrett topped the polls in their constituencies. Garrett received far more votes than anyone else in London. Each constituency or 'division' elected multiple members and each voter had as many votes as there were members, with no constraints on how they were used. This meant that a voter could 'plump' for a candidate by giving them all their votes, a provision that was designed to give voice to nonconformists but that favoured strong minorities generally and resulted in Garrett getting far more votes than there were electors. She found out afterwards that one man had plumped for her on the basis of a gown he saw her wearing: so much for *women* being excluded from the parliamentary franchise on the grounds of being unable to make rational informed choices. Davies had neither the fame, the popularity, nor the organization of Garrett, but still topped the Greenwich list, no mean achievement in the circumstances.[84] The other London candidate, Maria Grey, who had been persuaded to stand in Chelsea, only narrowly missed out.

---

[80] PT to ED, 11 November 1870, GCPP Davies 5/7; ED to HRT, 12 November 1870, *EDCL*, 349.
[81] ED to AM, 15 November 1870, *EDCL*, 350; ED to HRT, 14 November 1870, *EDCL*, 349–50.
[82] ED to AM, 15 November 1870, *EDCL*, 350–1; Stephen, 123.
[83] ED to HRT, 21 November 1870, *EDCL*, 351–2.
[84] ED to HRT, 21 November 1870, 25 November 1870, *EDCL*, 351–3; *Lloyds Weekly Newspaper*, 4 December 1870. Louisa Garrett Anderson, *Elizabeth Garrett Anderson* (Faber and Faber, 1939), 156.

244   DAVIES AND THE MID-VICTORIAN WOMEN'S MOVEMENT

Work started immediately and was demanding. The London School Board met first in the second week of December and determined thereafter to meet once a week for four hours, excluding meetings of its six standing committees, of which Davies sat on two, and local work arising from these in Greenwich, which was considerable.[85] For the three years of her tenure (she did not seek re-election) Emily had to structure her life, including the college at Hitchin, around this considerable London commitment.[86]

For some of the men on the school board, the novelty of having two ladies on board was evidently going to be a challenge. There was some discussion before the first meeting as to who should take the chair, prior to the formal election of a chairman, and Garrett seems to have suggested playfully that having received the greatest number of votes she should. Even Davies was horrified: 'It is not being a woman (tho' that probably enhances it) but your youth and inexperience that makes it strike me as almost indecorous to think of presiding over men like Lord Lawrence [a former Viceroy of India]...'[87] As Garrett commented to Skelton Anderson, 'Miss Davies is a good deal my senior [forty to her thirty-four], and if I live to be 100 she will still be so and will feel it as much as she did when I sat at her feet in girlhood. I enjoy thinking how I can crush her with the Recorder's [Russell Gurney, who was also elected to the board] and Mrs Russell Gurney's decided opinion on the other side.' She had been dining the previous night in exalted company (including Robert Browning, Jenny Lind the singer, Dean Stanley, and Lady Augusta) and 'ought to have felt luminous in the dark', but the observation as regards Davies was astute.[88] She did see herself that way. But she was also, as Garrett described her to Anderson a month earlier, 'my own clear sighted critical & honest friend who knows me thro & thro & entirely without glamour'.[89] And while the critical, honest, and without glamour friend could sometimes be a trial, she was a true friend.

When they turned up to the first meeting there was of course no question of Garrett taking the chair. Indeed, she and Davies were actually asked to sit apart from the rest of the committee. With Russell Gurney's support they resisted that, but before anybody could say anything another member was proposed as interim

---

[85] ED to FB, 5 January 1871, *EDCL*, 354–5; Stephen, 125–6. Davies was a member of the statistical committee, charged with estimating the need for new schools, and the bye-laws committee, charged with introducing local bye-laws to require compulsory attendance. The latter was something to which she was strongly committed and devoted considerable effort.

[86] Her attendance dropped off in the third year, when she was both mistress at Hitchin and overseeing the building work at Girton: Hollis, *Ladies Elect*, 88.

[87] ED to EG, 7 December 1870, *EDCL*, 539–40. Part of the context here is that the chairman, when duly elected, was entitled to receive a salary, unlike the other members. On this occasion Huxley moved, before the vote, that the salary be waived, and this was agreed. Lord Lawrence had no need of a salary. See 'The chairmanship of the London School Board', *Saturday Review*, 30 (17 December 1870), 767–8.

[88] EG to JSA, 8 December 1870, LSE 9/10/081.

[89] EG to JSA, 8 November 1870, LSE 9/10/074.

chairman. Lord Lawrence was then elected, and did them the honour of at least commencing 'Ladies and Gentlemen', which no one else had done, but they were just two out of fifty-one, and made to feel it. Garrett, at least, felt that the atmosphere in general was decidedly hostile, and at the end of the meeting Gurney escorted them discretely out through a back door.[90]

With time, of course, the men got used to their presence and appreciative of the hard work they put in, and from Davies's point of view this was exactly what she had long urged as the path towards the proper recognition of women: men and women working effectively together. But it would be a long time before the women were anything other than a very small minority and they inevitably found themselves stretched. For Davies, especially, fighting for equal and compulsory education for boys and girls (who tended to be taken out of school whenever needed to help at home), equal pay and recognition for male and female visitors, and female representation on management committees, in a field in which she was not particularly interested and a borough with which she was not familiar, it was very hard work.[91]

Davies's concentration on her new college, on girls' secondary education, and on the London School Board, rather than on the franchise, property rights, or the Contagious Diseases Acts, might be thought to situate her out of the mainstream of the women's movement. She certainly saw things differently. The higher education of women, in her view, was a necessary preliminary to gaining entry into the professions, which required higher levels of education. Improved education and the demonstration of public service were essential to gaining the franchise, which required the demonstration of an ability to make informed judgements. They were also essential in gaining equality in marriage, which could only come when women were considered equal in other respects.

Many commentators agreed. In September 1868 the *Spectator*, which had consistently argued for the improved education of women whilst arguing against the franchise and women's rights generally, lambasted 'those most hysterical in claiming women's rights' for neglecting its importance, and stressed especially the necessity of the higher education of women.[92] *Fraser's*, in its lead article of May1869, insisted that 'the only genuine remedies' for women's dissatisfaction with their abilities not being used 'must lie in the direction of improving feminine education and opening new areas to them in active life'.[93] *Macmillan's* took no party line but devoted significantly more pages at this time to the education of women than to other women's causes, as did the *Contemporary Review*. In the two years following Davies's article on her proposed college, it published another five

---

[90] EG to JSA, 15 December 1870, LSE 9/10/082.   [91] See Hollis, *Ladies Elect*, 83–7.

[92] 'Women's needs and women's rights', *Spectator*, 41 (19 September 1868), 1095–7. By 1871, Hutton had become a strong supporter of the college: 'The higher education for women', *Spectator*, 44 (14 October 1871), 1235–6.

[93] 'Women's education', *Fraser's Magazine*, 79 (May 1869), 537–52: 544.

substantial articles focused on the higher education of women plus two broader reviews of women's causes, both of which treated education as the central issue. In one of the latter Joseph Mayor, having identified some of the leaders of the women's movement (Becker, Faithfull, Davies, Cobbe, and Garrett: essentially those who would be both known to and respected by his readers), stressed that, while *university* education for women was not in his view appropriate, 'The topic…which is of most importance to us at the present time…is, that of female education, with which Miss Davies' name is chiefly associated.'[94]

[94] J. B. Mayor, 'The cry of the women', *Contemporary Review*, 11 (1869), 196–215: 205.

14

'A Good Age for Retiring into Private Life'

Early in 1873, three of the first intake from Davies's college sat the Cambridge tripos examinations in a hired room in the University Arms Hotel. Davies 'knitted away steadily by the fire', invigilating in person while Lady Rich covered in Hitchin.[1] On the first day of the classical tripos, the papers had been sent to the wrong address and arrived late. It wasn't the best way to begin, and Louisa Lumsden felt it sealed her third, but she passed with honours as did Rachel Cook (a second), and as had Sarah Woodhead, in mathematics, before them. From Davies's perspective, these tripos successes must have felt like an enormous triumph. Three women, students of the college she had fought so hard to set up, had passed the Cambridge degree examinations, with honours, in the traditionally valued subjects, and under the same conditions as the men: just ten terms of residence (in Rachel Cook's case, since she had started late, nine) and taking the little-go first. That surely was a vindication of her stance.

The following October the college, now officially named Girton College, moved into its new building outside Cambridge. The Waterhouse building was still unfinished. The walls were unpainted, the ground floor had no doors or windows, the bedrooms no curtains or blinds. There were draughts everywhere, the chimneys smoked, workmen's tools littered the corridors.[2] The building was, however, grand and imposing, as Davies had always dreamt it would be. The student accommodation was generous, on the model of the men's colleges. There was the nucleus of a library, built up from donations. And the students now had access to lectures in Cambridge, as well as those given in college, opening up their options in natural and moral sciences. On Sidgwick's urging, twenty-two of the thirty-four professors in the university had already opened their lectures to women, and more would follow.[3] Since these were part of their prescribed duties, moreover, there was no fee payable, so the costs to the college were merely those of a

---

[1] Louisa Lumsden, *Yellow Leaves: Memories of a Long Life* (Blackwood, 1933), 54.

[2] Recollections of Jane Frances Dove, Girton GCPP Stephen 2, extracts and quotation in Stephen, 283.

[3] Clough, 170; Stephen, 287. They were not allowed into the new Cavendish Laboratory. James Clerk Maxwell, though friendly with both Fenton Hort and James Stuart, was amused by the idea of women students but not supportive. Stuart, 191–2; Lewis Campbell and William Garnett, *The Life of James Clerk Maxwell* (Macmillan, 1882), 631; Isobel Falconer, 'Cambridge and the building of the Cavendish Laboratory', in Raymond Flood et al., eds., *James Clerk Maxwell: Perspectives on his Life and Work* (Oxford University Press, 2014), 86.

Emily Davies and the Mid-Victorian Women's Movement. John Hendry, Oxford University Press. © John Hendry 2024.
DOI: 10.1093/oso/9780198910237.003.0014

248 DAVIES AND THE MID-VICTORIAN WOMEN'S MOVEMENT

carriage to and from town.[4] There was also a resident tutor, Louisa Lumsden having stayed on in that capacity.

Davies remained acutely aware of appearances. She insisted on referring to Humphrey's lectures on anatomy and physiology as being on physiology only, 'as the word Anatomy may give the impression that the Lectures are different from what they are', and on her students being chaperoned.[5] Whatever fears she had about interference from either the undergraduates or the socializing ladies seem to have proved unfounded, however. Her students got on with their work, with only the builders' noise for interruption. Relations between Davies and Clough appear to have been cool at best, but the Girton and Merton Hall students must have mixed, with no apparent adverse consequences. Agnes Bulley, a student who had been denied the opportunity to sit for the tripos by Davies's strict time constraints, moved to Merton Hall; Edith Creak, a Merton Hall student reading for the mathematics tripos, attended lectures at Girton.[6]

Davies still found the office of mistress difficult. By Easter 1874, both the building work, in which she had taken a very close interest, and her term on the London School Board had finished, but by then she must have been exhausted. She was happy to lead daily prayers, but was uninterested in either the housekeeping or the individual students: uninterested, indeed, in the job as she had defined it. Having insisted that the mistress should be accountable to the executive committee and governing body, she found it uncomfortable to be in that position herself. She still had enough authority over the committees to get the results she wanted, but as the earlier incident over the little-go memorial had shown, she found the confusion of goals difficult to negotiate. Her temptation was to try and fix up behind the scenes what she wanted as mistress and that repeatedly got her into trouble.

The first upset after the move to Cambridge was not of her making at all, but followed on almost accidentally from developments at the University of London. The question of London degrees for women was raised again in convocation, in January 1874, when two motions were put down, one urging that women should be allowed to take the university's degrees, the other that they should be allowed to take the degrees in arts only.[7] On the suggestion of Hutton and Francis, both members of senate as well as of convocation, the question was referred to the next meeting of the annual committee of convocation in May. Meanwhile Henry Maudsley, an eminent doctor and member of the annual committee, wrote an article for the *Fortnightly Review*, combining an attack on Mill's *The Subjection of Women* with an explicit and full-blooded attack on the higher education of women as making them physically unfit for their duties as women.[8]

---

[4] ED to BB, 6 January 1874, *EDCL*, 418–19; ED to AM, 6 September 1873, *EDCL*, 409–11; Stephen, 287.
[5] ED to BB, 6 September 1873, *EDCL*, 407–9: 408. [6] ED to BB, May/June 1874, *EDCL*, 425.
[7] Willson, 111.
[8] Henry Maudsley, 'Sex in mind and in education', *Fortnightly Review*, 21 (1 April 1874), 466–83.

'A GOOD AGE FOR RETIRING INTO PRIVATE LIFE' 249

Maudsley's argument was familiar. Women were 'marked out by nature' for a very different role from men, namely that of mothers and nurses of children, and giving them the same education as men was not only inappropriate but positively harmful. The brain being in such close nervous communion with the bodily organs, the female mind was obviously completely different from the male, and must be educated differently. Where it was not, as was often the case in America, the effects of the excessive educational strain upon female health were often, as American physicians attested, disastrous.

The argument was familiar, but coming from an influential physician, not an anonymous journalist, it couldn't be ignored. After much discussion as to how best to respond, Elizabeth Garrett Anderson wrote a 'Reply' for the *Fortnightly*.[9] After gently castigating Maudsley for his unprofessionalism in using a literary journal to propagate opinions that should properly have been tested in the scientific literature, she stressed that the higher education of women as it was being introduced in England did not have the aims and objectives Maudsley had attributed to it, and was being carried out in a quite different way from the American examples he had cited. In particular, the deleterious consequences noted by the Americans arose largely, as they themselves stated, not from excessive mental exercise but from a lack of physical exercise and education. In England, physical exercise and hygiene had always been, as was readily evidenced, at the top of the agenda of those seeking to advance women's education.

It was an effective response, but the problem for Davies was that Bodichon thought that the article would be very harmful, 'because there is so much truth in it', and both Fanny Metcalfe and Louisa Lumsden (privately) agreed with her. Bodichon had always believed passionately in the importance of physical exercise and what she called 'hygiene' and had argued strongly when the college was set up that Elizabeth Blackwell should be appointed as a professor of hygiene, responsible for a programme of physical training.[10] She thought then and she thought now, as did both Metcalfe and Lumsden, that Davies didn't take that side of things seriously enough, that too many of the students were ill too often, that the housekeeping should be improved, and that somebody with the appropriate skills should be responsible for their physical health. As well as stating their views privately, moreover, and to Davies's irritation, Bodichon and Metcalfe also brought the matter up on the executive committee, where they criticized her more broadly for not taking enough interest in the students, some of whom felt lonely and neglected.

Davies agreed that health was important, but she argued that any formal training should be done at school age, and that as girls' schooling developed that would increasingly happen. The college should 'have a generally healthy system

---

[9] Elizabeth Garrett Anderson, 'Sex in mind and in education: a reply', *Fortnightly Review*, 21 (1 May 1874), 582–94.
[10] Hirsch, 247.

250   DAVIES AND THE MID-VICTORIAN WOMEN'S MOVEMENT

going on' and be ready to give occasional advice when needed, but at eighteen and over—an age at which they were often expected to be caring for husbands and children as well as themselves—women should be responsible for looking after their own health. Bodichon had said something to the effect that her own nieces at eighteen would still be babies, to which Davies retorted that in that case 'I think you should send them to a good school for a year before they come here. Our College is not a place for "young girls", any more than the other Colleges are for young boys. It is a place for young women. As to their feeling lonely, I'm afraid that cannot be helped.'[11]

As to the broader accusation, she admitted in a letter to Tomkinson that 'I don't think I am as genuinely sociable as the Mistress here ought to be....I always said I could not be as much to them in this way as Mistress as I could as Secretary, and it is so. One cannot play with them on quite equal terms as I used to do, and maintain authority as its sole representative besides.'[12] That she ever played with the students on quite equal terms was probably a figment of her imagination. She tried, but she wasn't naturally sociable, she disliked small talk, and they were always conscious of her authority, even if she wasn't.

To Bodichon she wrote that it was not in her nature ('it does not suit my "genius"') to mix casually with the students, and the college was not a family: 'My "idea" of the College is that of a society, not a family', in which the students should be treated as independent young women, not as dutiful daughters, and so long as she was mistress that was how it must be: 'I should like it to be understood that I am not ready to carry out any other "idea" than this which I have tried to explain & which I have had in view, more or less distinctly, from the beginning.'[13] The word 'society' here referenced the idea of a group of people bound together in a common venture, reflecting her conception of the men's colleges and perhaps also influenced, through Llewelyn, by Maurice's idea of a college as a fellowship embracing teachers and students alike. At the same time, of course, she insisted on petty rules such as the morning roll call and early gate hours, and viewed the mistress as being quite strictly *in loco parentis*. The balance was clear in her own mind, but it was not easy for others to understand.

In practice, Lumsden, as resident tutor, took on something of the pastoral role. Davies appears to have appreciated this, and at this point she even 'hop[ed] that some day Miss Lumsden may be able to be Mistress'. She had reservations, however. She told Bodichon that she thought that Lumsden would carry out her (Davies's) ideas, and when they discussed matters they almost invariably agreed, but that might have been because she agreed with everyone she talked to. In terms of energy, work, and mastery of business, she thought her weak.[14] Lumsden seems

---

[11] ED to BB, 12 June 1874, *EDCL*, 425–9: 426–7; Stephen, 291–3.
[12] ED to HRT, n.d., in Stephen, 280.   [13] ED to BB, 12 June 1874, *EDCL*, 425–9: 428–9.
[14] Ibid., 428.

'A GOOD AGE FOR RETIRING INTO PRIVATE LIFE'   251

also to have shared her view on Davies with Bodichon, and while on the surface they got on smoothly enough there was evidently tension. This was accentuated over the summer, as negotiations over Lumsden's contract proved difficult. Lumsden wanted significantly more than Davies (in her capacity as secretary, not mistress) was prepared to offer and seems to have used the demands of her family to play hard to get. She eventually agreed to continue for just two terms, on the proviso that she might have to resign at any moment.[15]

The next upset followed quickly on, when Davies sounded out Mary Kingsland, one of the students coming up to the natural sciences tripos, as to whether she would be interested in staying on after the examinations as a second resident tutor. Kingsland told Frances Dove, who was coming up to the same examinations and might well have wanted the position herself, and she told Lumsden, with whom she seems to have been quite close. In fact Dove only took an ordinary degree, and went to teach with Dorothea Beale at Cheltenham Ladies' College, but the damage was done.[16]

On hearing that Kingsland might be offered a tutoring post, Lumsden, according to Davies, said that if the terms were the same as hers she would resign. Kingsland was, in Lumsden's view, childish and socially inferior, and ignorant of conventional manners; she demanded in particular that she should not sit at high table, and should in other ways be treated as if still a student. 'I'm afraid we must give up our hope', declared Davies to Bodichon, 'of [Lumsden's] ever being fit to be Mistress. She has come out very badly in this business, having been so indiscreet as to discuss it, not only with two or three of the older Students, but with Miss Kilgour [one of the new intake]!'[17] Who told whom was disputed, but it was evidently all round the students, and from them reached Lady Stanley, and from her other committee members. Lumsden, having thought it over, withdrew her objections and Kingsland was in due course appointed, but the whole business was trying for Davies, who would have preferred to arrange things quietly behind the scenes and then get them rubber stamped by the executive committee.[18]

The next upset again arose from Davies sounding someone out about a tutoring post, and again concerned Lumsden, who had accepted her post for two terms only, but assumed that she could in fact stay as long as she wanted. In February 1875, Davies, who by this time would have been glad to be rid of her, sounded out Elizabeth Welsh, who had just passed her tripos examinations, about taking over after Easter. Welsh said she would only accept it if Lumsden had definitely refused to stay, and when approached Lumsden 'came hot and angry, & intimated that she had not intended to go, but that there might be no difficulty on that score, tendered her resignation'.[19]

---

[15] ED to BB, 12 August 1874, *EDCL*, 434.
[16] ED to BB, 4 November 1874, *EDCL*, 442–3.   [17] Ibid., 442.
[18] ED to BB, 4 November 1874, 10 November 1874, 19 November 1874, *EDCL*, 442–4.
[19] ED to BB, 22 February 1875, *EDCL*, 454–6: 455.

Davies was in a difficult position, entirely of her own making. Lumsden was temperamental, complaining and prone to ill health, and needed, in Davies's view, to be taught her place. 'It is evident that Miss Lumsden, by simply staying on & doing what she likes, is considered to be establishing a claim upon the College & we are supposed to be under an obligation to keep her as long as she likes to stay. This makes it desirable to assert our freedom of action before going further.'[20] There were the students' needs in terms of teaching to be considered, of course, but by this point that was for Davies a secondary consideration. Some of the students not taking the tripos might be asked to help. Whatever her faults, however, Lumsden was also very popular with the students, and a necessary bridge between them and the mistress. They wanted her to stay and—a symptom of the difficulties Davies was encountering—they made this point by appealing to Bodichon, with Constance Maynard, who was in her third year, writing on their behalf.[21] When Davies sounded out the executive committee she found that most— including both Bodichon and Adelaide Manning, whom she could normally rely on for support—were in favour of reappointing Lumsden.[22]

Davies conceded. She would not oppose the reappointment.[23] But almost at once the situation was escalated. The college statutes provided for a number of alumnae to sit on the governing body. The students didn't trust Davies to represent their views and wanted, naturally enough, to be represented on that body. The obvious person for that role was Lumsden, and asked to clarify her own position on reappointment, she apparently said that she would resign if she were not elected.[24] Fanny Metcalfe now took up arms. She was already unhappy with Davies's response to her in the wake of the Maudsley article, and with the way she was running the college generally. One of the issues that had been raised repeatedly by Lumsden was the poor quality, as she saw it, of the food, and this had become a bit of a sore point. On one hand Davies saw the comments as going too far, and heard from Lady Stanley that Lumsden was bad-mouthing the college housekeeping at home in Edinburgh. On the other hand Lumsden and Metcalfe thought that Davies was ignoring the housekeeping—which was, after all, the mistress's main responsibility—and trusting too much in the housekeeper.[25]

Having written round to the executive committee and gained the support of Shirreff and Bodichon, Metcalfe put forward a proposal in April, in her own name

---

[20] Ibid. At some point Lumsden also upset Davies, whether intentionally or otherwise, by returning with a group of students from a visit into Cambridge after the prescribed gate hours and offering no apology. HRT to BB, 1874–5, Girton GCPP Bodichon 3/26.

[21] CM to BB, 20 February 1875, Girton GCPP Bodichon 3/19.

[22] ED to BB, 22 February 1875, 28 February 1875, 12 April 1875, *EDCL*, 454–7.

[23] ED to BB, 28 February 1875, *EDCL*, 456.

[24] FM to BB, 28 March 1875, Girton GCPP Bodichon 3/22.

[25] FM to BB, 12 July 1874, Girton GCPP Bodichon 3/18; ED to BB, 22 February 1875, *EDCL*, 454–6. The housekeeper's name was Hammond. We know nothing else about her.

'A GOOD AGE FOR RETIRING INTO PRIVATE LIFE' 253

and Shirreff's, that Lumsden be elected to the governing body.[26] This was too much, and Davies's first thought was to get it promptly dismissed. 'To put a subordinate officer on the Governing Body', she exclaimed to Bodichon, 'seems so manifestly objectionable that I should hope not many would wish for it. You know I do not consider Miss Lumsden a suitable person in any case to be on a body which ought to be specially wise & self-restrained. If people will only have a little patience we can before very long put on a really satisfactory old Student, who will be able to attend meetings & will I hope by and by be of great use to us.'[27]

Davies hoped that the matter could be quickly disposed of, but once again her way of handling things led her into trouble. Metcalfe had apparently mentioned at a meeting of the executive committee her intention of proposing Lumsden, but she gave no formal, written notice, so Davies didn't put it on the agenda. When Metcalfe complained, she insisted that she had to adhere to forms, in case she should inadvertently invalidate the proceedings. She issued a supplementary agenda, but there was clearly tension in the air, and her mood can't have improved when Bodichon let her know that she intended to support Metcalfe's proposal.[28]

From Davies's perspective, there were two issues here. One was personal. If she was to have an alumna on the governing body it should be one she could rely on. The other was a matter of principle. If, as Davies insisted, the mistress could not be on the governing body, it seemed obvious to her that a tutor could not be either. On hearing of Bodichon's intention to support the proposal, she again argued on both scores. If a former student was to be elected it should be 'one who will represent the good feeling that now exists, undisturbed by rankling memories of past battles & discontents. It is quite possible that occasions might arise when Miss Lumsden's presence would be embarrassing & a real hindrance to free discussion.'[29] As a matter of principle, nobody should at the same time be a member of the governing body and hold an office inside the college. Her own case had been exceptional and, she insisted, very painful, and not something she would want to impose on anyone else. Electing Lumsden, or anyone close enough to the continuing students to act as a representative, would be worse. 'I have the strongest objection to this movement for putting the Mistress under the control of the Students—for that is what it comes to. I think the part taken by some of the Committee about Miss Lumsden & other matters has been most ill-judged & that such things ought never to be done again.'[30]

---

[26] ES to BB, 2 March 1875; FM to BB, 28 March 1875; FM to Mary Ponsonby, April 1875; Mary Ponsonby to FM, 5 April 1875; AM to BB, 6 April 1875; FM to BB, 7 April 1875, Girton GCPP Bodichon 3/20, 22, 26, 25, 23, 24; ED to BB, 22 April 1875, *EDCL*, 457–9.

[27] ED to BB, 22 April 1875, *EDCL*, 457–9: 458. She probably had in mind either Rose Aitken or Elizabeth Welsh.

[28] ED to FM, 24 April 1875, *EDCL*, 459; ED to BB, 27 April 1875, *EDCL*, 460–1.

[29] ED to BB, 27 April 1875, *EDCL*, 460–1: 460.

[30] ED to BB, 27 April 1875, *EDCL*, 460–1.

254 DAVIES AND THE MID-VICTORIAN WOMEN'S MOVEMENT

Davies rallied her troops. This time Adelaide Manning stood by her and Henry Tomkinson sent round a note expressing her views.[31] As in the past, her will prevailed, and Lumsden promptly carried out her threat and resigned,[32] but it was clear that she could no longer rely on that being the case. In castigating Lumsden, Davies had suggested that someone else might, in time, be more suitable, and a couple of months later Bodichon suggested that one of the recent graduates might be elected; but Davies insisted it was too soon, and again held out.[33] By this time, however, there was a general search on for suitable people to augment the body, and here Davies seems to have been out on a limb. She objected to two of the lecturers, proposed by Bodichon, and her own suggestion of her old ally Isa Craig Knox appears not to have found favour with the others.[34] It was time to move on.

Davies had already decided the previous year to retire as mistress that summer. She had never been comfortable in the role and had held it only because she couldn't trust anyone else to manage the move to Cambridge, with all the risks she felt that entailed. The move had now been made. The college was established and entering a period of steady growth, and with that, the grand building, and the location, finding a suitable new mistress promised to be much easier. Two other factors weighed heavily.

One was her mother, now elderly and often unwell. She had leant heavily on Jane Crow and Annie Austin to act as substitute daughters in her absence, but she could only impose so much and as time went on she must have felt that she really needed to be home much more herself than the mistress's role allowed. In her formal resignation she cited 'family circumstances' as preventing her from offering herself for reappointment.[35]

The other was her own state of exhaustion. She had been in intense project management mode for years. The seemingly constant battles with her own colleagues to get her way were draining, and she was locked into a vicious circle. The wearier she was, the less well she handled the conflicts, and the less well she handled the conflicts the more wearying they became. A letter to Frances Buss is instructive. Having established her North London Collegiate School as a private venture, Buss had changed its status in 1870 to that of an endowed 'public school', under a board of trustees, while remaining headmistress. This had enhanced the status of the school, enabled her to raise money for new buildings, and ensured the school's continuation once she retired, but meanwhile it had placed her in a similar position to Davies, under the control of a not altogether compliant board, and in her case a far from compliant chair: John Storrar, chairman of convocation at the University of London. Although he had served on and signed up to the

---

[31] AM to BB, 6 April 1875, JB to BB, 1875, Girton GCPP Bodichon, 3/23, 28.
[32] Lumsden, 57; FM to BB, 9 April 1876, Girton GCPP Bodichon 3/41.
[33] ED to BB, 27 April 1875, 2 July 1875, *EDCL*, 460–1, 463–5.
[34] ED to BB, 2 July 1875, 3 July 1875, *EDCL*, 463–5.   [35] Stephen, 295.

'A GOOD AGE FOR RETIRING INTO PRIVATE LIFE' 255

conclusions of the Schools Inquiry Commission, Storrar was still opposing the admission of women to the university, had his own strong views both as to what a girl's education should consist in and as to the superiority of his own sex, and seems to have been insufferably patronizing to Buss.[36] At some point in the winter of 1874–5 she wrote to Davies expressing her frustration and Davies gave her back some very hard, almost cruel advice: you brought this on yourself, it is only to be expected, and you just have to cope with it; you exacerbate it by flying off the handle and being discourteous when you should be keeping your cool. (Buss's first biographer and friend Annie Ridley described her temperament as 'gunpowdery'.)[37] Buss was clearly hurt, but she recognized her own temperament and it was a letter that could only have been written by a good friend. She must have realized that it said more about Davies's own frustrations than anything.[38]

On 22 April 1875, Davies wrote to Bodichon: 'I am 45 to-day: a good age for retiring into private life.'[39] Responding to Bodichon's reply, a fortnight later, she explained: 'I don't think you can have any idea of how the annoyances & anxieties of the last few years have sickened me of "public life". I suppose I don't show illness much, for it seems impossible to make people understand how worn-out I am. I have often felt as if I could bear it no longer—(I mean being the object as public servants are, for everyone to stick pins into.) & must throw it all up.'[40]

When Davies first considered giving up as mistress she had even considered giving up as secretary as well. The role increasingly required presence in Cambridge, and she was worried about how her relationship with a new mistress might work out.[41] This must still have been a possibility in the spring, as Lady Stanley then sounded out Bodichon as to whether Charlotte Burbury might possibly take the role.[42] In the event, she could not let go, and decided to stay on as secretary for the time being,[43] a decision made easier by the appointment of a mistress of whom she approved and on terms she approved. The new mistress would not be a member of the executive committee or governing body: Davies, as continuing secretary, was not going to give up control. She would, however, have effective control (power of nomination and veto) over the choice of resident tutors: on this, Davies had learnt from her own experience.[44]

---

[36] See Carol Dyhouse, 'Miss Buss and Miss Beale: gender and authority in the history of education', in Felicity Hunt, ed., *Lessons for Life: The Schooling of Girls and Women 1850–1950* (Basil Blackwell, 1987), 2–39.

[37] Annie E. Ridley, *Frances Mary Buss and Her Work for Education* (Longmans, Green & Co., 1896), 241.

[38] ED to FB, 1874–5, *EDCL*, 445–6; ED to BB, 22 April 1875, *EDCL*, 457–9. For Frances Buss's reaction, see Kamm, 184 ff.

[39] ED to BB, 22 April 1875, *EDCL*, 457–9: 459.

[40] ED to BB, 27 April 1875, *EDCL*, 460–1: 460.

[41] ED to BB, 12 June 1874, *EDCL*, 425–9: 429.

[42] HS to BB, 18 April 1875, Girton GCPP Bodichon 3/34.

[43] ED to BB, 27 April 1875, *EDCL*, 460–1.

[44] ED to BB, 22 April 1875, *EDCL*, 457–9; Stephen, 297. The committee minutes simply noted that a paper with these proposals was accepted. Girton GCGB 2/1/3.

256 DAVIES AND THE MID-VICTORIAN WOMEN'S MOVEMENT

An advertisement was placed inviting expressions of interest, which Davies presumably filtered before passing them on. The successful candidate, Marianne Bernard, was still in her mid-thirties, and with no obvious qualifications for the job, but she was happy to be guided by Davies and was, besides, a 'lady' of good family and very well connected.[45] She came from a prominent military family and was niece of the 1st Baron Lawrence, former Viceroy of India, the chairman of the London School Board during Davies's term there, and now amongst the supporters of the National Union for the Education of Girls of all Classes.[46]

The immediate impact of Davies's 'retirement' was not retirement at all. Back at home in London she could catch up on all her commitments there and continue to control the college through its executive committee. With the college growing there was new building work in hand, and with a building committee comprising Bodichon, Lady Stanley, and herself she could effectively control it, exchanging her ideas with her colleagues but using her own direct contact with Waterhouse and invoking Tomkinson as treasurer so as to get her own way. There was a small fly in the ointment, as Bodichon and Lady Stanley tried to co-opt Metcalfe to the committee, but Davies would have none of it. 'It puts a Secretary into a very awkward position, when members of a Committee take matters into their own hands & act without regard to the decisions of the [Executive] Committee....I do not see how a Committee can work if its members are not prepared to abide by its decisions & it seems to be specially the duty of a Secretary to take care that the business is carried on in conformity with the instructions given.'[47]

Bernard proved utterly pliable, taking Davies's advice on tutorial appointments, and generally following her instructions. 'If this is going to the Mistress,' wrote Tomkinson in response to a draft memorandum, 'is it not rather too much telling her what to do and how to do it? Wire pulling from a distance.'[48]

The downside was that Davies didn't get the rest she badly needed. She complained repeatedly of fatigue and of 'nervous weakness and irritability', exacerbated by that fatigue.[49] The following autumn, she took to her bed for a month, and decided to resign as secretary of the college, taking on instead the less onerous position of treasurer. Though a bachelor, Tomkinson had long been responsible for his sister Sophia and her children, her husband, the Bishop of Calcutta, having

---

[45] Stephen, 297. See also MF to BB, 8 January 1875, Girton GCPP Bodichon 3/31 and AC to BB, 18 May 1875, Girton GCPP Bodichon 3/30 for alternative proposals.

[46] Josephine Kamm, *Indicative Past: A Hundred Years of the Girls' Public Day School Trust* (George Allen & Unwin, 1971), 42. Bernard had taken a course at the Home and Colonial School Society, with which Davies was involved, but that would hardly have prepared her for involvement in university-level education. Her uncle was known to the public as the 'saviour of the Punjab' for his role in repelling the Indian Rebellion—saviour of British imperialism might be a more accurate moniker.

[47] ED to BB, 10 December 1875, *EDCL*, 477–8: 478. See also FM to BB, 9 April 1876, Girton GCPP Bodichon 3/41.

[48] HRT to ED, n.d., in Stephen, 302.

[49] ED to BB, 29 December 1875, *EDCL*, 479; ED to AM, 17 June 1876, in Stephen, 304.

slipped off a gangplank and drowned in the Ganges. In 1870 he had inherited the family estate, Reaseheath Hall in Cheshire, and it now suited him to spend more time there, renovating the house and attending to the estate.[50] In the summer of 1877, Llewelyn Davies's sister-in-law, Caroline, who had married George Croom Robertson, Professor of Philosophy at University College London, but remained childless, took over as secretary.[51]

By this time, not only was Girton fully established, but both it and Davies's other initiatives were bearing fruit elsewhere. Whereas the elections of 1870–1 had resulted in just three women being elected to school boards around the country (Davies, Garrett Anderson, and Becker), those of 1873 had elected twenty-eight and by 1877 there were seventy-one.[52] Thanks to the work of the Endowed Schools Commission, the number of endowed girls' secondary schools had grown from about ten to about a hundred. This was still a small number, and they were of varying sizes and qualities, but it was nevertheless a remarkable growth. The Girls Public Day School Company had opened thirteen high-quality high schools, with many more to follow,[53] and local initiatives had led to the creation of others, such as the Manchester High School for Girls, established in 1874.[54]

Most satisfying of all, for Davies, must have been the progress in respect of university degrees for women. Ahead of her May 1874 meeting of the University of London's annual committee of convocation meeting, a whole series of memorials were put forward, asking for degrees to be opened to women and rebutting the recent *Fortnightly Review* article by Maudsley, and at the May meeting the more general of the motions proposed in January, that women be allowed to take the university's degrees, was passed, apparently without a division. There was an amendment put forward, restricting the motion to the examination in arts, and proposing that successful candidates should receive certificates only, and not degrees, but this was defeated, eighty-three to sixty-five. Its proposer, ironically, was Arthur Creak, father of Edith, then studying at Merton Hall and attending classes in Girton towards the Cambridge mathematical tripos but, of course, unable to graduate. Meanwhile, another proposal was also put to the senate, by one of its own committees, recommending that the regulations and examination

---

[50] Sophia's son, who inherited Tomkinson's and other family estates, was Edward Cotton, later Sir Edward Cotton-Jodrell, who as a Conservative MP was a supporter of women's suffrage.

[51] Stephen, 304–5. Daphne Bennett creates a nice fiction about Tomkinson proposing to Davies, she refusing him and taking to her bed, and he going off in a huff—but it is purely the product of her imagination, with no evidence whatsoever to support it. Tomkinson was a very eligible bachelor and could probably have married whom he chose had that been his inclination, but I rather suspect it wasn't. Davies might conceivably have been tempted to retire into marriage, but certainly not to the Cheshire squirearchy.

[52] Patricia Hollis, *Ladies Elect: Women in English Local Government, 1865–1914* (Oxford University Press, 1987), 486.

[53] Kamm, *Indicative Past*, 207 ff.

[54] Sara Burstall, *The Story of the Manchester High School for Girls, 1871–1911* (Manchester University Press, 1911).

papers for the general examination for women be made identical to those for the matriculation examination.[55]

When the matters came to be discussed at senate in July, the question of the general examination was deferred. The motion on admitting women to degrees was passed, but with a wrecking amendment, stating that while the senate wished to extend the scope of what it offered to women it was not prepared to apply for the new charter that would be necessary for women to be admitted to degrees. Richard Hutton was by now very firmly on the women's side, arguing that there was no danger of women being masculinized (his earlier concern) and that 'You cannot distinguish between the foundations of a good education for a woman, and the foundations of the same education for a man.' They might assimilate different elements, but the knowledge was the same. The vice-chancellor, Sir John Lubbock, was also on side. But the voting was decisive against them: seventeen to ten. In the following months, the standardization of the matriculation-level exams was agreed, though they remained technically separate, and the question of degrees for women was effectively put on ice for another couple of years. But it was evident now that it would not go away.[56]

It was set off again by an Act of Parliament introduced in 1876 by John Bright and Russell Gurney, partly in response to developments in Edinburgh, where a group of students including Sophia Jex-Blake had got halfway through the courses for a medical degree before being debarred from getting it. The Gurney Act, as it was known, removed any restriction on the granting of qualifications for registration with the General Medical Council on the ground of sex. For the University of London, where there was a balance of opinion for admitting women to arts degrees but strong opposition to admitting them to professional degrees in medicine, this meant, perversely, that the senate was authorized to offer women medical degrees without any change to their statutes, but not arts degrees. Constitutional arguments followed because a change of statutes required the agreement of convocation, and there was much dispute as to whether or not convocation could be by-passed under the new law. On both senate and convocation there were groups wanting to admit women to all degrees, to arts degrees only, and to no degrees at all, as well as groups wanting to either elevate or reduce the power of convocation. Thanks to some loose wording in the Act, there was disagreement, too, as to whether if women were admitted to the degrees they would or would not become eligible for membership of convocation. The consequence was a mess. There was a growing mood for opening up to women, however, with Hutton, now fully converted, and Fitch among its leaders. The end result was that in 1878 a supplemental charter was accepted that enabled women to take all of the university's degrees, but not to be members of convocation. By 1880 the first

[55] Willson, 112–14.   [56] Willson, 114–16.

'A GOOD AGE FOR RETIRING INTO PRIVATE LIFE' 259

four women had graduated with BAs, with BScs and MBs following over the next two years.[57]

Degrees were followed by colleges. Bedford College immediately began preparing students for the London degrees and in 1882 Westfield College in Hampstead was founded, with Constance Maynard, one of the early Girton students, as principal. The architecturally grandiose Royal Holloway College in Egham, founded by the wealthy patent medicine entrepreneur Thomas Holloway, was opened by Queen Victoria in 1886 and admitted students the following year. Around the country, the university extension movement pioneered by James Stuart led to a number of 'university colleges', typically offering University of London degrees, and many of these took women from the beginning.

From 1873–4 and again from 1879–86, Llewelyn Davies was principal of Queen's College, and Emily hoped that it too might become a college of London University.[58] The principal's role was, however, an honorary, non-executive one. Executive power lay with the dean, first Edward Plumptre and then Henry Craik, and Queen's remained a girls' school.

Meanwhile, things also began to move in Oxford. In 1875 Oxford University introduced degree-level examinations for women, nominally separate from the men's tripos examinations but classed in the same way and formally certificated. Two women's halls would shortly be established, Somerville Hall and Lady Margaret Hall, as well as a Society for Home Students, providing for those who were living in Oxford but couldn't meet the residential costs of the halls. In 1879 Annie Rogers, daughter of the radical economist Thorold Rogers, completed the honours course for Literae Humaniores, achieving first-class level in both Mods (in 1877) and Greats.[59] The pattern of equal but different was followed in Scotland. The Ladies' Lectures at Edinburgh developed into the equivalent of a full degree, but without the degree qualification (this came in 1892), while St Andrews introduced a 'Lady of Arts' qualification in 1876.

Although Emily Davies retired from public life completely for a decade, and played only a small role thereafter, she didn't stop working. She continued to run the London Association of Schoolmistresses until its dissolution in 1888, by when there were national associations of headmistresses and assistant mistresses. She continued to encourage and coordinate girls' entries to the local examinations.[60] And she continued to dominate Girton, especially in respect of the building programme.

By the mid-1870s, Waterhouse was famous. Two of his most significant commissions, for Manchester Town Hall and the Natural History Museum in South Kensington (then part of the British Museum), were in progress and his

---

[57] Willson, 117–44.   [58] ED to BB, 6 January 1874, *EDCL*, 418–19.

[59] This was a twelve-term classics degree in two parts.

[60] See, for example, ED to BB, 14 October 1881, Girton GCPP Bodichon 1/182.

260 DAVIES AND THE MID-VICTORIAN WOMEN'S MOVEMENT

particular brand of warmly coloured brick and terracotta Victorian gothic was all the rage. From Davies's perspective the style combined the grandeur needed to give the college the dignity that it could not acquire from history with the warmth appropriate to a domestic building. But it was very expensive, the more so as she insisted on generous accommodation for the students (an environment in which they could study, have privacy, or relax with friends was, she felt, essential) and wide corridors (for a healthy and open environment, which Barbara Bodichon deemed essential). An American visitor reckoned that an American college would get two to three times as many rooms for the money.[61]

This meant that without Davies's oversight there was always a risk that future buildings might, for want of money, be done to a cheaper design, something she was determined to prevent. She was also determined that any money available should be spent on expanding the student accommodation rather than on decorations, gardens, or public rooms, as Bodichon, Fanny Metcalfe, and others would have liked. She could not bear the idea of turning away students who had the desire and ability to take up a place. For the college to be sure of surviving, moreover, she felt that it needed above all to reach a critical mass: at least two hundred students seems to have been her target.

By remaining on the executive committee and taking over as treasurer, Davies could effectively retain control over expenditure, both on the building programme and more generally, and she did. Among Marianne Bernard's appealing qualities (appealing, that is, to Davies), she seems to have shared Davies's careful approach to routine expenditure, whether on meals and housekeeping or on scientific apparatus. She supplied regular accounts and followed guidance.[62] This left more for building. Following eighteen new sets built in 1876 there were further extensions in 1879, and over these Davies kept full control. Only in 1884, when further building was undertaken, did she not entirely get her way. There had been several pleas for a library, which she had successfully resisted, insisting on the priority of student rooms, but in this case the building was made possible by a donation of £1,000 from Lady Stanley, given specifically for a library, and a large gift from Barbara Bodichon which covered £5,000 of the £12,000 cost and effectively allowed her to dictate terms. A library was built.

Two years later, an even larger donation was received, quite out of the blue, from the residuary estate of a wealthy widow, Jane Gamble. This time, Miss Gamble being dead and so unable to thwart her, Davies regained control, and twenty-seven new student sets were built. The college could now accommodate over a hundred students, and at this point Davies's attitude to building seems to have changed. She still wanted more student accommodation but in 1890 she put forward to the executive committee plans for a massive extension incorporating

---

[61] Stephen, 312.   [62] Stephen, 312–13.

not only about forty extra sets but new kitchens, a grand dining hall, and something she had probably long desired, a chapel.

Her proposals were rejected, the main opposition being to the chapel. Lady Stanley was particularly opposed. Though dutifully attending church, she had never been particularly religious herself, and her children included a prominent atheist, a Muslim convert, and a Roman Catholic priest. But the bulk of the committee concurred. The most urgent needs now were to improve the wages and conditions of the staff, and there was a general feeling that while the college had partly aligned itself, on Davies's insistence and against the advice of most of her colleagues, with the Church of England, to reinforce that by building a chapel would be anachronistic. Davies's response, recorded in a letter to Adelaide Manning (who had supported the proposal), was absolutely typical: 'There seems to be nothing to be done but to try when vacancies on the committee occur to fill them better.'[63] In 1891, Barbara Bodichon died, leaving the college another £10,000, and Davies sought to revive her plans, but to no avail. Lady Stanley, eighty-five years old but apparently undiminished, remained resolute. As one of the committee members had remarked to Davies after the previous year's meeting, however, 'You will get your way in the end.' And so she did. Lady Stanley died in 1895, and two years later Davies's building plans—including the chapel—were accepted.[64]

Meanwhile, one other area in which Davies continued to play a leading role in the college was in respect of its relations with the university, and its ongoing fight for recognition: first, for women to take degree examinations as of right rather than by private agreement with the examiners, which had to be negotiated afresh each year; and once that was achieved for them to receive degrees. This was an area in which Davies felt the need for personal control, for two reasons. First, she couldn't trust the university. Whilst everybody was very nice, they seemed to her to fall into two camps. There were the diehard conservatives, led by Edward Perowne, who were opposed to the higher education of women in general, never mind in Cambridge. And there were the radicals, led by Henry Sidgwick, who sought wholesale reform of the university but were not at all adverse to treating women as a special case and exempting them from things of which they disapproved, like the little-go. As in most institutions there was probably a body of opinion in between, but Davies didn't see it. Her second reason for maintaining control was a feeling that she couldn't trust her own colleagues on the executive committee not to backslide from the principles she had established.

The first attempts to advance things came from outside Cambridge. In 1877 Parliament passed a Universities of Oxford and Cambridge Act, setting up a committee of the Privy Council to consider revisions to the university statutes, and at

---

[63] ED to AM, 19 July 1890, in Stephen, 316.   [64] Stephen, 315–18.

262 DAVIES AND THE MID-VICTORIAN WOMEN'S MOVEMENT

that time a newly elected Liberal MP, Leonard Courtney, introduced an amendment enabling the university to examine women concurrently with men. It was heavily defeated. Then in 1880, after a Girton student, Charlotte Scott, had been marked as equal to the eighth wrangler in the mathematical tripos, Professor W. S. Aldis, principal of the College of Science in Newcastle (an offshoot of Durham University), and his wife got up a memorial to the university senate asking for the admission of women to both examinations and degrees on the same terms as men.[65]

This was done without any consultation and seems to have been welcomed by neither Girton nor Newnham. The risk to Girton was that it might prompt the university to introduce some special examinations or non-degree qualifications for women, as at Oxford. The risk to Newnham was that it might lead to a tightening up of the conditions under which their own students took the degree examinations. In the event the memorial secured over eight thousand signatures and could not be stopped, or even delayed, and both Girton and Newnham had to respond. In a reprise of previous encounters, Henry Sidgwick, convinced that the proposal was premature and potentially harmful, suggested that they present a common front. And Davies, of course, declined: 'I'm afraid it seems very ungracious to repudiate a common cause.... One feels a want of reciprocity in our not being ready to work with you, in return for your friendly help to us, but I do not see how we can help it.' Any association with Newnham risked appearing to sanction their heinous practice of presenting women for tripos examinations without having fulfilled the normal conditions. So two responses went in. That from the Association for Promoting the Higher Education of Women in Cambridge just welcomed any arrangements by which the informal taking of examinations could be put on a more stable footing. That from Girton, written by Davies and endorsed by the executive committee, stated that in the view of the college the performance of women had been sufficiently tested to justify their being admitted to the BA degree, but at the same time dissociated the college from the memorial.[66]

The memorial was not rejected outright. A syndicate was appointed to consider the matter and unsurprisingly, as Davies feared, that tended to follow the Sidgwick line. It proposed regularizing the admission of women to the little-go and tripos examinations, but not the ordinary degree examinations, on the same conditions as men, but with women free to substitute parts of the higher local examination for the little-go and so avoid the need for being examined in classics. Class lists for the tripos would be released (separately from those for men, of course) and certificates awarded as was by then happening in Oxford. From Sidgwick's perspective, and that of the Cambridge reformers in general, the little-go and ordinary degrees were historical anachronisms that they wished to

---

[65] Stephen, 323. Durham University Records UND/AA3/2A&B.   [66] Stephen, 322–4.

abolish. From Davies's much more conservative perspective, they had not been abolished and so must be respected. Nothing in the proposal prevented her from insisting that Girton students pass the little-go, however, and she could still ask the examiners privately for their assistance with the ordinary examinations. She was therefore forced into supporting the proposal, and indeed into supporting it with all the forces she could muster. She submitted a memorial from the London Association of Schoolmistresses, encouraged memorials from elsewhere, and worked her contacts hard to gain support for a memorial from non-resident members of the senate.[67]

A vote was set for 24 February 1881, and there was a panic about numbers. 'I have had a very strong letter from Professor Stuart,' wrote Davies to Bodichon, 'urging us to do all we can to send up voters. The Vice-Chancellor [who happened this year—the position rotated—to be Perowne] has declared war against us, and our friends are greatly alarmed.... If we can send up 200 voters we shall be safe.'[68] The panic was unjustified. A mere 32 voted against the proposal, with 398 in favour. There was overwhelming support for the examination of women, on almost the same terms as men.[69] But not on quite the same terms, and degrees were another matter altogether.

The question of degrees for women, now available at London, was not raised again at Cambridge until 1887. By this time, Caroline Croom Robertson, finding the secretary role too demanding, had become treasurer, with Frances Kensington, previously secretary at Bedford College, taking the bulk of the secretarial duties. Davies had once again become honorary secretary, effectively retaining control of the executive committee. Girton had a candidate for the classical tripos, Agnata Ramsay, who was known to be exceptional.[70] Millicent Fawcett had given an address the previous autumn in which she lamented the university's withholding degrees for women, and in conversation with her Davies had established, first, that Henry Sidgwick wanted degrees for women and would work for them when the time was right; second, that his policy was to wait for a remarkable achievement by a woman in the tripos examinations on which to pin a campaign; but third, that he would then campaign on his own terms, i.e. for degrees to be awarded with exemption from the little-go and at honours level only, not at ordinary level. Davies's response? To get in first and try to avoid, as last time, being forced into supporting Sidgwick's scheme. The ordinary examination was not so important in itself, but if the men had it the women should. The little-go was a hassle, but apart from her determination that women should not in any way

---

[67] Stephen, 324–5.
[68] ED to BB, February 1881, Girton GCPP Bodichon 1/173, in Stephen, 325.
[69] Stephen, 325–6.
[70] Better known as Agnata Butler, after she married Henry Butler, Master of Trinity and Josephine Butler's brother-in-law.

be granted an easy option, she still believed in the value of a classical education, and the compulsory Latin and Greek it entailed.[71]

First, form a committee, with reliable allies: Lady Stanley, Lady Goldsmid, Elizabeth Garrett Anderson, her brother Llewelyn, and from Cambridge George Liveing and Henry Jackson, a Trinity classicist, both now supportive members of her governing body. Then draw up a memorial. Then, having established her own terms, ask Sidgwick to join the committee. Sidgwick, since 1883 the Knightsbridge Professor (the chair earlier held by Maurice) and restored since 1885 to his Trinity fellowship, declined. He was not opposed on principle, he assured Davies, to men and women receiving the same degrees under the same conditions. But he was opposed to the conditions presently applied to men, in particular to the compulsory classics in the little-go. He was also opposed to anybody getting the poll degree, which he thought worthless, and while he hadn't been able to get rid of it for men he would resist strongly its extension to women. Indeed, he felt all this so strongly that he not only set it out in a letter to Davies but repeated it in a letter to the *Times*, asserting that what was asked for in the new memorial ran 'against the wish of the majority of those resident members of the Senate who have hitherto supported the extension of the educational advantages of the University to women'.[72]

Sidgwick clearly felt just as strongly as did Davies, and with such a public statement he removed any chance of the memorial succeeding: both reformers and conservatives would oppose it. Jackson sought a compromise, suggesting that if Sidgwick accepted the poll degree, Davies might forego the little-go. If Davies were to concede anything it would be the poll degree rather than the little-go, but she was in no mood for compromise at all and stood her ground. Another of the young Trinity fellows, Richard Archer-Hind, then got involved, however, and a kind of compromise was reached. The memorialists would indicate, in a covering letter, their willingness to accept an alternative to the little-go allowing women to substitute a modern language for Greek, and Sidgwick would withdraw his objections, though retaining the right to vote separately against the extension to women of the poll degree. From Davies's perspective, however, the damage was already done, for while Sidgwick might have made a formal concession, in practice it was no concession at all. His views were well known. The only real concession came, once again, from Davies, and this time it was to no effect. In February 1888 the council of the senate decided, albeit by the narrowest of majorities, not to consider the matter further. No syndicate would be set up. There would be no mechanism by which the proposal might be considered, let alone enacted.[73]

The question wasn't raised again for nearly a decade, and then the initiative came from Newnham, where Sidgwick's wife Eleanor (formerly Nora Balfour,

---

[71] Stephen, 327; ED to Henry Jackson, 27 July 1887, in Stephen 328–9.
[72] Stephen, 327; *Times*, 10 July 1887.   [73] Stephen, 329–30.

sister of the future prime minister, who had been a student at Newnham) was now principal. Marion Kennedy was honorary secretary. In late 1895 a meeting was arranged on the relatively neutral territory of the Kennedy home. Now at least it seemed as if Davies and Sidgwick might work together. This was probably the first time they had actually met in years and, presumably to her great surprise, Davies found Sidgwick 'very engaging'! A committee was set up including equal representations from Girton, where Elizabeth Welsh was now mistress, and Newnham, and various memorials were got up, the main one being from over two thousand members of the senate. Davies also penned a pamphlet sketching out the history of higher education for women and emphasizing that offering degrees now would no longer be the radical step it might once have been, but a natural, even conservative, evolution. The formal approach this time was more cautious than before, asking just for the council of senate to nominate a syndicate to consider under what conditions and with what restrictions, if any, women might be admitted to degrees—something that both Davies and Sidgwick could put their names to, and that could hardly be refused.

It was not refused, but phrased as it was, much depended on the membership of the syndicate, and here the conservative element won out. What was recommended, in early 1897, was the admission of women to titular degrees. Even this was too much, however, for the non-resident members, still dominated by conservative clergymen who, as time went on, could more and more easily make the railway journey to Cambridge to vote. In May the recommendation was overwhelmingly rejected.[74]

Davies finally resigned as honorary secretary of Girton in 1903, aged seventy-three, over the old argument as to whether or not the mistress should be a member of the executive committee. After Bernard had retired in 1885, Elizabeth Welsh had been elected mistress and had served on that body, but she was a Davies friend and protégée. When she retired, Davies took a stand on the issue in respect of the new (as yet not appointed) mistress and lost. It was not worth her while, she wrote to Adelaide Manning, continuing the struggle. Not only on this issue but on others too it was a constant fight, 'often useless and always painful'. The college was now going its own way. In other words: she could no longer control it. She remained a member of the governing body, continued to visit, and continued to remain involved, especially when it came to building, and continued to be honoured as founders are. But she gave up trying to direct things.

Meanwhile, in 1886, Mary Davies, Emily's mother, with whom she had been living for the past twenty-five years, died. Emily moved into rented rooms close to her brother, who had meanwhile moved across Blandford Square into Barbara Bodichon's former house, Bodichon, in poor health, now staying permanently

---

[74] Stephen, 331–4.

in Sussex. No longer tied to her mother, she travelled extensively, and once again became active in the suffrage movement. She joined the National Society for Women's Suffrage, and by 1890 she was on the executive committee of the central committee of that society.

By this time the 1882 Married Women's Property Act had extended women's control over the property they brought into a marriage, effectively providing for women in general the protection that rich fathers had long secured for their daughters through trust deeds. A woman's property was still not entirely her own, and would not be so until well into the twentieth century, but it was clear progress. In 1883, after years of campaigning by Josephine Butler and others, the Contagious Diseases Acts had finally been suspended, and in 1886 they were repealed. The 1886 the Guardianship of Infants Act, passed after several years of debate, didn't fundamentally alter the preferential rights of fathers and their appointed guardians over separated or widowed mothers, but it did at least allow the courts to take into the account the interests of the children concerned. And while an amendment to the 1884 Reform Bill to extend the suffrage to women had been heavily defeated, there was a sense that the issue was at least a live one in Parliament, as it had not been for some years.

In this context, interest in and activism for votes for women was on the increase, and by 1890 there were a number of rival organizations. In 1888 the National Society for Women's Suffrage, the body originally set up by Becker and Wolstenholme in 1867, had effectively split over divisions surrounding the admittance of political organizations (in practice, socialist organizations) and the extent of the franchise sought. The more radical group, including Wolstenholme, had formed the National Central Society for Women's Suffrage, while the more moderate Central Committee of the National Society for Women's Suffrage, which restricted its claims to those of widows and spinsters, continued as a separate organization, led by Lydia Becker and Millicent Fawcett. Davies thus found herself allied for the first time with the 'radical' Millicent, now widowed and living in London with her sister Agnes and daughter Philippa. Others involved in the society included her old colleague Lady Goldsmid, Jessie Boucherett, and Frances Power Cobbe. Nine years later, under Millicent Fawcett's leadership, the two groups re-merged as the National Union of Women's Suffrage Societies. In 1903 this split again, with the creation of the militant and socialist Women's Social and Political Union, led by Emmeline Pankhurst.

Needless to say, Davies remained through all this on the moderate wing, and as the militant movement grew she in turn grew increasingly active, speaking up for the 'old law-abiding school of women suffragists'.[75] She objected strongly to any expressions of support for the militants and was shocked by their growing resort

---

[75] Stephen, 349.

to violence. She wrote leaflets, joined demonstrations and deputations, directed tactics, and spoke at meetings. As the situation evolved, however, she found herself, also as often before, out of sympathy with her colleagues. Eventually, in 1912, after the prime minister Asquith had scotched all hopes of success by backing universal suffrage for men with no representation at all for women, the National Union decided to put its weight behind the Labour Party, as the only political party committed to women's suffrage, and this was too much. Davies resigned and joined instead the Conservative and Unionist Women's Franchise Association, as vice-president. This seems entirely fitting. Despite the strong influence of Mill and years of working with Liberals, she had always been at heart a political Conservative.[76]

Meanwhile, in 1902, thanks presumably to some improvement in her financial circumstances, Davies had taken a flat in Montagu Mansions, just south of the Marylebone Road. In 1908, she took a small terraced house in Belsize Park, South Hampstead. She died aged ninety-one on 13 July 1921, alert, rational as ever, and having voted—presumably for the Conservative and Unionist candidate, the engineer and industrialist George Balfour—in the 1918 election.

[76] Stephen, 349–53.

15

Conclusion

In this book I have explored the early years of the Victorian women's movement through a largely biographical account of one of its key members, with a particular focus on two contextual aspects: the variety of views within the movement as to what was desirable or practical, in terms of both ends and means; and the changing social and institutional structures and attitudes within which they all worked, which made possible some moves that weren't possible before, while hindering others. Apart from throwing new light on Emily Davies herself, I wanted to explore two developments in particular, in each of which she occupied a pivotal position. One was the transformation of the women's movement from what was essentially a minority, dissenting Unitarian phenomenon in the 1850s into what was already in the early 1860s a much more mainstream affair, cutting across religious divides, and increasingly implanted as the decade progressed within the established church, supported by key establishment figures. The other was an apparent division of the movement into three arms, one focused almost entirely on educational opportunities, another on the protection of vulnerable women, and the third on women's rights under the law. I also wanted to explore the space of public discourse within which Davies acted: a space of reasoned argument and response lying between the extremes of radical claims of women's rights and reactionary rejections of any change to the status quo.

The literatures on the women's movement and the history of religion don't overlap much, at least in the period covered here. Kathryn Gleadle and Ruth Watts have explored the dissenting origins of the women's movement and the links between Unitarian women's networks and radical Unitarian politics, but that relates mainly to a much earlier period.[1] Although the links persisted at a personal level, at least through the 1850s, they seem to have been of only marginal significance to the women's movement of the 1860s. Laura Schwarz has written on secularism, free thought, and the women's movement, but primarily in reference either to a later period or to the earlier overlap with radical Unitarians.[2]

---

[1] See, for example, Kathryn Gleadle, 'British women and radical politics in the late nonconformist enlightenment, c.1770–1830', in Amanda Vickery, ed., *Women, Privilege and Power: British Politics, 1750 to the Present* (Stanford University Press, 2001), 123–51; *The Early Feminists: Radical Unitarians and the Emergence of the Women's Rights Movement 1831–1851* (Macmillan, 1995); Ruth Watts, 'Rational religion and feminism: the challenge of Unitarianism in the Nineteenth Century', in Sue Morgan, ed., *Women, Religion and Feminism in Britain, 1750–1900* (Palgrave Macmillan, 2002), 32–52.
[2] Laura Schwarz, *Infidel Feminism: Secularism, Religion and Women's Emancipation in England, 1830–1914* (Manchester University Press, 2013).

Emily Davies and the Mid-Victorian Women's Movement. John Hendry, Oxford University Press. © John Hendry 2024.
DOI: 10.1093/oso/9780198910237.003.0015

CONCLUSION   269

Secularist innovations such as the Female Medical Society (whose Charles Drysdale once baffled Emily Davies with his insistence that female medics and Christian belief were incompatible)[3] remained on the fringes of the women's movement. Several writers have drawn attention to the freethinking of Elizabeth Wolstenholme,[4] but that only became evident towards the end of the period considered here, when it became a source of friction with her more conventional colleagues. The only significant attempt to explore the Church of England context is Helen Mathers's exploration of the evangelicalism of one of those colleagues, Josephine Butler.[5] This is an isolated example, however, and in some ways misleading. Evangelicals generally were amongst the strongest supporters of traditional gender roles, and while Butler was an evangelical in the emotional sense, in matters of doctrine and social practice both she and her husband were more aligned with the broad church. Indeed, George Butler had been reluctant to enter orders at all, given what he'd seen of theological disputes and clerical misogyny in Oxford, and had been persuaded to do so only once he was persuaded that being a good clergyman might be much the same as being a good man.[6]

In general, there has been remarkably little exploration of either the relationship between the women's movement and the established church or the transformation of the movement from one built upon dissenting women's networks to one cutting across religious divides, many of whose leaders were committed members of the Church of England. Given the overwhelming dominance of the Church of England and its teachings in English society at the time, and especially in the upper-middle reaches of society from which decision-making elites were mainly drawn, this seems a curious omission. The church, it seems, was so much part of the background as to be largely taken for granted by historians.

This neglect may be partly a consequence of a downplaying of the broad church movement within a grand historical narrative that has focused heavily on the evangelical revival of the early nineteenth century and has tended towards a binary classification of 'high church' or 'evangelical'. As I have argued here, in the context of the elite periodicals and lay intellectual discourse, broad church thinking was not only a prominent feature of the period under discussion, but arguably a dominant one. If we look for liberal perspectives, whether on theology, science, or the status of women, we find them either amongst the mainly atheist radicals or—and in greater profusion—amongst broad churchmen and their sympathizers. And given the dominance of Christianity within the culture, it was the

---

[3] ED to JC, 12 January 1864, *EDCL*, 90–3: 91.

[4] Schwarz, *Infidel Feminism*; Sandra Holton, *Suffrage Days: Stories from the Women's Suffrage Movement* (Routledge, 1996); Wright.

[5] Helen Mathers, 'Evangelism and feminism: Josephine Butler, 1828–96', in Morgan, ed. *Women, Religion and Feminism*, 123–38; 'The evangelical spirituality of a Victorian feminist: Josephine Butler, 1828–1906', *Journal of Ecclesiastical History*, 52 (2001), 282–312.

[6] Jordan, 15 ff., 28. The friendship of Arthur Stanley, after whom he named his second son, might well have been a factor here.

latter that was the more influential in establishment circles. Within the church, the broad church liberals remained a small minority, but under their influence the church itself grew significantly broader and more liberal. The established church of the early 1870s was much more accepting of theological differences and much more accommodating of scientific and social change than that of the mid-1850s. Traditional teaching on the subjection of women to men didn't go away, or if it did it was often replaced by religiously based pseudo-sciences of 'natural' female weakness and incapacity. But a space was created for the legitimation of alternative perspectives.

The broad church was not the whole story, of course, and at the beginning of our period it was not even a significant part of the story. In the late 1850s, Emily Davies, Elizabeth Garrett, Jessie Boucherett, and Emily Faithfull, all committed members of the Church of England, felt their religion no bar to joining the women's movement, something that would have been unthinkable even a decade earlier. What had changed in that decade, however, was primarily institutional and only secondarily related to religion. Three factors stand out, the first of which had to do with the workings of men.

Within the 'public' sphere of business and politics, men had long worked together across religious divides. In business this happened as a matter of course. In politics, the classic example was the abolitionist movement. This was led by the liberal evangelicals of the Clapham Sect, but with strong support from Unitarians like Bodichon's grandfather, William Smith. The evangelicals involved were doctrinally firm but politically liberal, rational intellectuals. Emily Davies's father and his sponsor, Bishop Maltby, were later examples of the kind. And in both their liberalism and their rationalism they found common ground with the Unitarians. Within the 'private' sphere, however, the women's networks were strongly constrained by religion. Women of the established church socialized with women of the established church; Unitarian women socialized with Unitarian women. There was some overlap with the Quakers, whose strict moral codes aligned with the evangelicals while their rational theological dissent aligned with the Unitarians. An overlap was created too by a gradual drift of both Quakers and Unitarians into the established church, as in the Davies family circle in Chichester. But a strict separation of spheres amongst the evangelicals effectively precluded their women from joining the activist Unitarian networks.

In the 1850s, the Law Amendment Society and its successor the Social Science Association again brought together members of the established church and Unitarians. The Law Amendment Society was dominated by members of the established church, in this case running across the spectrum from high to low. It also attracted members from across the political spectrum, from Radical to Conservative. Its defining characteristics, however, were that it was broadly progressive (and predominantly Liberal) and above all rationalist. Its central aim was to make the law more rationally consistent than would be the case without its

CONCLUSION   271

interventions. This approach chimed with that of Unitarians such as Matthew Davenport Hill, who became one of the society's key members, and as had been the case with abolition, pressing social concerns created a strong overlap of interest between Unitarian and Church of England activists. In this case the overriding concerns were with child poverty and criminality and the laws by which they were addressed. In practical terms, the churches couldn't work together and each set up its own system of reformatories. But men like the Unitarian Hill, the religiously flexible Lord Brougham, and the leading lay evangelical the Earl of Shaftesbury were equally committed to social and legal change.

It was due to Hill's prominence in the Law Amendment Society that Bodichon's book on the laws concerning women got taken up by that society, and largely due to Hill's influence, with Brougham's support, that the Unitarian women's network became an integral part of the Social Science Association. Once that had happened, the women's movement gained access to serious established church support, at least insofar as it addressed concerns that could be linked to traditional concerns of the church. SPEW provides the best illustration here. On one hand it was unquestionably the fruit of Bodichon's and Parkes's writing on women and work. It was located in Langham Place alongside the *English Woman's Journal*, owned and led by Unitarians. On the other hand it was the brainchild of Jessie Boucherett and was actively supported by the Earl of Shaftesbury with the nominal support of four bishops, all of whose interests lay not in opening up opportunities for women at all but in the alleviation of poverty, a traditional part of the church's work and an arena they sought to control.

More generally, the Social Science Association opened up the nascent women's movement to open view and open participation. As members of the movement reported on their activities to the annual congresses, those reports were themselves reported in the local and national press. The satires of the *Saturday Review* may have been harsh, but they told people that there was a women's movement. Papers like Cobbe's on university admission were very widely reported indeed. Moreover, the annual congresses were major events, attracting people who might not otherwise have got involved, Lydia Becker's attendance at the Manchester congress in 1866 being a prime example.

A second factor of some significance is that the group around Bodichon and Parkes was not just concerned with the politics of rights and opportunities for women. It was also a group of women earning their living, or seeking to earn their living, as writers and painters, and this went across religious divides. Parkes, Craig, and Procter were poets, and it was as poets as well as feminists that they knew each other. Parkes was brought up in the Unitarian family network, Procter was a Roman Catholic convert, Craig established church. Max Hays was a writer, of no known religion, and Lady Monson was Church of England, both coming into the movement from the artistic circles of Rome. So from the beginning Langham Place, though set up by Unitarians, cut across religions.

The third factor was Langham Place itself, together with the *English Woman's Journal*. This was the first time a women's movement had been centred on a physical place, and a formal institution, rather than being just a network of people. A consequence was that anyone could just turn up on the doorstep, as did both Jessie Boucherett and Emily Faithfull. Emily Davies arrived through a personal introduction, but there was somewhere for her to arrive at, and work there for her to do.

By the early 1860s, the women's movement was established as one running across religious beliefs, and it was at this point that the broad church became relevant. For Emily Davies and Elizabeth Garrett in particular, the contacts made through Llewelyn Davies were critical. Davies's various campaign committees, for example, were all multi-denominational, but there is no doubting the importance she attributed to having a prominent churchman in the chair. Dean Alford may not have had any specific interest in the education of women, but like other broad churchmen he was committed to an approach that saw social change as an opportunity for broadening and expanding the church's potential rather than as a threat to its authority. Broad church and especially Maurician affiliations also provided something akin to the Unitarian women's network for some of the women activists within the Church of England, women who rejected traditional church doctrine on the role of women, but for whom religious belief and its expression through church attendance, ritual, and prayer were deeply important. It gave them a home within the church, and in many cases a shared home.

The broad church perspective was also important in Cambridge University, a Church of England institution in which the religious question of the day was not one of high versus low, tractarian versus evangelical, but that of the uncertain boundary between Christianity and agnosticism. This was a defining issue for the broad church and the university's response, in the cases of Henry Sidgwick and Sedley Taylor, for example, key figures in the promotion of the women's colleges, was the broad church response of inclusiveness.

The other way in which the broad church promoted the women's movement was through its public support for their causes. Broad church writers wrote articles in support of women's causes, including property rights, improved schooling, admittance to the universities and professions and, in a few cases, the franchise. Broad church editors gave their pages to writers from the women's movement itself: Emily Davies, Millicent Garrett Fawcett, Frances Power Cobbe, Lydia Becker, Emily Shirreff, and others. This was not the only public support they received. The radical press and Radical politicians like the (Quaker) Brights and (the atheist) Mill were even more strongly behind them. From the perspective of the establishment, however, the Radicals, even though they might sometimes be admired for their personal qualities, were political extremists. The broad churchmen, in contrast, were part of the establishment, moderate progressives who were increasingly emblematic of how things might reasonably change. As the church at large grew broader and more tolerant under their influence, moreover, the causes of women, and especially the education of women, grew more respectable. It is most unlikely that the Bishop of Peterborough would have spoken up in support of Davies's college if she had not already had a core of church supporters. Lyttelton too, idiosyncratic though he was, might not have played as active a part as he did in advancing women's causes were they not being advanced by staunch members of the Church of England.

From a broad church perspective, society was changing, the role of women in society was changing, and the church needed to recognize, welcome, and respond to that rather than fight it. The approach was that of a church moderate rather than a church militant, however, seeking to run with society rather than ahead of it. It was reasonable rather than strictly rational, based as much on feeling and common sense as on logical argument. It tended, in consequence, to be strong in its support of moderate reforms whose time had come, but much less so in support of reforms for which society at large was not yet ready, even if they had reason on their side. Richard Hutton's *Spectator* articles capture this well. He was supportive of improved education for girls and broadening the scope for women's work, including in the professions. He was cautious about giving women the same education as men and came round only slowly to the idea that they might get university degrees. He persisted in thinking the time not yet ripe for giving them the vote, even on a feme sole basis. His logic was that they needed to be better educated first, but common sense told him that they needed to be seen to be better educated as well, before men would come round to the idea.

Davies shared some of this thinking, but like all those active in the women's movement she saw proposed reforms as ways of *bringing about* social change. She withdrew from the suffrage campaign and took no part in that for married women's property rights, but she would undoubtedly have been pleased had those campaigns succeeded. Far better the vote now than in twenty or fifty years time. For her the question of what objectives to pursue and when was partly a question of how best to use her own time and energy; partly a question of what she could control, of pursuing her own projects; partly a question of long-term objectives; and partly a question of strategy.

By the early 1870s, members of the women's movement were campaigning in three distinct areas. One was for the repeal of the Contagious Disease Acts (CDAs). Another was for changes in the law relating to women: married women's property and the franchise. The third was around educational opportunities for girls and women. These campaigns were motivated by three main objectives. One was the protection of vulnerable women from the abuses of male authority, be it violent husbands, magistrates, the police, or the clergy. Another was women's rights: above all the right to equality under the law, including the rights to vote and own property. The third was the opening of opportunities for women to freely fulfil their potential and so contribute to society. These were, of course linked. The claim of women's rights, in particular, included both the right not to be molested and the rights to university admission, employment, and entry to the professions. The motivations, however, though they might be combined, were quite distinct, and the combinations of campaigns to which women gave their active support and the rationales for doing so depended heavily upon them.

The concern with the protection of vulnerable women had deep roots in the Quaker and Unitarian networks of the 1830s and 1840s. Female abolitionists were at least as much concerned with the fate of women—planters' wives as well as their enslaved mistresses and daughters—as they were with principle of chattel slavery. It was also a central concern of the women's movement in its early stages. It is, I feel, where Bessie Parkes's heart lay. Ten years later, it is certainly what motivated Josephine Butler, leader of the campaign to repeal the Contagious Diseases Acts, and some of the Quaker women who supported her. For Butler this was explicitly a religious and moral issue, not a political one, and she grew to resent and sideline the support of Becker and Wolstenholme, both of whom took a different view.[7] Butler took little interest in the campaign for married women's property rights once the 1870 Act, which did little for women's rights but something to protect the worst abused, had been passed. She continued to support the suffrage campaign, but mainly in the hope that women voters would bring pressure on the government to address the issues she most cared about.

For Lydia Becker, in contrast, as well as for Helen Taylor, Clementia Taylor, and others, the central issue was women's rights and by far the most important efforts of the women's movement were those directed towards the franchise. For these campaigners, the protection of prostitutes was neither central nor seemly. Even the campaign for married women's property was, for Becker, a 'branch' issue, best severed from the main trunk. From this perspective, the history of the women's movement in the 1870s is one of competing personalities and differing judgements over how quickly and how best to advance the cause, as Becker and Manchester split from London, and Becker then split from her Manchester colleagues when Jacob Bright lost his parliamentary seat in 1874 and William Forsyth, who took up the parliamentary campaign, insisted on the explicit exclusion of married women from his bill.

For Elizabeth Wolstenholme and Ursula Bright (Jacob's wife), the rights of women and the protection of women were one and the same. From Wolstenholme's Radical and freethinking perspective, Victorian society, in its treatment of both women and the working classes, was rotten through and through, and every iniquity was the subject of a campaign. At the other end of the suffrage campaign, meanwhile, Millicent Garrett Fawcett also saw the various motivations as interwoven, but placed herself as much in support of opportunities as rights. Even more than Becker and in stark contrast to Wolstenholme, she sought to work within the structures of Victorian society rather than in out-and-out opposition to them.

[7] Williams, 157–8.

CONCLUSION 275

Fawcett was a Millian, but she knew Mill as a political economist, assisting her husband in writing on the subject and writing her own digest of his work, as well as an advocate of women's rights. For many people, especially after the publication of *The Subjection of Women*, the two were quite distinct, with Mill the intellectual being revered and Mill the feminist widely thought to be over-indulgent of his wife, Harriet Taylor Mill's obsessions. For Mill the intellectual, the freedom of women was not so much a question of abstract rights as one of the benefits to society from leaving everyone free to develop their potential, unhindered by law or convention, to the maximum. This was the doctrine that inspired Barbara Leigh Smith as a young women and Emily Davies and Elizabeth Garrett as they entered the women's movement, and it was the doctrine that underpinned all of Davies's work and to some extent all of the work for the education of women. The campaign for the ladies' lectures and examinations had nothing to do with rights and was only indirectly to do with protection. The central purpose was to provide opportunities for young women to study, for the benefit of the children they would subsequently teach. The purpose of the Girls Public Day School Company and like organizations was similarly to provide opportunities for girls such as already existed for boys, for the ultimate benefit of society as a whole.

We find it natural in the twenty-first century to think in terms of rights, and historians have tended to see the women's movement in the 1870s and beyond as focused on the franchise and the rights of mothers and married women, with education as something of a side show. In the 1870s people thought in terms of duties. The wrongs done to women were a concern: they represented a potential failure of duty, whether on the part of fathers, husbands, or others. But rights talk was considered extreme. And from this perspective the suffrage campaign hit all the wrong buttons. People varied in their views as to whether it would be sensible to give women a vote, all things considered, but the majority of legislators could never be persuaded that they were wronged by being denied it, as they might be wronged by the CDAs or by poor education. From that point of view, the CDA campaign and the educational campaign were both more salient than the suffrage campaign. Pro or anti, they were not, as the suffrage campaign undeniably was, laughing matters.

The difference, of course, lay in their perceived respectability or, to put it another way, the extent to which they challenged vested interests. The CDA campaign threatened the double moral standard that lay at the core of Victorian male hegemony, enforcing purity upon any woman who wished to be considered as a person at all. Improvements in education could also be seen as threatening to male superiority, but they needn't be so. They could also be cast as making better wives, better mothers, better teachers, and as providing openings for those who, through no fault of their own, might never be wives and mothers.

For Emily Davies, motivations aligned with both strategy and practicalities. The treatment of prostitutes seems to have been, for her, a medical matter, for informed professional judgement. She had never campaigned for women's rights, for the protection of prostitutes, or against the oppression of working-class women. She seems to have been ambivalent about the moral double standard in its social manifestations, objecting to restrictions upon young women in daily life whilst imposing similar restrictions upon her own students, questioning notions of respectability in private while obeying them in public. But we have no record of her ever discussing the question in its sexual aspect, and she quite possibly never thought about it. She was concerned about the franchise, as voting was one way in which women could contribute their perspectives and experience to the common good. But on a purely practical level, getting involved with the campaigns for legal reform would have meant playing second fiddle to Elizabeth Wolstenholme, whom she regarded as a traitor to the educational cause; Josephine Butler, whom she completely mistrusted; and Lydia Becker, who would probably have left her trailing in her wake. She could also read the periodicals and see that there was much more support amongst moderate liberals for women in education and the professions than there was for female suffrage.[8] The vote would come, but from a strategic point of view other things needed to come first. As a student of Mill she will have been conscious, as some of her reforming colleagues may not have been, that on his theories the franchise should be based on educational, not property, qualifications, so the first priority was for women to be educated, both to gain those qualifications and to demonstrate to men that they were capable of reasoning and sound judgement.

By the 1870s, education had also become her project. She had come to it by accident, her support of Elizabeth Garrett leading her first into university reform, then to the admission of girls to the locals, and only then to the reform of girls' secondary education. The issue suited her, however. It resonated with her own experience, denied the university education that her brothers received, and that had enabled Llewelyn to become a leading writer and intellectual as well as a distinguished churchman and social activist. It played to her intellectual strength. It enabled her to work with politically moderate and congenial colleagues. And in the case of the college she could, to a certain extent, keep control. For her personally, as she discovered if she didn't already know it, this was a major consideration.

Most of the others involved in the educational campaigns seem, like Davies, to have been more interested in opportunities than in rights. Barbara Bodichon was perhaps the most radical, but her preference, the more so as she grew older, was to inspire and back others rather than to lead herself. She was also a romantic, to

---

[8] Lydia Becker, in contrast, was so enthused by the franchise project that she believed it to be achievable in the very short term: Williams, 39. Martin Pugh has argued that it was more achievable than either contemporaries or historians have recognized, and attributes the failure in part to Becker's leadership: *The March of the Women: A Revisionist Analysis of the Campaign for Women's Suffrage, 1866–1914* (Oxford, 2002), 13, 73.

CONCLUSION   277

whom the college appealed. The educationists were also, far more than the suffragists, establishment figures, working within the accepted social structures of class, gender, and religion. Frances Buss, Maria Grey, Emily Shirreff, and even Lady Stanley were all deeply committed feminists, but they were also utterly respectable, good Christians, with not a hint of the radical or strong woman. For some of their more radical colleagues in the women's movement, this might suggest a lack of commitment, but it also meant that they could much more easily win over moderate opinion, work effectively with establishment figures, and so achieve change. Their reforms could be advanced, moreover, through institutional changes that didn't require the sanction of laws, which were never going, as things then stood, to be passed anyway. The rewards might be modest and slow to come, but they were at least there to be had.

Discussion of the public reception of the claims of the women's movement has tended to focus on their outright rejection. The barbs of the *Saturday Review* are irresistibly quotable, their underlying humour often missed. The owner, Alexander Beresford Hope, was a reactionary, an ardent opponent of the broad church and a misogynist, and the *Saturday* reflected that, but it could employ writers like Leslie Stephen—who would have disagreed with Hope on almost everything—and ran a nice line in satire. Proclamations from high as to the natural and innate weakness of the female sex are also highly quotable and not hard to find. Women, we read, are weak in body and mind, incapable of reasoned judgement, made unfit for motherhood by mental exertion, defeminized by exposure to the hustle and bustle of the world, and so on. But any reading of the better novels of the period—which as Anthony Trollope frankly admitted reflected the biases of their readers—will paint a different picture. Such views were held, certainly, but they were not typical. Women were seen as vulnerable, but as much on account of the constraints imposed on them by society and the subservient role they saw as their lot as on account of any natural weakness. A woman was expected to behave like a lady and to defer, outwardly, to the supposedly superior intelligence and wisdom of a man. But she wasn't assumed to be in reality any less intelligent, any less wise.

If we want to understand public resistance to the claims of the women's movement we consequently need to look not at the extremes but at more modest objections, more likely to be representative of mainstream opinion. Looking back to the views cited earlier in the book, one guide to the liberal end of the spectrum here might be Richard Hutton in his more conservative vein: cautious about women getting degrees, ambivalent about women's rights, and opposed to their getting the vote, at least for the time being, while recognizing the question as worth serious discussion, and trying to give it serious discussion. At the moderate conservative end of the spectrum might be Margaret Oliphant. Forced into making her own living following her husband's death, Oliphant had no qualms about women entering the public sphere. She negotiated her contracts and wrote on political as well as literary subjects, including several essays in *Blackwood's Magazine* on the claims of women. ('I suppose' she wrote later, 'I must have become...a sort of general utility woman for the magazine.')[9] But she was strongly opposed to the suffrage, or to changes in the marriage laws.

Somewhere between Hutton and Oliphant lay the bulk of the reading public, the relatively educated middle class, well illustrated, and well represented, by Trollope, whose major novels fall within the period covered here and who made repeated reference to the women's movement in his novels and lectures of the late 1860s.

Trollope was a progressive, open-minded Liberal, and a great respecter of female ability. His female characters are always sympathetically drawn: intelligent, capable, and wise, where his men are often foolish, shortsighted, or easily misled. Some (Madame Goesler, Miss Dunstable) blatantly challenge the ideology of separate spheres: they are free agents in a masculine world without any loss of femininity. He had no sympathy with the sexual double standard, which he viewed as immoral, both in its condemnation of the innocent and in its indulgence of the guilty;[10] or with men who abused their power and sought to control their wives. He was good friends with George Eliot, was friendly for a time with Emily Faithfull, and will almost certainly have met Bodichon, Davies, and others in the women's movement. He was at least half in love with an American journalist, Kate Field, of strong feminist persuasion. And yet he was also the most socially conservative of men, unable to escape the gender norms of his age. On the question of higher education for women, he seems to have been conflicted. Lecturing on the subject in the wake of Davies's campaigning he took refuge in the line that he could hardly object to young women spending their days reading novels rather than studying—but nor could he begrudge them the opportunity.[11] His treatment of a woman's 'profession' and the love elements of his plots are thoroughly conventional:[12]

When a girl asks herself that question,—what shall she do with her life? it is so natural that she should answer it by saying that she will get married, and give her life to somebody else. It is a woman's one career—let women rebel against the edict as they may; and though there may be word-rebellion here and there, women learn the truth early in their lives. And women know it later in life when they think of their girls; and men know it too, when they have to deal with their

---

[9] Margaret Oliphant, *Annals of a Publishing House: William Blackwood and His Sons. Their Magazine and Friends*, Vol. 2 (William Blackwood and Sons. 1897), 475, quoted in Joanne Shattock, 'Margaret Oliphant and the Blackwood "brand"', in Joanne Shattock, ed., *Journalism and the Periodical Press in Nineteenth-Century Britain* (Cambridge University Press, 2017), 341–52: 341.

[10] See, for example, his treatment of the 'fallen woman' in *The Vicar of Bullhampton*.

[11] Anthony Trollope, 'On the higher education of women', in *Four Lectures* (Constable, 1868).

[12] Anthony Trollope, *The Vicar of Bullhampton* (Bradbury, Evans, 1870), 246.

CONCLUSION 279

daughters.…Nature prompts the desire, the world acknowledges its ubiquity, circumstances show that it is reasonable, the whole theory of creation requires it.

This was what his audience would have expected. It was the convention, it was a convention that pleased him, and it was one that pleased them. But many of his books pivot on a situation in which there is a clash between convention, generally understood, and moral virtue in some specific case. A character has to struggle between what is expected and what seems right, and it is always virtue that triumphs. In real life, there should always be exceptions: exceptional people, exceptional circumstances. But that does not mean the conventions are wrong, or even that those who wrongly apply them—selfishly or unthinkingly—are wrong. They misread their duty, they don't fail in it.

Compare an 1860s novel of Trollope's with one of Oliphant's written at the same time, and you are in different worlds. With Trollope you are in the 1860s. With Oliphant, even if it's set in real time, and even though she is the younger by thirteen years, it feels more like the 1840s. What marks out the 1860s is a world in which old ideas are being questioned, conventions are being challenged, people are beginning to think for themselves. But it is a world that is not yet quite ready to break free, as the women's movement sought to break free. A world where the proposals of the women's movement could be debated and taken seriously as marking a direction of travel, but not yet one in which they could be acted upon, other than very gradually, cautiously, and in ways which put the institutions of family, class, and religion at minimal risk.

If Trollope and his characters could not be persuaded by a women's cause, it was most unlikely that Parliament could be, or those who steered opinion in the press, or in the towns and villages of England. Whatever their views of women as individuals, these men lived in a world of male supremacy, and it was a world they found reassuringly comfortable. The very word 'rights' carried unfortunate connotations, being associated with violent revolutionaries and more generally with the politics of France and America, both of which had proved to be violently unstable democracies and very far from comfortable. What distinguished Britain and more particularly England (Ireland bringing its own problems) from such countries was the stability of its institutions and the harmonious relations they supported. (Not all women, and not all working-class men, would have agreed with the 'harmonious' bit, but by the 1860s the great majority would have.) England, on this view, was a society held together by social conventions and moral virtues, typically expressed as duties. The law was a blunt instrument to be invoked only *in extremis*. In one sense it was not that important, since rarely invoked, but it should be changed only with great caution, at the risk of unintended consequences.

The most important institution was generally regarded as that of marriage, around which was set a soft version of the separate spheres ideology, framed as a practical and consensual division of responsibilities. Being practical it was not rigid. Women might engage in the public sphere as men did in the private. Women's control of their property might not be protected by law, but it was protected by convention. The allocation of voting rights, on this view, though set by law, was also based on convention and essentially a matter of practical compromise. Perhaps the convention should be changed, but only with due care in regard to the possible but unpredictable social consequences; and there was no great hurry. Most voting men voted responsibly, with wives and families in mind, and any extension of the franchise, even to female property holders, wouldn't make enough of a difference to justify the risks.

Looking at this from afar we see the authority of gender, the authority of class, the authority of the church, not to mention affinities with the authority of race. We see a story that serves to hide or legitimate continuing oppression, and that serves the interests of the oppressors. But we cannot deny that middle-class Victorians of this period did value the power of moral convention over that of the law, moral duty over rights, practice over theory, social stability over equity; or that most middle-class women were happy with things as they stood. Emily Davies understood this, and worked with it. She also believed that it was only through giving women education, on a par with that given to men, that their potential would be recognized and, just as important, that their desire to realize that potential, to enter the public sphere, to seek the vote, and play their part in the polity, would be awakened. If the claim for equal rights were to be successful, it required both the demonstration of women's ability to reason and make sound judgements and the recognition amongst women themselves that they had that ability.

The question that follows on naturally from the above is: what difference did it make? Did improved educational possibilities significantly advance the suffrage and other reforms, or were they a side issue? Which came first, new laws, reformed institutions, or changed ways of thinking? Given the very slow pace of change on all fronts, it's impossible to make any causal connections, but we can perhaps make a few observations.

At the broadest level of analysis, Gladstone's first administration was a bright spot for liberal reform—not unlike the Wilson administrations of a century later. Yet Gladstone himself was resolutely opposed to female suffrage. As the 1870s turned into the 1880s and 1890s, England grew more conservative. The influence of the broad church faded. Morality tightened round established norms. For the women's movement, progress on all fronts was painfully slow. Compulsory examination under the Contagious Diseases Acts was suspended in 1883 and the Acts were repealed in 1886,[13] but this was not so much a gain for women as restitution

---

[13] Their equivalents in India, where racial prejudice compounded gender prejudice, would last another decade.

CONCLUSION 281

of an earlier loss. Following the Custody of Infants Act of 1873 and the Guardianship of Infants Act of 1886, mothers were able to challenge for custody of their young children after divorce and the courts were obliged to put the welfare of the child above the claims of the parents. However, the default position remained that custody rested with the father: in law they were his children, and only in extreme circumstances could he be deprived of his duty to maintain them and his right to bring them up as he chose. After the modest gains of 1870, the 1882 Married Women's Property Act gave a married woman the ability to contract as if she were a feme sole, together with the legal rights and liabilities associated with that. It also gave her control over any property already owned, earned, or acquired after the passing of the Act. This was arguably the most important legal gain for the women's movement in the nineteenth century, both materially and symbolically. However, it was not retrospective, it included some significant reservations, and it failed to advance the claim for suffrage. It would be 1935 before women acquired the same rights over their property as men.

The suffrage battle, meanwhile, continued, but for many years to little effect. It was only with the Representation of the People Act of 1918 that women finally got the vote, and then only on much more restricted terms than men. Only with the 1928 Representation of the People (Equal Franchise) Act, over sixty years after the first suffrage campaign, did they gain electoral equality.

If we look at educational reforms, the overall impression is of distinct advances, but advances that were again very slow and always compromised by traditional gender norms.

At primary level, the number of women on school boards grew exponentially through the last thirty years of the nineteenth century, and their presence and contribution became accepted as normal. However, they were clearly resented by some men (most notably by Lady Stanley's son, Lyulph, who seems to have been particularly arrogant), and struggled to exert any authority.[14] They were able to argue for measures to improve the attendance records of girls and the salaries and fees of female teachers and visitors, but policy seems to have remained firmly in the hands of men, with women offering advice and doing much of the groundwork.

At secondary level, there was a rapid growth in larger and more academic schools: the proprietary high schools of the Girls Public Day Schools Company, the Church Schools Company, and newly endowed grammar schools; the endowed grammar and middle schools established by the Endowed Schools Commission and the Charity Commission; municipal girls' secondary schools; and public schools such as St Leonard's, Wycombe Abbey, and Roedean. Until

---

[14] Patricia Hollis, *Ladies Elect: Women in English Local Government, 1865–1914* (Oxford University Press, 1987), 95 ff., 486; see also Jane Martin, *Women and the Politics of Schooling in Victorian and Edwardian England* (Leicester University Press, 1999), 42 ff.

well into the twentieth century, however, these remained massively outnumbered by small schools on the traditional model. The 1895 report of the Royal Commission on Secondary Education, chaired by James (now Viscount) Bryce, estimated that proprietary and endowed schools between them were currently educating about nine thousand girls in total. Numbers for private schools were impossible to obtain, but they estimated that there were between ten and fifteen thousand such schools (boys and girls combined), with an average attendance of forty to fifty each.[15] Meanwhile the young women going on to university in the 1870s and 1880s, mostly from professional families, were still mostly taught at home, preparing for university entry by private study.[16]

The education of girls clearly did improve, at least for those whose parents wanted it, and Joyce Pedersen has argued that the new schools also provided valuable role models, as their mistresses were seen as women exercising authority on their own account.[17] As Carol Dyhouse and Sara Delamont have shown, however, this needs to be severely qualified.[18] In the first place, many schoolmistresses, even headmistresses, did not see themselves as educational authorities, but rather as fulfilling traditional schoolmistress roles. In the second place, almost all headmistresses were subject to male, and usually entirely male, governing bodies, who in turn saw them as employees, with only devolved authority. Not only in schools under the Church Schools Society but also in endowed and municipal schools generally, the dominant figures were often clergymen who viewed girls' schooling, however academic, as preparation for motherhood.[19] Even pioneers like Buss and Beale, forceful personalities both, had struggled with their governing bodies, and a headmistress appointed later in the century, and beyond, would be expected to know her place. An attempt in the mid-1870s by the Women's Education Union (successor to the National Union for the Education of Girls of all Classes) to persuade the Charity Commission to include women on the governing bodies of new endowed girls' schools fell on deaf ears. It was 'surrounded with much practical difficulty' and the commissioners could give no assurances.[20] The creation of local

---

[15] *Report of the Royal Commission on Secondary Education*, Vol. 1 (HMSO, 1895), 49–52. Jane McDermid, *The Schooling of Girls in Britain and Ireland, 1800–1900* (Routledge, 2012), 14.

[16] Carol Dyhouse, *Girls Growing up in Late Victorian England* (Routledge & Kegan Paul, 1981), 55. For the family backgrounds of Oxford and Cambridge women students through to the 1890s see Joyce Pedersen, *The Reform of Girls' Secondary Education in Victorian England: A Study of Elites and Educational Change* (Routledge, 2017).

[17] Pedersen, *The Reform of Girls' Secondary Education*.

[18] Dyhouse, *Girls Growing Up*; Sara Delamont, 'The contradictions in ladies' education', in Sara Delamont and Lorna Duffin, eds., *The Nineteenth-Century Woman: Her Cultural and Physical World* (Routledge, 2014), 134–63; 'The domestic ideology and women's education', in Delamont and Duffin, eds., *The Nineteenth-Century Woman*, 164–88.

[19] Dyhouse, *Girls Growing Up*, 61 ff.

[20] Dyhouse, *Girls Growing Up*, 63. Carol Dyhouse, 'Miss Buss and Miss Beale: gender and authority in the history of education', in Felicity Hunt, ed., *Lessons for Life: The Schooling of Girls and Women 1850–1950* (Basil Blackwell, 1987), 2–39, suggests that the exercise of authority was easier personally for the severe Beale than for the fun-loving and feminine Buss, but while the distinction seems accurate the conclusion doesn't necessarily follow: see Kamm for their various trials.

CONCLUSION   283

authority girls' secondary schools in the twentieth century increased provision, but the problems of status and authority proved even higher in the state than in the private sector.

Rather than being banished, the traditional ideology of separate spheres continued in modified form. Girls' secondary schools often taught in the mornings only, to allow girls to help at home, and the early twentieth century witnessed a revival of the emphasis on female domesticity, with practical training in 'domestic science' squeezing out more academic subjects.[21] Well into the century, girls' schools were still preparations for matrimony, with gender distinctions and in most cases social and class distinctions strictly maintained. Following the example of Buss's schools, the new proprietary and endowed schools were open to all above the 'elementary' class (it being assumed that anyone going on to secondary education would by definition be middle class), rejecting the fine class distinctions characteristic of traditional girls' schools. But one of the reasons Buss's schools and their followers were mornings only was to prevent the social mixing that would follow from an extended day with its necessary long break.[22]

In this context the role model presented to middle-class pupils was not that of an equal woman but a choice between that of a celibate careerist and that of a well-educated lady wife, neither of which presented significant challenges to the separate spheres ideology.[23] The perceived conflict between an education modelled on that of boys and a woman's femininity remained unresolved.

Some of this was also reflected at university level. While university provision for women expanded, with men and women taking the same examinations, it expanded only slowly. By the end of the century the number of women entering the Oxford, Cambridge, and London colleges combined was still little more than two hundred a year.[24] With the exception of Girton, all were what Martha Vicinus has termed 'family-style' colleges, with an emphasis on traditional notions of femininity.[25] The great majority of university graduates seem either to have become teachers or to have married and taken on the traditional female role of at-home wife and mother, and it would be many decades before women worked themselves into the professions.[26] This may have been because that wasn't what interested them: they wanted to become teachers, or to become educated lady wives. It must also have been because the professions proved resistant. Persuading

---

[21] Felicity Hunt, 'Divided aims: the educational implications of opposing ideologies in girls' secondary schooling', in Hunt, ed., *Lessons for Life*, 3–21.

[22] Delamont, 'The domestic ideology', 175–6.

[23] Dyhouse, *Girls Growing Up*, 78; Delamont, 'The domestic ideology', 184.

[24] Martha Vicinus, *Independent Women: Work and Community for Single Women 1850–1920* (Virago, 1985), 127.

[25] Ibid., 128–30.

[26] Gillian Sutherland, 'The movement for the higher education of women: its social and intellectual context in England, c.1840–80', in P. J. Waller, ed., *Politics and Social Change in Modern Britain* (Harvester Press, 1987), 91–116: 100–4; *In Search of the New Woman: Middle-Class Women and Work in Britain, 1870–1914* (Cambridge University Press, 2015), 18 ff.

284   DAVIES AND THE MID-VICTORIAN WOMEN'S MOVEMENT

the universities to educate and examine women was one thing. Persuading them to admit women as members was another. It would be 1948 before Cambridge finally awarded degrees to women, seventy-five years after Emily Davies's first students took and passed its tripos examinations.

Professional bodies were similarly resistant, if not quite so dilatory. Women could qualify as doctors, but it would be the early twentieth century before they were admitted to the Royal College of Physicians or the Royal College of Surgeons, and then only in minuscule numbers. And it wouldn't be until the 1920s, following the Sex Disqualification (Removal) Act of 1919, that the first women were admitted as barristers or solicitors. The first woman JP was appointed in 1919 and women were not admitted to the House of Lords until 1958.[27] Women began entering the civil service in the 1870s, but starting in the lower clerical grades few gained promotion to executive, let alone administrative, grades and it would be 1925 before graduate women could be recruited into the administrative class, on the same basis as men. Even those organizations that admitted women into professional or managerial positions, moreover, typically retained a marriage bar, making it almost impossible for a university-educated woman to both marry and pursue a career. This was often the case even in schools. In the major banks, the BBC, the home civil service, and other organizations the bar was removed only in the 1940s. In the foreign service it lasted into the 1970s. If a woman wanted to enter a man's world, the prince she had to pay was celibacy.[28]

The higher education of women did challenge and eventually change social attitudes, but it was a very long process. Educational reforms met a lot of resistance and were repeatedly adapted to accommodate the prevailing ideology. Similarly with legal reforms. Granted ownership over their property, wives continued to place it in their husbands' care. Granted the franchise, they voted as their husbands dictated. When changes came, they came as much through the practical demands of two world wars as through campaigns of any kind. And changes in the law, or in formal institutions, weren't always accompanied by changes in attitudes. Emily Davies's dream of a world in which women had equal educational and professional opportunities to men was not realized in practice until at least the 1970s, arguably much later, and long after women got the vote. One thing that has been historically validated, however, is the Victorian idea, which she shared, that social convention is more important than the law. It is now over 160 years since the women's movement was founded. Women in Britain have long had equality with men under the law. They are still to achieve it in the minds of men.

---

[27] See Christina de Ballaigue, 'The development of teaching as a profession for women before 1870', *The Historical Journal*, 44 (2001), 963–88: 965.

[28] Delamont, 'The domestic ideology', 178–81; for detailed figures and case studies see Sutherland, *In Search of the New Woman*.

Select Bibliography

Altholz, J. L. *Anatomy of a Controversy: The Debate over Essays and Reviews, 1860–1864* (Scolar Press, 1994).

Anderson, Louisa Garrett, *Elizabeth Garrett Anderson* (Faber and Faber, 1939).

Annan, Noel, *Leslie Stephen: The Godless Victorian* (University of Chicago Press, 1986).

ApRoberts, Ruth, *The Moral Trollope* (Ohio University Press, 1971).

Askwith, Betty, *The Lytteltons: A Family Chronicle of the Nineteenth Century* (Chatto & Windus, 1975).

Banks, Olive, *Becoming a Feminist: The Social Origins of 'First Wave' Feminism* (Wheatsheaf, 1986).

Bartley, Paula, *Prostitution: Prevention and Reform in England, 1860–1914* (Routledge, 2000).

Beer, Gillian, *George Eliot and the Woman Question* (Edward Everett Root, 2018).

Bennett, Daphne, *Emily Davies and the Liberation of Women* (Andre Deutsch, 1990).

Biagini, Eugenio F., *Liberty, Retrenchment and Reform: Popular Liberalism in the Age of Gladstone, 1860–1880* (Cambridge University Press, 2004).

Birkin, Andrew, *J. M. Barrie and the Lost Boys: The Real Story Behind Peter Pan*, revised ed. (Yale University Press, 2003).

Blackburn, Helen, *Women's Suffrage: A Record of the Women's Suffrage Movement in the British Isles, with Biographical Sketches of Miss Becker* (Williams & Norgate, 1902).

Bolt, Christine, *Victorian Attitudes to Race* (Routledge 1971, reprinted 2007).

Bolt, Rodney, *As Good as God, as Clever as the Devil: The Impossible Life of Mary Benson* (Atlantic Books, 2011).

Bostick, Theodora, 'The press and the launching of the women's suffrage movement, 1866–67', *Victorian Periodicals Review*, 13 (1980), 125–31.

Boyd, Julia, *The Excellent Doctor Blackwell: The Life of the First Woman Physician* (Sutton Publishing, 2005).

Bradbrook, M. C., *'That Infidel Place': A Short History of Girton College, 1869–1969* (Chatto & Windus, 1969).

Bradshaw's Descriptive Railway Handbook (1863, reprinted by Old House, 2012).

Brock, M. G., and M. C. Curthoys, eds., *The History of the University of Oxford*, Vol. 7: *Nineteenth Century, Part 2* (Oxford University Press, 2000).

Brougham, Henry, *The Life and Times of Henry Lord Brougham, Written by Himself*, 3 vols (Blackwood, 1871).

Brown, Sue, *Julia Wedgwood, the Unexpected Victorian; The Life and Writing of a Remarkable Female Intellectual* (Anthem Press, 2023).

Browne, Janet, *Charles Darwin: Voyaging* (Princeton University Press, 1995).

Browne, Janet, *Charles Darwin: The Power of Place* (Jonathan Cape, 2002).

Bryant, Margaret E. *The London Experience of Secondary Education* (Athlone Press, 1986).

Burman, Sandra, ed., *Fit Work for Women* (Croom Helm, 1979; Routledge, 2013).

Burstall, Sara, *The Story of the Manchester High School for Girls, 1871–1911* (Manchester University Press, 1911).

Burstyn, Joan, *Victorian Education and the Ideal of Womanhood* (Croom Helm, 1980).

Burton, Katherine, *A Memoir of Mrs. Crudelius* (privately printed, 1879; Forgotten Books, 2018).

286 SELECT BIBLIOGRAPHY

Bush, Julia, *Women against the Vote: Female Anti-Suffragism in Britain* (Oxford University Press, 2007).

Butler, Josephine, *Recollections of George Butler* (J. W. Arrowsmith, 1892).

Caine, Barbara, 'John Stuart Mill and the English women's movement', *Historical Studies*, 18 (1978), 52–67.

Caine, Barbara, *Victorian Feminists* (Oxford University Press, 1992).

Caine, Barbara, *English Feminism, 1780–1980* (Oxford University Press, 1997).

Caine, Barbara, *Biography and History* (Palgrave Macmillan, 2010).

Campbell, Lewis, and William Garnett, *The Life of James Clerk Maxwell* (Macmillan, 1882).

Chadwick, Owen, *The Victorian Church: Part One, 1829–1859* (A. & C. Black, 1971).

Chadwick, Owen, *The Victorian Church: Part Two, 1860–1901* (A. & C. Black, 1972).

Clough, Blanche Athena, *A Memoir of Anne Jemima Clough* (Edward Arnold, 1897).

Cocks, H. G., *Nameless Offences: Homosexual Desire in the 19th Century* (I. B. Tauris, 2003).

Colloms, Brenda, *Charles Kingsley: The Lion of Eversley* (Constable, 1975).

Cook, Hera, *The Long Sexual Revolution: English Women, Sex and Contraception, 1800–1975* (Oxford University Press, 2004).

Crawford, Elizabeth, *The Women's Suffrage Movement: A Reference Guide, 1866–1928* (Routledge, 2000).

Crawford, Elizabeth, *Enterprising Women: The Garretts and Their Circle* (Francis Bootle, 2002).

Davidoff, Leonora, *The Best Circles: Society, Etiquette and the Season* (Croom Helm, 1973).

Davidoff, Leonora, and Catherine Hall, *Family Fortunes: Men and Women of the English Middle Class, 1780–1840*, 2nd ed. (Routledge, 2002).

de Bellaigue, Christina, 'The development of teaching as a profession for women before 1870', *The Historical Journal*, 44 (2001), 963–88.

de Bellaigue, Christina, *Educating Women: Schooling and Identity in England and France 1800–67* (Oxford University Press, 2007).

de Groot, Joanna, '"Sex" and "race": the construction of language and image in the nineteenth century', in Susan Mendus and Jane Rendall, eds., *Sexuality and Subordination*, 89–129.

Delamont, Sara, 'The contradictions in ladies' education', in Sara Delamont and Lorna Duffin, eds., *The Nineteenth-Century Woman*, 134–63.

Delamont, Sara, 'The domestic ideology and women's education', in Sara Delamont and Lorna Duffin, eds., *The Nineteenth-Century Woman*, 164–88.

Delamont, Sara, and Lorna Duffin, eds., *The Nineteenth-Century Woman: Her Cultural and Physical World* (Routledge, 2014).

Delap, Lucy, 'The "woman question" and the origins of feminism', in Gareth Stedman Jones and Gregory Claeys, eds., *The Cambridge History of Nineteenth Century Political Thought* (Cambridge University Press, 2011), 319–48.

Delap, Lucy, Ben Griffin, and Abi Wills, eds., *The Politics of Domestic Authority in Britain since 1800* (Palgrave Macmillan, 2009).

Desmond, Adrian, *Huxley: From Devil's Disciple to Evolution's High Priest* (Penguin, 1998).

Dingsdale, Ann, '"Generous and lofty sympathies": The Kensington Society, the 1866 women's suffrage petition and the development of mid-Victorian feminism', PhD thesis (University of Greenwich, 1995).

Dowling, Linda, *Hellenism and Homosexuality in Victorian Oxford* (Cornell University Press, 1994).

Doyle, Don H., *The Cause of All Nations: An International History of the American Civil War* (Basic Books, 2015).

Dyhouse, Carol, 'Social Darwinist ideas and the development of women's education in England, 1880–1920', *History of Education*, 5 (1976), 41–8.

SELECT BIBLIOGRAPHY   287

Dyhouse, Carol, 'Good wives and little mothers: social anxieties and the schoolgirl's curriculum, 1890–1920', *Oxford Review of Education*, 3 (1977), 21–35.

Dyhouse, Carol, *Girls Growing Up in Late Victorian England* (Routledge & Kegan Paul, 1981).

Dyhouse, Carol, 'Miss Buss and Miss Beale: gender and authority in the history of education', in Felicity Hunt, ed., *Lessons for Life: The Schooling of Girls and Women 1850–1950* (Basil Blackwell, 1987), 2–39.

Dyhouse, Carol, *No Distinction of Sex? Women in British Universities, 1870–1939* (UCL Press, 1995).

Ellegård, Alvar, 'The readership of the periodical press in mid-Victorian Britain, II: directory', *Victorian Periodicals Newsletter*, 13 (September 1971), 3–22.

Ellsworth, Edward, *Liberators of the Female Mind: The Shirreff Sisters, Educational Reform and the Women's Movement* (Greenwood Press, 1979).

Faderman, Lilian, *Surpassing the Love of Men: Romantic Friendship and Love between Women from the Renaissance to the Present* (Women's Press, 1985).

Falconer, Isobel, 'Cambridge and the building of the Cavendish Laboratory', in Raymond Flood et al., eds., *James Clerk Maxwell: Perspectives on his Life and Work* (Oxford University Press, 2014), 67–99.

Fawcett, Millicent Garrett, *What I Remember* (G. P. Putnam's, 1925; reprinted by Forgotten Books, 2018).

Figes, Orlando, *Crimea: The Last Crusade* (Allen Lane, 2010).

Finn, Margot, *After Chartism: Class and Nation in English Radical Politics, 1848–1874* (Cambridge University Press, 1993).

Fletcher, Sheila, *Feminists and Bureaucrats: A Study in the Development of Girls' Education in the Nineteenth Century* (Cambridge University Press, 1980).

Forster, Margaret, *Significant Sisters: The Grassroots of Active Feminism 1839–1939* (Penguin, 1986).

Gill, Stephen, *William Wordsworth: A Life*, 2nd ed. (Oxford University Press, 2020).

Gillis, John R., *For Better, for Worse: British Marriages, 1600 to the Present* (Oxford University Press, 1985).

Girton College Register, 1869–1946 (Girton College, 1948).

Gleadle, Kathryn, *The Early Feminists: Radical Unitarians and the Emergence of the Women's Rights Movement 1831–1851* (Macmillan, 1995).

Gleadle, Kathryn, 'British women and radical politics in the late nonconformist enlightenment, c.1770–1830', in Amanda Vickery, ed., *Women, Privilege and Power*, 123–51.

Glenfinning, Victoria, *Anthony Trollope* (Hutchinson, 1992).

Goldhill, Simon, *A Very Queer Family Indeed: Sex, Religion, and the Bensons in Victorian Britain* (University of Chicago Press, 2016).

Goldman, Lawrence, 'Introduction: an advanced Liberal: Henry Fawcett, 1833–1884', in Lawrence Goldman, *The Blind Victorian* (Cambridge University Press, 1989), 1–40.

Goldman, Lawrence, ed., *The Blind Victorian: Henry Fawcett and British Liberalism* (Cambridge University Press, 1989).

Goldman, Lawrence, *Science, Reform and Politics in Victorian Britain: The Social Science Association, 1857–1886* (Cambridge University Press, 2002).

Gregory, Gill, *The Life and Work of Adelaide Procter* (Ashgate, 1998).

Griffin, Ben, *The Politics of Gender in Victorian Britain: Masculinity, Political Culture and the Struggle for Women's Rights* (Cambridge University Press, 2012).

Grosskurth, Phyllis, *John Addington Symonds: A Biography* (Longmans, 1964).

Gurney, Ellen Mary, ed., *Letters of Emilia Russell Gurney* (James Nisbet, 1902).

Haight, Gordon W., ed., *The George Eliot Letters*, 9 vols (Yale University Press, 1954–78).

288 SELECT BIBLIOGRAPHY

Hall, Catherine, 'The early formation of Victorian domestic ideology', in Sandra Burman, ed., *Fit Work for Women* (1979), 15–32.

Hall, Catherine, 'Competing masculinities: Thomas Carlyle, John Stuart Mill and the case of Governor Eyre', in Catherine Hall, *White, Male and Middle Class: Explorations in Feminism and History* (Polity, 1992), 255–95.

Hall, Catherine, ' "Going a-Trolloping": imperial man travels the empire', in Clare Midgley, ed., *Gender and Imperialism*, 180–99.

Hall, Catherine, 'The nation within and without', in Catherine Hall, Keith McClelland, and Jane Rendall, eds., *Defining the Victorian Nation*, 179–233.

Hall, Catherine, *Civilising Subjects: Metropole and Colony in the English Imagination 1830–1867* (Polity, 2002).

Hall, Catherine, Keith McClelland, and Jane Rendall, eds., *Defining the Victorian Nation: Class, Race, Gender and the British Reform Act of 1867* (Cambridge University Press, 2000).

Hall, Catherine, and Sonya O. Rose, eds., *At Home with the Empire: Metropolitan Culture and the Imperial World* (Cambridge University Press, 2006).

Harrison, Brian, *Separate Spheres: The Opposition to Women's Suffrage in Britain* (Routledge, 1978).

Harrison, J. F. C., *A History of the Working Men's College (1854–1954)* (Routledge & Kegan Paul, 1954).

Harte, Negley, *The University of London, 1836–1986: An Illustrated History* (Athlone Press, 1986).

Hilton, Boyd, 'Manliness, masculinity and the mid-Victorian temperament', in Lawrence Goldman, ed., *The Blind Victorian*, 60–70.

Hilton, Boyd, *A Mad, Bad, and Dangerous People? England, 1783–1846* (Oxford University Press, 2006).

Hilton, Mary, and Pam Hirsch, eds., *Practical Visionaries: Women, Education and Social Progress 1790–1930* (Longman, 2000).

Himmelfarb, Gertrude, 'The Victorian trinity: religion, science, morality', in *Marriage and Morals among the Victorians: And Other Essays* (I. B. Tauris, 1989), 50–75.

Himmelfarb, Gertrude, *The De-Moralization of Society* (Institute of Economic Affairs, 1995).

Hirsch, Pam, *Barbara Leigh Smith Bodichon, 1827–1891: Feminist, Artist and Rebel* (Chatto & Windus, 1998).

Holcombe, Lee, *Wives and Property: Reform of the Married Women's Property Laws in Nineteenth Century England* (University of Toronto Press, 1983).

Hollis, Patricia, ed., *Women in Public, 1850–1900* (George Allen & Unwin, 1979).

Hollis, Patricia, *Ladies Elect: Women in English Local Government, 1865–1914* (Oxford University Press, 1987).

Holohan, Marianne, 'British illustrated editions of Uncle Tom's Cabin: race, working-class literacy, and transatlantic reprinting in the 1850s', *Resources for American Literary Study*, 36 (1), 27–65.

Holton, Sandra, *Suffrage Days: Stories from the Women's Suffrage Movement* (Routledge, 1996).

Hoppen, K. Theodore, *The Mid-Victorian Generation, 1846–1886* (Oxford University Press, 1998).

Hughes, Kathryn, *The Victorian Governess* (Hambledon Press, 2001).

Hunt, Felicity, 'Divided aims: the educational implications of opposing ideologies in girls' secondary schooling', in Felicity Hunt, ed., *Lessons for Life*, 3–21.

Hunt, Felicity, ed., *Lessons for Life: The Schooling of Girls and Women, 1850–1950* (Basil Blackwell, 1987).

Jalland, Pat, *Women, Marriage and Politics, 1860–1914* (Oxford University Press, 1986).

Jones, Tod E., *The Broad Church: A Biography of a Movement* (Lexington Books, 2003).

Jordan, Ellen, '"Making good wives and mothers"? The transformation of middle-class girls' education in nineteenth-century Britain', *History of Education Quarterly*, 31 (1991), 439–62.

Jordan, Ellen, and Bridger, Anne, '"An unexpected recruit to feminism": Jessie Boucherett, the Society for Promoting the Employment of Women, and the importance of being wealthy', *Women's History Review*, 15 (2006), 385–412.

Jordan, Jane, *Josephine Butler* (John Murray, 2001).

Jordanova, Ludmilla, *History in Practice*, 3rd ed. (Bloomsbury Academic, 2017).

Kamm, Josephine, *How Different from Us: A Biography of Miss Buss and Miss Beale* (Bodley Head, 1958).

Kamm, Josephine, *Indicative Past: A Hundred Years of the Girls' Public Day School Trust* (George Allen & Unwin, 1971).

Kaye, Elaine, *A History of Queen's College, London, 1848–1972* (Chatto & Windus, 1972).

Kenny, Anthony, *Arthur Hugh Clough: A Poet's Life* (Continuum, 2005).

Kingsley, Frances, ed., *Charles Kingsley: His Letters and Memories of his Life* (Kegan Paul, 1878).

Kuhn, William M., *Henry and Mary Ponsonby: Life at the Court of Queen Victoria* (Duckworth, 2002).

Kuper, Adam, *Incest and Influence: The Private Life of Bourgeois England* (Harvard University Press, 2009).

Lacey, Candida Ann, ed., *Barbara Leigh Smith Bodichon and the Langham Place Group* (Routledge, 2001).

Lazlett, Peter, *The World We Have Lost*, 2nd ed. (Methuen, 1971).

Letwin, Shirley Robin, *The Gentleman in Trollope: Individuality and Moral Conduct* (Palgrave Macmillan, 1982).

Levine, Philippa, *Victorian Feminism, 1850–1900* (University Press of Florida, 1989).

Levine, Philippa, *Feminist Lives in Victorian England: Private Roles and Public Commitment* (Blackwell, 1990).

Lloyd, Edith M., *Anna Lloyd* (Layton Press, 1928).

Lorimer, Douglas, *Colour, Class and the Victorians: English Attitudes to the Negro in the Mid-Nineteenth Century* (Leicester University Press, 1978).

Lowndes, Emma, *Turning Victorian Ladies into Women: The Life of Bessie Rayner Parkes, 1829–1925* (Academica Press, 2011).

Lowndes, Maria Belloc, *I Too Have Lived in Arcadia* (Macmillan, 1941).

Lumsden, Louisa, 'The ancient history of Girton College', *Girton Review* (Michaelmas term, 1907), 13–21.

Lumsden, Louisa, Y*ellow Leaves: Memories of a Long Life* (Blackwood, 1933).

McAleer, Edward C., ed., *Dearest Isa: Robert Browning's Letters to Isabella Blagden* (University of Texas, 1951).

McClain, Frank Mauldin, *Maurice, Man and Moralist* (SPCK, 1972).

McClelland, Keith, 'England's greatness', in Catherine Hall, Keith McClelland, and Jane Rendall, eds., *Defining the Victorian Nation*, 71–118.

McCrone, Kathleen E., *Sport and the Physical Emancipation of English Women, 1870–1914* (Routledge, 2014).

McDermid, Jane, *The Schooling of Girls in Britain and Ireland, 1800–1900* (Routledge, 2012).

McWilliams Tullberg, Rita, *Women at Cambridge* (1st ed., Gollancz, 1975; 2nd ed., Cambridge University Press, 1998).

Malmgreen, Gail, 'Anne Knight and the radical subculture', *Quaker History*, 71 (1982), 100–13.

290 SELECT BIBLIOGRAPHY

Manton, Jo, *Elizabeth Garrett Anderson* (Methuen, 1965).

Manton, Jo, *Mary Carpenter and the Children of the Streets* (Heinemann, 1976).

Marcus, Sharon, *Between Women: Friendship, Desire and Marriage in Victorian England* (Princeton University Press, 2007).

Marcus, Steven, *The Other Victorians: A Study of Sexuality and Pornography in Mid-Nineteenth Century England* (Basic Books, 1966).

Martin, Jane, *Women and the Politics of Schooling in Victorian and Edwardian England* (Leicester University Press, 1999).

Martin, Jane, and Goodman, Joyce, *Women and Education, 1800–1980* (Macmillan, 2003).

Mason, Michael, *The Making of Victorian Sexual Attitudes* (Oxford University Press, 1994).

Mason, Michael, *The Making of Victorian Sexuality* (Oxford University Press, 1994).

Mathers, Helen, 'The evangelical spirituality of a Victorian feminist: Josephine Butler, 1828–1906', *Journal of Ecclesiastical History*, 52 (2001), 282–312.

Mathers, Helen, 'Evangelism and feminism: Josephine Butler, 1828–96', in Sue Morgan, ed., *Women, Religion and Feminism*, 123–38.

Maurice, Frederick, *The Life of Frederick Denison Maurice, Chiefly Told in His Own Letters* (Macmillan, 1884).

Meadows, A. J., *Science and Controversy: A Biography of Sir Norman Lockyer, Founder Editor of Nature*, 2nd ed. (Macmillan, 2008).

Mellor, Anne K., 'Mary Wollstonecraft's A Vindication of the Rights of Woman and the women writers of her day', in Claudia L. Johnson, ed., *The Cambridge Companion to Mary Wollstonecraft* (Cambridge University Press, 2002), 141–59.

Menand, Louis, *The Metaphysical Club* (HarperCollins, 2001).

Mendus, Susan, and Jane Rendall, eds., *Sexuality and Subordination* (Routledge, 1989).

Meritxell, Simon Martin, *Barbara Bodichon's Epistolary Education: Unfolding Feminism* (Palgrave Macmillan, 2021).

Midgley, Clare, *Women against Slavery: The British Campaigns, 1780–1870* (Routledge, 1992).

Midgley, Clare, 'Anti-slavery and feminism in nineteenth-century Britain', *Gender and History*, 5 (1993), 343–62.

Midgley, Clare, 'Anti-slavery and the roots of imperial feminism', in Clare Midgley, ed., *Gender and Imperialism*, 161–79.

Midgley, Clare, ed., *Gender and Imperialism* (Manchester University Press, 1998).

Milne, John Duguid, *The Industrial and Social Position of Women* (Chapman & Hall, 1857; reprinted by Forgotten Press, 2018). A revised edition with updated statistics was published in 1870 as *Industrial Employment of Women in the Middle and Lower Ranks*.

Mitchell, Juliet, and Ann Oakley, eds., *The Rights and Wrongs of Women* (Penguin, 1976).

Mitchell, Sally, *The Fallen Angel: Chastity, Class and Women's Reading* (Bowling Green University Popular Press, 1981).

Mitchell, Sally, *Frances Power Cobbe: Victorian Feminist, Journalist, Reformer* (University of Virginia Press, 2004).

Mitford, Nancy, ed., *The Stanleys of Alderley* (Chapman & Hall, 1939).

Morgan, Simon, *A Victorian Woman's Place: Public Culture in the Nineteenth Century* (I. B. Tauris, 2007).

Morgan, Sue, ed., *Women, Religion and Feminism in Britain, 1750–1900* (Palgrave Macmillan, 2002).

Morris, Jeremy, *F. D. Maurice and the Crisis of Christian Authority* (Oxford, 2005).

Morse, Belinda, *A Woman of Design, a Man of Passion: The Pioneering McIans* (Book Guild, 2001).

Murphy, Ann B., and Deirdre Rafferty, eds., *Emily Davies, Collected Letters, 1861–1875* (University of Virginia Press, 2004).

SELECT BIBLIOGRAPHY 291

Norman, Edward, *The Victorian Christian Socialists* (Cambridge University Press, 1987).

O'Donnell, Elizabeth A., ' "On behalf of all young women trying to be better than they are": feminism and Quakerism in the nineteenth century: the case of Anna Deborah Richardson', *Quaker Studies*, 6 (2002), 37–58.

Orwell, George, 'Charles Dickens', in *Shooting an Elephant and Other Essays* (Penguin, 2003), 49–114.

Palmer, Geoffrey, and Noel Lloyd, *Father of the Bensons: The Life of Edward White Benson* (Virgin Books, 1998).

Park, Trevor, *'Nolo Episcopari': A Life of C. J. Vaughan* (St. Bega, 2013).

Patrick, Graham, *F. J. A. Hort: Eminent Victorian* (Bloomsbury Academic, 2015).

Pearce, Colin D., 'Lord Brougham's neo-paganism', *Journal of the History of Ideas*, 55 (1994), 651–70.

Pedersen, Joyce Senders, *The Reform of Girls' Secondary Education in Victorian England: A Study of Elites and Educational Change* (Routledge, 2017).

Phillips, Ann, ed., *A Newnham Anthology*, 2nd ed. (Newnham College, 1988).

Pigou, A. C., ed., *Memorials of Alfred Marshall* (Macmillan, 1925).

Ponsonby, Magdalen, ed., *Mary Ponsonby: A Memoir, Some Letters and a Journal* (John Murray, 1927).

Poovey, Mary, 'Covered but not bound: Caroline Norton and the 1857 Matrimonial Causes Act', *Feminist Studies*, 14 (1988), 467–85.

Poovey, Mary, *Uneven Developments: The Ideological Work of Gender in Mid-Victorian England* (Chicago University Press, 1988).

Prothero, Rowland E., *Life and Letters of Dean Stanley* (Thomas Nelson, 1909).

Pugh, Martin, 'The limits of liberalism: liberals and women's suffrage 1967–1914', in Eugenio Biaggini, ed., *Citizenship and Communities: Liberals, Radicals and Collective Identities in British History, 1965–1931* (Cambridge University Press, 1996), 45–65.

Pugh, Martin, *The March of the Women: A Revisionist Analysis of the Campaign for Women's Suffrage, 1866–1914* (Oxford, 2002).

Pyle, Andrew, ed., *The Subjection of Women: Contemporary Responses to John Stuart Mill* (Thoemmes Press, 1995).

Raftery, Deirdre, 'Educational ideologies and reading for girls in England, 1815–1915', *History of Education Society Bulletin*, 59 (1997), 4–11.

Ratcliffe, Eric, *The Caxton of Her Age: The Career and Family Background of Emily Faithfull (1835–95)* (Images, 1993).

Rendall, Jane, 'Women and the public sphere', *Gender and History*, 11 (1991), 475–88.

Rendall, Jane, 'A moral engine? Feminism, liberalism and the English Woman's Journal', in Jane Rendall, ed., *Equal or Different*, 112–40.

Rendall, Jane, ed., *Equal or Different: Women's Politics 1800–1914* (Blackwell, 1987).

Rendall, Jane, 'Friendship and politics: Barbara Leigh Smith Bodichon (1827–91) and Bessie Rayner Parkes (1829–1925)', in Susan Mendus and Jane Rendall, eds., *Sexuality and Subordination*, 136–70.

Rendall, Jane, 'The citizenship of women and the Reform Act of 1867', in Catherine Hall, Keith McClelland, and Jane Rendall, eds., *Defining the Victorian Nation*, 119–78.

Rendall, Jane, ' "The real father of the whole movement?" John Stuart Mill, Liberal politics, and the movement for women's suffrage, 1865–73', in Amanda Vickery, ed., *Women, Privilege and Power*, 168–200.

Reynolds, K. M., 'The school and its place in girls' education', in *The North London Collegiate School, 1850–1950* (Oxford University Press, 1950), 106–38.

Richardson, Anna, et al., *Memoir of Anna Deborah Richardson: With Extracts from Her Letters* (privately printed, 1877; reprinted by Kessinger Publishing, n.d.).

292 SELECT BIBLIOGRAPHY

Ridley, Annie E., *Frances Mary Buss and Her Work for Education* (Longmans, Green & Co., 1896).

Roach, John, *Secondary Education in England, 1870–1902: Public Activity and Private Enterprise* (Routledge, 1991).

Robson, Ann, 'The founding of the National Society for Women's Suffrage 1866–1867', *Canadian Journal of History*, 8 (1973), 1–22.

Rosen, Andrew, 'Emily Davies and the women's movement', *Journal of British Studies*, 19 (1979), 101–21.

Royle, Trevor, *Crimea: The Great Crimean War 1854–1856* (Little, Brown, 1999).

Rubinstein, David, 'Victorian feminists: Henry and Millicent Garrett Fawcett', in Lawrence Goldman, ed., *The Blind Victorian*, 71–92.

Rubinstein, David, *A Different World for Women: The Life of Millicent Garrett Fawcett* (Harvester, 1991).

Russell, Bertrand, *Autobiography of Bertrand Russell*, Vol. 1 (Chatto & Windus, 1967).

Russell, Bertrand, and Patricia Russell, eds., *The Amberley Papers: The Letters and Diaries of Lord and Lady Amberley*, 2 vols (Hogarth Press, 1937).

Rutson, Albert, ed., *Essays on Reform* (Macmillan, 1867).

Schultz, Bart, *Henry Sidgwick: Eye of the Universe* (Cambridge University Press, 2004).

Schwarz, Laura, *Infidel Feminism; Secularism, Religion and Women's Emancipation in England, 1830–1914* (Manchester University Press, 2013).

Schwarzkopf, Jutta, *Women in the Chartist Movement* (Macmillan, 1991).

Searby, Peter, ed., *Educating the Victorian Middle Classes* (History of Education Society, 1982).

Searby, Peter, *A History of the University of Cambridge*, Vol. 3: *1750–1870* (Cambridge University Press, 1997).

Secord, James, *Visions of Science: Books and Readers at the Dawn of the Victorian Age* (Oxford University Press, 2014).

Shaen, M. J., *William Shaen: A Brief Sketch* (Longmans, 1912).

Shanley, Mary, *Feminism, Marriage and the Law in Victorian England, 1850–1895* (I. B. Tauris, 1989).

Sharp, Evelyn, *Hertha Ayrton, 1854–1923: A Memoir* (Edward Arnold,1926).

Shattock, Joanne, 'Margaret Oliphant and the Blackwood "brand" ', in Joanne Shattock, ed., *Journalism and the Periodical Press in Nineteenth-Century Britain* (Cambridge University Press, 2017), 341–52.

Sidgwick, Arthur, and Eleanor Sidgwick, *Henry Sidgwick: A Memoir* (Macmillan, 1906).

Sigsworth, E. M., and T. J. Whyte, 'A study of Victorian prostitution and venereal disease', in Martha Vicinus, ed., *Suffer and Be Still*, 77–9.

Sklar, Kathryn Kish, *Catherine Beecher: A Study in American Domesticity* (Yale University Press, 1973).

Spender, Dale, ed., *The Education Papers: Women's Quest for Equality in Britain 1850–1912* (Routledge & Kegan Paul, 1987).

Stanley, Arthur Penrhyn, *The Life and Correspondence of Thomas Arnold, D.D.* (B. Fellowes, 1844).

Stephen, Barbara, *Emily Davies and Girton College* (Constable, 1927).

Stephen, Barbara, *Girton College, 1869–1932* (Cambridge University Press, 1933).

Stone, James S., *Emily Faithfull: Victorian Champion of Women's Rights* (P. D. Meany, 1994).

Strachey, Ray, *Millicent Garrett Fawcett* (John Murray, 1931).

Stuart, James, *Reminiscences* (privately printed, 1911).

Sutherland, Gillian, 'The movement for the higher education of women: its social and intellectual context in England, c.1840–80', in P. J. Waller, ed., *Politics and Social Change in Modern Britain* (Harvester Press, 1987), 91–116.

SELECT BIBLIOGRAPHY   293

Sutherland, Gillian, 'Anne Jemima Clough and Blanche Athena Clough: creating educational institutions for women', in Mary Hilton and Pam Hirsch, eds., *Practical Visionaries*, 101–14.

Sutherland, Gillian, *Faith, Duty and the Power of Mind: The Cloughs and Their Circle 1820–1960* (Cambridge University Press, 2006).

Sutherland, Gillian, *In Search of the New Woman: Middle-Class Women and Work in Britain, 1870–1914* (Cambridge University Press, 2015).

Symonds, Richard, *Inside the Citadel: Men and the Emancipation of Women, 1850–1920* (Macmillan, 1999).

Szreter, Simon, *Fertility, Class and Gender Britain 1860–1940* (Cambridge University Press, 1996).

Thomas, Joyce, 'Women and capitalism: oppression or emancipation? A review article', *Comparative Studies in Society and History*, 30 (1988), 534–49.

Thomas, Keith, 'The double standard', *Journal of the History of Ideas*, 20 (1959), 195–216.

Thompson, Dorothy, 'Women, work and politics in nineteenth century England: the problem of authority', in Jane Rendall, ed., *Equal or Different*, 57–81.

Todd, Margaret, *The Life of Sophia Jex-Blake* (Macmillan, 1918).

Tosh, John, *A Man's Place: Masculinity and the Middle-Class Home in Victorian England* (Yale University Press, 1999).

Tuke, Margaret, *A History of Bedford College for Women 1849–1938* (Oxford University Press, 1938).

Vicinus, Martha, ed., *Suffer and Be Still: Women in the Victorian Age* (Indiana University Press, 1972).

Vicinus, Martha, *Independent Women: Work and Community for Single Women 1850–1920* (Virago, 1985).

Vicinus, Martha, 'Lesbian perversity and Victorian marriage: the 1864 Codrington divorce trial', *Journal of British Studies*, 36 (1997), 70–98.

Vicinus, Martha, *Intimate Friends: Women Who Loved Women, 1778–1928* (University of Chicago Press, 2004).

Vickery, Amanda, 'Golden age to separate spheres? A review of the categories and chronology of English women's history', *The Historical Journal*, 36 (1993), 383–414.

Vickery, Amanda, ed., *Women, Privilege and Power: British Politics, 1750 to the Present* (Stanford University Press, 2001).

Walkowitz, Judith R., *Prostitution and Victorian Society: Women, Class and the State* (Cambridge University Press, 1980).

Watts, Ruth, *Gender, Power and the Unitarians in England, 1760–1860* (Longman, 1998).

Watts, Ruth, 'Mary Carpenter: education of the children of the "perishing and dangerous classes"', in Mary Hilton and Pam Hirsch, eds., *Practical Visionaries*, 39–51.

Watts, Ruth, 'Rational religion and feminism: the challenge of Unitarianism in the nineteenth century', in Sue Morgan, ed., *Women, Religion and Feminism*, 32–52.

Webb, Diana, and Tony Webb, *The Anglo-Florentines: The British in Tuscany, 1814–1860* (Bloomsbury Academic, 2020).

Wedgwood, Barbara, and Hensleigh Wedgwood, *The Wedgwood Circle, 1730–1897* (Collier Macmillan, 1980).

Weeks, Jeffrey, *Sex, Politics and Society: The Regulation of Sexuality since 1800*, 3rd ed. (Pearson, 2012).

Westwater, Martha, *The Wilson Sisters: A Biographical Study of Upper Middle-Class Victorian Life* (Ohio University Press, 1984).

Wiener, Martin, *Reconstructing the Criminal: Culture, Law and Policy in England 1830–1914* (Cambridge University Press, 1990).

294 SELECT BIBLIOGRAPHY

Wigmore-Beddoes, D. G., *Yesterday's Radicals: A Study of the Affinity between Unitarianism and Broad Church Anglicanism in the Nineteenth Century* (James Clarke & Co., 1971).

Williams, Joanna M., *The Great Miss Lydia Becker: Suffragist, Scientist and Trailblazer* (Pen & Sword History, 2022).

Williams, Perry, 'Pioneer women students at Cambridge, 1869–71' in Felicity Hunt, ed., *Lessons for Life*, 171–91.

Willson, F. M. G., *The University of London, 1858–1900: The Politics of Senate and Convocation* (Boydell, 2004).

Woodfield, Malcom, *R. H. Hutton: Critic and Theologian* (Oxford University Press, 1986).

Wright, Maureen, *Elizabeth Wolstenholme Elmy and the Victorian Feminist Movement: The Biography of an Insurgent Woman* (Manchester University Press, 2011).

Index

For the benefit of digital users, indexed terms that span two pages (e.g., 52–53) may, on occasion, appear on only one of those pages.

Acland, Thomas Dyke, 11th Baronet 116–19, 126–7, 133, 135–6, 202
Adams, John Couch 199
Alexandra Magazine 104
Alford, Henry 36–7, 109, 122, 143, 150–2, 155, 160–1, 180–1, 195–6, 202, 243, 272
Alford, Marian 201
Algiers 27, 61–2
Amberley, Katharine, *see* Russell, Katharine
Amberley, Viscount, *see* Russell, John
American Civil War x, 4, 80–1, 144, 153–4, 221
Anderson, Elizabeth Garrett 57–8, 63–70, 74–5, 77–82, 90, 93–4, 102–3, 108–10, 115–16, 123, 127–9, 147, 150, 171, 179, 181–2, 211–12, 215, 231–2, 240–6, 249, 257, 264, 270, 272, 275–6
　and Contagious Diseases Acts 231–2
　and Emily Davies 48, 57–8, 80–1, 94, 243–4, 276
　and Henry Maudsley 249
　and John Stuart Mill 90
　and London School Board 240–5, 257
　and suffrage campaign 147, 150
　and women's higher education 211–12, 215
　marriage 211–12
　medical training 66–70, 77–9, 94, 108–10, 115–16
　qualification as doctor 240
　upbringing 57–8
Anderson, Skelton 211–14, 240–2, 244
Archer-Hind, Richard 264
Arnold, Matthew 83, 132–6, 140, 222
Arnold, Thomas 34, 46, 69, 153
Association for Promoting the Higher Education of Women in Cambridge 262–3
Aurora Leigh 29
Austin, Annie 56–8, 67, 74, 79, 179, 195, 200, 215–17, 254

Barton family 43–4, 56
Beale, Dorothea 114–15, 122, 137, 141–2, 237–8, 251, 282–3

Becker, Lydia 93, 160–2, 184–5, 194, 215, 223–4, 227–8, 231, 240, 245–6, 264, 266, 271–6
Bedford College 16 n.37, 23, 66–7, 83, 114–16, 121–2, 129, 212, 220, 259, 263–4
Beesly, Edward Spencer 37, 66–7
Belloc, Elizabeth, *see* Parkes, Bessie Rayner
Bernard, Marianne 256, 260, 265
biblical criticism 2, 35, 38
biography and history viii–ix
Blacker, Theodosia, *see* Monson, Theodosia
Blackwell, Elizabeth 23, 28–30, 64–6, 68–9, 179–80, 207, 231–2, 249
Blackwell, Emily 28–30, 179–80
Blackwood's Magazine 19, 34, 36, 102–3, 156–7, 225, 277–8
Bliss, George 43–4, 46, 48
Bodichon, Barbara 7–8, 17–18, 20, 24–9, 32, 62, 64–8, 70–2, 78, 80–1, 85, 92, 94–5, 97–104, 106–8, 114–16, 119–20, 129, 136–7, 139–41, 145–50, 155–7, 159–61, 171–4, 176–80, 185, 191–2, 195–6, 198–202, 207–11, 213–20, 228, 231–5, 249–56, 259–61, 265–6, 271, 275–8
　and *Brief Summary* 17–18
　and College for Women / Girton College 176–7, 179–80, 195–6, 198–202, 207–11, 213–20, 250–4, 256, 259–61
　and education of girls 114
　and *English Woman's Journal* 94–5, 98–100, 102
　and Emily Davies 79, 99–100, 102–3, 107, 200, 202, 207–11, 213, 253
　and higher education for women 172–4
　and hygiene 179–80, 249–50, 259–60
　and suffrage campaign 145–8
　and *Waverley Journal* 27–8
　and women and work 64–5
　marriage 28
Bonham Carter, Elinor 234–5
Bonney, Thomas 190, 199
Booth, Catherine 73–4
Booth, William 73–4

296 INDEX

Bostock, Eliza 23, 115–16, 121, 136–7, 140–1, 176–7
Boucherett, Jessie 30–1, 71, 93, 101, 106–7, 129, 139, 146–8, 150, 155–6, 159, 163, 227–8, 231, 266, 270–2
Bright, Jacob 146–7, 159–62, 223, 239, 274
Bright, John 151, 159, 221–2, 258–9
Bright, Ursula 146–7, 274
British and Foreign Anti-Slavery Society 23–4
British Association for the Advancement of Science 32–3, 38, 160–1, 194
broad church vii, 2–3, 34–40, 43, 46, 59–60, 69, 83, 85–7, 90, 117–20, 134, 136–7, 143, 151–3, 155, 165–6, 171–2, 174, 184, 186, 191, 198–9, 203–4, 222, 230, 237–8, 268–70, 272–3, 277, 280–1
Brodie, Benjamin 35–6, 116, 174
Brontë, Charlotte 28–9
Brougham, Henry, Lord Brougham 18, 25, 31–3, 47, 112–13, 133, 270–1
Browning, Elizabeth Barrett 29, 70
Browning, Robert 98, 177, 222, 241–2, 244
Bryce, James 135–7, 177–8, 180, 182–3, 188–90, 192, 202, 211–12, 214, 281–2
Burbury, Charlotte 209, 255
Burke, Edmund viii, 87–8, 143, 225
Burn, Robert 190, 199
Buss, Frances Mary 76, 114–15, 120, 127–30, 137, 139–42, 164, 185, 219–20, 233, 236–8, 241–2, 254–5
Butler, Agnata 263–4
Butler, George 185–8, 268–9
Butler, Josephine xiii, 87–8, 93, 160, 184–90, 192–3, 215, 227–9, 231–2, 236–9, 268–9, 274–6
Byron, Anne, Lady Byron 23

Cairnes, John Elliott 150
Cambridge, as location for College for Women 208–11
Camden School for Girls 236
Carlyle, Jane 71–2
Carlyle, Thomas 7–8, 152–3, 161–2, 222
Carpenter, Mary 23, 28–9, 32–3, 110–11
census, 1851 15 n.35, 29–30, 64
Central Committee of the National Society for Women's Suffrage 265–6
Chalker, Alfred 120–1
Chapman, John 17–18, 26–9, 67, 78, 108–10
Charles, Ebenezer 168
Chartism xii, 4–5, 22
Christian Socialism 36–8, 59, 66–7, 82, 103, 109–10, 117–18, 122–3, 152–3

Cheltenham Ladies College 114–15, 122, 137, 251
Clapham Sect 24, 44–5, 68–9, 270
Clarendon Commission 132–3
Clark, Edwin 200–1
class ix–xii, 4–8, 11–13, 15–16, 36, 45–6, 55–6, 59, 96, 131–2, 225–6, 228–30, 280
distinctions in education 7, 96, 114–15, 122, 130–2, 141–2, 237–8, 283
Clay, Walter 150, 155–6, 176–7
Clerical Subscription Act 1865 203
Clough, Anne Jemima 130–1, 136–7, 141–2, 177, 184–9, 191–2, 195–6, 204–7, 237–8, 248
Clough, Arthur Hugh 136–7, 185, 204
Cobbe, Frances Power xi, 9–10, 92–3, 100–3, 110–14, 144, 146–7, 150, 155–62, 167–8, 224, 231, 245–6, 266, 271–3
Codrington divorce case 105–6
Codrington, Helen 72, 105–6
Colenso, John 39–40, 87
Coleridge, Samuel Taylor 34–6, 46, 63
College for Women 86, 138–41, 163, 171–84, 188–9, 191–3, 200–2, 207–20, 233, 244, see also Girton College
College of Preceptors 119–20, 131–2, 141
Considerations on Representative Government 88–90
Contagious Diseases Acts 1866, 1869 184–5, 223, 230, 232, 245, 266, 273–4, 280–1
Contemporary Review 34, 36–7, 151–2, 155, 160–1, 167–8, 186, 194, 221, 233–4, 245–6
Cornell University 208–9
Cotton, George 117–18
Courtauld, Samuel 39
coverture 8
Craig, Isa 27, 30–1, 72, 98–101, 106–7, 109–10, 115–16, 121, 123–4, 144–5, 147–50, 173–4, 254, 271
Crimean War 3–4, 29, 60–1, 105, 117
Crompton, Charles 37
Crompton, Mary, see Davies, Mary (Emily's sister-in-law)
Croom Robertson, Caroline, see Robertson, Caroline Croom
Croom Robertson, George, see Robertson, George Croom
Crow, Annie, see Austin, Annie
Crow, Jane 56–8, 62–3, 66–8, 70, 73, 79, 81, 83, 98, 100–1, 106–7, 147, 150, 195, 215, 218, 254
Cushman, Charlotte 70–2
Custody of Infants Act 1873 17, 280–1

INDEX 297

damnation, eternal 36, 280–1
Darwin, Charles 5, 37–8, 152–3, 216, 222
Davies, Emily
    and Anna Richardson 76–7, 85–6
    and Anne Clough 136–7, 188, 192
    and Barbara Bodichon 79, 99–100, 102–3,
        107, 200, 202, 207–11, 213, 253
    and Bessie Parkes 99–102
    and Crow sisters 56–8, 67–8
    and degrees for women 108–10, 113–14,
        170–1, 174, 176, 183, 196–7, 213–14, 248,
        257–9, 261–5
    and education of girls 114–15, 118–21, 125,
        129, 133–5, 142, 165–7, 233–6
    and Elizabeth Garrett 48, 57–8, 80–1, 94,
        243–4, 276
    and Henry Sidgwick 202–3, 205–8,
        210, 262–5
    and Josephine Butler 192
    and London School Board 1, 236, 240–5
    and Louisa Lumsden 249–54
    and rights of women 84, 88, 90–2, 146, 159,
        163, 181, 237–8
    and school endowments 139
    and suffrage campaigns 145–59, 265–7,
        273–4
    Burkean vii–viii, 87–8, 143
    childhood and upbringing 41–56
    Millian vii–viii, 88, 91–2, 102, 135, 143
    neatness 81
    on imagination, faculty of 233–4
    political leanings 87–8
    precision 48–9
    religious beliefs 85–7
    sexuality 92–3
    women's movement, first encounter
        with 62–3
Davies, Henry 47–8, 55, 61–2, 66–7
Davies, Jane 44, 48–9, 52, 54–6
Davies, John 42–52, 79
Davies, (John) Llewelyn 36–7, 44, 47–8, 53, 55,
    58–60, 62, 66–8, 79–80, 82, 84, 86, 109, 115,
    117–18, 165–6, 176, 199–200, 241–2, 250,
    259, 272, 276
    and broad church 59, 86, 165–6
    and Christian Socialism 59, 82
    and F. D. Maurice 82, 85–6, 250
    and university education for
        women 196–7, 264
    support of Elizabeth Garrett 241–2
Davies, Mary (Emily's mother) 43, 48–9, 54–5,
    79–80, 178–9, 218, 254, 265–6
Davies, Mary (Emily's sister-in-law) 66–7

Davies, William 46, 53–5, 60–2
degrees for women 80–1, 102–3, 110–13, 122,
    125, 142, 157–8, 259
    University of Cambridge 170–1, 174, 176,
        183, 213–14, 261–5
    University of London 108–10, 113–14, 196–7,
        248, 257–9
Derby, 14th Earl of 3, 87, 148–9, 221–2
Dickens, Charles 30–1, 70, 203, 226
disabilities, women's 8–10, 22, 29–30, 223
Disraeli, Benjamin 3–5, 87, 148–9, 221–2
divorce 9, 17–19, 280–1
Dixon, William 225
double standard 11–14, 275–6, 278
Dove, Jane Frances 251
Drewery, Ellen 80
Drysdale, Charles 268–9
duty ix, 10–11, 20, 24, 40, 86, 101, 122, 146,
    164–6, 197, 226–7, 230, 248, 275, 279–80

Ecclesiazusae 95, 112–13
Edinburgh Review 34, 36–9, 225
education of girls 1, 7, 26, 52, 91, 114–21, 123,
    125–6, 129–42, 163–7, 185–7, 233–8, 245,
    257, 282–3
education of girls, arguments against 116, 118,
    122, 126–7, 167
Elementary Education Act 1870 5, 223, 238–9
Eliot, George 7–8, 43, 83, 85, 91, 95, 179–80, 278
employment for middle-class women 15–17,
    29–30, 75, 94, 96, 110, 135, 157–8, 166–7,
    169, 194, 212, 224, 230–1, 272–4, 278–9,
    283–4, see also Society for Promoting the
    Employment of Women
Endowed Schools Act 1869 223, 233–4
English Woman's Journal 27–8, 30, 64–6, 68, 70–3,
    75–7, 80–1, 94–103, 106–7, 117–18, 145, 231
Englishwoman's Review 106–7
endowments, see school endowments
enslavement, see slavery
Erskine, Thomas 36, 68
Essays and Reviews 37–40, 87, 221–2
eternal damnation, see damnation, eternal
Evangelicalism 12, 34–5, 39, 41–8, 51, 55, 57–8,
    71, 73, 153–4, 268–71
Evans, Marian, see Eliot, George
examinations
    Higher Local 191, 262–3
    Local 114–29, 132–3, 136, 138, 140–3, 171–3,
        204–5, 219–20, 233
    special, for women 168–9, 190–3, 195, 206,
        220, 257–8, 261–2
Eyre, Edward 152–3

298 INDEX

Faithfull, Emily 30–1, 68, 71–3, 82–3, 91–3, 96–104, 106–7, 110, 161–2, 245–6, 272, 278
Fawcett, Henry 89–90, 123, 127, 145, 147, 152–3, 159–60, 189, 204, 207–8
Fawcett, Millicent Garrett 57–8, 123, 159–62, 193–7, 202, 204–5, 207–8, 224, 263–4, 266, 272–5
Fearon, Daniel 135–7, 139–40, 234
Female Medical Society 169, 268–9
Field, Lucy 28–9
Fitch, Joshua 109–10, 123, 125–7, 132–3, 135–6, 140, 168, 171, 188, 190, 211–12, 217, 237–8, 258–9
Forster, William 233
Fortnightly Review 37, 154–5, 194, 224, 229, 248–9, 257–8
Foster, Charles 113
Fox, Eliza (Tottie) 18
franchise, *see* suffrage
Fraser's Magazine 34, 36–9, 102–3, 111, 155, 157, 186, 194, 245–6
Froude, James Anthony 96

Gamble, Jane 247–8
Garibaldi, Giuseppe 144
Garrett, Elizabeth (Lizzie), *see* Anderson, Elizabeth Garrett
Garrett, Louie, *see* Smith, Louie
Garrett, Millicent (Millie), *see* Fawcett, Millicent Garrett
Gaskell, Elizabeth 4–5, 28–9, 66–7, 101
gender and race x–xi, xiv, 224–5
gentleman, characteristics of xi, 6–8, 10–11, 51
Girls Public Day School Company 237–8, 257, 275, 281–2
Girton College 184, 213, 220, 247–57, 259–65, *see also* College for Women
Gladstone, William Ewart 3, 109, 123–4, 146–9, 151, 161–2, 221–3, 229, 232, 238, 280–1
Gloyne, Elizabeth 227–8
Godwin, William 22
Goldsmid, Louisa, Lady Goldsmid 113–16, 121–2, 146, 150, 174, 180, 183, 198, 202, 215, 264, 266
governesses, plight of 9, 16
Governor Eyre Defence and Aid Committee 152
Granville, 2nd Earl 109, 136
Gray, Charles 119–20
Great Exhibition 5, 56
Grey, Charles, 2nd Earl 46–7, 56
Grey, Maria 129, 235–8, 243, 261, 276–7
Griffiths, John 116–17
Grote, George 109, 168

Grote, Harriet 72
Guardianship of Infants Act 1886 266, 280–1
Gurney, Emilia Russell 68–70, 77, 82, 119–22, 127, 153, 179–80, 183, 195–6, 198–202, 208, 210–11, 215–18, 244
Gurney, Mary 237–8
Gurney, Russell 109–10, 115–16, 145, 147, 152–3, 176–7, 227–8, 244–5, 258–9
Gurney Act, *see* Medical Act 1876

Hack family 43–4, 48–9, 52, 55–6, 61
Hammond, Lemprière 135–6, 187, 234
Hampson, Jane 159–60
Hard Cash 84, 226
Hare, Alice, *see* Westlake, Alice
Hare, Julius 36
Hare, Katherine 159–60
Hare, Thomas 89–90, 159–60
Hastings, George 31–2, 71, 109–10, 115–16, 123–5, 150, 155–6, 173–4, 176–7, 180, 183, 196, 202, 227–8
Hawes, William 70
Hays, Matilda (Max) 68, 70, 92–100, 104, 271
Heywood, James 113–16, 143, 150, 180, 182–3, 202, 207–8, 215
Higher Education of Women, The 163–8
Hill, Matthew Davenport 18, 31–2, 231, 270–1
Hill, Octavia 78, 140–1
history and biography, *see* biography and history
Hitchin, *see* College for Women
Hobart, Mary, Lady Hobart 180, 182–3
Hobhouse, Arthur 229, 233
Hodgson, William Ballantyne 119–20, 124–5, 137
Home and Colonial School Society 131, 141
homosexuality 7–8, 14–15, 92–3, 95, 97
Hope, Alexander Beresford 127, 277
Hort, Fenton 58–9, 198–201, 230
Hosman, Hatty 70
Howitt, Anna Mary 25, 30
Howson, John 125–6, 129, 185
Hughes, Thomas 36–7, 82, 103, 152–3, 243
Hutton, Richard Holt 36–7, 83, 96, 102–4, 112–13, 127, 134–5, 143, 157–8, 167–70, 194, 196–8, 206, 217–18, 248, 258–9, 273, 277–8
Huxley, Thomas 5, 37–8, 78, 85, 152–3, 164–5, 177, 222, 241–2

imagination, Emily Davies on 233–4
improvement 5–6
Indian Rebellion x, 3–4, 153
Infant School Society 25

INDEX   299

Jackson, Henry 195–6, 264
Jamaica Committee 152–3
Jameson, Anna 29–31, 61–2
Jex-Blake, Sophia 78, 113–14, 258–9
Jowett, Benjamin 35–6, 38, 58–9, 222

Kay-Shuttleworth, James 237–8
Kennedy, Benjamin 209
Kennedy, Charlotte, *see* Burbury, Charlotte
Kennedy, Marion 209, 264–5
Kensington Society 144–5, 155–6
Keynes, John Maynard 202
Kingsland, Mary 251
Kingsley, Charles 36–8, 96, 123, 152–3, 190–1,
    222, 224, 227
Knox, Isa, *see* Craig, Isa

Ladies London Emancipation Society 144, 216
Ladies Sanitary Association 68–9
lady, characteristics of 7
Lamb, William, 2nd Viscount Melbourne,
    see Melbourne, Lord
Langham Place vii–viii, 27–30, 67–8, 70–3,
    80–2, 90, 92–107
Lawrence, John, 1st Baron Lawrence 244–5, 256
Lawson, Wilfrid 211–12
lectures for women 185–92, *see also* North of
    England Council for Promoting the Higher
    Education of Women
Leigh Smith, Barbara, *see* Bodichon, Barbara
Leigh Smith, Anne (Nannie) 28, 62–3, 74–5, 82,
    96–7, 178
lesbian, *see* homosexuality
Lewes, George 37, 154–5, 179–80
Lewes, Marian, *see* Eliot, George
Lewin, Sarah 72, 104
Lightfoot, Joseph 190, 196, 199, 211, 213–14
Liveing, George 117, 119, 127, 174–5, 189–90,
    199–201, 264
Lloyd, Mary 110–11, 150, 159–60
Local Examinations, *see* examinations, Local
London Association of Schoolmistresses 140–1,
    163–4, 177, 185–7, 233–4, 259, 262–3
London School Board 1, 81–2, 218,
    236, 244–5
London School Board, elections to
    1, 240–3
London Society for Obtaining Political
    Representation for Women 159–60
Lubbock, John 240–1, 258
Lucas, Margaret Bright 159–60
Ludlow, John 36–7, 103
Lumsden, Louisa 218–19, 247–54
Lyell, Charles 38, 177, 222
Lysistrata 95

Lyttelton, George, 4th Baron Lyttelton 123–4,
    132–3, 135–6, 138–43, 176–7, 180, 197–8,
    202, 211–12, 233–8, 272–3

Macaulay, Zachary 45
Macmillan, Alexander 36–7, 60, 155, 192
Macmillan, Daniel 36–7, 60
Macmillan's Magazine 34, 36–7, 102–3, 155,
    185–6, 193, 196–7, 224, 227, 245–6
Magee, William Connor 211–12
Malleson, Elizabeth 140–1
Maltby, Edward 46–7, 49–51, 53–4, 59, 270
Manchester Board of Schoolmistresses 140–1,
    170, 186–7
Manchester National Society for Women's
    Suffrage 227–8
Manning, Adelaide 134–5, 140–1, 148–51, 195,
    200, 243, 252, 254, 261, 265
Manning, Charlotte 23, 67, 80–2, 119–22, 124,
    140–1, 144, 179–80, 183, 198–200, 202, 216
Manning, Henry 47–8
Manning, James 67
Margaret Hall 259
Markby, Thomas 120, 126–8, 171–5, 188–90,
    204–5
Married Women's Property Acts 1870, 1882 223,
    229–30, 266, 280–1
Married Women's Property Committee 227–8
Marshall, Alfred 213–14
Martineau, Harriet 23, 28–9, 135
Martineau, James 35
Masson, David 36–7, 155
Matrimonial Causes Act 1857 18–19
Maudsley, Henry 248–9, 252, 257–8
Maurice, Frederick Denison 2–3, 35–40, 45, 59,
    68–9, 78, 82, 85–6, 102–3, 109, 119–20,
    122–4, 140–1, 143, 181–2, 189–91, 202,
    204, 207–8, 216, 222, 250, 264
Mayor, Joseph 194, 245–6
Medical Act 1876 258–9
medicine as a career for women 6–7, 64–5,
    68, 75–8
Melbourne, Lord 17, 53–4
Merryweather, Mary 25, 28–9, 98–9, 104
Merton Hall 205–8, 215, 220, 248, 257–8
Metaphysical Society 39–40, 222
Metcalfe, Frances (Fanny) 50–1, 182–3, 202,
    249, 252–3, 256, 260
Middle-Class Examinations,
    see examinations, Local
Mill, Harriet Taylor 22, 24, 88–90, 275
Mill, John Stuart vii–viii, x–xiii, 7–8, 37, 66–7,
    88–92, 101–2, 123, 135, 143–5, 147–9,
    151–62, 205, 222–5, 227–8, 234, 240–1,
    243, 248, 266–7, 272–3, 275–6

300 INDEX

Milman, Henry Hart 36–7
Milne, John Duguid 29–30
Milnes, Richard Monckton 18
Monck-Mason, Annabella 56
Monson, Theodosia, Lady Monson 30,
    97–8, 271
Moore, Amy 173–4
moral double standard, *see* double standard
morality 20, 40, 47–8, 83–6, 89–90, 160,
    225–6, 280–1
Morant Bay 152
Morgan, Sydney, Lady Morgan 71–2
Morley, John 37, 154–5, 161–2, 241–2
Mozley, Anne 45
Municipal Corporations (Elections) Act
    1869 9–10, 223, 239
Myers, Frederick 186–7, 189–92, 197,
    204, 206–7

National Association for the Promotion of Social
    Science, *see* Social Science Association
National Education League 238
National Education Union 238
National Reformatory Union 31–2
National Society for Women's Suffrage 227–8,
    265–6
National Union for the Education of Girls of all
    Classes 237–8, 256, 282–3
National Union of Women's Suffrage
    Societies 266–7
National Women's Rights Conventions 23–4
Newcastle Commission 139
Newcastle Society for the Employment of
    Women 74–5
Newnham Hall 205–6, 262, 264–5
Nightingale, Florence 3–4, 7–8, 29, 65, 221
Noilles, Helena, Comtesse de Noilles 30
Norris, John 120, 125–6
North British Review 29–30, 34, 36–7
North London Collegiate School 76, 114–15,
    120, 129–30, 139
North of England Council for Promoting the
    Higher Education of Women 188,
    190–2, 237
Norton, Caroline 17
nursing 29, 65, 70, 167, 171

obedience of wives to husbands 8–10, 13–14,
    122, 223, 229
Oliphant, Margaret 19–20, 102–3, 156–7,
    225, 227–9
On Liberty 89–90
Origin of Species 5, 37, 40
Orwell, George 226

Osborne, Sydney Godolphin 96
Owen, Richard 38
Owen, Robert 22, 25
Owenism 24–5

Palmerstone, 3rd Viscount 3–4, 87, 132–3,
    145–7, 221–2
Pankhurst, Richard 161–2
Parkes, Elizabeth Rayner (Bessie) 24–9, 32,
    61–2, 64–6, 70–1, 82, 93–102, 104–7, 123,
    129, 145, 147, 150, 156–7, 178, 271, 274
Parkes, Joseph 27, 95–6, 106
Pattison, Mark 35–6, 52–3, 174 n.29, 186
Payne, Joseph 237–8
Perowne, Edward 127, 190, 261, 263
Pipe, Hannah 130, 140–2
Plumptre, Edward 119–20, 124, 170–1,
    173–4, 259
Ponsonby, Mary 215
Porter, Mary 137, 140–1
Potts, Robert 117–21, 123, 126–7, 174–5
Princess, The 94–5, 173–4, 179, 182–3
Principles of Political Economy 88
Procter, Adelaide 65–6, 70, 72–3, 94–101,
    104–7, 271
professions, women excluded from,
    see employment for
    middle-class women
property, women's 8–10, 17–20, 27, 29–32, 67,
    71, 89–90, 92, 94, 163, 184–5, 223–30, 266,
    272–4, 279–81, 284
prostitution 12, 96, 223, 230–2
pudding 112
Pusey, Edward 51, 76

Quarterly Review 34, 36, 38–9, 194
Quakers 2–3, 16, 22–4, 32, 43–4, 48–9, 73–4,
    76–7, 87, 129–30, 270, 272–4
Queen's College 16, 36, 114–15, 119–22, 129,
    136–7, 141, 170–3, 176, 181–2, 259

race x–xi, 152–5, 161–2, 164–5, 224, 280
    race and gender, *see* gender and race
Ramsay, Agnata, *see* Butler, Agnata
Reade, Charles, *see Hard Cash*
Reader 36–7, 103, 164
Reform Act 1832 9–10, 22, 239
Reform Act 1867 88, 221, 223
Reform League 151–5
reformatories 23, 25, 31–2, 110–11, 270–1
Reid, Elizabeth Jesser 23, 30
Reid, Marion 22–3
Remarks on the Education of Girls 26
Representation of the People Act 1918 281

INDEX 301

Representation of the People (Equal Franchise) Act 1828 281
Rich, Julia, Lady Rich 215, 247
Richardson, Anna 7, 39–40, 78–9, 81–3, 85–8, 90, 92, 114–15, 126–7, 129, 136–7, 144, 159–60, 172–4, 188, 195, 207, 217
rights, women's
   language of 6, 17–20, 22–4, 31–3, 84, 88, 90–2, 94–5, 123, 146–7, 151, 157–9, 163–4, 181, 185, 196–7, 215, 221, 223–4, 226–8, 230–1, 237–8, 245–6, 268, 271, 273–81
   property, *see* property, women's
Robertson, Caroline Croom 66–7, 256–7, 263–4
Robertson, George Croom 66–7, 256–7
Robinson, Hugh 233
Roby, Henry 124, 132–3, 135–41, 174, 176–7, 180–1, 183, 196–8, 202, 215, 233–5, 243
Royal Holloway College 259
Russell, John, Viscount Amberley 37, 154–5
Russell, Katharine, Viscountess Amberley 161–2, 181–2, 211–12
Russell, Lord John 3, 146–9, 154–5, 221–2
Rutson, Albert 192–3, 195–6
Rye, Maria 30–1, 71, 96

Saturday Review 2, 19, 27, 32–4, 75, 95, 112–13, 125, 127–8, 149, 156–7, 161–2, 212, 271, 277
school endowments 91, 132, 135–40, 233–8
Schools Inquiry Commission 132–3, 135–40, 143, 164, 177–8, 180, 185, 187, 211–12, 233, 237, 254–5
Seeley, John 178, 183–4, 196, 198, 200–2
Self Help 5, 225
separate spheres x–xi, 12–17
Sewell, Elizabeth 130
sexual double standard, *see* double standard
Shaen, William 110, 113–14, 143, 198
Shaftesbury, 7th Earl of 30–1, 71, 73, 270–1
Shaw-Lefevre, George 226–8
Shirreff, Emily 129, 216–17, 236, 252–3, 272–3, 276–7
Sidgwick, Henry 178, 184, 189, 195, 202–10, 213–14, 222, 247–8, 260–5, 272
Sisterhoods 29, 70, 93, 100–1
slavery xi–xii, 4, 8–9, 23–4, 44, 80–1, 96, 144, 146, 153–4, 164, 223 n.4, 223, 226, 274
Smiles, Samuel 5, 225
Smith, Ben 24–5
Smith, Eleanor 137, 186
Smith, Goldwin 224
Smith, Julia 23–5
Smith, Louie 64–7, 69–70, 80, 93, 150, 159
Smith, Sydney 111

Smith, Valentine 65
Smith, William 24, 270
Smith-Stanley, Edward, *see* Derby, 14th Earl of
Smith-Stanley, Edward Geoffrey, *see* Stanley, Lord
Social Science Association 2–3, 31–4, 71–2, 80–2, 89, 109–10, 112–14, 123–5, 129, 132–3, 136, 139, 150, 155–7, 160–1, 164, 171–3, 227–8, 231–2
Society for Promoting the Employment of Women 27–8, 30–1, 68, 70–4, 76, 78–81, 98, 106–7, 209, 271
Society of Apothecaries 78–9, 108
Solly, Henry 80–1
Solly, Samuel 124
Somerville Hall 259
Somerville, Mary 109, 111
special examinations for women, *see* examinations, special, for women
Spectator 33–4, 36–7, 96, 112–13, 127, 157, 167–70, 206, 213, 229, 245–6, 273
Stanley, Arthur Penrhyn 34–7, 69, 136–7, 222, 244
Stanley, Edward, 2nd Baron Stanley of Alderley 181–2
Stanley, Henrietta, Baroness Stanley of Alderley 121–2, 136–7, 180–2, 184, 202, 215, 217–18, 237–8, 251–2, 255–6, 260–1, 264, 276–7, 281
Stanley, Kate, *see* Russell, Katharine
Stanley, Lady Augusta 136–7, 183, 208, 215
Stanley, Lord (Edward Geoffrey Smith-Stanley) 87, 135–6
Stansfield, Carolyn 159–60
stays 7
Steinthal, Samuel 188
Stephen, Barbara xii
Storrar, John 135–6, 254–5
Stowe, Harriet Beecher 144, 153–4
Strahan, Alexander 36–7, 167–8
Stuart, James 187–91, 200–1, 215–16, 259, 263
Subjection of Women 91–2, 223–5, 248, 275
subscription 35, 203
suffrage 9–10
   female 3, 22, 66–7, 88, 91–2, 144–50, 154–63, 171, 176–7, 209–10, 223–4, 227–8, 232, 237–8, 243, 245–6, 265–7, 273–6, 279–81, 284

Tait, Archibald 30–1, 35–6, 39–40, 222, 237–8
Taylor Mill, Harriet, *see* Mill, Harriet Taylor
Taylor, Clementia (Mentia) 23, 80–2, 113–14, 144, 146–51, 159–60, 223–4, 227, 241, 274

302 INDEX

Taylor, Helen 93, 145–7, 149–50, 155, 157–60, 167–8, 171, 173, 195, 204–5, 215, 274
Taylor, Peter 30, 113–14, 151, 159–60
Taylor, Sedley 180–1, 183–4, 202, 207–10, 214, 220, 272
teacher training 131–2, 138, 141–2, 233
Temple, Frederick 35–6, 38–40, 132–3, 222, 237–8
Tennyson, *see Princess, The*
Tidman, Paul 240–1
Tomkinson, Henry 91, 117–19, 124, 145–6, 176–8, 180–1, 183, 186, 196, 198, 202, 208–9, 215–16, 242–3, 254, 256–7, 257 n.51
Tractarians 39–40, 43, 48, 51, 53–4, 76
training for teachers, *see* teacher training
Transcendentalism 101
Trollope, Anthony 6–7, 11, 42–3, 45, 83–8, 277–9
Trollope, Thomas Adolphus 103–4
Tyndall, John 5, 177, 234

Uncle Tom's Cabin 144, 153–4
Unitarians 2–3, 16–18, 22–6, 28–32, 32 n.22, 35–7, 45, 67, 82, 101, 113–15, 130, 143, 175, 182–3, 207–8, 215, 268, 272, 274
Universities of Oxford and Cambridge Act 1877 217
Universities Tests Act 1871 203–4, 223
University College London 6–7, 45
University of Cambridge 5–7, 35–7, 177–8, 182–3, 202–4, 208–11, 222, 272
  degrees for women, *see* degrees for women, University of Cambridge
  intercollegiate lectures 187
University of Edinburgh 45, 124, 258–9
University of London 45
  degrees for women, *see* degrees for women, University of London
University of Oxford 35–6, 38, 42, 114–17, 126–8, 174, 177, 189, 259, 262, 268–9, 283–4

Vassar College 181–2
Vaughan, Charles 14, 117–18, 123–4
Vaughan, David 58–9, 117–18
Venn, John (logician) 190, 200–1, 211
Venn, John (rector of Clapham) 68–9
Verney, Frances Parthenope 221
Victoria Magazine 102–4
Victoria Press 27–8, 30–1, 70–2, 74–5, 98, 100, 102
Villiers, Henry Montague 73–4
Vindication of the Rights of Women 22
virtue, *see* moraity

Waterhouse, Alfred 172, 174, 176, 184, 198–9, 213, 247–8, 256
Waverley Journal 27–9
Wedgwood, Frances (Fanny) 119–20, 176–7, 216
Wedgwood, Julia (Snow) 38, 161–2, 215–16
Welsh, Elizabeth 251, 264–5
Westcott, Brooke Fosse 58–9
Westfield College 259
Westlake, Alice 123–4, 145
Westlake, John 109–10, 123–4, 127–8, 175
Westminster Review 18, 22, 24, 34, 37–9, 154–5, 159, 167–8, 224
Wilberforce, Henry 51
Wilberforce, Samuel 5, 30–1, 38–9, 78, 88
Williams, Eliezer 42
Winterbotham, Henry 211–12
Wollstonecraft, Mary 22
Wolstenholme, Elizabeth 136–7, 140–1, 144, 146–7, 159–60, 164–5, 174, 184–7, 189–92, 196, 204–5, 215, 227–32, 266, 268–9, 274–6
women and work, *see* employment for middle-class women
Women and Work 28–9, 64–5
Working Men's College 36, 59
Working Men's Club and Institute Union 80–1

Youthful Offenders Act 1854 31–2